THE CHILD WITH A HANDICAP

A CREED FOR THOSE WHO ARE HANDICAPPED

Howard A. Rusk, M.D.
Director, Institute of Physical Medicine and Rehabilitation
New York City

Last Christmas I received a message from a prominent American which impressed me greatly. I shared the creed it contained, by an unknown Confederate soldier, with many of the patients and staff of the Institute and other friends. The father of one of the patients was so deeply moved by it that he had it cast in bronze on a tablet which now stands in the lobby of the Institute as a constant source of inspiration to patients, staff and visitors. Since it has become a credo for the institute, we want to share it with the former patients and staff members and friends of the Institute.

"I ASKED GOD FOR STRENGTH, THAT I MIGHT ACHIEVE
  I WAS MADE WEAK, THAT I MIGHT LEARN HUMBLY TO OBEY...

I ASKED FOR HEALTH, THAT I MIGHT DO GREATER THINGS
  I WAS GIVEN INFIRMITY, THAT I MIGHT DO BETTER THINGS...

I ASKED FOR RICHES, THAT I MIGHT BE HAPPY
  I WAS GIVEN POVERTY, THAT I MIGHT BE WISE...

I ASKED FOR POWER, THAT I MIGHT HAVE THE PRAISE OF MEN
  I WAS GIVEN WEAKNESS, THAT I MIGHT FEEL THE NEED OF GOD...

I ASKED FOR ALL THINGS, THAT I MIGHT ENJOY LIFE
  I WAS GIVEN LIFE, THAT I MIGHT ENJOY ALL THINGS...

I GOT NOTHING I ASKED FOR — BUT EVERYTHING I HAD HOPED FOR

ALMOST DESPITE MYSELF, MY UNSPOKEN PRAYERS WERE ANSWERED
I AM AMONG ALL MEN, MOST RICHLY BLESSED."

Reprinted from IPMR, the publication of the Institute of Physical Medicine and Rehabilitation. A unit of the New York University — Bellevue Medical Center.

THE CHILD WITH A HANDICAP

A TEAM APPROACH TO HIS CARE AND GUIDANCE

Edited by

EDGAR E. MARTMER, M.D.

Past President, American Academy of Pediatrics

Associate Clinical Professor of Pediatrics
Wayne State University, College of Medicine

Chief, Division of Pediatrics, Harper Hospital

Senior Pediatrician, Children's Hospital of Michigan

Consultant in Pediatrics
East Side General Hospital
Crittenton General Hospital
Herman Kiefer Hospital
Receiving Hospital
St. John's Hospital
Woman's Hospital
Detroit, Michigan

CHARLES C THOMAS • PUBLISHER
Springfield   •   Illinois   •   U.S.A.

CHARLES C THOMAS · PUBLISHER
BANNERSTONE HOUSE
301-327 East Lawrence Avenue, Springfield, Illinois, U.S.A.

Published simultaneously in the British Commonwealth of Nations by
BLACKWELL SCIENTIFIC PUBLICATIONS, LTD., OXFORD, ENGLAND

Published simultaneously in Canada by
THE RYERSON PRESS, TORONTO

This book is protected by copyright. No part of it may be reproduced in any manner without written permission from the publisher.

© *1959, by* CHARLES C THOMAS · PUBLISHER

Library of Congress Catalog Card Number: 58-14082

With THOMAS BOOKS careful attention is given to all details of manufacturing and design. It is the Publisher's desire to present books that are satisfactory as to their physical qualities and artistic possibilities and appropriate for their particular use. THOMAS BOOKS will be true to those laws of quality that assure a good name and good will.

Printed in the United States of America

CONTRIBUTORS

Elizabeth M. Boggs, Ph.D.
Vice President: Programs and Services
National Association for Retarded Children, Incorporated

Z. Stephen Bohn, M.D.
Assistant Clinical Professor of Neurology
Wayne State University
College of Medicine
Medical Director
Michigan Epilepsy Center and Association

Eric Denhoff, M.D.
Medical Director
Meeting Street School for Handicapped Children
Providence, Rhode Island
Chairman: Handicapped Child Committee
American Academy of Pediatrics

Charles H. Frantz, M.D., F.A.C.S.
Chief of Staff
The Mary Free Bed Children's Hospital and Orthopedic Center
Grand Rapids, Michigan
Chairman: Department of Orthopaedic Surgery, Blodgett Memorial Hospital
Grand Rapids, Michigan
Orthopaedic Consultant: Eastern Orthopaedic School
Grand Rapids, Michigan

Benjamin M. Gasul, B.S., M.S., M.D.
Director, Pediatric Cardiophysiology Department
Cook County Children's Hospital and
Hektoen Institute for Medical Research
Clinical Professor of Pediatrics
University of Illinois College of Medicine
Attending Pediatrician (Cardiology)
Presbyterian, St. Luke's and Mt. Sinai Hospitals

Lee Forrest Hill, M.D.
Chief of Pediatrics
Raymond Blank Memorial Hospital for Children
Des Moines, Iowa

Samuel Karelitz, M.D.
Chief, Pediatric Division
The Long Island Jewish Hospital

Chairman, Committee on Adoptions
American Academy of Pediatrics

Clinical Professor Pediatrics
New York State Medical School at New York College

George A. Kopp, B.S., M.S., Ph.D.
Director, Wayne State University Speech and Hearing Center

Director, Speech and Hearing
Rehabilitation Institute of Metropolitan Detroit

Consultant, Division Dental and Oral Surgery
Cleft Palate Habilitation, Sinai Hospital

President-Elect, American Speech and Hearing Association

Harriet G. Kopp, B.A., M.A.
Director, Clinical Services in Speech and Hearing
Rehabilitation Institute of Metropolitan Detroit

Associate Editor, Journal of Speech and Hearing Disorders

Sherman Little, M.D.
Professor of Pediatrics and Professor of Pediatric Psychiatry
University of Southern California Medical School

Director of Psychiatric Services, Children's Hospital, Los Angeles, California

Charles D. May, M.D.
Clinical Professor of Pediatrics
Columbia University
College of Physicians and Surgeons

Elenora H. Moore, M.A., Ed.D.
Associate Professor of Elementary Education
Wayne State University

E. Gordon Murphy, M.B., B.S., D.C.H.
Clinical Assistant, Hospital for Sick Children
Toronto, Ontario, Canada

Clinical Teacher, Department of Paediatrics
University of Toronto

Alvah L. Newcomb, B.S., M.D.

Associate Professor of Pediatrics
Northwestern University Medical School

Chief, Pediatrics, Evanston Hospital

Attending Pediatrician, Children's Memorial Hospital

Letha L. Patterson, A.B.

"One of the Founders of the National Association for Retarded Children, Inc., the Minnesota Association for Retarded Children, Inc., and the St. Paul Association for Retarded Children, Inc."

Sheldon C. Reed, A.B., Ph.D.

Director, Dight Institute for Human Genetics
University of Minnesota

Conrad M. Riley, M.D.

Associate Professor of Pediatrics
Columbia University
College of Physicians and Surgeons

Saul J. Robinson, M.D.

Associate Clinical Professor of Pediatrics
Stanford University School of Medicine

Chief, Department of Pediatrics
Mount Zion Hospital

Consultant Cardiologist
Valley Children's Hospital

Albert D. Ruedemann, M.D.

Chairman, Department of Ophthalmology
Wayne State University College of Medicine, Detroit

Chief, Division of Ophthalmology
Harper Hospital

Albert D. Rudemann, Jr., M.D.

Instructor in Ophthalmology
Wayne State University College of Medicine

Pauline M. Ryman, M.A.

Director of Social Service
Henry Ford Hospital

HEYWORTH N. SANFORD, M.D.
Professor of Pediatrics
Chairman, College of Pediatrics
University of Illinois School of Medicine
Pediatrician-in-Chief, Research and Educational Hospital
Chief of Staff, Cook County Children's Hospital

EDWARD B. SHAW, M.D.
Professor of Pediatrics
University of California School of Medicine
Chairman, Department of Communicable Diseases
Children's Hospital, San Francisco

RALPH L. STEFFEK, ED. D.
Supervisor of Counseling
Extension Service and Coordinator for Extension Centers
The University of Michigan

JOHN C. SULLIVAN, PH.D.
Professor of Educational Psychology
College of Education, Wayne State University

SAMUEL M. WISHIK, M.D., M.P.H.
Professor of Maternal and Child Health
Graduate School of Public Health
University of Pittsburgh

HENRY H. WORK, M.D.
School of Medicine, Department of Psychiatry, Division of Child Psychiatry
University of California Medical Center
Los Angeles

To

Clifford G. Grulee, Marshall C. Pease and Henry M. Van Hook
Pediatrician   Philosopher   Soldier
Who have been my counselors

To

*The Members of the American Academy of Pediatrics who
have stimulated me through the years by their dedication
to the cause of improving the care of children*

and

To

*My wife, Helen and my son, William who have
encouraged me through the years.*

INTRODUCTION

Throughout the ages the child with a handicap has been a concern to his parents and to the social order. In primitive societies such a child, unable to withstand the hazards of nature or to defend himself against his enemies, was eliminated early in life. In other societies the child with a handicap was considered a hazard to the group. Because such a child required additional care, he interfered with the rapid movement of the group when danger threatened. In flight from an enemy, he might easily be captured. To prevent his becoming a victim of practices worse than death, his own group frequently decreed his early death.

The practice of eliminating the child with a handicap gradually disappeared. Wherever superstition and ignorance flourished, however, such a child was believed to be possessed by the devil or cursed by the gods. Treatment was determined by the whims of witch doctors, medicine men and high priests who encouraged credulity and fear. Kindness or cruelty marked the handling depending upon whether terror or solicitude was to appease an unpredictable god.

Although many societies dealt harshly with the child with a handicap, others, including the Hebrew, accorded them special care and consideration. The teachings of Christ mention the lame, the blind, the demon-possessed, the compassion He had for such individuals. During the middle ages physically handicapped individuals, especially dwarfs, were often shown humane consideration, rising to positions of influence and power. As a result many individuals with handicaps made lasting contributions to the literature, drama and art.

Awakening social conscience and modern medicine have gradually developed the realization that the child with a handicap is first of all a human being essentially no different from other children, that his handicap may be corrected or improved, and that he might be expected to participate in a range of activities open to all citizens. The child with a visible physical handicap was the first to receive the benefit of these changed attitudes. More recently the recognition that other handicaps are amenable to treatment has improved the outlook for almost every child.

No clear-cut definition as to what constitutes a child with a handicap has been reached. In the past, when attention was focused on the child with an orthopedic defect, the term "crippled child" was adopted. Today orthopedic handicaps are recognized to be important; but many other conditions including rheumatic heart disease, congenital heart lesions, cerebral palsy, other types of brain damage, eye and ear defects, speech defects, cranio-facial defects and emotional disturbances are recognized as being equally important. One definition which has been suggested is that any child with a physical, mental or emotional problem which interferes with normal growth and development is a child with a handicap. Such a definition, emphasizing the child as a whole individual, recognizes that handicaps may involve the mental and psychological well-being as well as the physical health of the affected individual.

The Children's Bureau of the U. S. Department of Health, Education and Welfare has estimated that there are 285,000 cases of cerebral palsy affecting persons under 21 years of age in the United States of America, 64,000 cases of cleft palate and hare lip under 18 years, 275,000 cases of epilepsy, 60,000 cases of serious eye defects, 1,000,000 children with orthopedic defects and 675,000 cases of rheumatic fever. Although these figures are incomplete and do not include many handicapping conditions, they serve to emphasize the wide spread distribution of handicaps among children. If all degrees of handicapping and if all types of handicapping conditions were to be included, some estimates indicate that 10 per cent of all children are handicapped.

Accurate information as to the number of children with handicaps is not available. While the fragments of statistical information concerning specific handicaps are known, the absence of standard classification procedures coupled with the lack of authority, funds and facilities to require the reporting of cases have prevented the assembling of complete, accurate and reliable data.

Not only is accurate information unavailable but also the change in incidence of handicapping conditions makes it difficult to compare data. The decrease in tuberculosis of the bone following the adoption of pasteurization of milk and the campaign to eliminate tuberculosis in cattle are illustrations. The increase in the incidence of blindness due to retrolental fibroplasia as more premature infants are saved, the recent marked reduction in the cases of retrolental fibroplasia following the discovery that high oxygen concentration was a contributing cause, the administration of prophylactic vitamin supplements to reduce the incidence of rickets as a cause of bone deformities, the almost universal use of poliomyelitis vaccine undoubtedly reducing handicapping from poliomyelitis are other illustrations.

During the past fifty years the practice of medicine has changed from the goal of saving individual patients to a broad program of preventive medicine. The establishment of public health programs and the prevention and treatment of communicable diseases have been made possible by the use of immunizing agents and new therapeutic measures including drugs and antibiotics. Advances in medical knowledge combined with increased availability of medical and hospital care, improved transportation facilities, better nutrition, increased education and an improved standard of living have enabled thousands of infants and children to survive who would have succumbed at the turn of the century. The number of children with handicaps who have survived has thus increased.

Continuing research will bring forth additional means of prevention as well as new and improved methods of treatment. However, research must be adequately supported and encouraged. A basic amount of money available on a continuing basis is essential to maintain a research program, although grants-in-aid or sums for specific research activities limited in time and purpose are a proper means of augmenting a research budget. Funds must be available in adequate amounts so that individuals capable of conducting worthwhile investigations in basic research problems will not be forced through economic pressure to leave the field in which there is great need for qualified personnel.

Every human being requires assistance as he passes through infancy into childhood, through childhood into adolescence, through adolescence into adult life. If a child has a physical, mental or emotional handicap, he may require assistance that will exceed the ability of his parents by themselves to provide. The need will depend upon the individual circumstances. Medical advice and treatment, special education, spiritual assurance and economic aid may be needed. Meeting the complex problems presented by this large segment of the child population which has handicapping conditions is challenging. Since children with handicaps are a matter of concern to the entire community, their problems become a community responsibility.

The objective must be to see that every child is cared for in such a manner as to assure recovery whenever possible, to secure the greatest degree of improvement when complete recovery is impossible and to assist the child to make a satisfactory adjustment to society, to his family and to his environment. Every effort must be made to enable such a child to become independent and to make his own contribution to society rather than becoming dependent on others. The ultimate goal of preventing the development of handicapping conditions whenever possible and of providing adequate care and treatment for every child who has a handicap will require a continuing expansion of present day activities.

The care and treatment of children with handicaps has undergone a complete transformation in the past decade. Great progress in understanding and accepting the child with a handicap has been made. The recognition that most handicapped children are normal individuals has shifted the emphasis from the handicap to the child. The conservation and cultivation of the abilities of the individual, the improvement of his disability so far as possible and the utilization of all available means to help him develop abilities replacing those which cannot be restored have become basic objectives.

This decade has been a period of great increase in community interest and activity in behalf of children with handicapping conditions. Public understanding of the problems with which the child is confronted is increasing. With the change in attitude by society, parents, losing the feeling of guilt, are accepting the child as he is. Physicians are recognizing their responsibility to the child, to his family and the need of a program for the child's whole care. Organizations interested in various types of handicapping conditions are expanding their programs. New groups concerned with special handicapping problems are being organized. The U. S. Department of Health, Education and Welfare through The Children's Bureau is stimulating state programs by providing statistical data, recommendations for care programs, consultation services and financial aid.

Progress in the development of adequate facilities is evident as community interest has increased. Some communities now have adequate facilities to enable a large proportion of children with handicaps to be restored to active and useful lives. Other communities, slow in recognizing the need, have made little effort to assure that every child with a handicap will have an opportunity to utilize his abilities to the utmost. Unfortunately, even in those areas where adequate facilities exist not all children are afforded their use.

Available facilities must be utilized to the fullest extent and to the best possible advantage. The various agencies involved need not lose their identity by participating in such cooperative effort. By avoiding duplication of facilities, each participating group can expend a greater effort in its particular field and serve the community better. When skills and abilities of all the various groups involved are brought into a closely cooperating unit, the spirit of rehabilitation makes possible the mobilization of all community resources. The Queen's Rehabilitation Program, a pilot project in New York City sponsored by the Association for the Aid of Crippled Children, is an example of how a community may provide the kind of restoration envisioned in this new concept of treatment of the handicapped. Here cooperative effort under good leadership has assured that all the resources of a community are available to the child with a handicap.

Since degree of recovery, care, or compensation may depend upon it, early recognition of the child with a handicapping condition is important. The parents most logically may be the first to recognize symptoms which are not considered normal and for which an explanation should be sought through consultation with a physician. However, teachers, social workers and recreational personnel are being trained to consider a child's related needs and to refer their observations to parents and physicians.

The evaluation of the child and diagnosis of his handicap is the first step in rehabilitation. The child should have a complete physical examination and such additional studies as may be indicated in the individual case. Special tests and examinations including vision, hearing and speech should be made. Many cases may require psychometric and psychiatric examinations, a social service investigation and an evaluation of educational and recreational needs.

As soon as the complete diagnosis is established, the parents profit most when an explanation of the handicap, when plans for treatment, and when consideration of such additional assistance as may be indicated is discussed with them. To assure the utilization of all available measures, the physician should be thoroughly familiar with the community resources. If certain special services are not available within the community, the physician needs to know where and how such resources may be obtained. These resources may include the various medical and surgical specialties, occupational therapists, physical therapists, recreational workers, visiting nurses, psychiatrists, dentists, teachers and geneticists.

No single solution or stereotyped program exists which can be adapted to assist every child with a handicapping condition. Each child presents a problem different from all others. His care must be individualized. After careful consideration of all the factors involved, including the child, his handicap, his family, the type of care and treatment required, the resources of the family and community resources, someone has to be responsible for arranging a program of adequate diagnosis and treatment. In most cases this person is the physician whom the parents consult.

The adequate treatment of some children requires the combined efforts of people trained in various fields of endeavor. When the program of rehabilitation for the child is being arranged, provision should be made for all who will be working with the child to work as a unit. If the child is of school age, the school staff may provide contributing members of the team. Whether he attends regular school, is a pupil in a special class or special school, or receives home teaching, the child with a handicap increasingly is under the observation and direction of staff members with professional training. During the process of rehabilitation, the emphasis will shift from one professional team member to another as the need at the time dictates. If the members of the team communicate with each other by discussing the program and progress of the child, the results will be much better than if each individual attempts to carry on his portion of the program independently. Since parents are an integral part of the team, every effort should be made to have them thoroughly informed at all times. The most important member of the team, however, is always the child, the patient whose recovery is the goal of the entire program.

One of the serious problems at the present time is a lack of adequately trained personnel. Young people should be encouraged to consider the many opportunities in the various types of activities including nursing, social service, physiotherapy, special education, play therapy and medical technology. Local community colleges should be encouraged to undertake some of the training at the service and technician level. Four year private and public colleges and universities should be assisted in expanding programs requiring higher levels of professional competency.

The interest of the public in the child with a handicap should continue to be encouraged and stimulated. Although funds available for work with the child who has a handicap have increased during the past decade, the need for funds will increase even more as programs continue to expand. Just as further education is needed to encourage parents to seek assistance as soon as a handicap is recognized, so continuing education of the public will be necessary to assure adequate support for voluntary and governmental programs.

THE EDITOR

PREFACE

The emphasis in caring for the handicapped child has shifted from an attention to the handicapping condition itself to a concern for the well-being of the whole child. Our present goal is to enable that child to progress in as normal a manner as possible in his physical, emotional, mental and social development. To achieve this objective, helping a child to become a mature, independent, self-sufficient individual, demands the complete co-operation and understanding between parents, teachers, nurses, physicians, therapists, social workers and others interested in welfare of children with handicapping conditions.

This book provides an introduction to a selected number of contributions which have been made in widely separated areas involving children with handicaps. Although these contributions contain a great deal of research data and medical information, the volume is not primarily a medical text. The materials may be read with profit by student or skilled practitioner. The editor assumes full responsibility for insisting that a need existed for a book which would enable a more general public to gain the viewpoint of the leaders in the field of the care of children with handicaps.

The authors of the various chapters are leaders in their respective fields. Their splendid co-operation in preparing the material presented is simply further evidence of their dedication to their work.

ACKNOWLEDGMENTS

I wish to express my sincere appreciation to the authors who have contributed the chapters which make up this volume. Ralph Steffek deserves special thanks for his editorial assistance and counsel. I am most appreciative of the clerical assistance of Edna Barker in the preparation of the manuscript.

The courtesy of W. B. Saunders Company for permission to use the figures which appeared in the August 1955 Issue of Pediatric Clinics of North America, the C. V. Mosby Company for a figure from Journal of Chronic Diseases—June 1956 and Dorothy G. Murray for permission to quote from "This Is Stevie's Story" is acknowledged with thanks.

Charles C Thomas and his associates have been most helpful throughout the preparation and publication of *The Child With A Handicap*.

E. E. M.

TABLE OF CONTENTS

	Page
Contributors	v
Introduction	xi
Preface	xix
Acknowledgments	xxi

Chapter

1.	The Role of the Physician	3
2.	The Role of the Parent	11
3.	The Role of the Psychiatrist	30
4.	The Role of the Social Worker	44
5.	The Role of the Teacher	57
6.	The Role of Adoption Agencies	74
7.	Counseling in Medical Genetics	82
8.	The Child with an Amputation	90
9.	The Child with Cerebral Palsy	128
10.	The Child with a Congenital Heart Defect	150
11.	The Child with a Convulsive Disorder	163
12.	The Child with Diabetes	177
13.	The Child who is Emotionally Disturbed	182
14.	The Child with Familial Dysautonomia	199
15.	The Child who is a Mongol	211
16.	The Child with Progressive Muscular Dystrophy	221

17.	The Child with Nephrosis	233
18.	The Child with Poliomyelitis	252
19.	The Child with Cystic Fibrosis	265
20.	The Child with Rheumatic Fever	241
21.	The Child with a Speech and Hearing Disorder	291
22.	The Eyes of Children	311
23.	Guides for Discipline	341
24.	Guides for Parents	351
25.	Guides to Play Materials	367
26.	Guides to Reading Materials	382
27.	Guides to Health Education Materials	385
28.	Guides for Community Programs	390
	Directory of Camps for the Handicapped	391
	Directory of Schools, Services and Other Facilities	391
	Additional Books on Handicapping Conditions and Rehabilitation	392
	Lists of Books for Children	397
	Index	398

THE CHILD WITH A HANDICAP

THE ROLE OF THE PHYSICIAN

Samuel M. Wishik, M.D., M.P.H.

Physicians heal the wounds of sick children to make them well, and they supervise the health of well children to keep them well. Most handicapped children, however, are neither sick nor well. Their continuing and complex needs are ever changing during the growth years. All the physician's ingenuity and understanding are called upon to diagnose and treat, to advise and plan, to support and help toward self-reliance. The twenty-five-point credo that follows tries to outline the standard of responsibility that the physician sets for himself in counseling the families of handicapped children.

1. I REALIZE THAT EXTERNALLY INVISIBLE CONDITIONS, SUCH AS HEART DISEASE OR DEAFNESS, CAN BE JUST AS CRIPPLING AS A PARALYZED LIMB.

As a matter of fact, when it is not obvious to other people that the child is handicapped, he receives less consideration than sympathy. A hearing aid, for example, not only improves the child's hearing but lets other people know that the child may be missing some of the conversation. When the child with a heart condition stops playing with the others at school, the teacher may interpret this lack of participation as a lack of social maturity if she does not know that such a child fatigues quickly.

2. WHEN A CHILD IS FOUND TO HAVE A HANDICAPPING CONDITION, I LOOK CAREFULLY FOR OTHER DEFECTS—BECAUSE MULTIPLE HANDICAPS IN THE SAME CHILD OCCUR MORE OFTEN THAN SINGLE HANDICAPS.

A study made in Georgia,[1,2] reports that a group of handicapped children had an average of two and two-tenths different major handicaps in various combinations, such as an orthopedic condition plus mental retardation, cleft palate plus hearing impairment, or strabismus (crossed eyes) plus a personality disturbance. This knowledge again emphasises the necessity of treating the child rather than a single diagnosis or handicap.

3. I DO NOT TURN A DIAGNOSIS INTO A LABEL FOR A CHILD. I DO NOT TURN ADJECTIVES INTO NOUNS. HE IS NOT "AN EPILEPTIC;" SHE IS NOT "A DIABETIC."

Within any diagnostic group a broad range of severity and types of involvement, from the extremely mild to the very severe, can be identified. No specific child can be described merely by a diagnosis, such as "cerebral palsied" or "mentally retarded." Almost any child, no matter how handicapped, has remaining capacities that outnumber his deficiencies. The child and his family must be helped by focusing on those capacities rather than on his limitations. Furthermore, the child deserves to be given the benefit of doubt. Only by a trial period of prolonged observation can the physician be sure that the child's seeming limitations are real.

4. WHEN CENTRAL NERVOUS SYSTEM INVOLVEMENT EXISTS, I KNOW THAT THE MANIFESTATIONS CAN BE NEUROMUSCULAR, SENSORY, INTELLECTUAL, CONVULSIVE AND EMOTIONAL, AND AT TIMES EVEN MORE SUBTLE AND ELUSIVE.

Mild behavior changes especially elude recognition. Such imperceptive disturbances that at times interfere with a child's education also elude recognition. For want of a better term, these children have been called "brain-injured,"[3,4] especially when the brain damage does not demonstrate itself grossly in the usual forms of paralysis, convulsions, or intellectual impairment.

5. I KNOW THAT VARIOUS MEDICAL SPECIALISTS CAN HELP AND THAT THERE ARE ELEMENTS IN THE CARE OF THE HANDICAPPED CHILD THAT ARE OUTSIDE THE FIELD OF MEDICINE.

The physician relies on the orthopedist, cardiologist, opthalmologist or other specialist when he recognizes need for consultation. The physician is less likely, however, to think of the educator, the social worker, or the vocational counselor.

6. I AM NOT AN AMATEUR PSYCHOMETRIST. I DO NOT MAKE FLIP JUDGMENTS ABOUT A HANDICAPPED CHILD'S INTELLIGENCE.

The flip prognosis comes back to plague the physician, whether he has erred on the side of optimism or pessimism. Like the lay person, the physician is not immune to being influenced by a peculiar facial expression, a strange voice or other unusual mannerisms that suggest mental retardation. Furthermore, it must be clear that the actual intellectual functioning of a child is affected by sensory disturbances, such as blindness or deafness, by emotional deviations, and by limitations in educational and social opportunities.

7. I TRY TO FIND OUT WHAT IS KNOWN ABOUT THE GENETICS OF A CONDITION, WITHOUT INJECTING MY OWN DESIRES FOR UNWARRANTED OPTIMISM OR PESSIMISM.

Telling the parents of a child with congenitally dislocated hips that chances are against the condition appearing in another child is not strictly correct if the approximate odds of another girl baby having the condition are about one in twenty as compared with about one in five hundred in other families.

8. I DO NOT MAKE DECISIONS FOR THE FAMILY. I LAY ALL THE FACTS CLEARLY BEFORE THEM SO THAT THEY CAN ARRIVE AT THEIR OWN SOLUTION.

When the parents have been told the approximate chances, to the extent that information is available, they alone can make the decision on whether or not to have more children.

9. I ADVISE PARENTS ON IMMUNIZATION, SAFETY, AND OTHER MEANS OF PREVENTING THEIR CHILDREN FROM BECOMING HANDICAPPED.

In counseling parents about their well children, emphasis must be given to the important and frequent preventable conditions that are occurring among children in the community. As long as accidents are the leading cause of death and disability of children in all age groups after the first birthday,[5] guiding parents in the rearing of healthy children is incomplete without the routine inclusions of advice about safety and accident prevention.[6,7,8,9,10] In our day, such words of caution may be more important than instructions on feeding.

10. IN THE HEALTH SUPERVISION OF WELL CHILDREN, I AM ON THE LOOKOUT FOR SIGNS OF INCIPIENT CONDITIONS THAT MAY LEAD TO HANDICAPS.

In the routine periodic examination of very young infants, careful measurements of the head circumference may be more valuable than frequent use of the stethoscope.

11. WHEN A CHILD HAS HAD AN UNFAVORABLE HEALTH EXPERIENCE

THAT HAS POTENTIAL FOR PRODUCING A PARTICULAR HANDICAP LATER, I CLASSIFY THAT CHILD ON MY RECORDS AS "SUSCEPTIBLE" OR "VULNERABLE" AND MAKE A SPECIAL POINT OF FOLLOWING HIM AND SEEING HIM PERIODICALLY.

The occurrence of convulsions in the first weeks of life or evidence of neurological symptoms with an attack of measles is a warning signal for the possible subsequent development of cerebral palsy in the same way, if not to as great an extent, as an attack of rheumatic fever is a warning that makes the physician watch carefully for later heart damage.

12. I KNOW THAT "CASE FINDING" IS MORE THAN FINDING A NEW CASE: AFTER THAT LOOKING FOR GAPS IN THE CHILD'S TOTAL REHABILITATION—PHYSICAL, MENTAL, EMOTIONAL, SOCIAL, EDUCATIONAL, AND VOCATIONAL—THIS ALSO IS "FINDING THE CASE" IN NEED OF CARE.

To the physician, the term "finding a new case" usually means that medical treatment is needed. When a physician who has been following a child with epilepsy, discovers, despite effective drug control of convulsions, that the child is not admitted to school because of the prejudices of the school authorities, the physician has "found" a case of a handicapped child—this time, handicapped educationally because of his neurological condition.

13. I AM WILLING AND ABLE TO WORK AS A MEMBER OF A PROFESSIONAL TEAM, RESPECTING THE CONTRIBUTIONS AND OPINIONS OF THE OTHER DISCIPLINES AND SUBORDINATING MY ROLE TO THE DECISIONS OF THE GROUP.

For example, the physician may advise the family to postpone elective surgery for psychological or educational reasons.

14. I CAN FLEXIBLY ASSUME VARYING DEGREES OF RESPONSIBILITY FOR DIFFERENT CHILDREN TO FIT EACH SITUATION BEST—SOMETIMES LIMITING MY ROLE TO GENERAL HEALTH SUPERVISION AND CARE OF INTERCURRENT ILLNESS, SOMETIMES SHARING WITH THE CONSULTANTS IN THE SPECIAL CARE OF THE HANDICAP.

This is a matter of give and take between the physician and the consultants.

15. ALTHOUGH I DO NOT HAVE TECHNICAL SUPERVISION OVER PHYSICAL THERAPY AND CERTAIN OTHER SPECIAL TREATMENTS, I INCLUDE THEM IN MY OVERALL ASSESSMENT OF THE CHILD'S NEEDS AND PROGRESS.

If the orthopedist recommends two years of frequent physical therapy to improve the usefulness of a limb by about 10 per cent, the family physician may raise the question of the balance between the probable improvement and the dislocation in the child's life that would have to occur to obtain it. When the physical therapist reports improvement in a child's walking after a year's treatment, the physician may interject his estimate of the contribution of time and growth to the child's progress.

16. I REALIZE HOW EASILY THE PRESENCE OF A CHRONIC HANDICAPPING CONDITION IN A CHILD CAN THROW THE FAMILY INTO MEDICAL INDIGENCY.

The economic effects on the family are both subtle and extensive. In addition to the mere cost of care, reduced earning capacity of the family, decreased earning potential of the child, as well as other incidental and hidden expenses often adversely affect the economic stability of the family.

17. I AM ACQUAINTED WITH THE PROGRAMS OF COMMUNITY AGENCIES, AND I COOPERATE WITH THEM IN THE CARE OF MY HANDICAPPED PATIENTS.

When, for example, the school health service refers a normal child to the private physician for supposed vision or hearing defect, the physician recognizes that an effective screening program in the school must produce a certain reasonable amount of over-referral in order to detect those who do need care. In another instance, when a handicapped child reaches his teens, the physician will consider possible referral to the Division of Vocational Rehabilitation of the State Department of Education.[3, 4, 5, 6, 7, 8]

18. I RECOGNIZE THE IMPORTANCE OF CONTINUITY OF CARE OVER A SPAN OF YEARS. IF I LOSE CONTACT WITH THE FAMILY, I CALL FOR HELP TO GET THE CHILD BACK UNDER MEDICAL SUPERVISION.

Although the private physician is not in a strategic position to keep after a family, the public health nurse can help to send the family back to him for continued observation.

19. I ENCOURAGE THE CHILD TO PARTICIPATE IN NORMAL SOCIAL GROUPS, AND I WORK FOR INCREASING HIS ACCEPTANCE BY THESE GROUPS AND BY THE COMMUNITY IN GENERAL.

Only by living with handicapped children and playing side by side with them can children grow up to be understanding adults, among whom some day will be those who are in a position to employ handicapped persons.

20. I PARTICIPATE IN DECISIONS, PLANS, AND ARRANGEMENTS FOR THE EDUCATION OF THE CHILD.

Here the physician has a very important set of responsibilities. The dual goals in the education of a handicapped child are on the one hand to keep him in as normal a setting as possible and on the other hand to give him whatever special education he needs. The balance between these two goals is a delicate one that depends to a large extent on the physician's diagnosis, recommendations, and periodic reappraisals. For example, restricted types of education, such as instruction by a teacher for the homebound or in a residential school are abnormal situations that are not the best solution for most handicapped children. The physician helps to interpret this information to over-protective parents.

21. TO NON-MEDICAL PROFESSIONAL PERSONS I INTERPRET MEDICAL INFORMATION THEY SHOULD HAVE ABOUT A HANDICAPPED CHILD.

The physician should interpret certain information to the teacher about the medical condition of a child in her class, such as: the nature of the condition, its cause, treatment, general prognosis, relation to physical activity, infections, diet, nutrition, personality, and the expected attitudes of others.

22. I PARTICIPATE IN ADVISING ABOUT PLANS AND ARRANGEMENTS FOR THE CHILD'S FUTURE VOCATION.

Planning for a child's future vocation should start early. The plan should not be too rigid and should be neither too delimiting nor too unduly encouraging to the family and the child. School counseling resources as well as vocational rehabilitation services should be called upon.

23. I ADVISE AND SUPPORT THE FAMILY IN THE DIFFICULT DECISIONS THEY MAY HAVE TO MAKE ON INSTITUTIONAL PLACEMENT FOR THEIR CHILD.

Even when a child's handicap is very severe, the values in the parents' eyes of keeping the child at home are the final factors in their decision concerning whether or not to place the child permanently in an institution. Many values may be derived from home and family care, both for the child and for the others in the family. If parents decide to keep a child, the physician can furnish them with concrete roles and responsibilities that will help them to give the child more effective care and to make their situation more bearable and meaningful.

24. I HELP TO ADVISE PARENTS' GROUPS AND OTHER ORGANIZATIONS OF CITIZENS ABOUT HOW THEY CAN IMPROVE SERVICES TO HANDICAPPED CHILDREN.

In recent years, an increased number of groups of parents organizing for the improvement of community services for children with one or another handicap have appeared on the American scene. These groups are enthusiastic and sincere individuals who at times let their enthusiasm run away with them. Because they lean strongly on the physician for guidance, the physician too may show a tendency to run away with the group, interjecting his personal opinions into his advice without first discovering what patterns of organization of services have been tried and have been successful elsewhere.

25. I STRIVE FOR THE IMPROVEMENT OF MY COMMUNITY'S RESOURCES FOR THE CARE OF HANDICAPPED CHILDREN.

This avowal ties in with the previous comment about guidance of citizens' groups. Two common and unfortunate tendencies in the development of new services are first, to establish a completely new service apart from any existing ones, and second, to set up a specialized service for one or another diagnostic group or condition. By and large, a program is much more likely to be on a sound basis if it fits in with existing services. Individuals and organizations should focus on the needs of children as a total group rather than on one or another specific condition handicapping some children.

This credo is the code of feeling and action of an understanding individual, a competent physician, and a conscientious citizen.

REFERENCES
Technical
1. Wishik, Samuel M.: Handicapped children in Georgia: a study of prevalence, disability, needs, and resources. *American Journal of Public Health*, 46:195, 1956.
2. Wishik, Samuel N.: *Handicapped children in Georgia: a study of prevalence, disability, needs, resources, and contributing factors. Implications for program administration and community organization*, 1956.

3. Strauss, Alfred A., and Lehtinen, Laura E.: *Psychopathology and Education of the Brain-Injured Child*. New York, Grune & Stratton, Inc., 1947.
5. Dietrich, Harry F.: The role of education in accident prevention. *Pediatrics*, 17:297, 1956.
6. American Public Health Association, Committee on Child Health: *Health Supervision of Young Children: A Guide for Practicing Physicians and Child Health Conference Personnel*. New York, American Public Health Association, 1955.

Lay

4. Lewis, Richard S.: *The Other Child: The Brain Injured Child*. New York, Grune & Stratton, Inc., 1951.
7. American Academy of Pediatrics, Committee on Accident Prevention: *Rx: Are You Using the New 'Safety' Vaccine?* New York Metropolitan Life Insurance Company, 1952.
8. The Children's Medical Center: *Accident Handbook: A Home Accident Guide*. Boston, The Children's Medical Center, 1950.
9. Dietrich, Harry F., and Gruenberg, Sidonie M.: *Your Child's Safety*. New York, Public Affairs Committee, Inc., 1955.
10. Prudential Insurance Company of America: *Safety . . . Your Child's Heritage*. Newark, Prudential Insurance Company of America, 1951.

THE ROLE OF THE PARENT*

Letha L. Patterson, A.B.

Of all life's problems, those presented by the child with a handicap require the highest quality of teamwork; teamwork within professions, among professions and between professional and lay people, especially parents.

Teamwork has been defined as: working with everyone in sight to get a job done.[1] The persons most plainly in sight and usually most anxious to help are the mother and father of the child with a handicap. Too often (at least in the past) we parents have been overlooked or ignored.

Parents can furnish the most complete family and case histories; must make the weighty decisions, carry out the plans and bear the physical, emotional and financial obligations involved. We are the ones who must learn to understand the child, as well as ourselves, in relation to living with overwhelming questions and with only the promise of inadequate answers.

Professional workers are now according the parent couple a most important status as members of the team. In recent years the term "interdisciplinary" has grown to include parenthood. Such a concept must be encouraged.

As the mother of a retarded child, it is not my intention to speak for all parents of all handicapped children, nor even for parents of all the mentally handicapped. Most of my thinking stems from six years of active participation with parents of retarded children. Admittedly, it is highly colored by my husband's and my own experience with our twelve-year-old son who is quite handicapped, although he is educable. The child's relatively high verbal and low performance abilities made it extremely difficult

---

*Based in large part on an article: Some Pointers for Professionals. *Children*, 3:13-17, January-February, 1956.

[1]Leirfallom, Jarle: Eight Goals for County Welfare Boards. *Minnesota Welfare* IX:24-25, May, 1954.

to secure and accept the help we needed. It is my hope that our experience will serve a useful purpose through the suggestions offered here.

THE PROBLEM MUST BE DEFINED EARLY

It is axiomatic that a problem cannot be solved without knowing what it is. The first and basic problem is to understand the child with a handicap. Medical, psychological, educational and social planning depend on an adequate appraisal of the child's present status and his potential ability for the future. Parents have often been denied guidance in this very fundamental first step.

The problem of inadequate professional service is recognized by many professional people. Dr. Grover Powers has written, "Here are major problems perhaps as old as human life itself but still too low on the totem poles of medical respectability and of scientific concern. We have recognized the problems but too many of us have done as the priest and Levite in the ancient parable—we have 'passed by on the other side' . . .

. . . When there is no cure, we doctors sometimes capitulate too easily to therapeutic defeatism forgetting that the physician is just as responsible for alleviating as for curing; action is just less urgent, not less vital."[2]

Thanks to a realistic and more widespread acceptance of handicapped children by their parents and an enlightened society which appears ready to extend more opportunities to the child with a handicap, professional workers are now able to improve their day-to-day services to such families. Many institutions are developing training programs which will prepare professional workers more adequately for their future responsibilities.

It has been my privilege to serve on a panel with the father of a deaf child and the mother of a blind child before classes of medical students. One alert young man posed this question after all three parents had stressed the importance of early definition of our problems: "What can the physician do when he is not sure himself and doesn't want to worry the parents?"

"Just be honest with us," was the reply.

[2]Powers, Grover F.: John Howland Award Address: The Retarded Child and his Family as a Challenge to Pediatric Practice, Research and Education. *Pediatrics*, 12:217-226, August, 1953.

It requires great sensitivity and intuition to take a mother's couched remarks and detect that they spell "worry." Often parents are concerned just as early as the physician is, but we are unable to express our fears and worries. Frequently, however, hints are offered that help is actually desired—whether that means waiting a while or consulting with specialists immediately. He is a wise counselor who will acknowledge his limitations.

One psychiatrist put it this way: "When I am faced with a worried mother or father I have got a problem. Either there is something wrong with the child, something is wrong with the parents, or both. If I can't identify the trouble, then I am obligated to get this family to someone who can."

Many serious problems may develop when parents of children with handicapping conditions are denied an early definition of the problem with which they are confronted.

Confidence in professional competence is often lost. "Why doesn't this baby have a soft spot?" I asked my pediatrician when the child was very young. "Oh, you just had a lot of good calcium when you were carrying him," he replied.

"Why is this baby's head so misshapen and assymetric?" I asked a short time later. "Go home and look in the mirror. Your head isn't so symmetrical, either," was his answer.

In view of the exasperating feeding problems and the poor neuromuscular activity of our boy, these were significant questions. Such supposed to be satisfying, but incompetent answers, only served to bulwark my natural defenses towards the truth when it was finally given us by a physician skilled in diagnosis, a skill which I had expected of my pediatrician.

Parents may lose confidence in themselves. When a mother asks intelligent questions of a series of doctors about developmental lags over a long period of time and is still met with the authoritative, "Oh, give the child time. If you don't stop worrying, you'll turn out to be a neurotic mother," she turns out to be just that. This has insidious psychological effects, particularly when an in-law says to the mother, "Well, if I had that child" and the husband pays no attention to the mother's worries and blames the child's lag on her inability to manage with the youngster.

This is particularly discouraging when a young mother has no previous child with whom to compare the development of the youngster with a handicap and no previous opportunity to prove her competence as a mother.

Parental uncertainty breeds emotional ills. When parents are denied a positive approach to their problems, there is a tendency to vacillate between overprotection and rejection of the child. The child with a handicap is often the first to feel the effects of emotional unrest, particularly that of the mother, thus adding psychic wounds to further complicate the original handicap. This emotional unrest can spread to the normal children and the marriage partner. In such a vicious cycle our strength becomes exhausted and we may find ourselves wanting, when we are finally brought to grips with the problem. Too many mothers and fathers have had to plan for a child with a handicap primarily in terms of family disintegration rather than on the basis of the needs of their children.

Perpetuation of the shibboleth that there IS something shameful in having a child with a handicap. Some parents, in uncovering the true causes of retardation, have been incensed that we and the public have been denied the already-discovered truths. Many physicians, because of the poor cultural attitude, have deemed it a kindness to let parents identify their problem for themselves, never recognizing the devastating family and cultural impact they were making to keep our problem in the Dark Ages. Parents have risen to the challenge to bring about education of the public and professional workers must help. As one parent has stated: "We need society on our team, too."[3]

PARENTS MUST UNDERSTAND THEIR PROBLEMS

Parents need to understand the implications of their problem. They are entitled to a straight-forward, understandable explanation of their child's conditions presented in a simple manner. Words like "idiot," and "feebleminded," which may be excellent and descriptive clinical terms, are no longer appropriate in communicating with parents. Unimaginative writers and purveyors of so-called humor have distorted the meaning of such words with connotations of social or moral deficiency in the mentally normal.

---

[3]MacDonald, J. Clifford: The Role of the Parent in the Proceedings of training institute co-sponsored by New York Medical College and the National Association for Retarded Children, Inc., New York, New York, March 14-17, 1956, pp. 75-77.

Most parents do not understand medical terminology and its use should be avoided in so far as possible.

The child psychiatrist we consulted for help with our problem was sensitive to the use of words. Such terms as "moron", "feeble-minded" and even "mental retardation" were avoided in the course of his study. He avoided technical terms without making us feel that he was talking down to us. He always referred to our child as "your son," "your lad," or by the child's first name, in a manner which enabled us to think more about the boy's problem and less about our own hurt feelings.[4]

PARENTS MUST SEE THAT THIS IS THEIR PROBLEM

Parents should not be expected to solve the problem of a child with a handicap by themselves. They often need assistance in recognizing that it is fundamentally their problem.

One method is for professional counselors not to take the problem over for them.

Many well-intentioned counselors in the past thought they knew what was good for parents and recommended, even insisted on, a definite plan, particularly that of institutionalization. Denial of the existence of the child is not the solution for either the child or his parents. Abandonment is not the answer to the problem. Experience has proven that if parents are robbed of their responsibility for planning for the care of their child serious emotional problems are created.

Only as parents are helped to work through their problems can they achieve real peace of mind. If we do not plan for our child ourselves, if someone else makes the decisions, we have not really made up our own minds and so must keep going over the ground again and again. We may never be at peace with the solution which was reached for us.

Administrators of institutions say that the best help for families in adjusting to their child's placement is for the parents themselves, with adequate professional guidance, to have decided that placement is best for the child in relation to the total family welfare.

Few people realize how much professional, unsolicited, and untried advice parents receive from well-meaning people, including

---

[4]Jensen, Reynold A.: The Clinical Management of the Mentally Retarded Child and the Parent. *American Journal of Psychiatry*, 106:830-833, May, 1950.

neighbors, relatives, friends and even strangers standing on street corners. When, with guidance and example, we see this as our problem, we are better able to shut out the unsolicited and often conflicting advice and rely on our own judgment.

We need professional support to help us feel competent and develop confidence that we will ultimately make correct decisions for proper care in our particular case. Assurance is needed that there is no failure if we change our plan when circumstances change, for life situations and a child with a handicap present different problems at different times. Professional counselors can help us explore the possibilities for solving our problem; support us in adjusting to our decisions; act as a continuing sounding board against which we can bounce our own thinking, and lend us a good, sturdy shoulder on which to lean when we falter under our load.

ENLISTING RESOURCES

Presenting a family with an evaluation and prognosis for their child is only the beginning. We must have practical guidance for the day-to-day management of our individual problems. Parents differ in the quantity and quality of information they can absorb during the different phases of their problem. What they want and need depends on the individual but many of us have had to search for this practical knowledge and assistance.

When we began our search more than six years ago, a scarcity existed in printed material on the subject of mental retardation. Today there are many fine publications available to parents.

Regardless of what parents are able to read and absorb, many need encouragement to depend upon their own observations and judgment and most will have questions to ask. We often continue to need support from someone, whether our child is at home or away, particularly in those days which follow the confirmation that our child is permanently handicapped.

It seems inevitable in these days of specialization, that the pediatrician will be the key leader in enlisting auxiliary resources—the one most responsible for manning and directing the team. After the clinical studies he may very well be able to turn this leadership over to the social worker; or perhaps to the teacher or special services director in the schools, or to the administrator of a residential institution. In some cases he will always stay in the leadership role, or at least need to stand ready to accept it when the family seeks his counsel.

More and more we are seeing clinics which house the professional team, the pediatrician, the psychiatrist, the psychologist and the social worker, all under one roof. This is ideal from the parents' viewpoint because it is very trying to carry a child with a handicap from one waiting room to the next in order to gather resources into one piece. Many of our children with handicaps have developed anxiety in regard to red brick buildings, to say nothing of their mothers.[5]

Not all physicians have easy access to specialized clinics and so it becomes a part of professional competence to know the auxiliary resources and programs in the community and state so as to put families in touch with child and family welfare agencies. He may even need to take leadership in developing social resources. Many existing social welfare agencies are rising to the challenge to better interpret and inform the public of their services but the physician has the responsibility to seek out and know these services and facilities first-hand.

One parent voiced this criticism: ". . . they (physicians) do not know the institutional setup and do not take the trouble to find out what facilities are actually available and suitable for the child, nor do they refer parents to positive sources of information on these topics."[5]

Much of the needless "shopping around" with the attendant expenditure of energies and money could be avoided if, at the time of the initial contact by the parents, the physician knows the resources available.

THIS IS A FAMILY AFFAIR

The core of the problem is inherent in the child with the handicap, but around this are a constellation of problems. When one member of a family suffers, all suffer, and we must concern ourselves not only with the "total child look" but also with the "total family look." For this reason both parents should be present whenever possible and especially at the first consultation regarding a child's handicap. Professional workers frequently overlook the

[5]Zwerling, Israel: Initial Counseling of Parents with Mentally Retarded Children. *The Journal of Pediatrics,* 44:469-479, April, 1954.

fact that fathers are parents, too. If is very difficult for a mother to go home and restate, interpret and answer questions about a problem she does not clearly understand herself. Often the problem with its fears has brought about a lack of communication between mother and father. This is particularly true of a young married couple or when the retarded child is the first born. Establishing adequate communication is difficult in any marriage and finding the words to support one another in this problem has seemed impossible to some of us. We have needed an objective person through whom to talk.

Unfortunately, all husbands and wives are not like the one who, when he learned that their little daughter would not progress like other children, said to his wife: "Honey, we don't know what lies ahead of us, but whatever it is, we can handle it because we are strong people."

Many parents find the words and strength to support one another, but a definite responsibility for this support falls upon our professional counselors. The family must have unity of spirit, purpose and understanding if the needs of the child and the total family are to be met successfully. A child with a handicap is a powerful force for either unity or disunity. Nothing seems more tragic than to have a mother and father out of phase, with one or the other refusing to face reality; refusing to "place" the child (if that seems desirable), or threatening to "walk out" if a certain course is not followed.

PREVENTIVE PSYCHIATRIC ASSISTANCE

The greatest advances in medicine have been in the field of prevention. We need to look more closely for ways to prevent emotional breakdown within these families. A much better evaluation of parents, themselves, in the initial stages of counseling, seems indicated. Gifted, average, or limited, any of us can find our problems complicated by our own emotional makeup or an unstable marriage. Professional counselors must learn to watch for the evidence, and listen for the cues given that all is not well within the family.

After a long and perilous muddling through their problems, a few parents have expressed the wish that they had consulted a marriage counselor or a psychiatrist early because they have recognized that the child and his handicap was not the only problem and perhaps not even the most serious problem. They had been unable to gain the cooperation of their marriage partner, however, and saw little point, or lacked the courage, to go alone. Many of these couples, it seems certain, could have been led to appropriate help if the physician had focused his attention on the total family unit. This points to a need to interview the husband and wife separately when attitudes are to be evaluated.

Here we are delving into preventive social work and preventive psychiatry, the success of which depends largely on public education. We need to educate the public that social workers don't work exclusively with the poor and that psychiatrists are not just concerned with the insane. Any family can have a problem too big for them, and often parents need help in gaining insight to preserve or improve their mental health. Surely this attitude will ultimately prevail so that the physician can utilize these resources promptly and properly.

THIS IS A MARRIAGE PROBLEM

Too few recognize the marital hazards that a child with a handicap presents and only recently have parents gained courage to discuss these intimate facets of their lives. An endurable marriage can become unendurable under the stress of the many problems which arise when a child is handicapped. The fear of pregnancy, the emotional strains which interfere with normal sexual response, many subtle factors can enter to produce emotional breakdown, divorce, or result in two peoples' living under one roof going through the motions of being married, but isolated beyond imagination.

The majority of us cannot be told the exact cause of our child's condition but in most cases we can be assured that our chances for producing another defective child are no greater than those of any other couple contemplating procreation. Many families need this professional support in order to "try again" with any sort of equanimity. This assurance, however, cannot be given indiscriminately because there are cases where the chances for repeating the experience are great. We see far too many families who have been given false assurance or no guidance whatsoever and are now burdened not with one, but with two and even more mentally subnormal youngsters. In many of these cases the probability could have been forecast by genetic counseling.

The physician can be of great help to parents if he will give simple explanations of the already known causes, including some insight into the laws of human heredity. Many parents who have not studied the biological sciences interpret "inherited" in terms of having descended from a defective person like the bar maid in the Juke-Kallikak mis-research. If they are thinking of this as an underlying cause, and that both sides of the family would have needed to contribute to the picture, if they understood even the chance coming together of recessive genes, such couples could look across the breakfast table without the hate and hurt that go with blaming "his family tree." This is particularly important when one of the marriage partners comes from a family which has exhibited the defect.

Here, again, we need more public education in such matters. The time has come to make heredity respectable since we all have it. Any couple may produce a defective child, via either heredity or accident and thoughtful scientists are coming to the view that even those pathological conditions dependent on heredity turn out to be physical diseases when adequately studied. What consolation for parents of children with handicaps to have.[5]

ACCEPTANCE OF CHILDREN WITH HANDICAPS

"Acceptance" actually begins with this understanding of possible causes. All couples need to know that they do take chances when bringing children into the world. We are more prepared to accept a loss, just as any gambler must be prepared to lose if we know the facts.

Acceptance begins (or should begin) long before that child with a handicap has made his appearance. It should start in the child care and marriage courses, in pre-marital counseling, at the first visit to the obstetrician. Not in a fear-producing manner because the chances are excellent for producing promising children and certainly prospective parents have more important thoughts with which to concern themselves than, "Will this child be all right?"[4] But the facts must become public knowledge if for no other reason than to gain public support in research to close in on the uncertainties that do exist.

We talk a great deal about "accepting" children, but few seem to understand what is involved once a child presents a permanent handicap.

Acceptance, here, is no simple act but a multi-faceted and continuing process. To effect it, parents need great support in developing maturity and maintaining their mental health.

Yes, there is acceptance of the child as he is, with his handicap, and not as we had dreamed he would be, but it is more. It means accepting a reasonable prognosis so that we are realistic in our expectations of him. Further, there is the acceptance of our marriage partner, other children and their needs. There is acceptance of ourselves, our limitations, our feelings, some of which we cannot understand without help, and finally, there is the acceptance of living with an ever-present problem day in, day out; year in, year out, with all the stresses that go with it.

There is another dimension to acceptance, that of living with the plan chosen for our child. Many who have worked hard to effect improvements for the retarded, find themselves in a state of retroactive acceptance. With increased knowledge and understanding of the problem and the improvement in community facilities, it is often difficult to adjust to the decisions and mistakes that were made because of inadequate knowledge and guidance at the time of decision.

The statement, "Parents are good parents, when to the best of their ability, understanding, and circumstances, they provide as adequately as possible for the total needs of their children,"[6] has been of great help to many in understanding their basic responsibility for their children.

PARENTAL ATTITUDES IN ACCEPTANCE

The first and most immature attitude is that of ignoring, or pretending to ignore, reality. Initially, parents may refuse to admit that a problem exists and think, hopefully, "it just can't be." Unfortunately, there has almost seemed to be a conspiracy to help us develop this symptom of mental illness. Many of us have needed no encouragement in our attempt to escape from reality. The primary role of friends and counselors to troubled people is to

---

[6]Jensen, Reynold A.: Personal Communication.

discourage escape from the reality of the problem and to encourage the seeking of help for its solution. Although we often beg for it, we get enough "sugar coated solace" in the form of false hope from our friends, without getting generous doses of this bitter pill from professional counselors.

The next phase in development of emotional maturity is the accusing "scapegoat" stage. Parents admit that there is a problem and then proceed to blame: themselves, their mate (particularly his family tree), and by all means, the obstetrician, who only rarely deserves the discredit. This is a dangerous stage where moral principles may get jettisoned while thoughts dwell on suicide, murder, running out on a family or perhaps only drowning oneself in alcohol. Here we may find gross rejection of the child. Here may be the "cold frame" for many of the problems we create for ourselves, the incubator for the famous guilt-complexes.

Given proper knowledge and led to proper resources, with proper sustaining support and counseling, many parents can survive this phase very well. But this is the time when too many counselors have left us alone with our problems, thinking that there are certain things we would just have to work out for ourselves. There are, but we must not be left to do it by ourselves.

The final stage of maturity is admitting frankly that we have a problem, concerning ourselves not so much with the "who" and the "why," since most of us never find out anyway, as with the "what are we going to do about it?"

"Even the most unaccepting parent," says Dr. Leo Kanner, "is not a villain. The different types of attitudes are deeply anchored in the emotional backgrounds of the individual parents."[7]

As public education advances and professional assistance improves it is noted that parents are coming earlier and are receiving, more objectively, the expert help which they need, thus avoiding much suffering and the emotional scars that some of us older parents bear. Such unintentional and avoidable trauma can and will be prevented by education, specialized training and an increasing supply of skilled professional workers. Parents and parent-inspired organizations are hastening that day.

---

[7]Kanner, Leo: Parent Counseling in the Proceedings of a training institute co-sponsored by New York Medical College and the National Association for Retarded Children, Inc., N. Y., March 14-17, 1956, pp. 78-83.

PARENTAL ATTITUDES IN PLANNING

Dan Boyd, a New Jersey parent, has described three stages in the growth of a parent of a mentally retarded child: (1) Why did this happen to me? (Self-pity). (2) What can I do for my own child and family? (3) What can we do for others?[8]

These stages can be intermingled. The fact that a parent is working on a self-help organization does not necessarily mean that he has grown in relation to his own problem. Some can be stage 3 leaders, without having graduated from stage 1. These families are very hard to help. It often takes a long period of time and great skill on the part of professional counselors and their parent counterparts to help such parents make realistic plans for their own child.

Most parents, however, mature quite rapidly under the stimulus of the group. Self-pity fades when they find that they are not alone. Soon they are seeking to learn from and emulate the parents who are meeting their problems successfully. Before they realize it they are experiencing the healing that goes with helping another family. Some move on to be eager for all parents to have access to the organization which has rescued them from desolation.

Even these mature stage 3 parents may find themselves confined to stage 2 when problems arise in their homes or when previous decisions must be reviewed. During these times parents can be very difficult. Then professional counselors may need to lend great support while feeling "nothing but plain, simple, humble reverence before the mystery of our misfortune," to use the words of John Cowper Powys.[9]

SELF HELP ORGANIZATIONS—A RESOURCE

More and more, parent organizations are proving to be an important resource. Parents are regularly urged by professional counselors to join such a group for the value they will receive as well as the contributions they can make. "Parent counsel com-

---

[8]Boyd, Dan: The three stages in the growth of a parent of a mentally retarded child. Pamphlet. Nat. Assoc. for Retarded Children, Inc., New York, New York, August, 1953.

[9]Powys, John Cowper; The Meaning of Culture, New York, W. W. Norton & Co., 1929.

mittees" often function to receive referrals from professional sources because they find that parents who have successfully faced their problems offer a special kind of help to new families which supplements the help that professional counselors give. When we say, "We know how you feel," there is no questioning our sincerity. Here, too, it is important for both a mother and a father to visit with the new couple for this improves communication within both families.

There is great therapeutic value in parents' working together in organizations to help one another, although it has its problems. While most families benefit from membership in a group, others seem to find better adjustment outside. A few parents appear to be hurt by such membership. Much depends on the maturity of outlook and leadership of the group and whether the new member is receiving adequate professional assistance outside the group.

There is an optimum length of time for active participation in a self-help group which varies with individuals. "Occasionally, parents in their devotion to group activities may find an outlet for their problems at the expense of the child."[10] It is very easy for persons emotionally involved with a "cause" to let it consume them to the exclusion of other important areas of living. Our professional counselors can serve in an excellent guardianship role to guide us when they see us overdoing or using group activities to escape other responsibilities.

THE PROFESSIONAL-LAY PARTNERSHIP

Dr. Martha M. Eliot, former Chief of the Children's Bureau has said: "When officials of public agencies ask what kinds of services should be provided for retarded children, my advice is 'ask the parents' . . . (they) are often best qualified to say what help they need, thoughprofessional persons will have to provide the hows."[11]

Clearly the professional-lay partnership is essential, for in it lies our great hope for cultural progress in complicated social problems which carry us across all lines and cross-country through

---

[10]Richmond, Julius B.: Self-Understanding for the Parents of Handicapped Children. *Public Health Reports*, *69*; 702-4, July, 1954.

[11]Eliot, Martha M.: Unpublished address to the Nat. Assoc. for Retarded Children Inc., Boston, 1954.

the fields of medicine, psychology, education and social work. Our challenge becomes one of learning how to work together; of recognizing that there are problems, defining these problems and devising techniques for solving them; of defining our separate roles and evolving adequate methods of communication in order to serve more effectively together.

Dr. I. I. Rabi has stated: "Wisdom is by its nature an interdisplinary quality and not the product of a collection of specialists."[12] Certainly the parent who has lived with the problems of a child with a handicap, and has delved into the many aspects of such problems can bring a certain wisdom that may be denied the professional worker viewing the situation from his own discipline.

The emphasis must never be on the discipline but on the child and family which the various disciplines strive to observe.

"An immature, inexperienced professional worker may throw a potentially effective program into disrepute by attempting to prove that his or her profession has the major contribution to make to the family."[13]

Asked which professional counselor proved most important to them, parents might reply, "Our minister," just as quickly as, "Our physician." One parent did say, "The only real help we have had has come from other parents."

SOME PITFALLS IN WORKING TOGETHER

Parents are serving as members of the team, not only in helping with their own child, but at staff level—doing parent counseling, serving as speakers and teachers before professional audiences and are also consultants in planning and effecting services, facilities and techniques. It is important for professional people to be clear in their own minds what our status is at a particular moment, for these require a different level and type of communication, different ethics, manners and responses. We must do a great deal more thinking and writing in this virgin field if we are to reach

---

[12]Rabi, I. I.: Scientist and Humanist—Can the Minds Meet. *Atlantic Monthly*, pp. 64-67, January, 1956.

[13]Richmond, Julius B.: Health Supervision of Infants and Children. *The Journal of Pediatrics*, 40: 634-50, May, 1952.

true effectiveness in this very essential and creative area of working together to meet the needs of suffering people. We have some very real problems.

When we are working in partnership with lay people who are emotionally involved with a problem, we must always recognize that the work may be therapeutic and that the relationship is one of emotional support. It is very taxing to maintain an accepting attitude throughout the many stages of parental adjustment and maturity. Success can be highly rewarding but failure may prove quite serious.

We need to abandon any attitude that professional people always do certain things well and that lay people can't do certain things well; that professional workers always understand, and that lay people cannot understand the technicalities of a problem.

Parents of children with handicaps, standing as a symbol of human need, possess a freedom often denied to professional workers. They often have special skills, knowledge and experience which enable their earning the status of "professional laymen," a status worthy of the same respect afforded the professional members of the team.

Sometimes parents need to be encouraged to maintain and be proud of stating their point of view as parents. Our questioning of the status quo should not be construed as a threat to professional workers, nor should our professional friends encourage us to set up camp in professional or "bureau" quarters, for to do so dissipates our unique value to society.

As is so often the case, our main problems stem from inadequate communication. Here, intelligent parents can prove of great value by encouraging adequate communication between the various disciplines. Often parents find themselves acting as interpreters and inter-communicators. We are probably the first to ask, "What do you mean? Give us a working definition of that term if it is necessary to conversation." If our professional counselors can make themselves meaningful to us, they will be meaningful to their professional partners. We parents see so much knowledge that needs to be broadcast across professional lines.[5]

Specialization does not lend itself easily to plain talk. Further, the English language is beset with multiple meanings, with single words meaning different things to different people. Professional people need to be wary, particularly when using technical language before the public audience.

For example, the use of psychiatric terms, such as "anxieties, hostilities, frustrations, guilt-feelings" and other emotionally-charged words to describe our feelings, without adequate explanation as to what is meant, frequently does harm to parents who are striving to understand their problems. We need constructive help rather than explanations which do not explain, and frequently further confuse us. One authority appearing on a TV panel used the term "guilt-feeling" which caused a mother to write: " . . . Is not what appears to be 'guilt-feeling' to professionals, merely concern with the child's welfare, mingled with grief over his handicap?"[14]

Dr. Julius B. Richmond, pediatrician of the State University of New York Medical school, has said, "All parents experience some feeling of guilt about illness in their children . . ."[15] Dr. Hyman S. Lippman, child psychiatrist at the Wilder Child Guidance Clinic in St. Paul, Minnesota, expressed it as, "All parents of handicapped children must experience anxieties and frustrations."[16] Dr. Reynold Jensen, child psychiatrist at the University of Minnesota medical school, has written, "It seems natural for many parents of retarded children to feel some hostility towards the physician who leads them to come to grips with their problem."[17]

Ah, now we understand. These appear as natural feelings and the use of these psychiatric terms, alone or in sequence, is not meant to convey emotional ill-health, parental inadequacy, or that parents are responsible for their child's handicap. It is helpful for parents to know that these reactions are typical.

Now consider the warning given by the father of a deaf child. To frustrate a child's ability at lip-reading by obstructing his view of the speaker's mouth is just as bad as whispering in front

---

[14] National Association for Retarded Children, Inc.: New York. *Children Limited*, 4-5, June, 1955.

[15] Richmond, Julius B.: Lecture before National Society for Crippled Children and Adults, Chicago, No. 13, 1953. (Paper based on this lecture entitled, Self-Understanding for the Parents of Handicapped Children. *Public Health Reports*, 69: 702-4, 1954.

[16] Personal Communication

[17] Personal Communication

of him. In discussing matters with the parents (which are not harmful for the child to hear), the counselor should use care not to obstruct his mouth with his hand or turn his face too far away from the youngster. Thoughtful parents will often help by seeing that the child is placed so as to have a clear view.

The mother of a blind child told of the eye specialist who kept saying, "Look at me, Terry" to the lad, not realizing that to "look" meant to "feel." When the little boy kept putting his hands up to the physician's face, the doctor became annoyed. As it turned out, the child had no control over the position of his eyeballs.

Professional and lay people have much to learn from one another. We need each other and must create opportunities for discussing our problems and viewpoints in an atmosphere of freedom. Lay people need professional soundness for their efforts and professional workers often need the lay impatience and discontent which seems always to precede our greatest cultural progress.

IMPORTANCE OF PROFESSIONAL ATTITUDE

One significant and final conclusion can be drawn: The attitude of our professional counselors is most important. Most parents seem able, ultimately, to forgive inadequate knowledge and service, if their professional counselors have shown that they cared that people were troubled, were earnestly trying to understand and to help. Professional arrogance and jealousies, however, leave some parents suspicious and bitter. Parents are very sensitive to any patronizing attitude and find it difficult to understand when professional workers are unwilling to take the time to hear the truth which they can impart to help us all gain larger truths.

There are some who hold that in professional training too much emphasis is placed on "objectivity" and not enough on "loving kindness." Certainly, we parents expect professional counselors to be objective about our problems, but about us, never. Help can never be offered without regard and feeling for parental sturggles.

In seeing a good play, we are transported with the hero and heorine through a couple of hours of struggle with their problems. If it is an excellent play, we come away enriched with new insight and count it a well-spent evening. Skilled professional counselors learn to view our problems through our parental eyes in much the same manner. The term "empathy" is appropriate here. It is only through "empathy" that support, reassurance and guidance can be given.

"Feelingly persuaded" to find that we are, parents reveal many strengths. With professional help to convert our problems into the greater good for mankind, to discover the sweetness in the uses of our adversity, we parents do find meaning in our suffering.

The rewards for professional counselors in terms of satisfaction in helping parents of children with handicaps are great, perhaps more than most realize. Actually, it is as inspiring for parents in the field to observe the growth of professional workers, as it is rewarding for them to observe parents develop in stature and strength.

Through such a partnership it is possible for us all to become more effective people.

THE ROLE OF THE PSYCHIATRIST

Henry H. Work, M.D.

THE many handicapping conditions described in this book present the child thus involved, as well as his parents, with a variety of problems which the ordinary child never faces. Some of these conditions concern the development of the handicapped child's personality and the pattern of his emotional life. Though his rate of growth may be considerably different from the non-handicapped child, the fact that the child with both congenital and acquired handicapping conditions, by virtue of his own growth, faces all of the ordinary problems of living, is emphasized. Out of the confusion engendered by the way that his handicap is cared for, as well as by the way his general growth is proceeding, come problems which add to the handicap and which often make the life of such a child more difficult than need be in terms of the handicapping condition alone.

Our culture is much more tolerant of handicapped individuals and has gone further in an attempt to care for them than many previous or even existing cultures. Partly this tolerance exists because our culture exhibits a very real concern for every citizen, a feeling that everyone is equally entitled to the rights and privileges of membership in that citizenship and that acts of birth or subsequent misfortune are not in themselves socially discriminating. Our way of life, therefore, tries to make provisions for the care of each individual in proportion to his needs. More than in most other countries our culture makes an effort to see that each person grows up in his own right. If that person has disabilities which make it difficult for him to grow, our culture tries to provide services and facilities which will assist him.

On the other hand, many people in our culture express concern about contact with or employment of handicapped individuals. Such concern may grow out of fear which conflicts with the humanitarian instinct of the individual. Such fear is often supported by manifest morbid curiosity. Although a good deal of "There but for the grace of God go I" philosophy is expressed in our culture, the ability to make such an assertion may not be sufficient to permit an individual to assist others. In fact, such a philosophy may even interfere with the kind of associations that a non-handicapped individual has with the handicapped.

Important as is the acceptance of the handicapped individual by our culture, those persons who would aid the handicapped child must assess the way in which he grows, the way he conceives of himself in relationship to others. Such a conception may make the difference between an individual adjusted within his handicap, and therefore able to function, and an individual who is totally crippled and more than disabled by virtue of his handicap. Everyone concerned with serving the needs of the handicapped is aware that the total amount of the disability is no measure of the individual's feeling about himself. The Helen Kellers have long since proved this. However, many workers who minister to children with paralytic conditions are aware that very mild handicapping injuries may sometimes be much more important than severe ones. The fact that children who are blind or who are more totally disabled with such a condition as cerebral palsy have made adequate adjustment is of no advantage when trying to help the child with even a small handicap understand his own place in the social system.

Consideration of the variety of factors which play upon an individual either born with a handicap or developing one during the childhood years emphasizes the seeming major importance of the shape of the body. As each individual grows, a picture develops in his awareness of what he is like and how he functions. This graphic understanding has been named the "body image." As the relationship of the appearance of people to the way that they function has been studied, researchers have become aware that the individual's conception of himself is a very important factor in determining the manner in which he will function. In fact, the closer that the individual's body image comes to coincide with the way that others view him, the more likely he is to be a well-adjusted individual able to utilize all of his functions.

Such a body image is built out of the perceptions that an individual has as he grows. This body image is greatly modified by the way that these perceptions are permitted to function. Thus, the ordinary growing child with considerable curiosity explores all parts of his body, tests out the functions of his various muscles, finds out for himself what he can see, hear, feel and smell, and gradually begins to build up a picture of his own body and its functions in relationship to the outside world. Obviously, this process is either enhanced or made more difficult by the comments of people around him. A child may gain a more optimistic or a more discouraged view of his own body in the light of the opinions of his parents and friends.

The handicapped child not only has a distorted body on which to build certain percepts, but also he may lack certain sensory equipment which will assist him in making this image. To that extent the worth of the body image may also be distorted and there may be lacking the feeling of confidence that grows out of a good and well developed image. A child has a body image not only of his whole body, but also of the different parts of his body. The handicapped individual may gain a distorted picture of his body as a whole because of his particular focus of attention on that part of his body which is different from the ordinary.

Treatment is influenced by the picture that the individual has of himself. The manner of approach to the patient is through his concept of himself as it has developed over a period of years. Many of the exaggerated aspects of an injury stem from the irrational development of such a picture of oneself. Not only does the individual feel that he is different, alone, strange, or otherwise altered, but also fears and depressions rising from relatively small injuries complicate the picture of the handicapped. Considering the feeling of wholeness that most persons have about themselves, the smallest injury can alter this picture and give rise to a rather irrational and consequently fearful approach to the handicap.

During the war, individuals often suffered very superficial skin wounds. The soldiers' feelings about these superficial wounds frequently interfered with future combat duty. Since their feeling for wholeness had been somewhat shattered these soldiers felt that their whole bodies had been changed, or might be more severely damaged.

If the congenitally handicapped individual were to grow in isolation, he might form a picture of himself which would not include the concern about difference or strangeness. However, such a child has parents. The kind of body image which a congenitally handicapped child has of himself is formed not only by himself but by his parents. The parents are immediately, and oftentimes in overwhelming fashion, concerned about any handicap that is present at birth. This parental concern may be less noticeable in the case of certain internal defects, but is strikingly apparent when there is disfigurement of the skin, bones, muscles or extremities. This attitude is easily and quickly communicated to the growing child. Thus the image which the congenitally deformed child develops includes the same ingredients as are seen in the older child. The sense of inferiority, the sense of difference, and the sense of shame become particularly prominent.

Many congenital disabilities and those which occur early in life tend to interfere with normal physical growth of the child. At times, this interference with growth is complicated by the attitudes of the parents whose tendencies to restrict the activity of the child may further interfere with physical growth. More important, however, the activities of the parents in relation to these children interfere with the social and emotional growth of the child.

No matter what the handicap, the child's needs include the basic needs of an ordinary child. Usually these needs are met during infancy by the abundance of care that is offered to such small children. Our whole culture insists that the infant be kept dependent and nurtured. This kind of care is as easily given to the handicapped child as to the ordinary child. Because of his dependence on the parent and because of the considerable concern on the part of the parent, more care is frequently given the handicapped child.

With the ordinary child, however, the end of the first year marks a period in time when his dependence becomes less and when he begins to strike out for himself. Many of the handicapping conditions of childhood, such as cerebral palsy, amputations, blindness, deafness, etc., interfere with the child's ability to attain this independence. This interference does not, however, alter the need that such a child may have to become independent. A very considerable conflict may arise during the second and subsequent years as the child strives to gain a status for himself, to build up a more independent image of himself, and to function on his own. The parents, for a variety of reasons, must continue to care for the child. In so doing they may reinforce a dependence which may interfere with the child's emotional growth.

Such a condition is most graphically illustrated by the case of a child mildly paralyzed with cerebral palsy. This child was a problem to the therapists and physicians as he grew because the amount of his hemiplegic handicap was not sufficient to account for his failure to utilize the assistance that was being offered. An appointment was made to see the mother alone. At this time she was able to express her very extreme concern lest any of the child's activities injure him further. This concern had grown out of a very real feeling over what she fancied had occurred during her pregnancy which she had equated with causing the child's disability. To help her understand what her concern was doing to hamper the development of this particular child took a great deal of time. This mother was making very determined efforts to hold this child back and not to permit him to use what abilities he had. This parental hinderance is not an uncommon phenomenon. The child's emotional growth is crippled by the extreme zeal and devoted care which the parents wish to offer.

Unique or different kinds of emotional handicaps do not necessarily parallel each of the varying physical handicaps. The longer the disability persists the greater likelihood that emotional difficulties will develop. The common psychological symptoms of anxiety, fear, shame, and a sense of failure, often leading to depression, are all found in a variety of handicapping conditions. The strength of these symptoms and their importance to the patient depend on the manner in which his rearing has been handled.

Over recent years knowledge of the role of the mutual relation of parent and child in the growth process has greatly increased. This knowledge has indicated that the personality of the mother has much to do with the normal growth of a child, and that the kind of care which she offers may or may not enhance such growth. This maternal influence is uniquely true of the handicapped individual since the amount of care is even greater than is usually offered to growing children without disability.

Since a variety of concerns on the part of parents are immediately apparent, the fact that the parent feels considerable guilt when a child becomes ill and develops a changed body because of it is not surprising. The mother whose child develops poliomyelitis resulting in subsequent paralysis is immediately overwhelmed by concerns about what she might have done to prevent this illness. Doctors and others are frequently besieged with questions—"What might I have done?" "Could I have done this?" "Do you think I should have taken him out of doors?"—as soon as such an illness develops. Such guilt concern lingers over a long period of time. In fact, the subconscious effect continues to haunt the parent (and the parent's dreams) for years with each difficulty in which the child finds himself.

Such guilt or self-blame is natural and to be expected. In fact, parents have such common concern for their children that it would be highly unlikely that any parent should not have some concern lest something happen to his child. Any parent who did not have this normal concern would be considered a cruel or callous individual.

At the same time, the guilt may continue to interfere with the actual care of the child. This consideration becomes important in all handicapping conditions. The child who is born with a congenital defect elicits in his mother as much guilt as the child who suffers a broken leg because his mother has allowed him to play in the street. No easy measure of the depth of this guilt is available, but the individual concerned with helping the handicapped must be aware that it is present most of the time and that it may be a very important source of interference with the care of the child. Nor is it uniquely self-blame, because it includes the element of "Why did this happen to me?" as much as "What could I have done?". The parents' ways of answering these questions are often expressed in the care of the child.

The most common manifestations of rather severe guilt is the oversolicitous, over-sympathetic parental attitude. Particularly there is a decided effort on the part of the parent not to let anything further happen to the child. This determination becomes again of major importance when the physician considers the factors that interfere with the independent growth of the child, the giving of freedom, and the opportunity to carry out the child's own curiosity. The over-protection may so severely restrict the field of activity of the child that despite his handicap he grows up in a relative vacuum, unable to utilize whatever talents he has as an individual, over and above the handicapped portion of his body.

Shame also plays a large role in constricting the environment of the child. Such a shame is equally built out of the cultural experiences of the parent and the feeling that everyone not only considers her child different but does blame her for the defect. Such shame is extremely common throughout our culture, despite the tolerance that we have of differences among people. Many people still remain who are either scornful, frightened or concerned whenever they meet handicapped people. The parent sees this as morbid curiosity, a scorn and fear which engenders embarrassment on the part of the parents of disfigured or handicapped children and leads them to isolate their offsprings from contact with the outside world. Such parents try to protect their child from having experiences which can be potentially damaging. Other children are very prone to make remarks about handicapped individuals, and the stares and covert remarks of adults make the parent very hesitant about allowing the child outside the home. This parental concern interferes with those parts of the child's social growth which includes some knowledge of other children, or of the general environment and ways of coping with the environment. The handicapped child is left in the position of knowing a very limited portion of his total milieu and therefore having a restricted social maturity.

Even when the world and the community might accept the handicapped individual, the parents may make the assumption that this is not true because they themselves do not accept the handicap. Commonly, parents become so overwhelmed by the handicap, especially if it is a disfiguring one, that they make the assumption that the rest of the world feels exactly the same way. They therefore assume that because the child is so different, he is totally unable to adjust. Parents thus set up a constant barrier of dependence, just as has been noted previously.

Contrariwise, a certain number of parents adopt the mechanism of denial. They refuse to admit that a handicap is present. They accuse the child of malingering, or they may wander from clinic to clinic searching for someone to tell them that nothing is wrong. Such parents are a very common source of concern to medical and rehabilitative personnel. They present a very real burden because of the defensive method that they have set up to blot out the recognition of the handicap. In these situations the child is almost totally lost. When the people on whom he depends for help and support deny the presence of any difficulty, no matter how apparent that handicap may be, the child cannot understand what is happening. Furthermore, these parents are frequently less receptive to psychological assistance than the ordinary parent suffering from either shame or self-blame. Therefore the problem of assisting the child remains constantly harrassing, one that is never solved.

Despite the feeling of guilt that is engendered in parents, many of them also adopt the feeling that the care of the child is primarily or even entirely a matter of duty. This rationalization is particularly noticeable when the parent's own childhood was an unhappy one or marked by the same sense of duty. When this does occur, underlying hostilities which may at times be very close to the surface must be prepared for. This suggestion may seem out of keeping with the rest of the material which has been presented, but it is true that over a period of time parents encounter increasing difficulty in the care of their children. Parents so burdened may demonstrate this hostility very openly or with a very thin disguise. They may even demonstrate such ill feeling by the way that they overdo the medical care, sticking with needless rigidity to diets or painful schedules of medication. The overprotective attitude which has been described as coming out of guilt may equally come out of hostile-aggressive feelings which a parent may have toward a child. The "Why did it happen to me?" question may eventually turn to an expression of anger against the child because it did happen.

The care of any handicapping condition does present very honest and very difficult burdens on the parents. The mere extra amount of attention, the visits to physicians, and all of the factors which limit the activities of the parents are bound to give rise to feelings of ill will toward the child. Whenever such feelings develop in the parent, guilt again ensues and a distorted pattern is started which includes a greater anxiety and concern on the part of the parent, over-protection in the attitude toward the child, and the subsequent difficulties that have been previously noted. However, when a whole household revolves around a handicapped child and his needs, a feeling of burden quickly builds up in parents and in other children. Not only does this excessive care make a child self-centered and dependent on others (because he expects the same treatment from outsiders as he gets from his family), but it increases the feeling of overwhelming care on the part of the parents. The burden increases chronically with time.

Dependence is a comfortable state in infancy. As a child grows and becomes aware of what abilities he has, regardless of his limitations, such dependence becomes a more uncomfortable situation for any individual because of the vulnerability which is inherent in it. This same vulnerability is strikingly noticed when one goes to assist an older individual who is partially handicapped in any fashion. Graphic pictures of individuals rejecting help, clinging to their own crutches, wishing to push their own wheelchairs are highly expressive of the very severe concern the dependent individual has lest too much be done for him.

The reaction of the individual against being totally dependent is seen not only in children who are congenitally handicapped. In these children the dependence is a prolonged one, and the child may lack the ability to demonstrate his independence and to fight his way out of it. The child who, however, becomes handicapped by virtue of accidents or illnesses in later life finds himself in the same situation in relation to parents and friends. The common anxieties of parents show themselves very quickly in their effort to make the child dependent. Such efforts, sympathetic and considerate as they may be, have the same effect as the repression of independence in the growing individual. Just as the growing child's independence demands a way of expression, so the dependent position in which the later-time handicapped child is placed causes him to suffer from inability to utilize his remaining capacities and to expand his own horizons.

The ordinary child learns through curiosity, through imitation, and through a considerable freedom. This freedom is a very important element for the handicapped as well as the ordinary child. Not only must he achieve a certain amount of independence, but also he needs a freedom to explore and to try out his abilities.

Certain individuals are so badly handicapped that it becomes difficult to permit them any kind of freedom. Too often parents, in themselves concerned, tend to exaggerate the extent of the disability and are very concerned about permitting freedom. Carlson's classic way of his sudden ability to walk in front of the runaway horses is a beautiful example of the over-protected child who is suddenly released and finds abilities of which he was not aware. On the other hand, as the handicapped individual grows and as his dependence on others is either maintained or enforced, he comes to think of himself as highly inferior. He develops a sense of being in a minority group.

What resources have we to cope with the problems of dependence, vulnerability, loneliness, and the concerns of those who care for handicapped individuals? Being aware of the problems which we have described, and the ways in which handicapped individuals accept, reject or merely surrender to the reality of their defects, gives us a basis not only for understanding but for assisting the individual who is so handicapped.

Throughout this chapter stress has been directed to the effect of the handicapping situation on the total personality of the individual. Obviously, in caring for such an individual the physician must approach him also as a total personality. As Menninger says, "The disability is not so much what the examiner perceives it to be, as it is what the patient perceives it to be. It is the patient who suffers this pain, its continual presence, its effects on his feelings of dignity and worth, its crippling effects on his total functioning."

When a handicapped individual is old enough so that contact can be established and the problem discussed, something must be learned about the feelings that he has about himself. Those who would help must understand what his personal concept is, and what his body image is like. Those who would help must listen to his description of his difficulties. Those who would help must try to understand what the social crippling has been, in addition to the physical crippling. How great the dependence of the individual is must be explored in order to learn how vulnerable he feels because of this dependence. Equally, it will be necessary to explore the extent of either denial of the illness or rejection of help. Just as shame has been described in the parents, considerable embarrassment on the part of the individual in relationship to society and his place in it may exist. He, too, may feel a sense of guilt for having been a burden to others.

The problem of dependence is not unique to the handicapped individual. Many otherwise ordinary children are cared for by parents who over-emphasize the frailty of the child to try to enhance the infantile state and who make every effort to keep the child dependent. When this occurs, the child is described as "emotionally immature" even though his body may be normal in size and his understanding may be equal to the tasks of his age. The care of such children involves a going back and an understanding of the infantile or early state of the child. The child must be helped to develop a new relation with another adult and fight his way again to maturity.

Some of this development involves the subject of motivation. Children and adults who are overly dependent on others and are, therefore, immature, are frequently not at all motivated to help themselves. Such motivation grows only slowly out of the contact and out of the new identification with an inspiring adult. Inspiration is not denied by modern psychotherapy wherever it is properly used as a source of help to individuals who have become overly dependent. Inspiration is not the same as over-sympathy, or over-indulgence, such as these patients have known before. Inspiration involves setting a new and rather difficult example to be followed. The therapist has a peculiar opportunity in that he is not as involved with the handicapped individual as the parents or family who have had such a child in their care.

Those who care for handicapped children have a unique opportunity to demonstrate an attitude toward them which is similar to the encouraging attitude established and demonstrated toward other ill persons. A new kind of standard needs to be developed to which such children can identify. Such a standard is not devoid of pity, but it does not use pity in a maudlin fashion. Encouragement is fostered within the limits of the disability, and everything is done to stimulate self-activity rather than dependence.

In the problem of the social adjustment of the child there is always a concern about schooling. Most frequently such children are either protected from school or they are isolated and taught in unique situations which frequently support their dependence.

This position does not mean that the handicapped child should by any means be forced into a school situation with which he cannot cope. While it is ideal to get the child into as normal a school setting as possible, that child must not be placed in competition with children whose abilities are far greater than his. The impact of a handicapped child on a school situation in itself alters the character of the school setting. The handicapped child must frequently be moved into a school situation by graduated steps.

Initially this may mean merely the getting of the child out of the home into a protected school setting which does not offer competition but which places him with peers in his own handicapped situation. At least this breaks the particular dependent bonds of home and offers him an opportunity for independence in a restricted setting. Many children never get beyond such a setting, but there are those who can be helped to achieve some stability here before being prepared to move on to a more ordinary type of schooling.

The same principles and criteria which apply in the care of the patient apply to an understanding of the problems of the parents. The shame, the guilt, the self-blame and the unique concern that parents have, not only because of the defect in their child, but because of their feelings about the world around them, have been delineated. The fact that parents not only blame themselves, but become angry at the outside world and then at the child who has been the cause of their difficult situation has been stressed.

It follows, from such a description, that most of the attempts with the parent must be made to understand which of these many factors, or how many of them, are operating in any one situation. This attempt is often difficult to do. In the ordinary medical setting a parent presents the child, focuses attention on the child, and wants help for the child. When help is offered to parents, or when an attempt is made to try to understand parental feelings, parents frequently infer that the child is being deprived. Quite frequently parents initially resent any focus of attention on themselves.

Once given an opportunity to talk, however, parents quickly break down this barrier. During a relatively short series of contacts it is often possible to establish a relation with a parent wherein he can talk about the feelings which have existed since the time of onset of the handicapping condition. When this understanding can occur, the parents are able to bring out their own feelings of concern and anxiety, and to begin gradually to talk about themselves.

This envolvement of parents should by no means be done abruptly. To point out these feelings to a parent in the initial contact would be just as wrong as to accuse him of poor care of the child. Over a period of time a rapport can be established which can lead to an unburdening of the parents' problems. This development is nearly always possible in the usual medical contacts because the care of these children is a chronic process requiring frequent visits for the evaluation of change in the child.

During such a period of time, anyone concerned with the family situation can begin to make a contact which is separate from the child. When such a contact can be made, the parent then can begin to look upon himself as an individual and to begin to talk about his or her own problems in the care of the child. Such an isolation from the specific problems of the child is highly necessary; without it assistance for the child cannot easily be attained.

Many parents experience guilt about talking about themselves because of their sense of duty and the special concern they have that everything be done for their child. To break through this barrier is possible by helping them to understand the common principles which have been described, principles which suggest that the growth of the child is highly dependent on the kind of care which surrounds him. Once parental pride can be understood and accepted, once parental feeling of loneliness and grief can be felt and permitted to be expressed, a basis for an understanding of their relationship to the child can be established and advice can be given as to how much they may do and where to limit their activity.

Merely telling parents not to be over-solicitous, merely telling them to push the child into newer activities accomplishes little if an understanding of their concern about the child has not been delineated. When, however, this has been done, parents themselves can be led to a stage where they can set a better example for the child and thus serve as the inspiration for the motivation which the child himself so badly needs.

In summary, handicapping conditions have a very gross effect on the social and emotional development of the child. The fear, the blame, and the guilt that the parent feels (as well as the frequent antagonism toward the child), serve as a basis for a change in the rearing of such an individual. These feelings blind the parent to those basic needs which are similar to those of the ordinary child. They interfere, therefore, with normal growth by enhancing dependence and by not giving the child the ordinary freedom of learning. In many instances such freedom is greatly limited, but it is often more limited by the unique concern of parents about such a child.

Assistance for the patient comes from understanding his feelings about his illness, from discovering what his concept of himself is, and by correctly appraising the difficulties which he faces. This understanding, rather than sympathy for these difficulties, can offer a new kind of motivation to the handicapped individual. Work with the parent primarily includes an understanding of whatever basic bad feelings may be tending to interfere with the ordinary care of such a child. Such an understanding permits the parents to handle the child in a fashion not dissimilar from that which they offer to the rest of their children. Eventually, such an understanding removes the hostility that parents feel toward the child because of their own guilt, their own self-blame, and their own anxiety as to what may happen in the future.

That the emotional stability of a handicapped child can be fully restored is only rarely possible. On the other hand, many barriers to the progress of the handicapped child are quite needless, in many instances these barriers can be removed.

THE ROLE OF THE SOCIAL WORKER

Pauline M. Ryman, M.A.

Ideally the social worker functions as a member of a multi-discipline team which is involved in the care and treatment of the child with a handicap. These multiple services are needed, not just because the doctor has insufficient time to undertake the whole task, but because many different kinds of skills and knowledge are required to offer comprehensive services to the child, services which the doctor may not be professionally trained to offer. In this comprehensive approach, the various professional members of the team work together sharing the same objectives for the patient and his family, sharing the written records and case conferences which offer the opportunity for exchange of thinking and planning, respecting the skills of the other members of the team, and supporting the others in a mutual effort to contribute to the well being of the child and his family.

The social worker contributes to the care of the child with a handicap through direct service to the patient and the parents, through community organization and planning, and through consultation about social and emotional problems with other persons who are involved in the care of the child. In an opportune position to recognize the gaps in community services to meet the needs of children with disabilities, the social worker may make an important contribution in community planning by bringing to the attention of those who are responsible for community planning the needs which she observes in her daily practice.

The professional social worker has completed two academic years of graduate study leading to a master's degree in an accredited school of social work. Although she may employ various processes in social work according to the needs of the situation, casework is the process most frequently utilized. Social casework is a method employed by social workers to help individuals find a solution to problems of social adjustment which they are unable to handle in a satisfactory way through their own efforts. Three generally recognized casework processes include psycho-social study, diagnosis and formulation of treatment plans, and the treatment itself. Treatment may involve modifying the environment, giving support to patient and parents, or bringing about a change in attitude through giving of insight. Doctoral programs in social work are designed for those who plan to go into teaching, administration, or research.

The social worker may come in contact with the child wherever the child and his family present themselves for service. This presentation may be in the hospital, school, in camp, in a community agency, in an institution for children with handicaps, or in a guidance clinic.

The medical social worker who usually practices in a hospital or a health agency is available at certain critical points in the life of a child with a handicap. In most settings she enters into the situation only upon the referral of the physician. Orthopedists, neurologists, and pediatricians are particularly oriented to seeking collaboration of the social worker in treatment of their patient. Out of 4,832 hospitals reporting on this subject to the American Hospital Association in 1952, only 723 (17.5%) had a social department. More than half (410) of the 723 departments were in hospitals of over 250 beds. Nearly half of these departments had only one staff member.[1] Since it is probable that many infants with correctible congenital anomalies are born in hospitals lacking these specialized services, every physician and nurse should be well informed regarding the resources for providing and financing the medical services needed in such cases.

The most adequate resource for planning and treatment of children with serious physical defects is the state program for crippled children. Fortunately today every state and territory has an organized program for the child with a handicap, programs which provide the best possible medical and surgical care for all children who are in need. Although many states base eligibility entirely upon medical need, some states impose financial eligibility requirements. Parents who are in a position to do so are required to make some financial contribution. Paradoxically the state program for handicapped children often offers a better quality of service to low income families than is available at any price to those well able to purchase it. This paradox is due primarily to the fact that most state programs provide for the multi-discipline approach. All aspects of care are well integrated to provide a comprehensive service and an adequate follow-up.

One of the important contributions of the social worker to the multi-discipline group is the social study. Even though an adequate social history is undertaken at the beginning of the contact with the family, this study cannot be considered a static kind of evaluation. If a family is to survive and to function adequately, it must achieve a state of homeostasis. This state, however, may be disturbed when any member of the family is subject to new pressures. A family is a constellation of constantly shifting relationships made up of multiple interacting variables. Parents who at one point may be able to cope quite adequately with the problems presented by a child with a handicap might decompensate rapidly if the marital situation deteriorates, if the health of either parent fails, if unemployment occurs, or if other members of the family develop acute problems which create new stresses. Caseworkers with recent experience in working with parents of children with cerebral palsy have commented upon the value of the home visit in obtaining a better understanding of family relationships and of the place of the child in his family.

The caseworker is able through interviews with the parents to make an assessment of the strengths and limitations of the family and to evaluate their ability to cope with the problems presented by the child. The caseworker attempts to determine the meaning of this particular illness or disability to this particular family. Sharing of this information with other members of the treatment team makes possible the formulation of treatment plans which take into account the ability of the family to participate. Parents need to be made aware of the resources available to assist them with their particular problems. At the appropriate time other agencies in the community may be utilized to meet the needs of the child and his family. The parents should be prepared for referral to other agencies so that they are able to use the services more effectively.

The referral process consists of much more than giving the name and telephone number of an agency. The caseworker must be thoroughly familiar with the function of the agency, its eligibility and intake policies, its policies regarding fees, and the obligations of parents who apply for services. Most important she must not only assess the readiness of the patient and family to accept a referral but also she must determine the appropriateness of the agency for meeting the need of a particular patient at the time of referral. As new problems arise with which assistance is needed, supportive relationship with the caseworker must continue and be available to parents throughout the long treatment period. The parents must see the social worker as a helping person who is interested in their problems. Parents should be encouraged to seek further help as the situation changes. The changes may relate to the medical problem, to the family situation, or to the social and emotional adjustment of the child.

If the marriage relationship is satisfactory, pregnancy is usually a happy time for a young couple. Each anticipates with pleasure the birth of the baby. If the child is "born different" either partner may consider this a reflection of his adequacy. Either or both may react with disappointment, anger, frustration, or antipathy toward the child. Either may be overwhelmed by a sense of guilt and may wonder how this experience could have happened to him. Such an experience is one of the most difficult situations for a couple to face. At such a time they should be surrounded with understanding professional people who are able to offer the emotional support needed. Through a relationship established with the caseworker at the time of the birth of the child, parents may express their feelings of disappointment and anxiety.

Unfortunately the advent of a child with a handicap is often imposed upon an unstable marriage. Such an additional stress aggravates the relationship and results in projection of negative feelings on the spouse or the family. Either parent may choose to accept or deny the presence of difference. Either may establish defenses which mask a problem and which make the offer of professional help difficult. The physician who is too reassuring may blind himself to the existence of emotional problems in parents.

If feelings in regard to the handicapped child are not sufficiently handled at the time of birth, they may flare up when the next child is expected. Parents who have given birth to a child with a handicap are entitled to expert professional advice regarding the hereditary aspects of the problem. If the social worker in her contacts with parents discovers anxiety in regard to the possibility of another defective child, she may direct them to sources of expert help in this regard. If chances of their having another defective child are great, they may want advice regarding contraception or sterilization. Most marriages cannot bear up under the constant fear of repeated pregnancies with the possibility that other children may also be defective.

The stresses imposed by the presence of a child with a handicap sometimes cause marital relationships to deteriorate to the point where marital counseling is indicated. In some instances such counseling may necessitate a referral to a family caseworker agency where this service is available. Such situations provide an opportunity for a family caseworker to collaborate with the medical social worker who may be involved with the child and his family in regard to medical treatment. The family caseworker can take into account the impact on family relationships of the presence of the child with a handicap in the family. Social workers involved with such children and their parents have observed that one of the most important determinants in the mother's ability to handle her child's problems is the understanding and emotional support which she receives from her husband. If either marital partner is so emotionally immature that he cannot permit the other parent to give to the child the time and attention needed, a constant situation of friction is created which has a damaging effect on all concerned.

Prompt and adequate treatment to overcome deformities may be indicated. The child with a handicap wants to appear as little different as possible from a normal child at the time that he begins to relate to those outside the immediate family. The social worker may assist the family to accept medical recommendations for hospitalization and surgery. She may prepare the child as well as the parent for these experiences. All of those concerned with the care of the child must appreciate the significance of hospitalization to him. The effects of separation on both the young child and his parents must be understood and dealt with skillfully. Liberalization of visiting privileges and the presence of the parent while a child is undergoing painful procedures tend to reduce anxiety. Formerly the medical worker worked alone to offset many of the irritants in the hospital environment which might have an unfavorable effect upon the child and her family. Due to the recent trends in education for nursing, medicine, and hospital administration, all of those involved in the care of the sick child are becoming more sensitive to his needs and work together to make the hospital experience as satisfying as possible to him.

A few of the more progressive hospitals are experimenting with social group work services for hospitalized children. Such programs usually start with the organization of a recreation program but with much more extensive objectives. The group worker, a professionally trained individual who has completed two years of graduate training in an approved school of social work, must recognize the distinctive elements in the personality of each child as that child struggles to grow up, to adjust to the separation from his parents and friends, and to cope with the frustration of illness in a strange environment of the hospital. The social group worker must see the child as a whole with his family background and cultural pattern, with his particular illness, and with its meaning for him. Occasionally he will need to explain to the child the restrictions of the medical treatment and hospital care. By means of guided group experiences the social group worker in a hospital may help individuals to develop and to use their capacities for personally satisfying social relationships, to deal with problems presented by their environment, and to use the resources of this environment in a constructive way.[2]

The social group worker, usually a member of the social service department in the hospital, works closely with the medical social worker who may have a relationship with the individual child patients in the group as well as with their parents.

The social worker frequently functions in programs for the blind, the deaf, or the hard-of-hearing child. As in other handicapping conditions these children present special problems to parents. That these children be provided with adequate diagnostic and treatment facilities and that special training facilities be made available at the proper time is important. Counseling with parents and children may help to overcome some problems and prevent others. Since many small communities lack special training facilities, these children may be faced with the additional problem of long separation from their families in order to obtain an education. Under such circumstances to preserve family ties and to maintain the interest of families in their children is especially important.

The medical social worker may also be useful as children become acutely ill with sequelae which may constitute a permanent or temporary disability. This assistance includes work with patients with polio, with rheumatic fever, with amputation due to malignancy or acute infection, with disabling conditions which are recognized as the child develops such as muscular dystrophy, and epilepsy, or with disabilities acquired as the results of accidents. In those instances where the child is old enough to establish a relationship with another person, the caseworker may work with the child as well as the parent.

The caseworker assists the family in meeting their fears of chronic illness, disability, and disfigurement. The caseworker must be sensitive to the feelings of the family toward treatment and toward use of appliances. Usually there is the advantage of time in continued contact with the patient and his family. The caseworker must provide a thoughtful long-range service, and she must offer her help at the tempo geared to the needs of the patient and his family.

Ilene Blackey has referred to the medical social worker as the "professional glue by which various aspects of the hospital service are brought together in behalf of the patient."[3] The social worker serves a motivating, facilitating, coordinating role in addition to the service which she provides directly to the patient and his family.

Those social workers who are involved in the treatment of children with physical handicaps should keep in mind at all times that the presence of a physical handicap at birth or a handicap acquired later need not constitute a handicap in regard to adjustment to life. Since the child with a handicap is first of all a child, he has the same emotional needs as a normal child. Because of the additional problem imposed by the physical disability, he may require more emotional support from his parents and others about him than a normal child would need. Because of advancing medical knowledge, many physical disabilities can be almost completely overcome before the time the child starts to school. If his social and emotional adjustment are adequate, he may be able to lead a normal satisfying life and to achieve the same amount of independence as a physically normal person. The caseworker, sensitive to stress factors in family relationships as they affect the child and as they affect the parents in their ability to relate to the child, must be able to offer the support which is needed.

Parents must impart a feeling of courage and self-confidence to the child. Every child has to feel that he belongs. He must develop a sense of trust in those about him. From the beginning he must sense the feeling of security which loving and warm parents can give him. He takes a cue from the attitudes he finds in his home. If the parents are cheerful and matter-of-fact and if in their attitude he can sense a loving acceptance, he acquires the security that he needs in order to develop and grow up with his handicap. Some parents find difficulty achieving this attitude toward the child. If their own conflicts in relation to the child's deformity can be minimized, they can then be more helpful to the child in relation to his own attitude. Parents may require support in placing limits on the child with a handicap because of their over-concern for him and because of their need to overprotect him.

The caseworker should be constantly alert to the possibility of providing as many normal life experiences as possible to the child with a handicap as well as to his family. This possibility of course includes adequate schooling, the opportunity to develop fully any talents which he may possess which help him to compensate for areas of activity in which he cannot participate. Summer camp experience often offers an opportunity for a child to develop new skills as well as to give his family a period away from him. The provision of sitter service to allow young parents to have a social life apart from the child is important to maintain stability in the marriage. In one community a group of medical students organized a sitter service which was made available to parents of children with cerebral palsy. This service provided the students with a valuable opportunity to observe the problems presented by such a child in his home and to his family, and the parents were able to go out and enjoy a social evening with the assurance that the child was being well looked after by a person who had some familiarity with medical problems.

Some parents have difficulty in adapting to a well child after having had a long experience in considering the child "sick." As an example a child with a congenital heart defect may have been restricted in physical activity and in general treated as a sick child. Following corrective surgery he may have become for all practical purposes a normal child. The parent as well as the child may need help in making this transition.

The social worker has an important contribution to make in the preventive area. Good prenatal care often prevents the occurrence of congenital anomalies. Because the social worker often becomes involved with expectant mothers early in their pregnancy, she can urge them to seek adequate prenatal care from a qualified obstetrician who can give sound advice and care during pregnancy. As workers become more familiar with some of the elements which determine prematurity, they can help to eliminate some of the stresses in families which may precipitate premature birth or which may create unfavorable attitudes toward pregnancy. The medical social worker who encounters a young woman with a physical condition which is a contra-indication for a pregnancy may make available advice regarding contraception. Since nutrition is important to the well being of a pregnant woman, social workers in public agencies, alert to the importance of this factor, can suggest food menus and consult in regard to nutrition so that expectant mothers can have an adequate diet.

The child with mental retardation presents special problems to parents. In general the social worker's approach to this type of problem is similar to that of the child with a physical handicap. Depending upon the degree of retardation, institutionalization is sometimes indicated. If institutionalization seems to be the best plan both from the standpoint of the child and the parents, the caseworker may offer a valuable service in helping parents move toward a plan by attempting to relieve any feelings of guilt which may exist in regard to placement of the child. The social worker does not exert pressure on the parents to arrive at a decision regarding institutional care. Fortunately due to the activities of parent associations, state legislatures have improved the quality of care which is available in state institutions. Parent groups have also helped parents to become aware that their problem is not an isolated one but a problem shared by many other parents. Improved facilities in communities for the training and socialization of retarded children have tended to relieve the problem to some extent and to make it more possible for some parents to keep retarded children with them in the home. The social worker may assist parents in facing the apparent hopelessness of some situations. Parents must not deplete their emotional, physical, or financial resources, or mortgage their future in a futile effort to seek a cure for an apparently untreatable condition. Where warrented reassurance should be offered, all professional people who come in contact with parents need to be prepared to handle overt and latent anxieties which exist in relation to such problems. If another kind of expertness is needed to provide factual information, this expertness should be made available. Sometimes the parents benefit from the opportunity just to be heard by an understanding listener.

In instances other than those of mental retardation, consideration either of foster home or institutional care of a child with a severe handicap must be made. The child welfare worker can become active in regard to planning for foster care, in working with the child, with his natural parents, and with the foster parents. She may continue to provide supervision as long as the child remains in foster care.

In recent years children with congenital anomalies have become eligible for adoption. Formerly they were not considered adoptable and accumulated in children's institutions. Due to improved medical and surgical procedures, many correctible defects are overcome early. Adoptive parents are able with interpretation from the caseworker in the adoption agency to accept such children and to provide them with all of the advantages available in a normal home situation.

The child with emotional problems, even though his physical endowment is normal, may be even more handicapped than the child with a physical disability. Parents with children of this type may present themselves to a variety of agencies. They may come to the attention of the school, the court, the family and children's agencies, or the pediatric clinic. Social workers in all these settings must be well equipped to recognize this type of problem and to refer parents to the proper source of help for themselves and for their disturbed children. This problem is presently complicated in most communities by the fact that both out-patient and in-patient facilities for this type of treatment are vastly inadequate. Long waiting lists are the rule at most treatment centers.

The social worker may participate in one of several ways with the child who is emotionally disturbed. Since she usually functions in an intake capacity, she is usually the first person to interview the parent. After the intake conference at which time a decision is reached regarding acceptance of the patient, the caseworker may work with the parent while the psychiatrist works with the child. It is usually not considered possible to modify the child's problems if the parents are inaccessible to treatment. Some social workers offer direct treatment to disturbed children. Group workers also function in settings offering this type of care, both in out-patients and in residential treatment centers.

As in the case of the physically handicapped child, a social worker has an important role to play in regard to prevention of emotional disturbances in children. The social worker should be aware of the impact of crisis situations on children such as occur in acute or chronic illness or absence from the home of the parents, of the effect of marital incompatibility on children, of the impact of the presence of a physically handicapped child on other children in the family, of the effect of separation on children, of the importance of adequate recreational programs and group experiences, and of the traumatic effects of material deprivations such as inadequate diet, crowded housing, and feelings of insecurity due to unemployment. Recognition of these factors should result in bringing into play appropriate resources for offsetting undesirable influences.

At the time of the establishment of the State Crippled Children Program under the Social Security Act of 1935, provision was made for medical social consultation on a federal level. States were encouraged to create similar positions. Since this pattern of organization has been followed in most states, the contribution of the medical social work consultant has had a marked effect upon the formulation and application of policies. The consultant contributes her knowledge of casework philosophy to the administrator of the state program, usually a physician, and to other members of the treatment team. She is able to evaluate the effect of policies and procedures on the patient and his family and to recommend changes to improve and to extend services. As an example, some states required a court commitment in order to make the services of the state agency available to the child. Social workers, observing that this procedure served as a deterrent in acceptance by parents of agency services because it aroused fears that parents were actually relinquishing responsibility for decisions in regard to treatment, worked for more appropriate procedures. Actually the original intent of the court procedure was based on the fear that parents might fail to follow through with complete treatment and that the original investment of tax funds in the child's care might be lost through incomplete treatment. Gradually a more enlightened attitude has emerged. Consent and cooperation of parents is now sought through a casework approach rather than through legal channels. Most states have now modified their laws to make the court procedure unnecessary.

Many problems presented by patients and families can be met by other members of the treatment team or by changes in the institutional setting. The medical social consultant may contribute to the understanding of the multiple facets of the problem through interpretation and sharing of information with other team members.

At least one social work consultant is included in the professional staff of most of the voluntary health agencies who provide medical or health education services. In these situations the consultant usually functions in program planning, policy formulation, and consultation with others on the treatment team rather than in providing direct service to patients. The social worker is being utilized increasingly in interdisciplinary teams engaged in research on problems related to children with handicaps, as well as in other medical research.

In summary, the social worker in the hospital, in the family agency, in child welfare, in public welfare, in the school, in the court, in the child guidance clinic, in children's institutions, or in the official or voluntary agency offering medical service contributes to the care, adjustment, and rehabilitation of children with various physical and psychological problems. She assists parents to solve their problems presented by these children, offering assistance employing casework, group work, and consultation. Through her participation on the multi-discipline team involved in medical care and rehabilitation of the child, the social worker established her unique professional role.

REFERENCES
1. *Social Work in Hospitals*. Published by U.S. Public Health Service, 1955, Department of Health, Education and Welfare.
2. *Helping Hospitalized Children Through Social Group Work*, Coyle, Grace L., and Fisher, Raymond. *The Child*, April, 1952.
3. *Social Work*, Vol. 1, No. 2, April, 1956, Eileen Blackey.

THE ROLE OF THE TEACHER

Ralph L. Steffek, Ed.D.

To its innumerable admirers, the United States of America has always been more than a geographic location, more than a form of democracy, more than a nation of free people. The United States of America has stood for a way of life, a way of life which has emphasized the opportunity for the fullest development of the unique capacities of every individual. The United States of America has been the embodiment of the idea that every person has worth and dignity. The United States of America has been the tangible demonstration of mankind's fondest hope, a dynamic society within which every man, woman, and child possesses inherent rights and within which every citizen is expected to think critically, to respect differences, and to serve the community according to his talent and ability.

To achieve this brave concept, responsible citizens have devoted themselves for more than a hundred and fifty years to the nurturing of a system of education which would strengthen the basic principles of freedom, equality, and self-government which undergird American democracy. In organization, program, and outlook, these citizens have insisted, American education shall be committed to the ideal of individual liberty, shall reflect a respect for a government of law, and shall serve all of the children of all of the people. To underscore their determination, these citizens have caused to be written: "Religion, morality, and knowledge being necessary to good government and the happiness of mankind, schools and the means of education shall forever be encouraged."

Creating a system of education whose organization, program, and outlook would reinforce the basic principles of freedom, equality, and self-government has been the significant achievement of the American people. Starting with little but a dream of a way of life that would grace all men with dignity, these Americans have had to root out the aristocratic assumptions that education is the prerogative of privilege, that education is to be controlled by and for an elite, that education, except for cases of charity, is to be limited by wealth, class, caste, race, or religion. In place of these totalitarian notions, Americans have had to engrain the declarations that education shall be the heritage of every child, that education shall be universal and compulsory, that public education from the nursery school through the university, as a matter of public policy, shall be supported and controlled by civil government, a basic obligation of a free society.

The creation of a system of education which would reflect these democratic aspirations has required the American people to undertake several major responsibilities. They have had to recruit and train a vast corps of teachers. They have had to design and construct hundreds of thousands of schools simply to house the school age population. They have had to develop and produce a multitude of teaching materials including a vast range of textbooks, courses of study, laboratory equipment, films, recordings, resource units, and furniture and equipment designed to serve the needs of a population ranging from five years of age through twenty-one. Most important of all, they have had to evolve and gain acceptance of a set of values making possible the expenditure of a portion of the national income for the support of education.

A constantly expanding population has contributed to the magnitude of these self-imposed tasks. A study of *Table I, United States Population and Education Statistics, 1900-1970,* indicates that during the first half of the twentieth century the nation's population doubled and that the rate of increase is accelerating. This increase in the number of children for whom educational opportunity has had to be provided, coupled with the fact that an ever-increasing percent of eligible children and youths are continuing to enroll in American schools, accounts for the fact that three times the number of teachers who served American education in 1900 are presently needed to provide every child with a competent instructor, a number which will increase to five-fold by 1970. And although a severe shortage of qualified teachers continues to prevent the full realization of the ideal in American education, the facts continue to insist that even the present partial achievement is without parallel in the history of mankind. Thousands

TABLE I
United States Population and Education Statistics, 1900-1970

Year	United States Population	Population 5-13 Age	Population 14-17 Age	Percent and Number Enrolled in Schools		Population 18-21 Age	Percent and Number Enrolled in Schools		Teaching Staff
1900	76,094,000	15,000,000	6,131,000	698,000	11.4	5,931,000	238,000	4.0	515,000
1910	92,407,000	17,134,000	7,254,000	1,117,000	15.4	7,335,000	355,000	4.8	637,000
1920	106,466,000	20,124,000	7,869,000	2,500,000	31.8	7,334,000	598,000	8.1	819,000
1930	123,077,000	22,267,000	9,369,000	4,804,000	51.3	9,027,000	1,101,000	12.2	1,032,000
1940	132,122,000	19,942,000	9,847,000	7,072,000	71.8	9,754,000	1,494,000	15.3	1,091,000
1950	151,683,000	22,285,000	8,445,000	6,392,000	75.7	8,925,000	2,659,000	29.8	1,235,000
1960	170,000,000*	33,000,000*	11,187,000*	9,172,000*	82.0*	9,581,000*	3,260,000*	34.0*	1,750,000*
1970	190,000,000*	45,000,000*	15,500,000*	13,500,000*	85.0*	14,512,000*	6,500,000*	45.0*	2,500,000*

*Estimated
Sources: U. S. Bureau of the Census
U. S. Office of Education

of teacher training schools have had to be built and to be staffed. Courses of study have had to be determined. Certification standards have had to be set, research in a multiplicity of fields to have been undertaken. To have developed the means to have trained even the present army of teachers to their present capacities is an achievement which is dwarfed only by the even larger challenge which must be met during the last half of the twentieth century. America must train over two and a half million persons to become teachers by 1970.

School enrollment statistics confirm observation. The opportunity for schooling is increasingly being extended to every child. Community leadership is accepting the child who is mentally exceptional, physically handicapped, maladjusted, or educationally exceptional as a logical extension of its public commitment to make educational opportunity a heritage of every boy and girl. Schooling for the mentally retarded and the mentally superior, for the orthopedically handicapped and the emotional maladjusted, for the child with lowered vitality or with speech or reading problems, for the child who is deaf, hard of hearing, blind, partially sighted; in short, schooling for the total range of the school age population is today a reality in scores of communities throughout the United States.

In those communities where educational opportunity for the full range of the school age population is not the accepted public commitment of community leadership, at least one role of the teacher is clear. In such areas the teacher has the professional responsibility for cooperating in the creation of a more favorable climate of community opinion. As an individual who should stand up to speak for children, the teacher must create the opportunities to say to public groups, "As this nation's strength among nations lies in its human resources, children are this community's most important single asset." To the parent, he must find the occasions to emphasize, "If your child is to be this community's most vital concern, you have the responsibility for meeting and banding together with other parents who are as concerned as you for the well-being of their children." A brief review of the efforts of parents of children with cerebral palsy, childhood nephrosis, mental retardation—to cite but three examples—is convincing proof of the power of even a single devoted individual to move a whole community to dare to harness its best effort in behalf of its children.

Although many parent groups have successfully moved their community leadership to accept the responsibility for providing schooling for the child with a specific handicap, more effective educational gains have been scored when such groups have merged their leadership and resources in a cooperative community effort to improve their schools. Individuals or groups who want assistance in such a cooperative community effort may receive a free copy of *How Can We Organize for Better Schools?* by writing to the National Citizens Commission for the Public Schools, 2 West 45th Street, New York 36, New York. The pamphlet is one of the clearest and most comprehensive guides for helping community leaders organize and sustain effective action to strengthen school programs.

Because of their direct relationship to children, teachers are in a key position to understand that effective programs of education represent the combined efforts of a complex of factors. They know that although educational activities constitute a significant operation of the federal government, education continues to remain largely a state function. They know that although federal programs have spurred local communities into action, these vast educational programs are largely uncoordinated and that the Office of Education, a unit within the Department of Health, Education, and Welfare, has not yet been charged with integrating the federal effort. Consequently the forty-nine state systems of education in the United States operate almost independently of one another . . . Thus American educational policies are largely embodied in state constitutions, in state statutes, and in decisions of state supreme courts.

The state constitutions give the state legislatures almost complete authority over education within their states and usually make the state superintendent of public instruction responsible for its general supervision.

In the main, the state legislatures, in turn, have delegated this constitutional authority over to officers, boards, or agencies on a state, county, township, or local level.

Such districts, the administrative units which actually organize and offer the educational program for children, are almost always independent units of government, almost always entirely separate from city, township, or county units of government. Each such local board of education operates as a policy-making unit, determines the scope of the educational program to be offered locally, employs personnel, establishes the length of the school year, adopts salary schedules. Legally, these district boards can exercise only the powers granted to them by the legislature in general statutes. Such statutes, generally known as a School Code, require the establishment of school districts, provide for the election of boards of education by registered voters living within those school districts, define the rights, duties, and responsibilities of parents, children, and school officials, regulate matters of safety within the school building, and provide a formula for the distribution of monies appropriated from the general fund of the state or collected by the state for the support of education.

The local superintendent of schools is usually the executive officer of the local board of education. He has immediate charge of the entire school system. He nominates all candidates for employment, promotion, transfer, or dismissal. He usually prepares the annual budget, interprets it for adoption, and administers the budget after it has been adopted by the board of education. He directs the planning of new buildings, administers all of the schools, curriculums, and classes established by the board. He directs the instruction, the promotion, and the graduation of students. He executes the policies of the board and serves as its professional advisor.

Superintendents of schools and administrators generally are aware of the fact that their ability to discharge these many responsibilities is largely dependent on the quality of the school staff and upon the effectiveness of communication among and between board members, school staff, and the community whose educational aims are to be met. While he should be "the educational conscience for his community," the teacher who is identified with his profession can be the unifying force assisting school superintendents and administrators to understand more fully the aspirations that parents do have for their children. At the same time, such a teacher can help parents to accept the responsibility for providing administrators with both the financial means and the public support needed to translate those aspirations into actual programs.

As a member of a school staff, every teacher has the professional responsibility for helping to shape the educational philosophy of his school, for establishing educational goals, and for determining the educational procedures which he and his colleagues will pursue to achieve those goals. Publishing a statement of these objectives establishes criteria by which not only the staff itself but also the public to be served can determine whether the educational program implements the philosophy. One such statement, written by William G. Carr and published by the Educational Policies Commission in *The Purposes of Education in American Democracy*, lists the objectives of American Education under four over-reaching purposes as follows:

THE OBJECTIVES OF SELF-REALIZATION

The Inquiring Mind. The educated person has an appetite for learning.

Speech. The educated person can speak his mother tongue clearly.

Reading. The educated person reads the mother tongue efficiently.

Writing. The educated person writes the mother tongue effectively.

Number. The educated person solves his problems of counting and calculating.

Sight and Hearing. The educated person is skilled in listening and observing.

Health. The educated person understands the basic facts concerning health and disease.

Health Habits. The educated person protects his own health and that of his dependents.

Public Health. The educated person works to improve the health of the community.

Recreation. The educated person is a participant and spectator in many sports and pastimes.

Intellectual Interests. The educated person has mental resources for the use of leisure.

Aesthetic Interests. The educated person appreciates beauty.

Character. The educated person gives responsible direction to his own life.

THE OBJECTIVES OF HUMAN RELATIONSHIP

Respect for Humanity. The educated person puts human relationships first.

Friendships. The educated person enjoys a rich, sincere, and varied social life.

Cooperation. The educated person can work and play with others.

Courtesy. The educated person observes the amenities of social behavior.

Appreciation of the Home. The educated person appreciates the family as a social institution.

Conservation of the Home. The educated person conserves family ideals.

Homemaking. The educated person is skilled in homemaking.

Democracy in the Home. The educated person maintains democratic family relationships.

THE OBJECTIVES OF ECONOMIC EFFICIENCY

Work. The educated producer knows the satisfaction of good workmanship.

Occupational Information. The educated producer understands the requirements and opportunities for various jobs.

Occupational Choice. The educated producer has *selected* his occupation.

Occupational Efficiency. The educated producer succeeds in his chosen vocation.

Occupational Adjustment. The educated producer maintains and improves his efficiency.

Occupational Appreciation. The educated producer appreciates the social value of his work.

Personal Economics. The educated consumer plans the economics of his own life.

Consumer Judgment. The educated consumer develops standards for guiding his expenditures.

Efficiency in Buying. The educated consumer is an informed and skillful buyer.

Consumer Protection. The educated consumer takes appropriate measures to safeguard his interests.

THE OBJECTIVES OF CIVIC RESPONSIBILITY

Social Justice. The educated citizen is sensitive to the disparaties of human circumstance.

Social Activity. The educated citizen acts to correct unsatisfactory conditions.

Social Understanding. The educated citizen seeks to understand social structures and social processes

Critical Judgment. The educated citizen has defenses against propaganda.

Tolerance. The educated citizen respects honest differences of opinion.

Conservation. The educated citizen has a regard for the nation's resources.

Social Applications of Science. The educated citizen measures scientific advance by its contribution to the general welfare.

World Citizenship. The educated citizen is a cooperating member of the world community.

Law Observance. The educated citizen respects the law.

Economic Literacy. The educated citizen is economically literate.

Political Citizenship. The educated citizen accepts his civic duties.

Devotion to Democracy. The educated citizen acts with an unswerving loyalty to democratic ideals.

Just as no man can make up another man's sleep, so no published set of educational goals and objectives can be taken over and be said to represent the goals and objectives of a particular school or school district. However, such listings can be the spur to action, the basis for discussion, the challenge to discipline thought to the point where each individual has a reasoned basis for formulating his answer to "What is good for children?", "What should be our purposes in education?" And since schooling is a community responsibility, the community must share in shaping the answers to these key questions.

Educational procedures based upon the accumulated insight into how children and youth grow and develop and into how creative power, imagination, and the thrill of living can be released in every child command every teacher to insist upon at least the following decalogue:

1. **Every Child Is Unique**

Upon conception, he differs from every other child in his genes, his inherited potential.

Since this potential is affected by a host of pre-natal conditions such as the day-by-day state of his mother's physical and emotional well-being, her nutrition, her age, the number of children she had previously born, every child is patently different from every other child at the moment of his birth.

These differences continue to influence every child's further growth and development so that every child continues to exhibit a uniqueness in the pattern and the rhythm of his growth, in the unfolding of his intellectual capacity, in the tempo and vigor of his activity, in his sensitivity to the world about him.

In view of this vast range of individual differences, the teacher must require class sizes and work loads consistent with being able to know children as individuals. Every child deserves to be accepted each day for what he is, a unique individual.

2. **Everything That Grows Has A Groundplan**

And every child has his.

On the basis of this unique groundplan, the human being emerges, grows, and develops, each part having its time of ascendancy, each part developing in physiological time, in a general sequence but in a pattern and rate that is individual, each part forming a functioning living being.

Growth and development, however, encompass more than physiological changes in size, complexity, and proportion or in qualitative changes in cell, muscle, bone, teeth, hair, pigmentation. Growth is concerned with behavior and achievement, with motor coordination and mental processes, with social behavior and emotional control. Although every child in general passes through the same successive stages of growth and maturity, neither the child nor the adults about him control physiological time.

The teacher then has the responsibility for being competently informed, for understanding what is fact and what is fiction, and for encouraging parents, peers, and community leadership so to understand. Every teacher has the further responsibility for using this information to determine whether schooling is in accord with the growing body of our present understanding of how children really do grow and develop and to modify the curriculum in such manner wherever necessary that the lag between what is known and what is practiced is minimum.

3. Every Child Has Needs

Every child's capacity to be an intellectually, emotionally, socially functioning human being is directly related to the extent that his basic human needs have been and are being met. He needs to be wanted, to be loved, to be appreciated, to be accepted for himself.

Every child needs to develop a sense of trust, to have satisfying experiences, to be assured that the world is a dependable place.

Every child needs to develop a sense of autonomy, to have the opportunity to assert that he is a human being, that he is a person who is permitted choices.

Every child needs to develop a sense of initiative, to have leeway to show enterprise, imagination, creativity.

Every child needs to develop a sense of accomplishment, to be engaged in real tasks that he can carry through to completion.

Every child needs to develop a sense of identity, to clarify who he is, what roles he may be able to play in society.

Every child needs to develop a sense of intimacy, an ability to love and be loved.

Every child needs to develop a parental sense, an understanding of his capacity to produce and to care for children of his own.

Every child needs to develop a sense of integrity, to absorb his culture's ideals into his being, to root honor, faith, fairness, self-discipline into the core of his personality.

These needs speak to the point: every teacher has a clear role. He must mobilize competence, initiative, engenuity to live imaginatively with children while they are subject to his influence in school.

4. Learning Is Experience

Learning is doing.

Learning is participating, undergoing, reacting.

Learning is more than memorizing, more than listening and repeating, more than knowing the content of a book.

Learning is incorporating into one's being attitudes, appreciations, skills, habits, patterns of behavior, values. Learning is a function of the total environment of the individual. Learning is constant and complex, never simple or static. Learning takes place with every experience which a human being undergoes.

Meanings, attitudes, skills, values, appreciations are incorporated into a human being, become part of the human personality, slowly or rapidly depending upon the "realness" of the conditions under which learning takes place and upon the "readiness" of the learner. Both conditions are determined by the learner since every learning situation is dominated by the goals and purposes set or accepted by him alone.

Schooling, the actual experiences which children undergo under the guidance of the school, consists of those experiences for which the school has some responsibility, some opportunity for selecting, shaping and directing.

5. Behavior Is Caused

Behavior is based on purpose.

Every child is a social being, an ever-changing personality who is affecting and being affected by his total environment, consciously and unconsciously manipulating people and things in ways he discovers to be appropriate to bring him the satisfactions his manifold needs demand. The resulting interaction determines what he seeks from the world and how he goes about seeking it in his culture. When his purposeful behavior satisfies his basic human needs, "positively-charged" meanings for his life result, meanings which become the selective influence shaping his further purposes. When his purposes are thwarted, he learns a different set of meanings and these "negatively-charged" meanings become the selective factors shaping his further purposes.

The study of human behavior has already provided teachers with a host of insights into why individuals behave as they do. Psychologists and psychiatrists are now able to predict the kind of deviant behavior which a child will exhibit on the basis of their recognition of influences which are presently affecting him. Since a motivated learner learns more readily than one who is not motivated, the teacher must be a practitioner of basic mental hygiene principles. He must be prepared to consider the effects of intrinsic and extrinsic motivations, his use of marks, rewards, and punishments. He must understand that every child brings to every task a level of aspiration which has been conditioned into him by his past experiences, that every child needs practice in setting realistic goals for himself, and that realistic goal-setting leads to healthy individual growth.

6. Readiness Is A Condition

A child's readiness is actually a whole succession of stages of growth when his ability to learn to do equals his ability to do. As muscles get larger and stronger, as bones lengthen and cartilage is replaced with true bone, as motor and sensory nerves become coated with insulating sheaths which permit more differentiated action, as the brain develops new patterns of structural organization, the infant lifts his head, smiles, focuses upon an object. Behavioral growth develops with physical growth.

As the child acquires a background of experience, as he learns a sense of trust, as he develops a sense of autonomy, as he gains a sense of initiative, as he acquires a sense of identity, he passes through a series of readinesses, for language, for numbers, for emotional and social adjustment, for the learning of those innumerable skills, attitudes, values, appreciations which he has been conditioned to seek in his environment. Again, readiness cannot be forced in advance of natural growth.

Every teacher knows the importance of learning to read in our society. Every teacher must know that factors similar to those that contribute to "Reading readiness" must be understood and translated into effective curricular considerations if the child who comes to school is to have the kind of experiences which will contribute to his becoming a fully functioning member of our society.

7. Schooling Is A Cooperative Undertaking

The home is the most effective educative agency of our time. It nurtures the growing child during his most formative years. It indoctrinates and inducts him into the ways and values of his culture. It provides him with his initial identity within his community. It assumes primary responsibility for his welfare.

Although the evidence indicates that a child's experience during his early years is a major significance to him and that the home exerts a powerful continuing influence, the evidence also indicates that crucial phases of growth and development occur during childhood, adolescence, and young adulthood. The community in all of its aspects—churches, the press, schools, movies and television, and all of the myriad varying facets of community organization—combines into a potent educative force.

The experience which children have under the guidance of the schools is of particular concern to the entire community. Schools must reflect the whole community's most determined planning for the wholesome optimum growth of every child. The community looks to the school staff for evidence that the welfare of children is reflected in the entire school program. Thus, the beliefs, skills, attitudes, and understandings of these purposes by custodians, clerks, bus drivers, cafeteria workers—the whole corps of "non teaching" school employees is as important as is the knowledge, training, attitudes and skills of teachers, administrators, nurses, librarians—the professional staff. Each plays a significant role in determining the quality of schooling.

8. Good Schools Make Better Communities

Good schools reflect deeply-felt values.

Where every human being has worth and dignity, schooling and a concern for the general welfare is likely to have status, value, and importance. The intensity of these values and the values themselves are communicated to the young at home and throughout the community by the choices that constantly assert what is important to adults.

Where children are truly prized, the community expresses its concern for the influences that give feeling-tone and meaning to what young people experience. The good teacher is sought out, encouraged, given public support in his effort to add quality and depth to schooling.

Our population statistics indicate clearly that by 1970 America must have a minimum of two million, five hundred thousand teachers prepared for the stimulating opportunity of meeting the formal education needs of the school age population. The recruitment of young men and women who are warm interesting people in their own right to become America's teachers is a challenge of prime importance. Any child can attest that good teachers make good schools. Any citizen can demonstrate that good schools make good communities better.

9. Every Child Is A Hope

> Hope springs eternal in the human breast:
> Man never is, but always to be blest.
> —ALEXANDER POPE

That parents should have warm expectations for their off-spring is normal. That a nation should have plans to assist with the full-flowering of the promise which exists within every human being is its mark of greatness. In America each child merits schooling to the full extent of his capacities.

The total school age population includes children with capacities for learning that range from the extremely limited to the almost infinitely unlimited. It includes children with bursting vitality and energy and those who are limited to a minimum of vigor and activity. It includes children with a legion of differences in body structure, motor coordination, social orientation, emotional depths, and special talents. It includes children who are well and healthy and children who bear the effects of disease, impoverishment, accidental injury, and all the ills to which human flesh is heir to. The promise that is America demands that schooling, too, be the inheritance of all these, our children.

However, effort must be redoubled to identify, as early as possible, the children to be served. Through the annual school census, through medical examinations of infants and children where-ever these are performed, through training programs for teachers and special school personnel, schools must locate every child whose schooling needs may differ. Once located, every effort must be made to develop programs of schooling consistent with the individual needs of every child.

10. America Is Promises

Seeing all children and young people as America's faith in our future as a nation that deserves the commendation of history, the members of the Midcentury White House Conference on Children and Youth defined in their pledge to children the full scope of the role which must be played by every person who has the privilege of touching the life of a child.

> From your earliest infancy we give you our love, so that you may grow with trust in yourself and in others.
>
> *WE* will recognize your worth as a person and we will help you to strengthen your sense of belonging.

WE will respect your right to be yourself and at the same time help you to understand the rights of others, so that you may experience cooperative living.

WE will help you to develop initiative and imagination, so that you may have the opportunity freely to create.

WE will encourage your curiosity and your pride in workmanship, so that you may have the satisfaction that comes from achievement.

WE will provide you with the conditions for wholesome play that will add to your learning, to your social experience, and to your happiness.

WE will illustrate by precept and example the value of integrity and the importance of moral courage.

WE will encourage you always to seek the truth.

WE will provide you with all opportunities possible to develop your faith in God.

WE will open the way for you to enjoy the arts and to use them for deepening your understanding of life.

WE will work to rid ourselves of prejudice and discrimination, so that together we may achieve a truly democratic society.

WE will work to lift the standard of living and to improve our economic practices, so that you may have the material basis for a full life.

WE will provide you with rewarding educational opportunities, so that you may develop your talents and contribute to a better world.

WE will protect you against exploitation and undue hazards and help you grow in health and strength.

WE will work to conserve and improve family life and, as needed, to provide foster care according to your inherent rights.

WE will intensify our search for new knowledge in order to guide you more effectively as you develop your potentialities.

As you grow from child to youth to adult, establishing a family life of your own and accepting larger social responsibilities, we will work with you to improve conditions for all children and youth.

Aware that these promises to you cannot be fully met in a world at war, we ask you to join us in a firm dedication to the building of a world society based on freedom, justice, and mutual respect.

SO MAY YOU grow in joy, in faith in God and in man, and in those qualities of vision and of the spirit that you will sustain us all and give us all new hope for the future.

THE ROLE OF ADOPTION AGENCIES

Samuel Karelitz, M.D.

Until very recent years the handicapped child was considered unadoptable, or at least a poor risk. As late as 1948, 80% of the adoption agencies represented at a workshop on adoption sponsored by the Child Welfare League of America indicated that they considered the handicapped child to be unadoptable. Implicit was the assumption that to be accepted by agencies the child had to be suitable for adoption, i.e. that reasonable assurance could be given the adoptive parents that the child had potentialities for normal physical and mental development.

The more progressive adoption agencies required of the children for whom they assumed responsibility, and for whom adoption was considered possible as well as advisable, that the child's heredity background be free of mental defect or disease that might be transmissible and that the child's physical and mental development be progressing normally. This attitude was well described by Alice Lake [1] as follows: "Only two decades ago adoption was considered a risky business and few couples dared to take the chance. Social workers, with no overwhelming demand for children, cautiously placed only blue ribbon babies whose health and forebears were impeccable . . . Barely half a dozen years ago, a baby eligible for adoption through a reputable agency carried a gilt-edge guarantee. . . A cloudless heredity and a little body unblemished by defect was assured as a matter of course. Less risk than in natural parenthood was the keynote of the transaction. Not astonishing is the fact that, in the past, prospective adoptive parents expected perfect babies."

As the number of childless parents increased with the growth of the population, as the nation's economy improved and the individual family became more secure economically, adoption became more acceptable and was considered more realistically. The demand for children increased at an astonishing rate. In some areas the ratio of the demand to the availability of white children reported by authorized adoption agencies ran as high as 10-20 to 1. The failure of the agencies to satisfy the demand for perfect babies has resulted in a greater interest in the handicapped child.

By 1951 the number of adoption agencies which considered the handicapped child unadoptable was reduced to 47% from 80% in 1948. 40% of all the agencies considered that a dubious heredity did not preclude the child from adoption. By 1955, the number of adoption agencies which accepted children with manifest handicaps, both physical and/or mental, and with doubtful genetic heritage had increased greatly. The philosophy of the board members of adoption agencies, of the case worker, and of adoptive parents had changed. Workers in the adoption field, no longer feeling hopeless about handicapped children, have accepted the challenge to place these children in adoptive homes.

Belle Wolkomir, in an article entitled "The Unadoptable Child Achieves Adoption"[2] related that of the children refused by an adoption agency since 1938 as unadoptable and therefore placed in foster homes, one hundred made a favorable adjustment and were adopted by the foster parents. This experience of the Foster Home Bureau of the Jewish Child Care Association of New York is cited to illustrate the fact that, in light of our present experiences and beliefs, the concepts of our best adoption agencies of fifteen to 20 years ago were inaccurate. These children who have found happiness in family living might have been deprived of this normalizing experience had the then current criteria for adoption been adhered to rigidly.

The present concept of the adoptability of a child is based on the attitudes and conviction which were expressed by representatives of a large number of persons from various disciplines who met in 1955 and 1956[3] to survey concepts of modern adoption procedures and to set up standards for ideal adoption practices. Social workers, psychiatrists, psychologists, representatives of the clergy, of law and medicine, of genetics and anthropology, and of many national child welfare groups, including the Federal Children's bureau, were represented.

The tentative conclusions of this group, pertaining to the question of adoptability, were as follows:

(a) It is advantageous for any child of any age to be placed for adoption if he does not have a family of which he is part, and if a family can be found to give him the advantages of family life.

(b) Any child can be considered adoptable who can gain from family life and who has the capacity to develop in a normal environment, and for whom a family can be found which will accept him with his history and capacities. His history and examination should be such that there is reasonable assurance that the child has ability and potentialities for adjustment, that his handicaps are not such as will interfere with development of a sound child-parent relationship. He should have the capacity to find and give satisfaction in family living and not require a kind of care which no parent is expected to be able to give.

(c) Not only infants but older children and those with special needs may bring the satisfaction of parenthood.

(d) Even if a child's state or prognosis is not wholly favorable, adoptive parents may be found who, after being given full knowledge of the facts, are prepared to accept him.

Normal, well adjusted adults, given the opportunity, can weigh the risks of reasonable unknowns, arrive at a decision, and find a healthy way to adjust to the results of their decision.

To find such adoptive parents and to present the handicapped child honestly and fairly, the social worker must appreciate the true state of the child's handicap, must understand its implications, and should himself be free of former adoptive prejudices. He must be convinced of the suitability of the child for adoption and of the advisability of placement with the particular family. He must not read into the condition a handicap over and above the actual existing defect. He should interpret the defect on an individual basis, and not generalize. Paralysis due to polio can vary from an almost insignificant muscle weakness to a serious disability. If the case worker presents the condition as: "The child has some paralysis which resulted from polio," the adoptive parents may react with suspicion. They might not be disturbed if the condition were described as: "A lucky child who is now immune to polio and has fortunately emerged with only a slight weakness." Similarly, "This baby has a dislocated hip which will require at least six months in a cast," could be phrased as, "This child has a dislocated hip which with good treatment over a considerable period can be corrected so that his gait and posture will be quite normal." A handicapped child is often denied adoption, not because adoption is a poor solution for him, but because of fear that the adoptive parents would be hurt. The social worker who places babies should consider the remarks of Elizabeth Fairweather[4] regarding the placing of babies less than three months of age: "Let us concentrate less on our fears of unknown factors in a child and try harder to develop greater ability to know our adoptive applicants and to realize that they can offer us healthy nutritive soil in which a new life can develop."

In more than 25 years of association with an adoption agency, as pediatrician, the writer has had to help decide the adoptability of many handicapped children, many with genetic backgrounds of possible crippling diseases. Although these decisions had to be made in accordance with the prevailing policy, nevertheless some deviations were permitted. Each handicapped child has been regarded as an individual, different from all others, who presented specific and particular problems which had to be considered separately. Once it was decided that the child was suitable for adoption, it was recommended that adoptive parents be sought who could understand the problem and its implications. Placement in a particular home was discouraged unless it was quite clear to the agency case worker, to the psychiatrist, and to others of the staff that the adoptive parents would be able to accept the child with the handicap and would derive satisfaction from such a child. It occasionally happened that prospective adoptive parents requested children who were not generally acceptable. The motives of such persons were carefully checked to eliminate the possibility of personality disturbances of a pathological degree. When placement was made after careful evaluation of the child and after careful selection of the parents, adoption was regularly successful.

Congenital syphilis was, prior to 1945, generally regarded as a contra-indication for adoption. No physician would permit his client, the prospective adoptive parents, to accept such a child. Even after it had been amply demonstrated that syphilis could be cured, the social implication of the disease and the old fear that one could not be sure of a complete cure seemed to be reason for physicians to refuse to permit the prospective adoptive parents to take a child cured of syphilis. A child born with congenital syphilis is adoptable if cured of the infection as evidenced by negative serology, healed bones, and absence of central nervous system pathology. Inquiry of some leading authorities on the subject of syphilis has led to the opinion that a child who has remained well and with a negative Wasserman for one year after antibiotic treatment may be considered cured of the disease.

Congenital heart disease, of the acyanotic type, such as septal defects which are non-symptomatic, or patent ductus arteriosis, which is amenable to surgical correction, should not preclude placement. With progress in the surgery of heart disease, many conditions heretofore considered hopeless will become reparable and will convert non-adoptable to adoptable. Children have been placed in adoption with extra digits, absent digits, webbed fingers, knock knees, bow legs, clubfoot, dislocated hips, large hemangiomas of the skin, other birth marks, harelip, cleft palate, pigeon breast, funnel chest, hernias, and with non-progressive hydrocephalus. Infants have been placed after treatment for subdural hematomata, who, after several months of observation seemed unaffected. Children have been placed who developed deafness because of maternal German measles in the first trimester of pregnancy but who were otherwise unaffected. Children also have been placed who seemed to have escaped serious damage after having erythroblastosis. Children have been placed with mild spasticity following birth trauma. One such child now attending a cerebral palsy clinic is the favorite of the entire group. She is happy in her adoptive home, and her parents are delighted with her. Her progress is a great source of pride to them. The mother is not obviously affected by the so-called martyrdom bestowed upon her by well-meaning friends who look with surprise and question this adoption. More recently, children with such defects as poor vision, diabetes, asthma, and with paralysis due to polio, and some with other defects have been accepted by agencies and successfully placed in suitable homes. Children with a family background of epilepsy and mental retardation are being placed. Children with such defects as harelip, hernia, clubfoot are relatively easy to place in adoption. Children with some defects are difficult to place. They take much more time and effort of the case workers and are costly, almost prohibitive for agencies which are closely budgeted.

A realistic attitude toward the adoption of handicapped children may be summarized as follows:

(1) Infants with congenital infection or defects, which are correctible, may be, can, and should be placed in adoption. Most of the orthopedic conditions, soft tissue defects, hernia, harelip, congenital syphilis, and non-cyanotic congenital heart disease are in this category. In general, it is easier to place a child whose syphilis has already been cured, or whose hernia has been repaired, or whose extra digit has been removed, or whose harelip has been repaired. However, some adoptive parents prefer to have the child earlier, feeling that the earlier the child is in their home, the more successful will be the child-parent relationship. The adoptive parents may prefer medical attention of their own choice and to participate in the treatment of the child. These are matters for the case workers to survey with the adoptive parents.

(2) Children who have recovered from bacterial meningitis, viral encephalitis, fractured skull, erythroblastosis and other severe conditions are suitable for placement, unless the consequences of the disease are too debilitating.

(3) Children with some permanent handicaps may also be placed in adoption. Visual defects, deafness, paralysis following polio, or birth injury and congenital absence of a part or of a whole extremity do not preclude suitable placement. In the case of congenital anomalies of the genito-urinary tract, each situation should be considered separately. Only a very rare case (one whose kidneys are so injured that the expectancy for life is very short, a few months to a year) of this type might be considered unadoptable.

(4) Normal children of siblings with hereditary diseases, such as Tay Sachs, Niemann-Pick may be placed in adoption after observation beyond the period during which the disease becomes manifest. In most instances a year will suffice. In the case of cerebellar ataxia, this highly hereditary disease may not become manifest until the third decade. If the child never develops the disease, he obviously deserves adoption. If the disease does appear, it is likely to become manifest after the child has grown to maturity. It is rarely seen in early childhood. Should the child develop the disease later, he certainly would be better off with a family to look after his needs. He should, therefore, not be deprived of

a home, nor should some childless couple be deprived of the opportunity of having this child for many years.

(5) Children born with other recessive genetic conditions may be offered for adoption, but each must be evaluated individually. A child in whose family there is diabetes, asthma, or epilepsy should not be deprived of the opportunity of adoption. Even the child who has an electroencephalogram which indicates epilepsy but has a past history of none or only some convulsive episodes should be acceptable for adoption. Several such patients who have had only two or three convulsive attacks in their first 15 years of life have made excellent adjustments.

(6) Children born of mentally retarded parents, especially if one or both are retarded because of central nervous system infection, trauma, or tumor, may well be suited for adoption. Mental retardation is generally accepted as a serious handicap in adoption. While many regard an I.Q. of 85 as minimum for adoption, Dr. Charles Bradley of Portland, Ore.[5] finds that an increasing number of people will accept children with an I.Q. of 75. After good care within a family constellation, a child with an I.Q. of 75 might improve and be able to adjust well to family life. The study of Skeels and Harms[6] is pertinent. They found "that children of mothers of low intelligence or from fathers with low occupational status, or from a combination of both, placed in adoptive homes in infancy, attain a mental level which equals or exceeds that of a population as a whole."

While handicap in adoption is interpreted as any physical or mental defect which seriously affects the child, some would include race, color, and religion when these interfere with the best possible solution for the welfare of such a child. It is important to note that the problem here is not the child; the "handicap" is really that of the agency in not finding a suitable home. It is not a "handicapped child," but, instead, a handicap for the child, if the child is of mixed parentage and a suitable home is not available, or if because of religion alone, a child is deprived of an opportunity to be adopted. A greater awareness of the problem of placing all children in need of adoption has encouraged many agencies to develop inter-racial programs. The adoption committee of the Louise Wise Services, for example, has succeeded in placing a considerable number of colored children and children of mixed racial origin. Each child successfully placed is given the security that is his right, a security which he could not experience in an institution or a foster home. Generally those working in adoption feel that children should be placed in homes of the same religion. Indeed, the law of many states so prescribes. But many people now believe that if a child is to be deprived of an opportunity of family life merely because of religion, such a barrier should be crossed if it is to the advantage of the child.

That we have arrived at the current attitudes toward the adoptability of the handicapped child is gratifying. The belief is now widely held that no child is or should be barred from the opportunity of being adopted unless after careful investigation he is considered to be unable to gain from family life, not to possess the capacity to develop in a normal environment, or for whom a family cannot be found which will accept him with his history and capacities.

Dr. John Bowlby, Director of the Child Guidance Department of the Tavistock Clinic in London, England,[7] has written: "To dub a baby unfit for adoption is usually to condemn him to deprived childhood and an unhappy life . . . . Such children grow up to reproduce themselves. They are a source of social infection as real and serious as the carriers of diphtheria and typhoid."

REFERENCES

1. Lake, Alice: *Saturday Evening Post*, July 31, 1954, p. 28.
2. Wolkomir, Belle: *Child Welfare League of America Bulletin*, vol. XXVI, No. 2, Feb. 1947 "The Unadoptable Child Achieves Adoption."
3. National Conference on Adoption—Child Welfare League of America, Jan. 26-29, 1955.
4. Taft, Ruth: *Child Welfare*, June, 1953, p. 5.
5. Bradley, Charles: Paper read at National Conference on Adoption—Child Welfare League of America, Jan. 27, 1955.
6. Skeels, Harold M., and Harms, Irene J.: *Genet. Psychol.*, 72:283-294, 1948. Children with inferior social histories; their mental development in adoptive homes.
7. Bowlby, John: Quoted by Alice Lake, see ref. No. 1.
    Bowlby, John: Maternal care and mental health—A report prepared on behalf of the World Health Organization as a contribution to the United Nations Programme for the welfare of homeless children. *World Health Organization, Monograph Series*, No. 2, pp. 179.

COUNSELING IN MEDICAL GENETICS

Sheldon C. Reed, A.B., Ph.D.

An old story, many times told, has significance. On hearing about Darwin's theory of evolution, a lady cried: "Descended from the apes! My dear, we will hope that it is not true. But if it is, let us pray that it may not become generally known." To her, it was terribly degrading to be related, however distantly, to an ape. Eventually the news became generally known, and most people grew reconciled to the fact.

Contrariwise, many people point with pride to their descent from one or more of the passengers who came to America on the Mayflower. My own ancestry contains a sprinkling of those courageous souls who opened up the New World. They cheerfully accept the implication that all their good traits were inherited directly from a few of those now famous progenitors. They ignore the fact that four or five thousand ancestors made an equal contribution to their heredity. People accept the concept of heredity for traits which they admire and reject it for the traits from which they shrink.

Medical genetics is usually concerned with deleterious traits, many of them actually lethal. The counselor's client does not wish to learn that his problems have a genetic basis. He wants to be told that albinism is not hereditary, this his albino child is just an exaggerated Scandinavian! If three consecutive generations of congenital cataract are present in a family, the client will favor the less probable interpretation of recessive heredity rather than accept the more likely hypothesis of a dominant genetic mechanism because with recessive heredity the chances are smaller that the trait would reappear in subsequent children. Many parents of the mentally retarded reject the concept of heredity because to them this implies a Jukes or Kallikak kind of family which naturally no one would wish to acknowledge.

If the sincere client fundamentally does not wish to accept the concept of heredity for himself, though he may be willing to accept it for others, what effect does this attitude have upon the counselor and the counseling? Since the counselor wants to make his client receptive to positive suggestion, the counselor may attach undue significance to environmental accident, infection, or other non-genetic cause for the appearance of the trait in question. The counselor may overrate the probability of an environmental etiology and underrate that of heredity. However, if the trait is dependent upon a Mendelian dominant or recessive gene for its expression, the counselor must point out this fact with tact and understanding.

The counselor cannot afford to overrate the influence of environmental factors such as German measles and automobile accidents because the lady involved cannot be expected to have a second case of measles at the right time to explain the second abnormal child. As many physicians have found to their surprise and regret, lightning does strike twice in the same place and in the same way quite frequently. If the trait is a Mendelian one, and the chances of a repetition of the trait are one half or one fourth for each subsequent child, there is a reasonable probability that the client will return after having produced a second affected child.

Today's young people have accepted very literally the philosophy that every couple should have a family. If the couple is infertile, many of them then attempt to have their reproduction stimulated at the fertility clinic. That the children be spaced according to the medical and economic situation and that they be wanted are the only apparent limitations to the philosophy. Otherwise, the sky is the limit, and the American population is growing with joyous planned abandon.

The present compulsion to produce a family makes the position of the genetic counselor rather difficult. No matter how catastrophic the genetic situation may be, many young couples feel compelled to complete their family. Let me illustrate with a recent counseling case. The wife had been totally blind for several years, her eyes having been enucleated because of glaucoma. Her sister is also blind for the same reason. The husband has very poor vision because of congenital cataracts. His father has the same difficulty. The couple have one child, a baby representing the third generation of cataracts and with a poor prognosis for vision. Statistically speaking, the couple have at best an even chance at each conception of initiating a child with normal vision. The husband and wife were aware that both eye defects were genetic and wanted to know what their chances were of producing normal children.

Genetic counseling only rarely goes beyond educating the couple so that they understand what the chances are of a repetition of the abnormality in subsequent children. However, in the above case it seemed necessary to point out to the couple that they faced a dilemma even if their subsequent children had normal vision. That the normal child was likely to feel out of place and have psychological problems contingent upon its failure to correspond to the other members of the family was a new concept to them.

The question of how far the genetic counselor should go in making suggestions is worth consideration. In the United States there are a dozen heredity clinics, and in all of them the policy is uniform. The counselor does his best to explain the genetic and environmental factors involved in the situation with the expectation that the couple will then make an appropriate decision as to their subsequent reproduction. Definite advice as to future decisions is never given by the counselor. Since he cannot place himself in the client's position, he, therefore, cannot make the decision for the couple. At the time of the conference the husband and wife may not have stabilized their thinking and may not know what they will decide eventually.

Though the biologist knows full well that all traits, good and bad, result from the interaction of heredity and environment, to deny the role of heredity is more or less "fashionable." The open questions concern when and how the genetic and environmental factors function. Many of the people who verbally deny the concept of heredity, in actuality are found to be more pessimistic about their heredity than the facts require. Some actually think that having had one affected child all their subsequent children will be affected. Though such cases are encountered, they occur too seldom to be of concern to a particular couple. In many cases these apprehensive couples have been re-contacted several years after the conference. The counseling seems to have been helpful in reducing their worries and to have encouraged them to have larger families than they had previously thought wise.

A young minister and his wife had refrained from having children because the minister's brother had convulsive seizures. The couple were in doubt as to the magnitude of the chances they would be taking if they had children. Both husband and wife were requested to have electroencephalographs taken. The wife's brain potentials appeared normal, but the impression obtained from reading the husband's E.E.G. was one of dysrhythmia, indicative of petit mal seizures. The counselor explained that half of their children should display the dysrhythmia; but that like their father, most of them would not have seizures even though the dysrhythmia was present. At worst not more than one in eight of their children would be expected to develop seizures. When contact was re-established five years later, the minister was not only serving three rural churches simultaneously but had fathered four children in the five years.

Unfortunately the world is not entirely without its shadows, and in some cases the genetic counselor cannot tell the couple that there is no chance of a repetition of a particular abnormality in a subsequent child even though he would like to do so very much. In some cases the decision had been made before the person appeared for counseling. An illustration of this situation was presented by a twenty-four year old mother who came to Dight Institute after several years of trouble due to cystic fibrosis of the pancreas in two of her four children. One of the sick children had died, but the other child was still living at the age of six though half of his life had been spent in hospitals. Since the expenses each year had been much greater than their total income, they had lost their automobile, their house, and part of their ambition. The more recent expenses were borne by "county papers." The county had a legal right to any property they might accumulate until their debts to it were paid. Since the mother had already had two cystic fibrotic children, she was aware of the fact that "lightning does strike twice in the same place." She had already made her decision to limit her family to her two normal children and the two afflicted ones. She had come to the Dight Institute merely to check on what she had learned elsewhere: The chance of a repetition was still 1 in 4 for this disease at each subsequent pregnancy. She wanted to be sure of this before going ahead with a sterilization procedure.

Other serious diseases handicap children and force parents to take action that, otherwise, they would not consider proper. Two such afflictions are the sex-linked traits for hemophilia and pseudohypertrophic muscular dystrophy. Cystic fibrosis of the pancreas depends upon what is called autosomal recessive inheritance with one quarter of the children from carrier parents being affected, boys and girls in equal numbers. With the sex-linked traits, the mother is the carrier and produces sons, half of whom are affected, the other half being completely free and not even carriers of the heredity forces. The daughters are all free of the disease, but half of them are carriers and can produce sons, half again affected. Thus, a carrier mother will expect half of her sons to be affected if she carries a sex-linked trait.

Since sex-linked traits place the responsibility entirely upon the mother, many counselors emphasize factors which will serve to share the responsibility for taking preventive measures to both parents. An older couple had produced five boys, three of whom had developed the sex-linked type of muscular dystrophy and were incapacitated in order of their ages. The three boys were being cared for by the mother but were a heavy burden for her. She was greatly upset and disturbed to discover that she was pregnant at the end of her reproductive life. The couple had asked for a therapeutic abortion as a way out of an intolerable situation. As in the previous example, the couple had decided what they wished to do and were at the Dight Institute to make sure that they had their genetics straight.

Some families have to contend with more than one kind of anomaly. Their reactions to the traits which had appeared in their children are of considerable interest as demonstrated by the summary of a recent conference. The husband had a harelip and a cleft palate with reasonably good repair. The first child was premature, had a harelip and died. The second and third children were normal. The fourth child was hydrocephalic and had to be delivered by Caesarian section. Because of the fact that the mother had had influenza during early pregnancy, it is possible that the hydrocephalus was due to meningitis and not genetic in the strict sense. Without any genetic consultation the couple had requested donor insemination, and their obstetrician had made two unsuccessful attempts. At this point they heard of the Dight Institute and came for consultation.

The couple did not fear the repetition of harelip and cleft palate. They had faith in the ability of the plastic surgeon to repair the damage. But they were perturbed about the possibility of a repetition of the hydrocephalus, or spina bifida, even though it would seem likely that their affected child was the result of an infection. Even if the child were a result of genetic damage the chance of such repetition is only about three per cent for this particular anomaly. The couple had ninety-seven chances out of one hundred of a normal child at the next pregnancy. The chances of a repetition of harelip and cleft palate are from ten to fifteen per cent with confidence that it is genetic because of its previous appearance in both the father and the child.

The interesting features of the above case are that the mother is determined to have five living children which means three more pregnancies, all of which, to them, would be fraught with danger. They were not concerned about the fairly large chance of a repetition of the less serious anomaly, harelip and cleft palate, but were disturbed by the very small chance of a serious defect of the central nervous system. The conference seems to have been helpful in removing some of their unnecessary fears about the repetition of hydrocephalus in a subsequent child. It also encouraged them to complete their family without outside assistance. Donor insemination, useful where the husband is actually sterile and in some genetic situations, would seem to be of questionable value in this particular situation.

A final point warrants consideration. This is the matter of imparting negatively charged information to the client. Not to tell the patient anything that will cause anxiety and thus be damaging to him is good common sense if applied thoughtfully. However, the withholding of certain information may sometimes result in disaster. To apply insurance principles of producing a little apprehension in every client in order to protect a small percentage of these clients from serious mental distress at a later date is certainly proper. A case in point can be demonstrated by genetic counseling for Mongolism.

[The frequency of Mongoloid children goes up with mothers over thirty-five years of age at a rapid rate, one third of the affected children being born to mothers over forty years of age.] As the Mongoloid child is often the last child the family had expected to have, no subsequent children will be produced and consequently few families demonstrate a repetition of the anomaly. Therefore, it might seem wisest if all mothers producing a Mongoloid child were assured that there is no chance of a repetition of the defect. This would be positively charged information which the family would be happy to obtain. However, for the young mother who has produced a Mongoloid child this information would be false. A small but real chance exists this mother would produce a second or even a third Mongoloid child. Having been educated to believe that this could not happen to her, the mother will experience a shock severe and much more distressing than if she had taken a calculated risk and lost. The following family history demonstrates both sides of the picture:

A twenty-three year old mother gave birth to a Mongoloid boy, then to a normal girl, and at the age of twenty-nine to a Mongoloid girl. All three pregnancies were completely uneventful. Before the second and third children were born, the mother, assured by two physicians that there was no danger of a second Mongoloid child, had come to believe it. Without warning, the second abnormal child was presented to the mother, with resulting psychological trauma, as she made the diagnosis herself. The mother required some months to recover her mental equilibrium. At this stage the couple appeared for counseling.

Upon examination of the hands of the couple, the counselor noted that the husband showed a striking "simian crease" of the left hand and a less pronounced demonstration of it on the right hand. The wife's hands were normal. The creases on the husband's hands suggested that there was something more than accident concerned with Mongolism. The couple was warned that there was a small but real chance that they might yet produce a third Mongoloid child. They were quite willing to accept this possibility and were relieved to find that the chance was small. Being prepared for the worst, the couple have since produced two normal children and have a sense of elation from having won in the biological lottery.

To explore the possible genetic influences involved in all the conditions enumerated in the present volume, which is devoted to the handicapped child is not contemplated in this short chapter.

If the reader has a question in mind, it will be worth-while to obtain an appointment for a conference at a counseling center. The counselors at these centers are dedicated people who will give their all to help those who wish to come to them.

The reader who wishes to pursue this subject will find much of the significant literature in this field in: *Counseling in Medical Genetics*, by S. C. Reed, published in 1955, by W. B. Saunders Company, Philadelphia.

LOCATION, NAME OF INSTITUTION, AND PRINCIPAL COUNSELOR OF SOME OF THE HEREDITY CLINICS

Location	Institution	Counselor
Berkley, California	University of California	Curt Stern
Salt Lake City, Utah	Laboratory of Human Genetics, University of Utah	F. E. Stephens
Austin, Texas	The Genetics Foundation, University of Texas	C. P. Oliver
Norman, Oklahoma	University of Oklahoma	L. H. Snyder
Minneapolis, Minnesota	Dight Institute, University of Minnesota	S. C. Reed
New Orleans, Louisiana	Tulane University	H. W. Kloepfer
Ann Arbor, Michigan	Heredity Clinic, University of Michigan	J. V. Neel
Columbus, Ohio	Institute of Genetics, Ohio State University	D. C. Rife
Toronto, Ontario	Hospital for Sick Children	N. F. Walker
Winston-Salem, N. C.	Department of Medical Genetics, Bowman Gray School of Medicine	C. N. Herndon
Montreal, Quebec	Department of Medical Genetics, Children's Memorial Hospital	F. C. Fraser
New York, N. Y.	New York State Psychiatric Institute	F. J. Kallmann
Boston, Mass.	Children's Cancer Research Foundation, Harvard University	A. G. Steinberg

THE CHILD WITH AN AMPUTATION

Charles H. Frantz, M.D., F.A.C.S.

Prior to the Industrial Age, amputation in civil practice was primarily reserved for uncontrolled infection, gangrene, and complicated compound fractures. Generally speaking, these were few as compared to the "en masse" incidence produced by war.

This has now changed. We are in the midst of and seemingly fast progressing through the Industrial Age with a myriad of highly complex machines, incredibly fast accelerating vehicles and mechanized farm implements. The advancements of medicine, enlightening us in the treatment of degenerative diseases and affording control of infectious diseases by antibiotics, may be overbalanced by the phenomenal increase in the incidence of trauma. During World War II, approximately seventeen thousand individuals in military service became amputees. In the same period of time, there were sixty-five thousand civilian amputations per year. This figure represents some children in the total. However, no one knows with any degree of certainty the child amputee population in the United States.

In the past few years, we have come to realize that children in our society as a population group are subject to the same traumas as the adult. Children are passengers in cars, ride bicycles on busy highways, wander into railroad yards and construction areas. Children on farms are exposed to combines, tractors, cornpickers and other mechanized implements that are dangerous to the uninitiated.

A recent analysis of well over two hundred non-congenital child amputees revealed that 68% were due to trauma (vehicular accidents, farm-tool accidents, power-tools and railway accidents). The child is the victim of mechanization as well as is his parent.

Society requires functional rehabilitation of the handicapped. Many amputees are returned to a wage-producing job and are economically sound citizens. The child amputee as a segment of the population and an important potential in the coming generation must be rehabilitated. Present day interest indicates that juvenile amputees as a group, within the Crippled and Afflicted definition, are receiving more attention in medical centers. Juvenile amputee clinics and training centers are being developed throughout the country to evaluate, fit limbs and train the young amputee.

THE NATURE OF THE CHILD AMPUTEE

The child is a plastic growing human; he is a system of muscles and nerves operating in space. He possesses a progressively developing skeleton with a wide range of adaptability. His motor patterns are not fixed; they are constantly improving, and do so on a predetermined time scale with ever-increasing skill as he approaches maturity. Various reconstructive procedures on children afflicted with poliomyelitis have demonstrated that most children learn new or altered functional patterns with comparative ease.

Observations on the juvenile amputee corroborate this concept of rapid adaptation to altered functional demands as manifested by learning bi-pedal progression on an artificial leg and acquiring prehension skill with an upper extremity prosthesis. The speed with which the child learns patterns with an a-sensory appliance is something astonishing. No child, however, can be pushed beyond his kinesthetic level. Initial clumsy responses will gradually become cleverly coordinated acts as the child develops.

An analysis of a large group of juvenile amputees has revealed several important and pertinent facts:

1. Short stumps, excessive scar formation, neuromata, spur formation and phantom limb likely to plague the adult are seldom causes of dysfunction;
2. Careful examination of the child and his stump will seldom indicate the necessity for surgical conversion or stump refashioning;
3. The juvenile's problem is usually the need for a comfortable, mechanically sound prosthesis and training in its operation.

It has been observed that the young amputee does much better with an artificial limb than an adult, possibly because of these basic facts. He grows up with this prosthesis as a necessary mechanical component for his activities. His kinesthetic sense seems to develop with and be dependent upon its presence. The young wearer using his limb constantly knows no other motor patterns during his growth and maturation. The child may develop a sensory feed-back of his equilibrium and proprioceptive sense to a degree never reached by the adult amputee.

As a member of a family group, a child develops his character traits and habits proportionately to the influence of the parents and older siblings. Parental cooperation in maintaining a progressive program of limb-wearing is very important. Patterns initiated early in life exert a lasting influence. Properly guided, coached and disciplined in the daily use of a prosthesis, the young amputee comes to accept the device to the same degree as he does his clothing, eating habits, household chores and school.

Juvenile amputees should not be classed as crippled in the same sense as the post-poliomyelitis victim or the cerebral palsied. What is left of an extremity or segment of a limb is usually freely movable and capable of developing muscle power. There is no central nervous system impairment and the remainder of the body is normal, thus presenting no other motor handicap. This is most advantageous to the child in his rehabilitation program, when compared to a severely paralyzed poliomyelitis victim and congenital or post-traumatic cerebral palsied child.

CLASSIFICATION

Two types of juvenile amputees are encountered in medical centers.

1. *Non-Congenital Amputees (Post-traumatic and surgical):* The etiological factors contributing to this group include acute trauma, necessitating immediate removal of a limb. Explosions, vehicular accidents, power-tool and railroad accidents lead the list.

A second group within the non-congenital type is the elective amputation in childhood not having an immediate relation to acute trauma. The leading etiological factors in this group are subacute infection (gangrene following fractures, etc.), tumors, thermal injuries and nerve injuries.

2. *Congenital Amputees:* Statistical analysis of three hundred

fifty young amputees revealed a higher incidence in clinic records of congenital amputees appearing for care from one year to six years, over the non-congenital type. This revelation is quite understandable. Toddlers and kindergarten aged children are more closely guarded in the home environment. They do not wander far from the front yard. They are less liable to trauma. As the child approaches elementary school age, his radius of activity and wanderings enlarges, thus exposing him to more environmental trauma. The incidence of non-congenital amputees (post-traumatic and surgical) rises at the sixth and seventh years of life and continues to do so into the teen-age period of life.

The congenital type of amputee consists of two major groups:

(a) The true congenital amputation;

(b) The appendicular abnormalities which may be treated as amputees.

The true congenital amputee has been born with a complete or partial loss of an extremity. The stump or segment of the extremity varies little from the stump of the non-congenital (surgical) amputee. There may be some changes in the skeletal structures by roentgen examination. However, his prosthetic problem does not differ from the non-congenital type (Figure 1).

The appendicular abnormality which may be treated as an amputee requires considerable exercise in judgment as to whether he be fitted with a non-standard prosthesis primarily, or converted surgically to a more satisfactory stump and fitted with a standard prosthesis (Figure 2).

AMPUTATION LEVEL AND PROSTHETIC TYPE

Through the years it has been observed that the higher the amputation level the greater the loss of function (Figures 3 and 4). The loss of a hand is a severe handicap. However, the length of the forearm is preserved, elbow function is unimpaired, and what push-pull activity remains can be executed at a natural distance from the body. A prosthetic device applied as a substitute for a hand can be fitted over the forearm; the natural action of the elbow remains uninhibited. The opening of the terminal device may be activated by one single cable hooked to a harness (Figure 5).

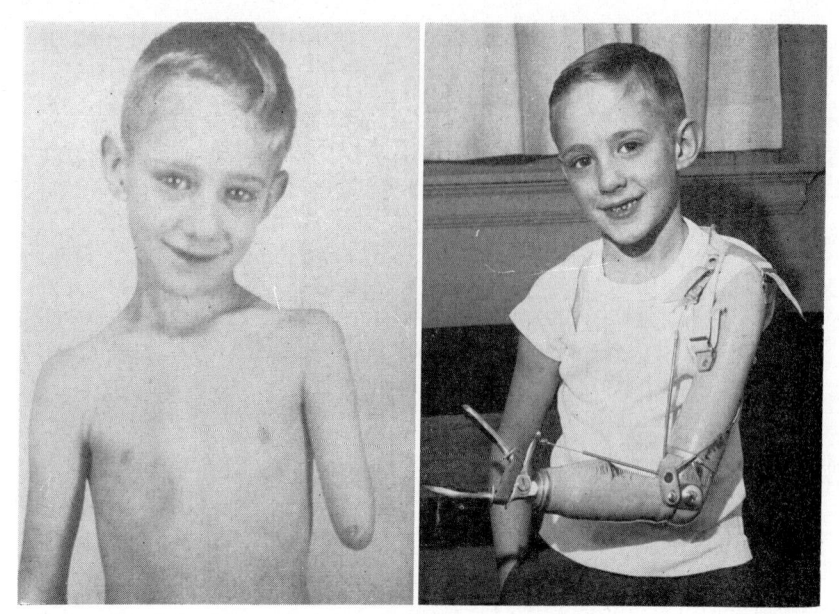

FIGURE 1. *Left.* Congenital amputation in a boy of eight years. Anatomically this is an elbow disarticulation. The stump is long and cylindrical in contour. *Right.* Fitted with a conventional type of above elbow prosthesis.

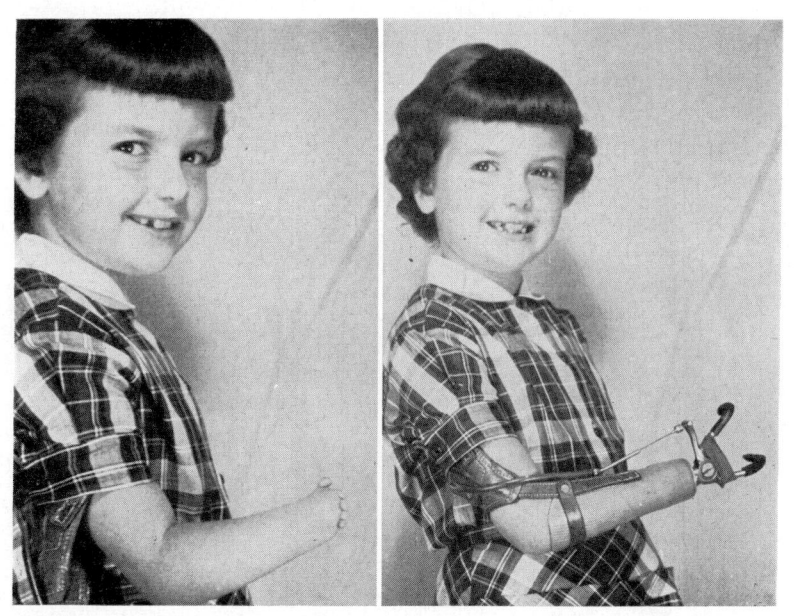

FIGURE 2. *Left.* Congenital absence of the hand. *Right,* Child fitted with a wrist disarticulation type of prosthesis.

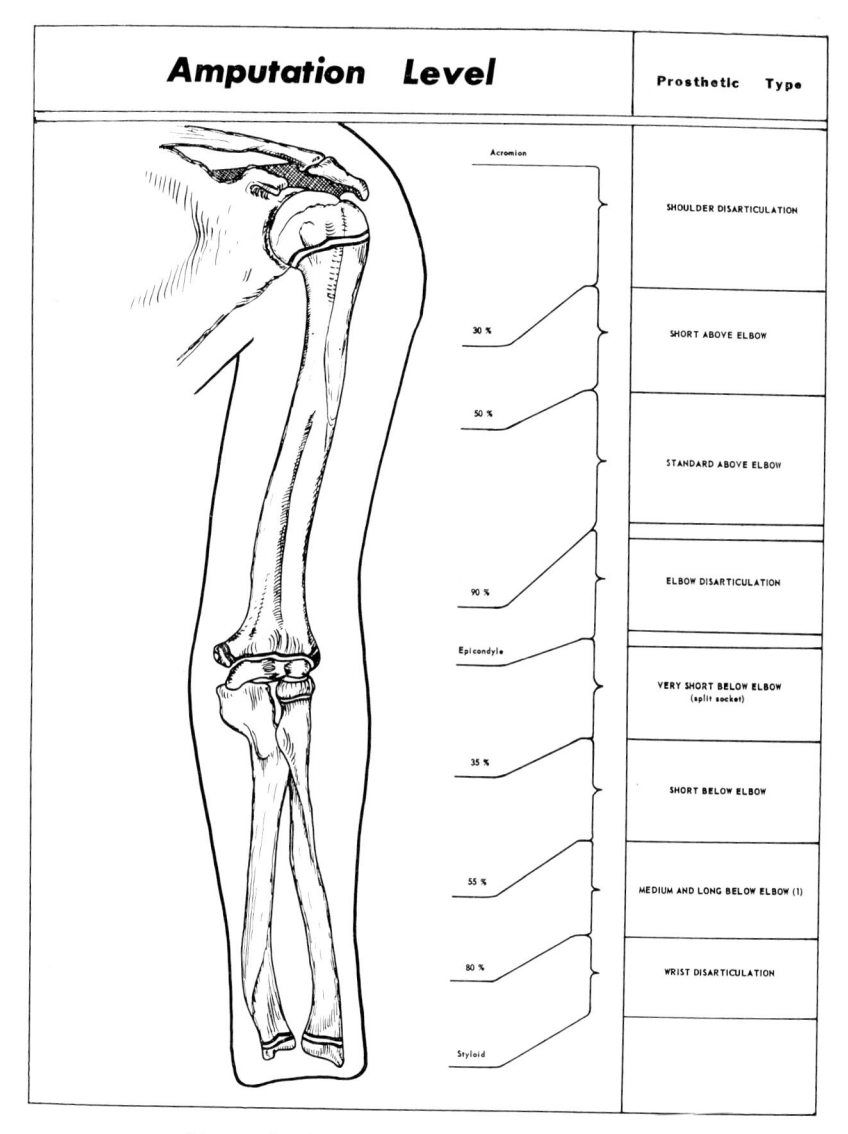

FIGURE 3. Arm amputation levels in children.

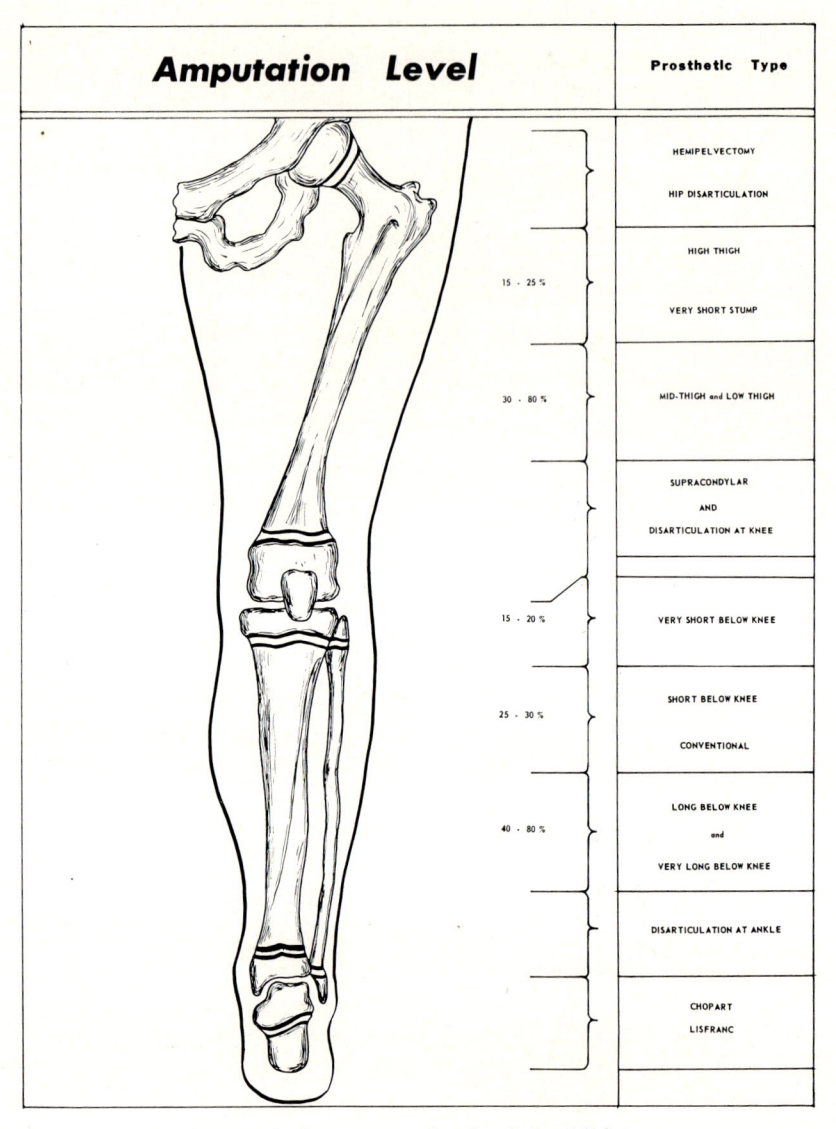

FIGURE 4. Leg amputation levels in children.

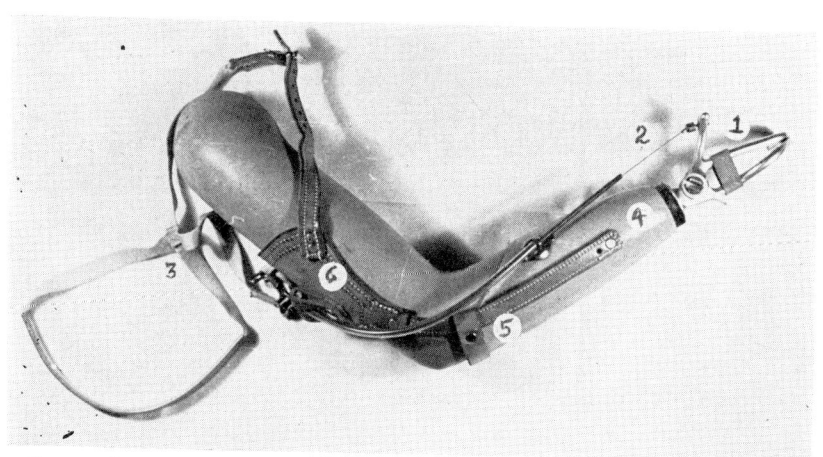

FIGURE 5. Typical below elbow upper extremity prosthesis which enables the amputee to have normal elbow motion and control. 1. Terminal device or hook. 2. Cable which operates the hook. This is operated by the opposite shoulder, through the figure of eight harness (3). 4. Plastic forearm socket encasing the stump. 5. Flexible leather elbow joint. 6. Leather triceps pad also a stabilizer. This is a single control motor system. The amputee opens the hook by the increase in cable tension. His elbow control is a natural pattern.

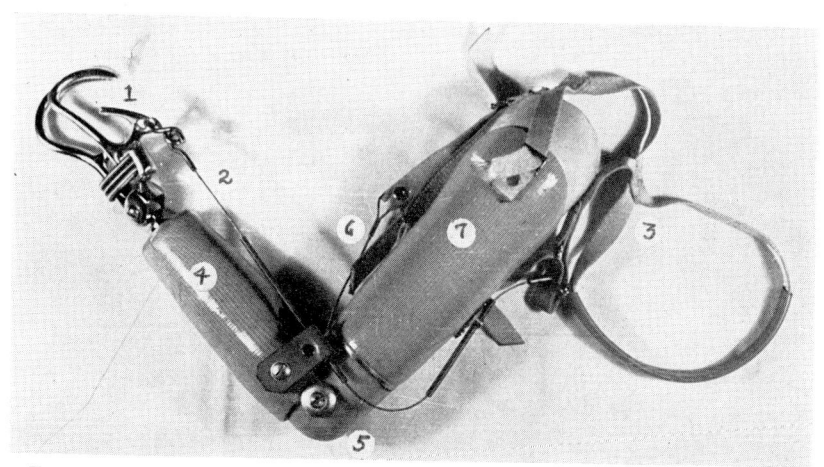

FIGURE 6. Typical above elbow prosthesis. The amputee must master a dual control system, the operation of the terminal device and the mechanical elbow. 1. Terminal device or hook. 2. Cable which operates the hook. This is operated by the opposite shoulder through the figure of eight harness (3). 4. Plastic forearm to provide length to the extremity. 5. Mechanical operating elbow joint. This can be locked in eleven positions ranging from complete extension (180°) to 40° of elbow flexion. 6. Short cable hooked to figure of eight harness (3) which locks and unlocks the mechanical elbow. 7. Plastic stump socket.

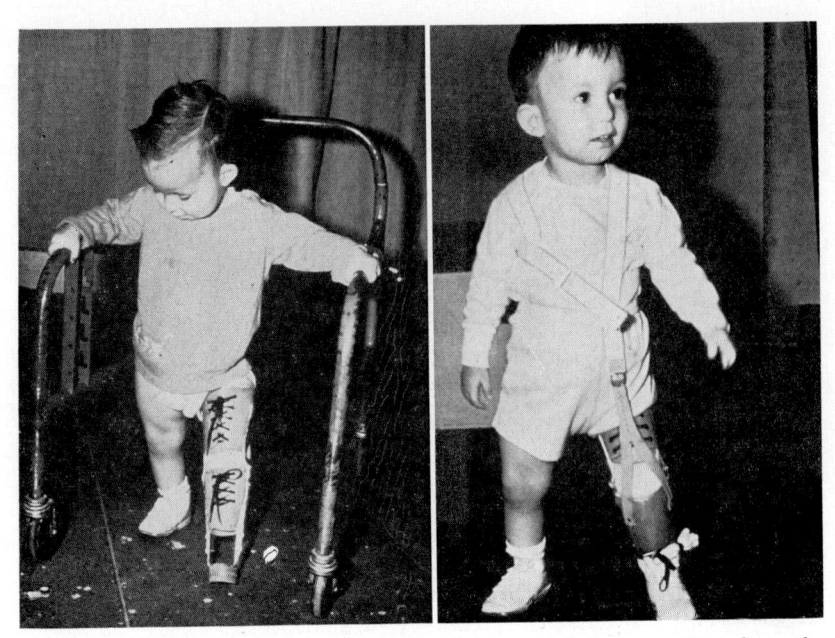

FIGURE 7. A sixteen month old child with a congenital amputation above the ankle joint initially activated with a leather socket and small disc for a foot. Early attempts at walking were aided by a small chair followed by a mobile walker. At eighteen months the child walked independently after being fitted with a small rubber foot and an adequate harness.

    The loss of an arm just above the elbow is a much more severe handicap than the loss at the wrist. Remaining function is limited to a short distance from the body. Prosthetic restoration must restore adequate length, terminal device operation (as a substitute for a hand) and a mechanically operating elbow joint. The prosthetic problem here is much more complex than the below-elbow situation and more difficult for the amputee to master (Figure 6).

    These considerations are matched in the lower extremity, but not in such a complex manner. The loss of the foot and a part of the lower leg is met by the application of an artificial foot, wood or plastic socket for the below-knee stump, a hinged knee joint and a thigh cuff. The amputee activates his knee joint in a natural manner, with the ability to place the prosthetic shin piece and foot at will, when walking (Figure 7).

    Amputation above the knee is a much more serious handicap. The loss of the natural knee has many implications and com-

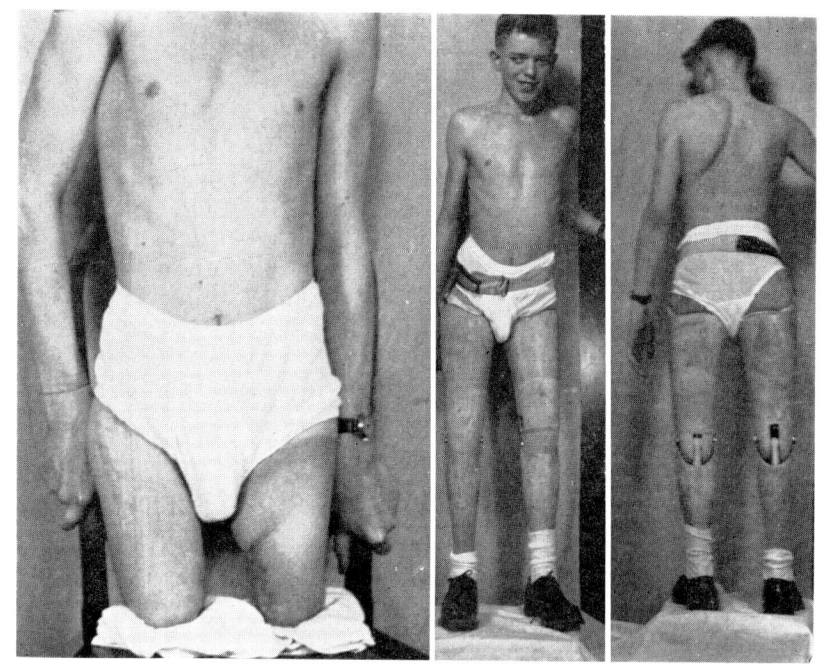

FIGURE 8. Loss of both lower extremities at fourteen years of age. At fifteen years, after being fitted with suction socket prosthesis, this boy is able to walk with two canes. This type of prosthesis does not require harnessing in most cases.

plications in fitting, alignment and the learning of a natural walking pattern. The fear of falling, faltering balance and instability must be alleviated with a properly functioning prosthesis (Figure 8).

Amputation levels are designated anatomically for clarification and for correlation with the type of prosthesis best suited for the level.

The science of prosthetics has improved by leaps and bounds since World War II. The fabrication of sockets is an exacting process. The advent of plastics has widened the field of media with which to work. More mechanical components are available, offering much more efficient operation of artificial limbs.

POST-TRAUMATIC AND SURGICAL AMPUTEES

Children who have a surgical amputation at an early age in life are in many respects quite different than the adult amputees. They are more tolerant than the adults, more adaptable to the

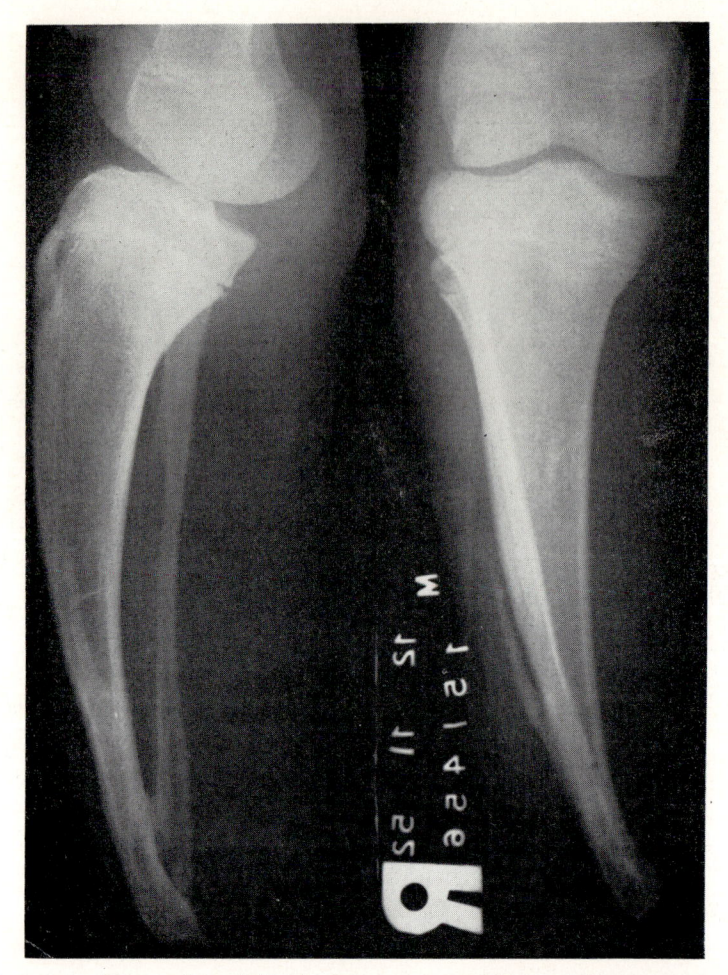

FIGURE 9. X-ray of the tibia of a fourteen year old boy which was amputated at the age of six. Note the bowing effect of the tibial stump and the tilt of the proximal epiphyseal plate.

change in motor patterns demanded for prosthetic motivation, and they are not plagued by complications likely to beset adults.

Long bone growth in a normal person is one phase of an orderly, proportionate, total skeletal maturation. The young child in whom this process is incomplete and who undergoes an amputation, in many instances will demonstrate alteration in the form and internal architecture of long bone stumps after wearing an artificial limb a few years.

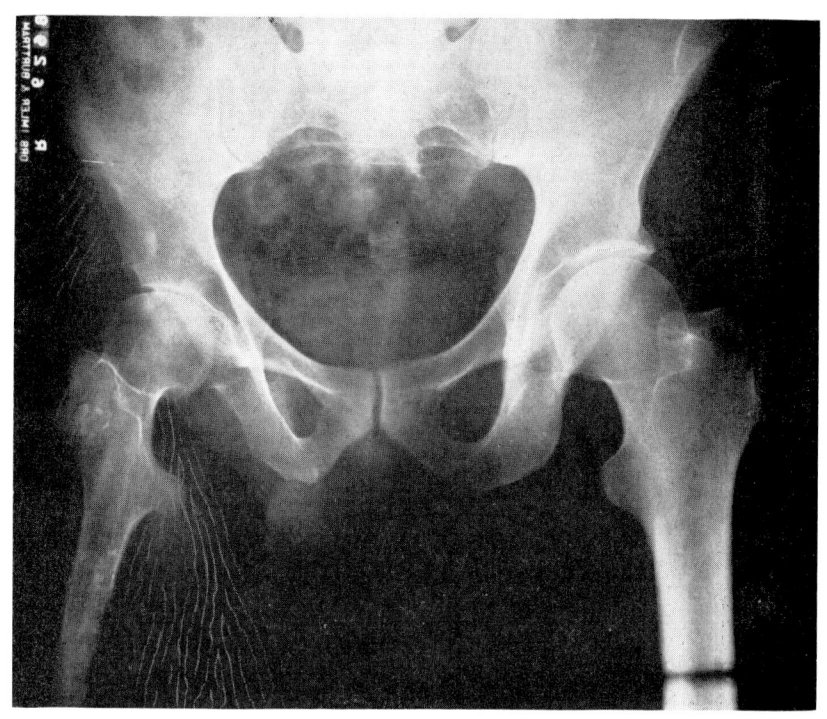

FIGURE 10. X-ray of the pelvis of a thirty-five year old male. The right leg was amputated at the mid thigh level at six years of age. Note the smaller femoral head on the amputated side. There is a coxa valga and a change in the contour of the lesser trochanter.

Many children with below-knee amputations prior to the age of six or eight years exhibit characteristic x-ray changes in two or three years. The tibia develops an anterior type of bowing or kyphosis. The proximal tibial epiphyseal plate will tilt backward. There may be a varus type of deformity in the tibial shaft (Figure 9).

The pelvis of a young amputee will demonstrate an asymmetry. The ilium on the amputated side is smaller than the normal side The femoral neck is in the valgus position and the lesser trochanter demonstrates an altered contour. These changes occur regardless of how soon the young amputee is made to bear weight, or what type of prosthesis is employed (Figure 10).

The upper extremity amputee also demonstrates characteristic bony changes. The above-elbow amputee after wearing a pros-

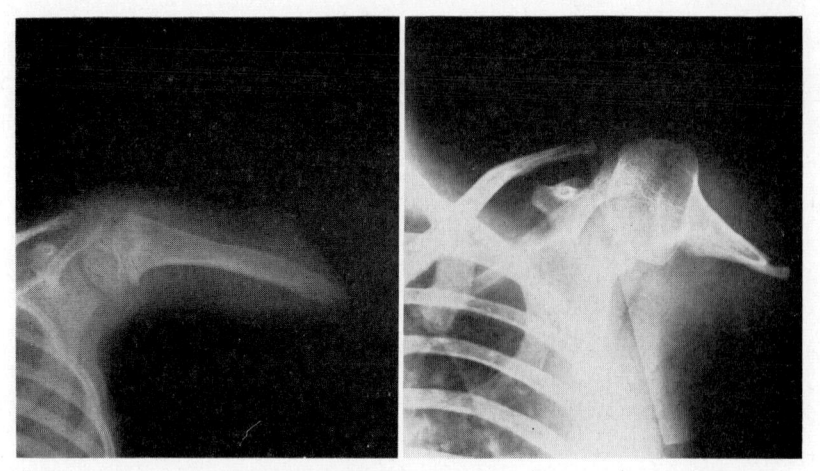

FIGURE 11. *Left.* X-ray of the upper arm stump (humerus) of a thirteen year old boy. Amputation was performed at nine years of age. Note the bowing of the proximal humeral shaft and varus attitude of the humeral head. *Right.* X-ray of a very short humeral stump of a girl twenty two years of age. The extremity was amputated at twenty months of age. The humeral head continued to grow but the growth of the shaft was arrested.

thesis a few years demonstrates humerus varus. Medium or long below-elbow stumps may reveal a bowing of the radius and ulna. The younger the amputee, the greater the possibility for changes in bony contour (Figure 11).

Such manifestations of adaptive skeletal changes, so far as can be determined, do not modify functional results. These are only anatomic alterations in skeletal contours, demonstrating the adaptability of the growing skeleton.

The child possesses great reserves in his adaptation. Tissues involved in operative procedures of amputation seemingly have the magic power of "youth" in the healing response. Degenerative changes in the vascular system are not encountered. Widespread tissue tolerance is the rule. Skin grafts will endure in a child wearing a prosthesis.

Spur formation at the end of the bony stump very seldom complicates the future of the child amputee. The femoral stump is the most common site of spur formation. It is transverse and medial. The humerus, tibia and fibula will demonstrate spur formation less frequently than the femur. Very seldom are they of clinical significance.

Scar formation about the stump in the child does not often become a barrier to prosthetic socket fitting, as it does in the adult. Children do not complain of scar tenderness or its formation. All amputation stumps have neuromata buried within the soft tissues as the result of nerve cutting. Properly buried and buffered by the soft tissues, they are not painful. Neuromata become painful only when irritated by pressure, friction or by traction when caught in the scar. In a series of 196 amputees operated by many surgeons using varying techniques, only 3.2% developed painful neuromata necessitating surgical excision.

Bursitis is not a common complication in juvenile amputees. It may develop at the end of the stump from an improperly fitting socket, especially in the lower extremity. Elementary school age boys who literally "pound" their prostheses may occasionally develop bursae at the fibular head and over the tibial tubercle.

The sensory counterpart of the leg or arm can be imagined or "felt" by the adult. Most adult amputees never lose their phantom limb. This phenomenon is not a complication unless it changes its nature. In some unfortunate individuals, painful phantom limb occurs. This is a very serious complication and difficult to treat. The phantom distal elements of the limb removed by amputation (the foot or hand) are very painful. The imagined extremity burns or aches, and there may be sensations of insects crawling under or on the skin. The bone may feel as if it were protruding through the skin, or the toes may feel as if they had been crushed by a hammer blow.

The child amputee does not experience painful phantom limb. The younger the child at the time of amputation, the more likely he is to completely lose the phantom. Amputated at the age of six, a child will have lost his phantom by the age of twelve. He cannot "call up" the image of his lost extremity. Apparently the immature and still developing "sensory counterpart" of his body, existing in the mind, may continue to develop "incomplete" as the child continues toward maturity. Older children never mention phantom limb unless quizzed. They must close their eyes to "conjure up the phantom."

Young amputees between the ages of six and ten or eleven years of age are confronted with a complication peculiar to youth and not experienced by adult amputees.

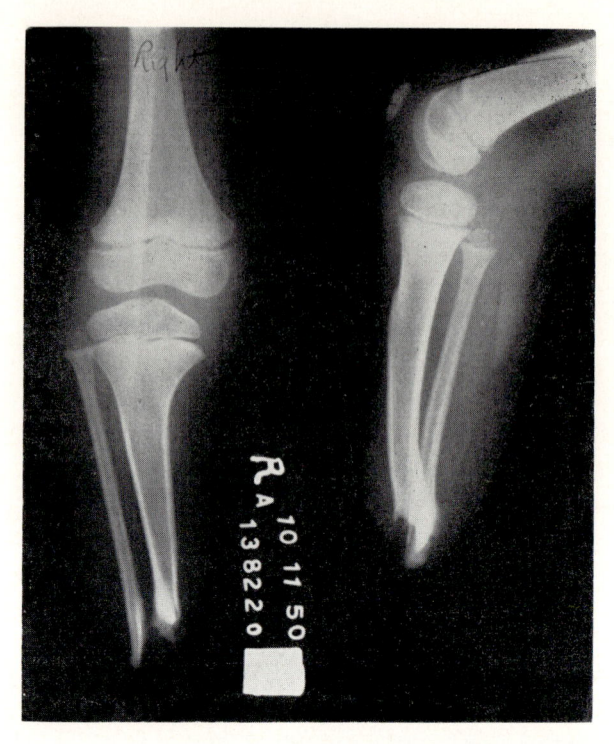

FIGURE 12. X-ray of the below knee stump of an eight year old boy. One year previously when the amputation was done the fibula and tibia were equal in length. The fibula has grown more rapidly than the tibia and is beginning to protrude through the soft tissues of the stump.

In many instances, the bony stump continues to grow distally. Six months to a year from the date of amputation the stump end may become red, tender to pressure and a distal tension of the soft tissues and skin is evident. Untreated, this situation becomes progressively more painful. Eventually, untreated, the bony stump protrudes through the soft tissues (Figure 12).

This phenomenon is called "overgrowth." It is a disproportionate growth between the bony stump end and the surrounding soft tissues. The x-ray of the stump will demonstrate an elongation of the bone end, tapering off to a spicule. The medullary canal may be visible, but narrows down to a sharp terminal point of cortical bone.

Clinically, this complication is encountered most often in the fibula. Occasionally, the tibia and humerus will become involved.

Seldom is it seen in the forearm; if so, the radius is more often the offending agent. This complication must be treated surgically by bone resection.

CONGENITAL AMPUTEES

True congenital amputations offer no difficult problem in fitting with standard prostheses. They do not bring to mind the familiar problems of the surgical amputation, i.e., site of election, scars, spurs, neuromata, phantom limb and overgrowth. None of these considerations are of major importance in this group

Since the amputation was present at birth, scar does not exist in the surgical sense, development of neuroma does not occur, spur formation does not take place, inasmuch as there has been no surgical disturbance of the periosteum. Phantom limb has not been encountered in a congenital amputation. Apparently there is no sensory counterpart of the complete extremity.

Overgrowth usually does not exist in the congenital amputee's stump. This phenomenon has occurred, however, when a congenital amputee's stump has been revised and the bone (periosteum) disturbed.

APPENDICULAR ABNORMALITIES

Congenital variations from the normal extremity development are legion. Classification is most difficult from an anatomical standpoint. The abnormalities of the upper extremity have been recorded in a detailed study by Birch-Jensen. The lower extremity to date has received so such analysis. Fundamentally, the goal in attempting to rehabilitate the child is an acceptable degree of function in the fields of prehension and ambulation. Whether this goal is met by appropriate footgear, sole lifts, bracing, primary attempts at prosthetic fitting or surgical procedures depends upon experience and a projection of the patient's status to mature years (Figure 13).

Families of handicapped children will more often than not accept non-surgical treatment initially. Should a child be rehabilitated by the application of a non-standard prosthesis and training in its use, the parents are encouraged. Not infrequently, when told that surgical correction is necessary before rehabilitation can be initiated, there is reluctance. For the good of the patient,

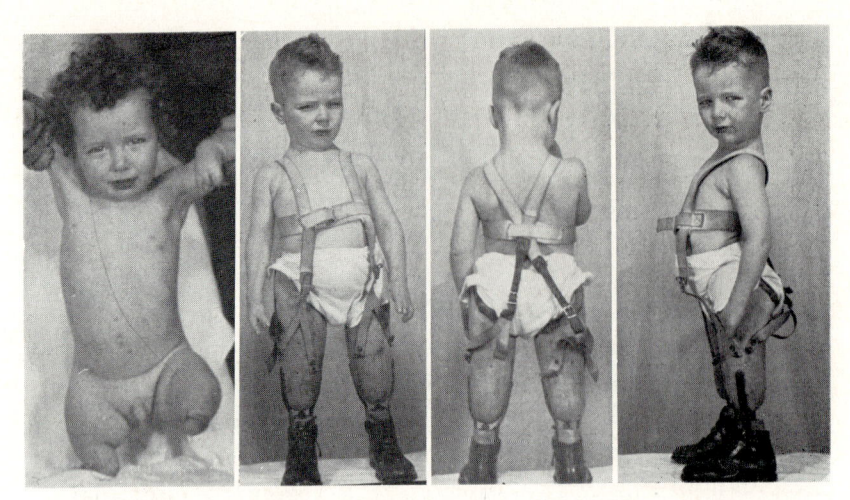

FIGURE 13. A child with a number of intrinsic anomalies involving all four extremities including bilateral syndactilism with a split hand on the right. X-ray examination reveals two rays for the right hand and three for the left. He has bilateral congenital dislocation of the hips, the right femur is short and the right fibula is absent. At fourteen months he moved like a quadruped with soft tissue flippers representing feet. At sixteen months he was fitted with bilateral prostheses having articulated ankles but no knee action. A harness with shoulder straps and a chest band was provided. The boy developed standing balance in a period of three months. One month later he was able to walk unaided.

it is more desirable to attempt rehabilitation of the child without surgery. Later, the necessity for plastic reconstruction may become evident; the cooperative parent will have anticipated this necessity and there will be no hesitation relative to surgery (Figure 14).

Amputations are thought by many to be basically mutilating and an admission of defeat. Many surgeons and families are reluctant to consider converting a grotesque non-functioning congenital abnormality of the foot to a classical amputation stump. The tendency to postpone a possible surgical procedure to a later date in the child's life is ever present.

What of the future? What will functional adaptation be? What consideration must be given to adaptation during the school years relative to psychological and sociological adjustments? Will there be cosmetic considerations for recreational activities?

In any program of management wherein amputation may be recommended as a reconstructive procedure for congenital ab-

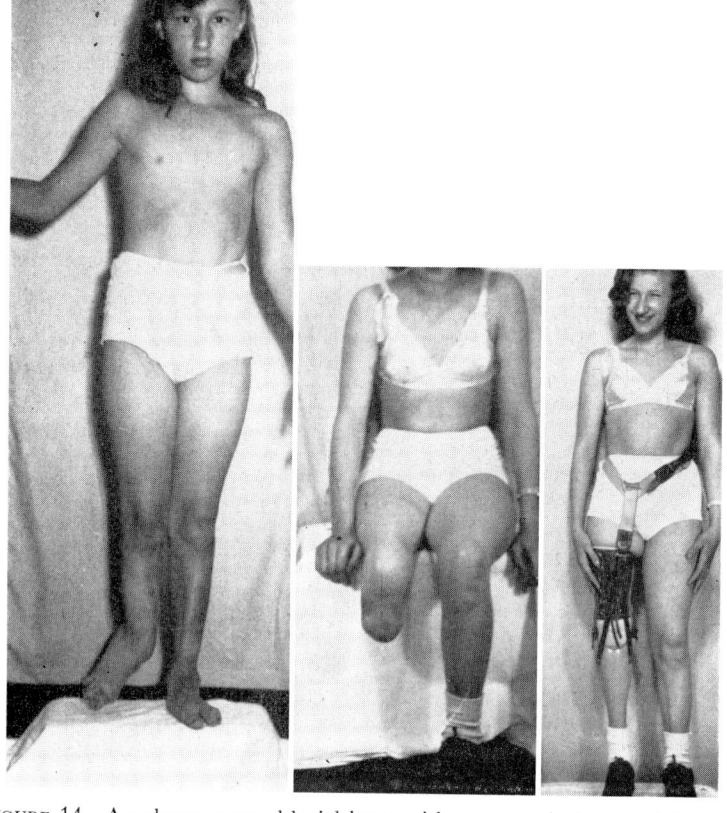

FIGURE 14. An eleven year old girl born with a congenital short tibia which was bowed anteriorly and a deformed foot. She walked with a short brace and a three inch lift on her shoe. This child and her parents asked for a conversion amputation and she now wears a conventional below knee prosthesis.

normalities, caution must be stressed. Reconstructive procedures have value only if function is improved. Each case must be individualized; skill and discretion should be the rule. It is unwise to consider amputation as a primary approach. Should amputation be the answer to the functional problem, the surgeon must have available an expert prosthetist and facilities for training the young amputee.

An approach to a situation by amputation and a well-fabricated prosthesis is no more radical than multiple reconstructive operations and bracing, if the patient functionalizes the prosthesis well.

The surgeon who makes a decision to amputate or disarticulate an anomalous part should have his treatment so planned for the future that he is able to offer a careful and detailed explanation of the entire problem to the family of the young patient. The parents must appreciate what is expected to be accomplished and the steps necessary to obtain the anticipated goal.

CONSIDERATIONS FOR THE AGE OF PROSTHETIC FITTINGS

Too often in the past, many children have gone empty-sleeved or have ambulated with crutches because of a negative approach to the child amputee problem.

Many times, the statement has been made: "Nothing should be done now; let's wait until Johnny can handle an artificial limb." Wait for what? A serious error is committed in assuming that the rapidly growing child needs only crutches until he reaches a relatively late stage of his maturity. In such thinking, the fact that growth and development are dependent upon exercise and functional activity is overlooked.

The amputee must obviously have the potential skill for the proper control and function of the prosthesis. This potential implies motor and emotional development to a stage where the child will tolerate and mobilize the appliance. When this stage has been reached, if the prosthesis is comfortable and mechanically sound, adequate training will produce good function.

The best performance with artificial limbs is seen in those who are fitted at an early age. There are variations in the chronological development of the motor skill, some children progressing more rapidly than others. It is not unusual to observe a child who stands or walks as late as twenty months. Children between fourteen and eighteen months learn to stand and walk in an artificial limb (Figure 15).

In the upper extremity, the pattern of development likewise is an orderly progression of motor behavior. The child develops index finger-thumb prehension at forty weeks. His grasp is good, but release is not coordinated. At two years he is turning door knobs, demonstrating pronation and supination. When two years old, the child is able to put on his shoes and unbutton some of his front buttons, and is able to manipulate clay into various

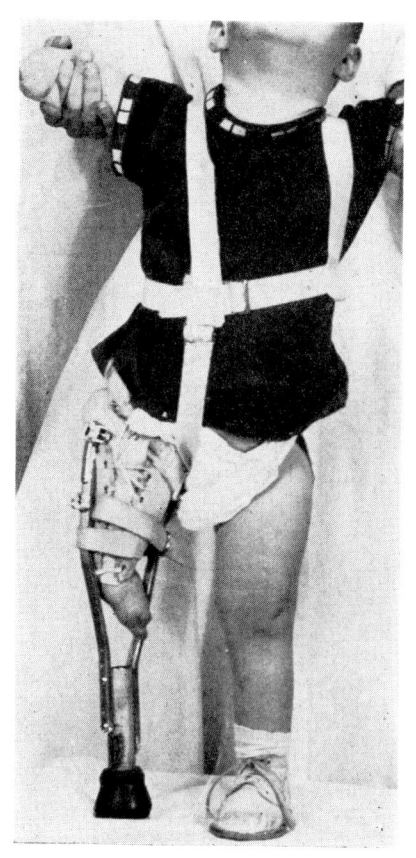

FIGURE 15. An example of an anomalous extremity primarily fitted with a prosthesis. This twenty three month old child was born with an extremely short right leg and a rudimentary foot. He has been fitted with an aluminum pylon tube of prosthesis. The rudimentary limb is encased in a soft leather, lacer cuff.

forms such as flat cakes and balls. Attempts at finger motor coordination will reveal a fine tremor.

At four years, he is dressing and undressing himself, and manages buttons and pencils and crayons fairly well. He is able to copy a square and follow a line in cutting with scissors. Psychologically, the child is responsive, is proud of his accomplishments and will accept verbal instruction. The four year level of intellectual and motor development has proven to be a very satisfactory period for applying an upper extremity prosthesis. The appliance, whether an above-elbow or below-elbow type,

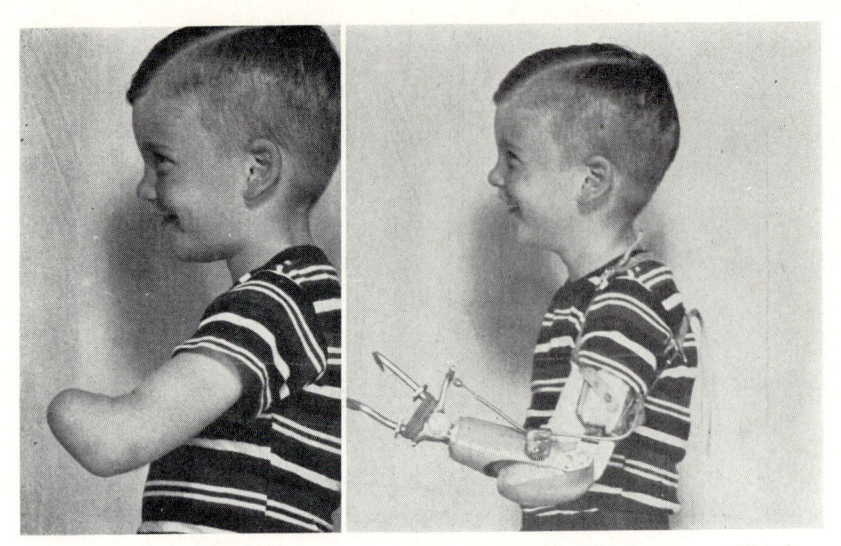

FIGURE 16. An example of congenital amputation of the forearm. This boy was fitted with a prosthesis at four years of age. He has adjusted to it and is accepted wholeheartedly by his age group.

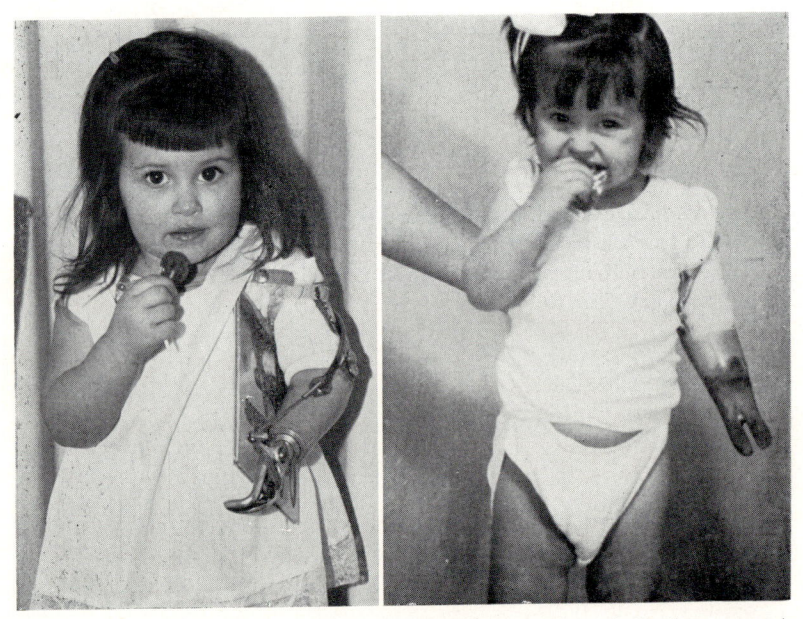

FIGURE 17 A. An example of a congenital amputation of the forearm. At seventeen months of age showing a passive split end type of prosthesis. *Right*. At twenty four months fitted with a voluntary opening terminal device. *Left*.

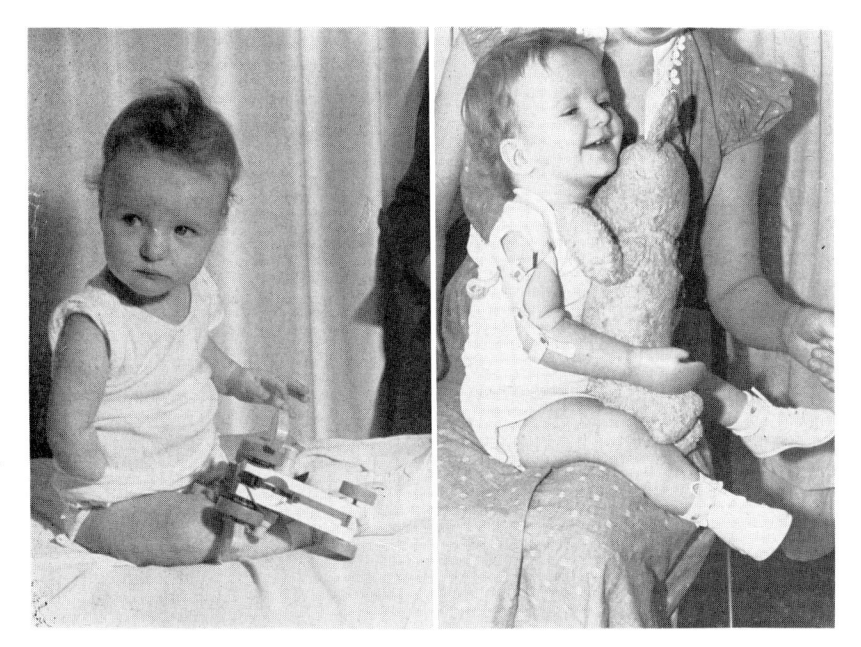

FIGURE 17 B. Another example of typical short below elbow congenital amputation. At eight months of age a plastic forearm shell and a semi rigid passive mitten was fitted. Within a month the child used the prosthesis as a support in creeping. (Developed by the Army Prosthetic Research Laboratory.)

can be fitted and the child will readily operate a voluntary-opening terminal device. An artificial arm applied at this age will allow a full year of training and wearing so that a good performance may be expected when he enters kindergarten (Figure 16).

Recent clinical experimentation has indicated that prosthetic tolerance can be obtained as early as six months, and this can be maintained through the stages from six months to the previously discussed four year level (Figure 17A and 17B).

In the very young upper extremity amputee, prosthetic tolerance is obtained but terminal device operation will closely parallel the child's motor prehension kinesthetic development, and in toddlers this is not well developed. It has been observed that children as young as twenty four months will develop the ability to operate a voluntary-opening terminal device (Figure 17A).

Young amputees should attend public school. Elementary teachers and principals should recognize the handicap and participate in the everyday training of the amputee. Unfortunately, in some instances amputees are prohibited from attending public schools. Normal environment is important to the child psychologically, and most young amputees are able to perform on the same level as their playmates. It is sometimes amazing how fast the child learns after proper fitting of the prosthesis and adequate instruction in its use.

PARENTAL ATTITUDE

Experience with three hundred young amputees and their families has demonstrated almost universal acceptance of a prosthetic device. Occasionally, parental cooperation is lacking. Without the complete understanding and cooperation of both parents, the success of a young amputee's rehabilitation program cannot be anticipated.

The lower-extremity amputee or his family seldom, if ever, refuse the opportunity for an appliance. The necessity for independent ambulation is recognized without argument. The fact that a lower-extremity prosthesis can be completely covered by clothing in the young male, and fairly well camouflaged in the young female, may unconsciously smother arguments to delay the application of a limb or to refuse it. The thought of their youngster walking without the use of crutches or a cane is a very pleasant one to parents. This is doubly true if the prosthesis is disguised and not apparent to the casual observer.

The upper extremity prosthesis is more difficult to disguise. Cosmetic hands for adults are in use every day, and the arguments of "hand or hook" continue. It has been shown that the two-fingered hook is more universally satisfactory for function than a mechanical hand. More adults use hooks than use hands. The cosmetic hand is an acceptible terminal device for an upper extremity prosthesis in social spheres and when the job demands are those of meeting the public with little need for skillful or intricate manipulations.

Efficiently operating and cosmetically pleasing hands for children will be available in the limb industry in the very near future. These will be voluntary-opening and voluntary-closing devices, and will be scaled in size from six or seven years of age upward (Figure 18).

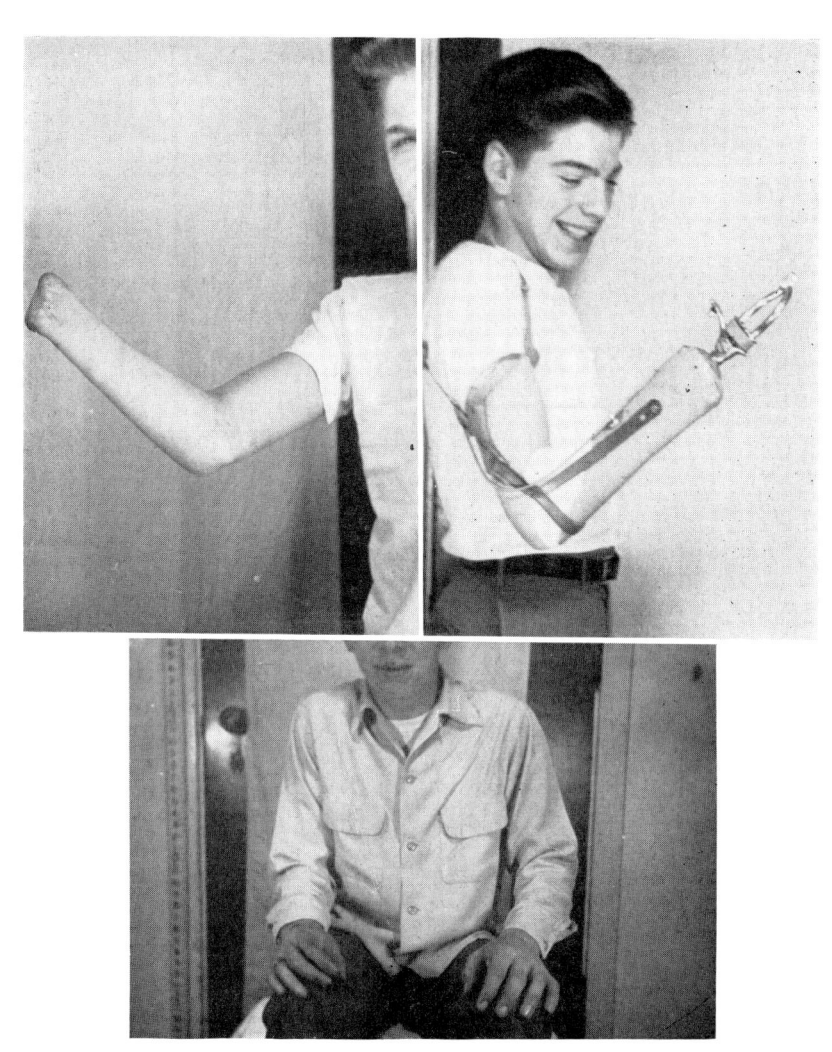

FIGURE 18. This sixteen year old boy lost his hand as a result of an explosion at thirteen years of age. He is a skillful worker and uses a voluntary opening type of terminal device. For social occasions he wears an APRL* voluntary closing hand with a cosmetic glove.

Not infrequently, there is a tendency for parents to reject an upper extremity prosthesis. This rejection usually pertains to girls, with reluctance exhibited by the mother. The reason given is the unsightliness of the hook.

*Army Prosthetic Research Laboratory. Washington, D.C.

In the congenital group, this reaction may be more truly based on a sense of guilt and the fear of a hereditary taint. The young congenital upper extremity amputee by the age of four years has learned to be quite skillful with a short below-elbow amputation stump (the most common congenital amputation of the upper extremity) (Figure 16). This skill is offered as a second excuse for not wanting a prosthetic device placed on the child. Many small tasks are completed with relative ease utilizing the fold of the elbow to hold small objects and utensils. In calling attention to this accomplishment, the mother may be refusing to accept the presence of a functional handicap. Practical considerations from a functional standpoint will demonstrate the child is able to operate only in areas close to the body. One upper extremity is quite short, and the normal side is brought in closer to the torso. The young amputee thus is not functioning efficiently.

Very seldom does the parent of a post-traumatic or surgical amputee refuse the aid of an upper extremity prosthesis. The child had two normal extremities prior to the incident or episode causing the amputation; he or she had developed normally as a two-handed person. The sudden absence of an upper extremity is more of a handicap here than in the congenital type. Usually the parent and child seek functional restitution.

When there is evidence of reluctance to accept the device, the problem may be solved by a conference with the family and a demonstration to the parents of a child with a similar amputation who has been wearing a prosthesis for a year. In most instances, the functional accomplishments of this child will stimulate the family to seek a similar result with their youngster.

CINEPLASTY

The cineplastic amputation is defined as one in which the stump is so formed that the patient may activate the prosthesis by a muscle motor within the muscles of the stump itself.

A metal, plastic or ivory peg is placed through the tunnel to transmit muscle power to the prosthesis by means of cables or cords. Experience has demonstrated that only those motors placed within the muscle belly are successful. This basic criterion to date has limited the location of muscle motors to the upper arm and pectoral region. Before cineplasty is considered, the amputee

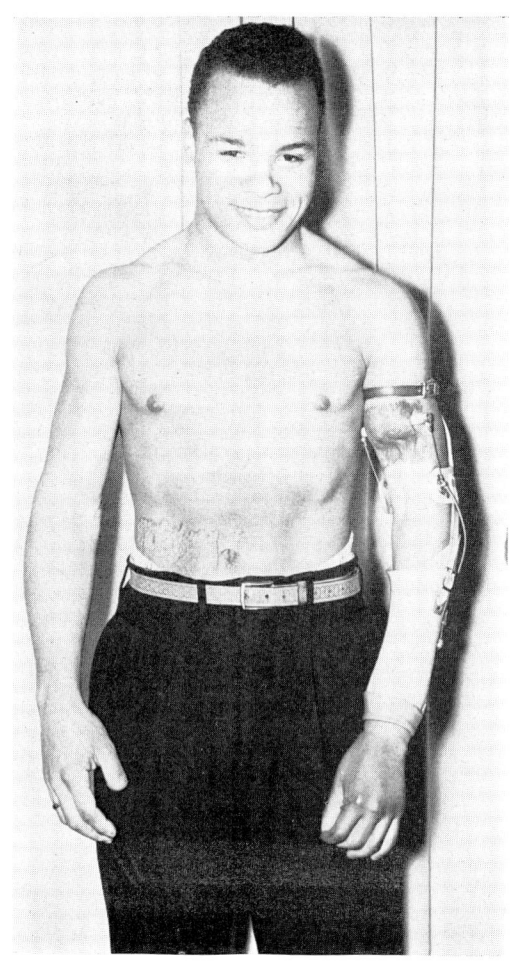

FIGURE 19. Cineplasty type of amputation. The biceps muscle of this seventeen year old boy has been split to afford a muscle motor for operating the terminal device of his below elbow type of prosthesis. (APRL hand and glove.) The muscle motor allows greater control of the terminal device and eliminates the need for harnessing.

must have a stump of adequate length, the muscle considered for the motor must have adequate excursion and power, and the skin must be healthy (Figure 19).

It is quite evident that before surgery is performed, the muscle or muscles must be exercised rigorously to develop strength and excursion.

Post-operatively, when the tunnel is well healed (three weeks), the motor must be activated by regular, graduated exercises. Resistance to contractile power is gradually increased.

Six to eight weeks after the operative procedure are needed to build up sufficient power and excursion to operate a terminal device.

The skin tunnel demands meticulous care. Daily cleansing with soap and water is necessary. Small alcohol sponges may be used to clean the tunnel.

The advantages of cineplasty over the conventional amputation are:

1. It does away with harnessing the opposite shoulder;
2. The terminal device is operated directly from the stump and the amputee is said to develop a proprioceptive sense or "touch" with his terminal device not possible with conventional harnessing. This sense, or "feedback," is highly theoretical.

Adult experience with cineplasty indicates many failures. The limited success has not been due to lack of physical conditioning, surgical technique or inadequate prosthesis. Emotional, mental and cultural background must be taken into consideration. Occupational qualifications are very important. Enthusiastic, fastidious individuals may be well-suited for the cineplastic procedure. Their hygienic habits, occupational and recreational pursuits may suggest great advantages with a motorized muscle.

Laborers, farmers and others following a "heavy-duty" type of occupation may fail to be benefited. Slovenly individuals with poor hygienic habits have continual trouble with the skin in the tunnel.

The "type of person" is given first and foremost consideration. Will he happily go through the pre-operative and post-operative conditioning and be able to have maintenance service easily available for physiological and prosthetic complications?

The cineplastic procedure in the child has not been universally accepted. It is suggested that cineplasty is the answer in congenital cases of amelia and phocomelia of the upper extremity. This is by no means universally true.

The young child, housed as an in-patient at a training or rehabilitation center, may be trained to perform in an acceptable manner. He is, however, a member of a family group, and when discharged to the care of his family his progress will depend upon the care and understanding of his parents. The responsibility of the parents in the follow-up care of growth problems and maintenance of prostheses is all-important. The cooperation of some families utilizing clinic service has not been satisfactory.

There are many unknown factors in the growing child relative to cineplasty.

Will hypoplastic muscles continue to develop during the maturation period to a sufficient degree to have justified a tunnel, offering much more function than conventional types of prostheses? Will the tunnel migrate with growth of the skeleton and soft tissue elements?

The type of person the child is destined to be is unknown. The occupational destiny of the young amputee is undetermined; his mental potential is not known and may be limited. What kind of a family and background does this potential candidate have? The parents may be indifferent, not particularly neat and tidy in their habits, or not possessing those attributes that make for a well-ordered home with environmental influences conducive to good physical hygiene. How far is this young amputee's residence from the hospital, clinic and prosthetist? It should be within a reasonable traveling distance, so that medical and prosthetic service is easily obtained for frequent clinical check-up examinations.

A decision to convert a young child to a cineplastic amputee should be made cautiously. The surgeon must be conservative. If a clinic team makes a decision for cineplasty, all facilities for pre-operative and post-operative conditioning should be readily available. The prosthetists must have experience in harnessing this type of amputee.

It is unwise for a surgeon to attempt cineplasty in a child under fourteen years of age. At this age of life, the youngster is close to maturity and physically strong and active. Children under fourteen years should not be considered for cineplasty except in those institutions that have had considerable experience in the complete management of cineplastic amputations.

THE REHABILITATION PROGRAM

Since World War II, the successful rehabilitation of veteran amputees has been the result of a team approach. The Armed Forces and the Veterans' Administration have demonstrated that a group of specially trained individuals offering their diversified skills in handling amputees will obtain much better end results in placing veterans back in wage-producing work than any one individual's endeavor.

The team consists of a surgeon, physical and occupational therapists, prosthetic instructor and prosthetist. These individuals must work as a unit and have at their command the equipment necessary to obtain the desired results.

For the past ten years this approach has been followed at the Mary Free Bed Children's Hospital and Orthopedic Center† for handling the child amputee. Properly equipped institutions must have out-patient service, in-patient facilities and cooperating prosthetists.

The program evolves into the following pattern:

1. Initial examination and evaluation—Out-Patient Service
2. Physical Therapy—If indicated
3. Prosthetic Fitting
4. Occupational Therapy
5. Prosthetic Training
6. Schooling and Recreation

   —In-Patient Service

7. Maintenance Follow-Up—Out-Patient Service

The initial examination is conducted in the out-patient clinic. The family may or may not have been contacted by a field social worker of some agency, acquainting them with available facilities. At this first examination an attempt is made to judge what program of correction will be best for the child. The stump is examined to determine its adequacy for a prosthesis and possible need for therapy or surgical care. If the young amputee has been a limb wearer, he is made to perform in his appliance. Functional skill is determined and deficiencies are looked for. There may be a need for modification of the prosthesis, or it may be discarded. If the child is a recent amputee, a regime of physical

---

†Grand Rapids, Michigan.

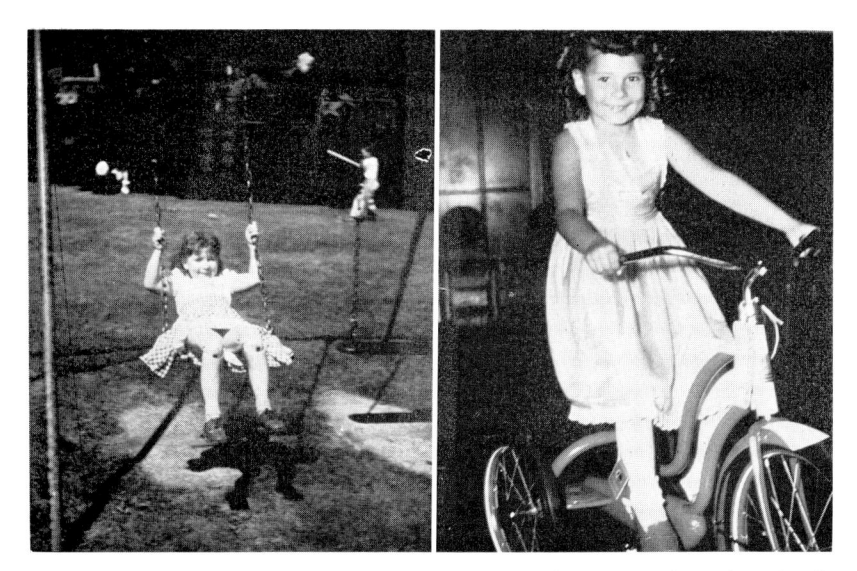

FIGURE 20. This eight year old girl lost both her legs at the above knee level. She has been fitted with a suction socket type of prosthesis and after intensive in-patient training is able to walk without outside aid.

therapy may be necessary to build up muscle power, mobilize proximal joints and condition the stump.

Questions by the parents are answered, and the child's problem and possible future accomplishment are explained to them. Here rapport is made with the family. If the child is wearing a prosthesis and has faulty habits, it may be adjusted or a prescription for a new appliance may be initiated. The training period may be estimated for the parents' satisfaction, and in-patient instruction ordered.

Two phases of physical therapy may be necessary: basic conditioning of the stump, musculature and proximal joint; and elementary instruction in prosthetic function and control.

All muscle groups must be developed to obtain maximum effectiveness in operating a prosthesis. A full range of motion of the joints is necessary if contractures exist they must be worked out. Stretching, passive motion, active motion and resistive exercises may be necessary to properly condition the fresh amputee.

The prosthesis may require four weeks to fabricate, preparatory to initial fitting. This first fitting is judged satisfactory only when

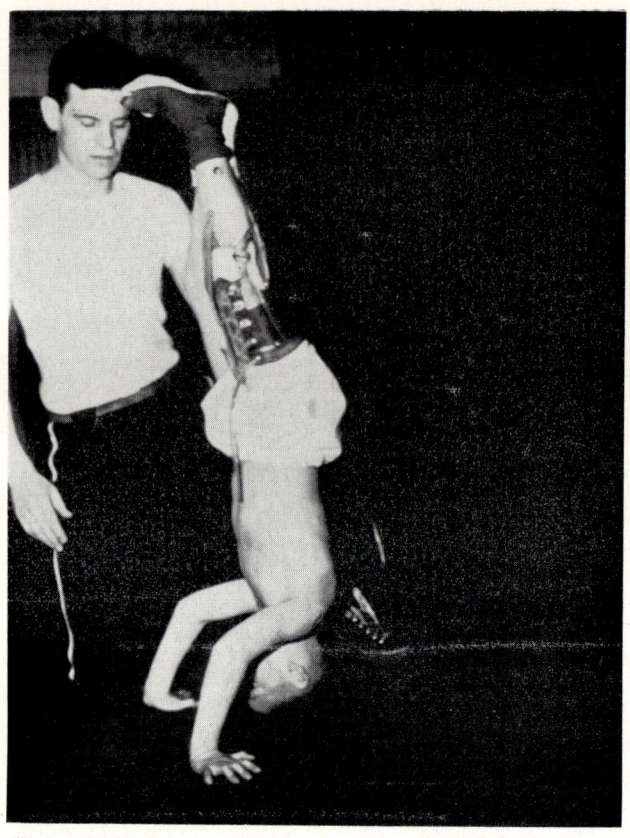

FIGURE 21 A. This nine year old amputee is an excellent swimmer, plays baseball and competes with his playmates on an equal basis.

a check-out examination has been made and the prosthesis judged to be comfortable, mechanically sound and properly aligned.

Occupational therapy and prosthetic training begin when the new appliance is accepted. The purpose of the training function is to teach the use of the prosthesis. The child is shown the practical utility of the appliance in everyday living. The occupational therapy department is equipped with games, manually and power-operated tools motivating the child's interest and affording means of muscle-building dexterity and the "feel" of the appliance (Figure 20).

During the in-patient training period, the young amputee should attend school in a commensurate grade. Contacts with

FIGURE 21 B. Working on a trampoline develops stump tolerance to shock, weight bearing, a sense of balance and skill.

other children offer an "outlet" with the new limb. Diversional activities are designed to augment prosthetic training. Birthday parties offer social contacts. Out-of-door activities, such as roller-skating, shuffleboard, bow-and-arrow classes, volley-ball, and so forth develop the competitive spirit and allow the young amputee to "participate" (Figures 21A and 21B).

When a child is judged ready for discharge, a final check-out examination should be made on his prosthesis. It must meet minimum standards for the child's age and level or type of amputation. His skill in operation and control of the device must be improved over his initial check-out procedure.

The parents should be in attendance at or near the day of discharge, to see their youngster perform with the prosthesis. They should be briefed on the operation and harnessing of the limb and informed of the techniques of stump care. The return appointment for out-patient check up is then made.

The parent should accompany the young amputee on his first school day. The grade teacher must be made acquainted with the prosthesis and observe what her young charge can and cannot do. His classmates should see the appliance and observe its operation. Usually when young minds full of curiosity are satisfied and no mystery exists, little further attention is directed toward an unusual circumstance in the body or activity of their schoolmate. This is one of the first major steps in accomplishing rehabilitation. The handicap has been accepted and mastered. The young amputee is now part of a group.

The follow-up program is met by regularly scheduled visits to the out-patient department. Four to five visits a year are a minimal number to meet the demands of growth and mechanical failures. The immature amputee continues to grow and being well trained will not particularly "nurse" his appliance. Elementary school age boys are very active in sports, and exact a punishing toll on their protheses. Fect break down, ankle joints spring, terminal devices bend, cables fray and break (Figure 22).

It is unwise to allow a young amputee to continue wearing an improperly functioning artificial limb. This is of great importance in the upper extremity amputee. Immediate repair allows continuity of function, and economically it is cheaper than a new appliance.

The youngster increases in height quite rapidly from nine to thirteen years. Adjustments in the length of lower extremity prostheses sometimes are necessary each three months to correct a limp due to the short prosthetic side. Sockets must be relieved for growth in muscle mass and the maturation of bony prominences.

Occasionally, teen-agers may not become good wearers of upper extremity prostheses. There is a tendency to put them aside for "this or that reason." Such a habit may become chronic with less and less time spent in the appliance. Return out-patient visits will aid in correcting this deficiency. The team personnel will pick up this failure by observing a lag in skillful acts and the lack of wear about the moving parts of the prosthesis. If the prosthesis is comfortable and mechanically sound, two reasons usually account for the failure to wear the artificial limb (Figure 23):

1. Parental cooperation is not satisfactory;

2. In-patient training has been inadequate (time element or calibre of instruction).

FIGURE 22. This sixteen year old boy with a left side below knee amputation plays basketball on a normal competitive basis with those of his age group.

Correction of this situation should be met by a conference with parents, pointing out the necessity for more supervision and encouragement. Rarely an emotional problem may come to light. This may have to be met by psychiatric investigation. Usually, these personality problems are encountered during the initial in-patient period, and occur in the older congenital upper extremity amputees.

(*See Figure 23 A, B, C, D, E, F on pages 94, 95 and 96*)

FIGURES 23 A, B, C, D, E, F. This nine year old girl with a congenital amputation on her left forearm was fitted with her first prosthesis at four years of age. She is able to perform all common tasks without difficulty due to the excellent terminal device control she has developed.

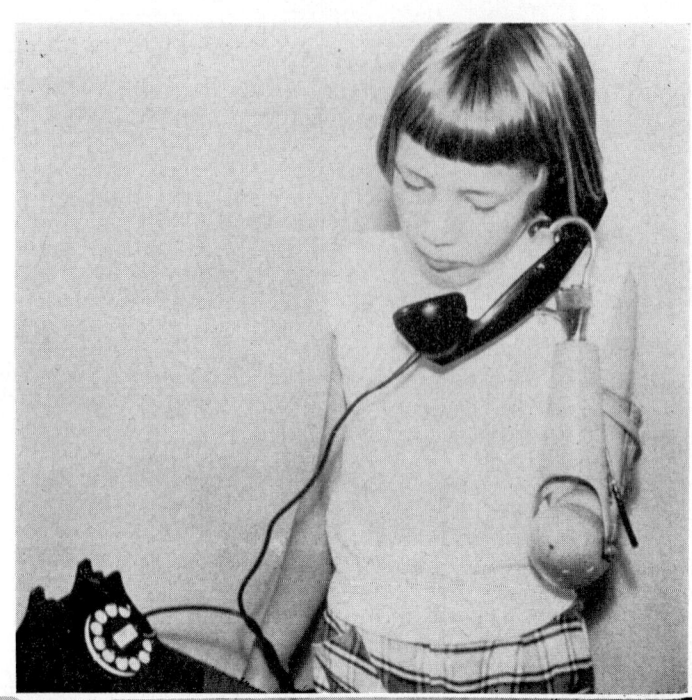

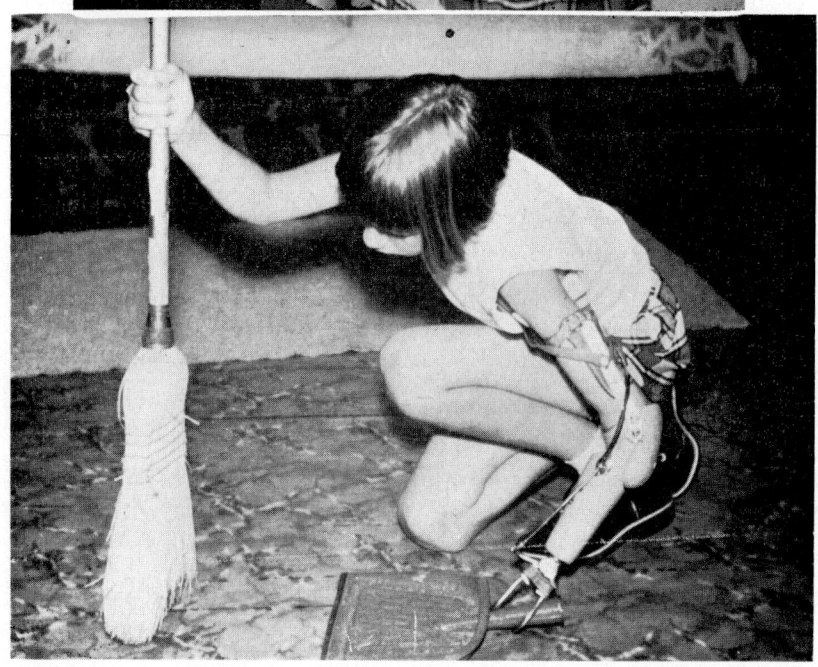

Figures 23 A, B

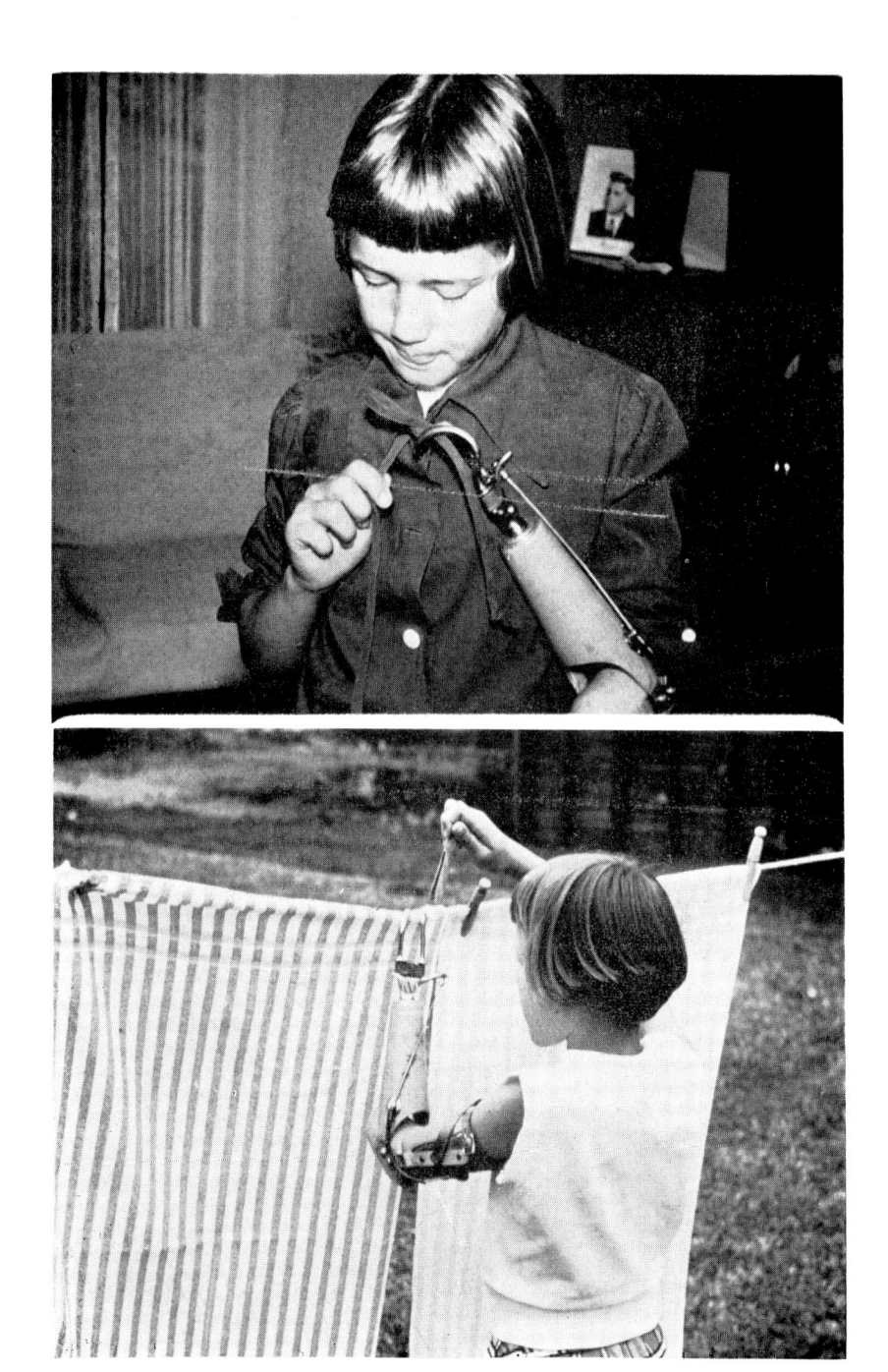

Figures 23 C, D

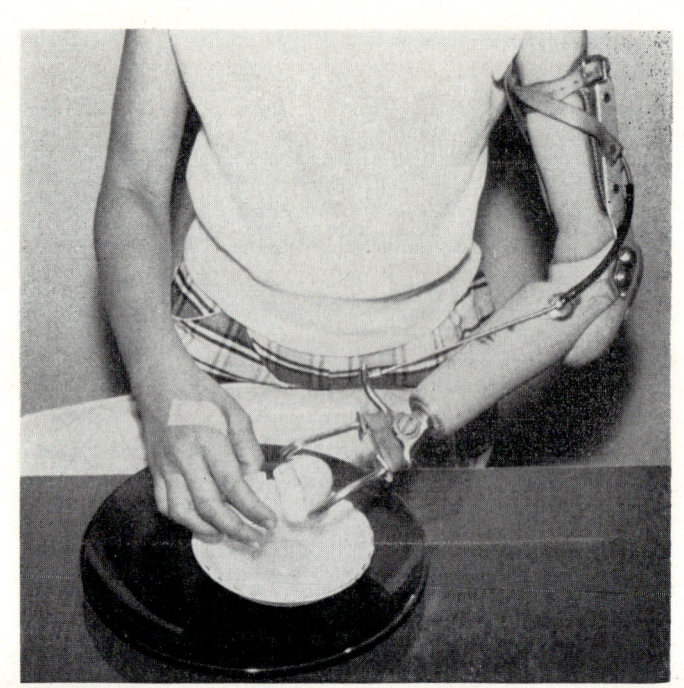

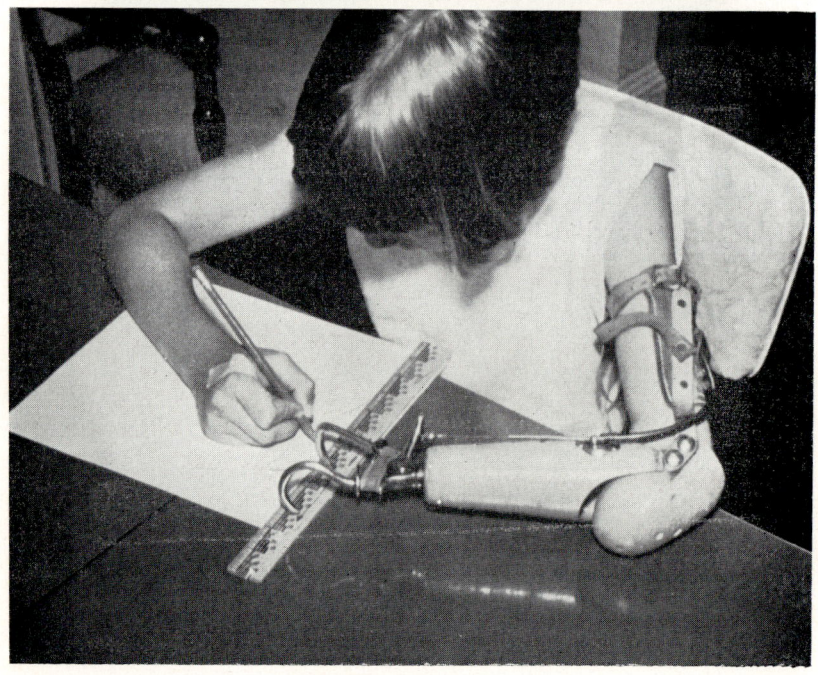

Figures 23 E, F

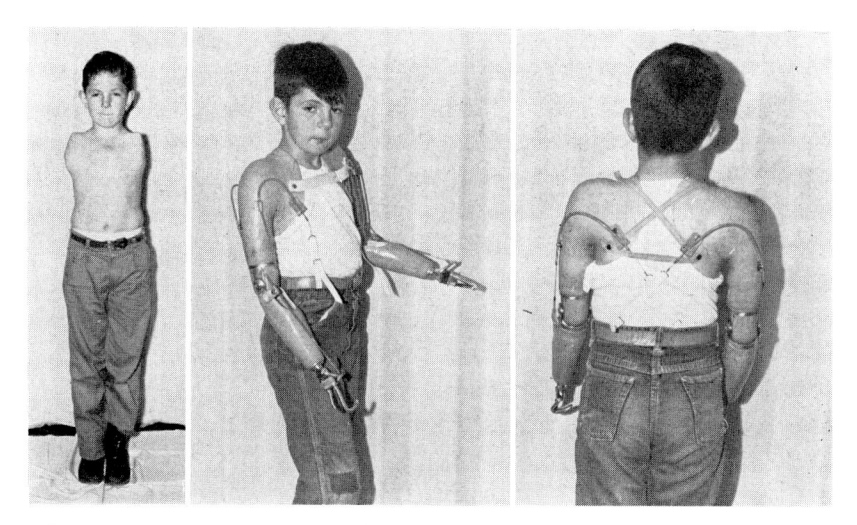

FIGURE 24. This ten year old boy has a congenital absence of the upper extremities (amelia). This deformity is a shoulder disarticulation from a prosthetic standpoint. He has been fitted with caps of laminated plastic over the stumps. The elbow locking mechanism is operated by a cable attached to his belt, the terminal device control is attached to the opposite thigh encircling it. This is a very severe type of handicap which requires long hours be spent to master prosthetic skill. Such individuals, through necessity, developed very skillful acts with the toes and excessive ranges of motion in the knee and hip joints.

Unhappy social impacts upon young elementary school upper extremity amputees may be, at times, temporarily difficult to cope with. Children are spontaneous and undiplomatic. A very common term encountered by the youngster in the second, third or fourth grade is "Captain Hook." A few young amputees have deeply resented this cognomen. Most children well trained and with understanding parents can ride over this period without frustration or resentment.

The well organized juvenile amputee training program with efficient out-patient follow-up services, with the aid of wholehearted family cooperation, will produce a high percentage of well adjusted, skillful young amputees (Figure 24).

127

THE CHILD WITH CEREBRAL PALSY

Eric Denhoff, M.D.

In the past, the term "cerebral palsy" implied Little's Disease—a spastic paralysis resulting from birth trauma. Today, the American Academy of Cerebral Palsy defines cerebral palsy as any abnormal alteration of movement or motor function arising from defect, injury or diseases of the nervous tissues contained within the cranial vault. Such a condition may occur before, during, or after birth.[1] Since neuropathological studies have demonstrated that children with enuromotor disability (cerebral palsy), mental deficiency, epilepsy, and behavior disturbances of organic origin have identical findings at post mortem, these clinical entities have been grouped together and called the "Brain Damage" syndrome.[2] Since no proof of brain damage is indicated in many post mortems of cases of individuals who had evidenced cerebral malfunction, a better term would be "Syndromes of Cerebral Malfunction."

Although the cerebral palsied child may present any combination of signs or symptoms which reflect cerebral malfunction, such as neuromotor disability, convulsions, vision, hearing, speech, tactile or perceptual problems, and mental, behavioral and emotional disturbances, the finding that differentiates cerebral palsied children from others in the syndromes is the neuromotor disability. This disability may be a spasticity, weakness, incoordination, rigidity, tremors or involuntary motions, alone or in mixed varieties. Dysfunction may be limited to a single limb or may involve the entire body. Dysfunction may vary in degree of severity and may change from time to time in relationship to the growth and development of the damaged nervous system. Similarly the other elements within the syndromes may gain or lose significance during childhood. For instance, a child with a spastic hemiplegia may have difficulty in walking as a toddler, with use of his eyes and hands as a six year old, with seizures as a ten year old, and with emotional instability as an adolescent. Frequently cerebral palsied children are diagnosed with multiple disabilities, such as blindness, deafness, cleft palate, and congenital heart disease. The same etiologic factors may be responsible for both the cerebral palsy and the additional handicaps.

INCIDENCE

The present incidence of cerebral palsy is difficult to estimate due to improved diagnosis, changing birth rates, inadequate registration and methods of computing incidence. Anderson,[3] on the basis of obstetrical data, estimates there are over fifty thousand infants born each year in the United States who will be neurologically handicapped. Wishik[4], basing his report on a Schenectady County, New York, house-to-house survey, estimates that in the United States there are between 1.5 and 3.0 cerebral palsied persons of all ages per 1,000 population, and that cerebral palsy results in one of every 170 live born infants. The United Cerebral Palsy Association's recent estimate indicates that there are 550,000 cerebral palsied persons in the United States, and that in New York State alone, cerebral palsy clinics are treating 4,841 patients. This figure does not include patients being treated by private physicians.

This data indicates that the number of known cases of cerebral palsy is on the increase. This increase may be due to better methods of case finding and to earlier diagnosis. However, Anderson's statistics correlate with impressions of pediatricians that although the number of severe cases of "Little's Disease category" are diminishing because of improved obstetrical methods, nevertheless, the numbers of mild cases of those who can be classified within the "Cerebral Malfunction Syndromes" are increasing because of fetal salvage. If these impressions are substantiated during the years to come, more children with milder degrees of cerebral palsy and related disorders should be diagnosed than heretofore.

Currently, 20% of cerebral palsied children require only occasional special services or none at all. 35% need special out-patient and/or educational services, while 45% need in-patient and/or custodial care. Within the two latter groups over 50% of the cases need services for mental retardation, speech, hearing, and visual problems, while over 25% need special care for treatment of convulsions. Since children with brain damage carry the defect for life, most of them require long term treatment and guidance.[5] Although significant improvement is not possible in most children and although some children get worse in spite of treatment, the majority are capable of learning self help and limited adjustment in a prolonged treatment-training program which involves parents as well as the patient.

ETIOLOGY

Cerebral palsy occurs during the prenatal, paranatal or postnatal period in the majority of cases. Approximately ten per cent (10%) of all cases are genetically determined, eighteen per cent (18%) are of prenatal origin, 35% are due to causes in the paranatal (obstetrical) period, and 18% may be found in the postnatal period. In 20%-40% of specific cases, the cause may be unknown.

Genetic Causes. Although anomalies of the germ plasm resulting in abnormal development of the fetal brain are not common, families where siblings or relatives have the same type of afflication have been noted. The progressive neurologic disturbances, such as Wilson's Disease or Schilder's Disease are of genetic origin and perhaps constitute the majority of the 10% that comprise this group. However, these disorders are not included in the recent classification of the Academy of Cerebral Palsy. Increasing evidence appears to indicate that the "pile up" effect of repeated exposure to roentgen rays has mutational effects in successive generations, some of which adversely affect the nervous system.

Prenatal Causes. Although a large number of infectious, metabolic, chemical, and irradiation agents may be found capable of producing brain damage in the prenatal period in animals, in the human being viral infections (rubella, toxiplasmosis and occasionally chickenpox) bacterial infections, (tuberculosis, syphilis) deep x-ray irradiation to the gonads, and metabolic disorders (toxemia of pregnancy, maternal diabetes) have been proven to produce deformities in the human embryo. Recent studies of the irradiation effects of atom bomb exposures indicate that such irradiation does have deleterious effects upon the embryo. Mental deficiency and microcephaly are among the handicapping conditions found in infants of mothers who were close to the center of the atomic explosion at a time when they were pregnant.[8]

Paranatal Causes. Birth injuries still account for the largest group of cerebral palsied youngsters. The 1951 New Jersey study demonstrated that 38.9 per cent of the children studied were in this category.[9] Vascular injury secondary to anoxia has replaced the traumatic delivery as a prime causative agent. Improper analgesia, anesthesia and resuscitation contribute to the group. Although prematurity still accounts for a large number of cases (30%), postmaturity also contributes its quota of brain damaged infants. Precipitate delivery, prolonged labor, premature rupture of membranes, Caesarean delivery, placental hemorrhage associated with pathologic maternal conditions, such as pelvic outlet disproportions, uterine contractibility abnormality, and placental complications are responsible for the great majority of cases.

Postnatal Causes. In the postnatal period, encephalitis, pneumonia, subdural hematoma, lead poisoning, hypoglycemia and other such causes account for most of the cases. A previously large number of cases due to kernicterus are now being reduced because of our knowledge of RH incompatibility, hyperbilirubinemia and the preventative advantages of the replacement transfusion. Some cases of kernicterus are correlated with prematurity, congenital hemolytic anemia with jaundice, and anoxia.

Since carefully controlled clinico-pathologic and clinico-anatomic correlations are not possible, the problem of the etiology of cerebral palsy is a vexing one. Although many "causative factors" have been identified, other etiologic agents are yet to be found. One small but well controlled study produced as many brain damaged children in a normal group of newborns as in a highly suspected group studied at identical periods. An unusually high number of previously unsuccessful pregnancies in both groups of mothers was the only common denominator.[10] Currently, a long range attack on etiology and neuropathologic correlations of cerebral palsy has been initiated by the National Institute of Neurologic Diseases and Blindness groping to find logical answers to such a compelx problem.

Summary. To summarize, although there are widely diverse causes of cerebral palsy the common denominator appears to be oxygen lack in association with a great variety of genetic, mechanical, infectious, and metabolic agents. Recent studies also suggest that maternal constitutional factors may make the difference between those infants who undergo brain damage and those who escape the effects of anoxia.

DIAGNOSIS

A diagnosis of cerebral palsy can be achieved from an accurate history and physical examination. Laboratory tests may be needed to confirm clinical impressions. In the history, the presence of epilepsy, mental retardation, or chronic neurologic disorders in the family, vaginal bleeding, acute or chronic illness during the mother's pregnancy, or an abnormal or difficult delivery contributes to the diagnosis. A knowledge of cyanosis, prematurity, postmaturity, jaundice, or infection during the postnatal period increases the index of suspicion. A report of severe feeding or sleeping disturbance, head injury, delayed development, and seizures during infancy is additive.

The physical examination may reveal a number of abnormal findings or a paucity, depending upon the age of the patient and the type and degree of the handicap. Generally, one may find strabismus, increased deep reflexes or pathologic reflexes, and hypertonicity in a spastic child. A child with dyskinesia may present nystagmus, vision, speech and hearing loss, hypermotility of the extremities, and variable deep reflex changes. Some children receiving anoxic insults early in utero may demonstrate maldevelopment of the eyes, ears, palate, heart and toes—the popular stigma of mental deficiency. Diagnostic criteria at the infancy, toddler, and school age levels are outlined.

Infancy. Cerebral palsy is infrequently diagnosed at birth since there is a paucity of abnormal neurological signs at this time. A brain damaged infant may be found to be hyperirritable or extremely listless. Hyperirritability may lessen as cerebral edema and bleeding recedes. On the other hand, a listless baby usually reflects anoxia with the medullary centers affected. Usually, later there is evidence of severe neuromotor disability. However, as a general rule the brain-damaged neonate appears normal for several weeks. Only as the stress of development is placed upon the damaged cortex, mid-brain, and lower centers, do the neuromotor difficulties become apparent. These first appear as sleeping or feeding difficulties with stiffening, arching, or excessive grunting. The diagnosis is made with growth and development.

The sleep disturbance and sucking and swallowing inadequacies which normally disappear within the first three months of life persist and even increase in intensity in cerebral palsy. Complaints become excessive even while the physician tries to rule out milk allergy, cholasia, or chronic indigestion. Weight gain and tissue turgor may be poor, and anemia is common. During these early months the only apparent physical indication of cerebral palsy may be a general lag in motor development. However, spasticity almost always appears before six months, whereas athetosis may not appear until after the first year. In infancy, spasticity may effect the lower extremities more severely than the upper extremities. The head, neck and upper extremities are more severely involved in the young athetoids. As the spastic infant grows, the thighs are frequently held in an adducted position because of increasing adductor muscle tightness. The infant exhibits a tendency toward "scissoring" of the legs on stimulation. As the spastic child grows, deep reflexes increase; and the stretch reflex and clonus may be noted in the affected limbs. Increasing periods of hypertonicity especially when the limbs are moved are now recognized. If physical therapy is not started, secondary contractures are prone to occur. In the athetoid infant, the arm and leg movements become more purposeless when the child is stimulated. Tension, or intermittent stiffening spells when reaching for objects, is more apparent as the infant grows. Straightening of the arms with clenching of the fists is characteristic.

In both groups of babies, eye difficulties in the form of strabismus and nystagmus may now be recognized. Internal strabismus is most common. The nystagmus associated with cerebral palsy is frequently jerky in character, sometimes fast or slow. In the athetoid infant a paralysis of upward and downward gaze develops, but this may not be recognized until the baby is old enough to look for objects. Most parents believe their baby was perfectly normal until his first illness which usually starts with a convulsion. Although parents may feel the seizure was responsible for the cerebral palsy, the seizure was probably the first manifestation of stress placed upon a damaged brain unable to maintain the developmental pace.

Between ten and eighteen months, when patients usually come for special diagnostic aid, certain neurologic patterns are present to substantiate the diagnosis. These usually are the persistence of infantile reflexes such as the grasp reflex, the sucking reflex, the tonic neck reflex, the Moro or startle reflex, the reflex of being held by the heels, and the extensor thrust reflex. Usually the presence of the Moro or startle reflex in which the baby reacts to loud noise by stretching out and sharply bending both arms and legs, and the presence of the tonic neck reflex in which when the infant's head is turned firmly to one side the arm and leg of the opposite side contracts, indicates severe damage when present after the first year. The extensor thrust reflex in which affected parts of the body may be forcibly thrust into extension without reasonable provocation is common of athetoids or severe spastic quadriplegias.

Pre-School and Older Children. As the child grows the diagnosis of cerebral palsy becomes easier especially in the more severe cases. In the very mild cases hitherto unrecognized, the youngster may present the cerebral palsy in the form of an organic behavior disturbance or a mild form of incoordination or clumsiness. Children with spastic hemiplegia or quadriplegia represent the largest group at the cerebral palsy nursery school. Spastic hemiplegia is not difficult to recognize since the child usually holds his arm pressed against the body with his forearm bent at right angles to the upper arm and his hand bent against the forearm. The fist may be tightly clenched with the fingers pressed firmly into the palm in a fixed position. On the other hand in a milder case the diagnostic sign may only be a peculiar over-extended appearance of the fingers with rotation of the wrist when the child reaches for items. In the young child the leg may be more spastic than the arm. A hemiplegic youngster may walk on his toes or on the outer ball of his foot while the leg rotates inwardly with the knee bent in a limited position. At rest the foot may be held in an equino-varus position, the big toe hyper-extended in the Babinski position. The child with the quadriplegia involvement may be unable to sit or walk unsupported and usually has poor control of all his extremities. Balance is poor, and contractures from the pelvic muscles to the muscles of the lower extremities are common.

A child with athetosis or other types of dyskinesia may differ from the spastic child by a variety of abnormal movements. In sitting or walking, the head may be drawn back and the neck may be thick and bull-like. The mouth may be open and the tongue protruding, and drooling may be excessive. The face may be mask-like at times but break into a grimace as the child tries to talk. Any or all of the limbs may be involved. The fingers particularly may be over-extended and almost constantly active when not at rest. Feet may turn inwards and the toes may tend to be held backwards. The athetoid may walk with a writhing, lurching, stumbling manner and with a good deal of incoordination of the arms. The overflow may be variable depending upon confidence or fear. When he is calm and well rested he may walk surprisingly well. Athetoid movements may be sub-classified as tremor, rotary, shudder or among others of twelve recognized types.

The ataxic child is easily recognized by the high-stepping, stumbling, lurching gait. When walking downhill he may suddenly fall on his face. He may totter and suddenly stop as he walks uphill. Nystagmus is common, tremors of the head are usual, and overshooting when reaching for toys is characteristic. Speech may be monotonous and drawling. There are varying degrees of ataxia as there are varying degrees of spasticity and athetosis.

Developmental Diagnosis. The comparison of the development of cerebral palsied children against the Gessel standards for normal children is a reliable aid in early diagnosis. The majority of cerebral palsied children fail to maintain their normal expectancy for their age group particularly after the first four to six months of life. Whereas the normal infant can hold his head erect from the prone for short periods during the first month of life, the average age of attaining this for a cerebral palsied youngster was 12.4 months. Whereas the normal infant usually reaches for nearby objects from 3-5 months, most cerebral palsied children reach for items at 14.5 months. Sitting without support which occurs normally from 6-8 months, does not occur in most cerebral palsied infants until 20.4 months. Speech is similarly delayed so that the average age for onset of this item in cerebral palsied youngsters for single words is 27.1 months, whereas the normal infant can speak single words by 11 months. Standing, and walking alone, are similarly delayed in cerebral palsied infants at 27.5 months and 32.9 months respectively. The average age for development of 2-3 word sentences in cerebral palsied children is 37.4 months as compared to under 30 months in most normal children. In general, the developmental progress of cerebral palsied youngsters demonstrates that they require more time to achieve developmental items which require more skill or maturity. The attainment times of walking, talking, and speech on the average are more prolonged than times of achieving head control, and reaching and sitting without support. The time intervals between acquiring more mature skills also become increasingly prolonged. For differential diagnosis in those children with specific sensory handicaps only, such as hard of hearing, the ages of achieving developmental items are normal except those which involve hearing and speech. The relationship of development rate and intelligence correlates with developmental progress and intelligence in cerebral palsy children only in relationship to speech achievement. In a small group of normal children a significant difference existed between those children who spoke sentences before the thirty month level and those who spoke after thirty months. Those who did not speak sentences until 30 months or later were found to be retarded in intelligence at or below the borderline range of intelligence.

Associated Handicaps. Since cerebral palsy is actually the neuromotor component of the larger cerebral malfunction syndromes, other handicapping conditions will be found in cerebral palsied children. In children referred to a nursery school[11] 50% were mentally retarded, almost 80%-90% had convulsive disorders, and at least 30% had an organic behavior disorder or emotional disturbance. Speech, hearing, visual, and perceptive disorders were also present in a large number.

Mental Retardation. To differentiate between the child with primary amentia and neuromotor disability and the cerebral palsied child who is mentally retarded because of cerebral malfunction is important. Both types can be found, but the outlook obviously is much brighter in those children with retardation caused by brain damage.

Behavior and Emotional Disturbance. Cerebral palsied children have the same behavior and emotional problems as normal children. However, more cerebral palsied children than normal children have hyperkinesis which is characterized by loss of emotional control, hyperactivity, impulsiveness, poor attention span, distractibility, listlessness, and irritability. Because parents and teachers frequently do not recognize that cerebral palsied children can have poor emotional control, emotional disturbances secondary to the primary disability—anxiety, acting-out and neurotic behavior—occur frequently. Behavior problems in children evidencing cerebral palsy are related both to organic factors and environmental conflicts with family and society.

Convulsive Disorders. Although the incidence of convulsions in cerebral palsied children is reported to be between 25% and 60%, in one group of carefully studied children, most of them developed seizures.[12] Seizures are classified as major motor seizures, minor motor seizures, and mixed seizures. In cerebral palsied children, major motor seizures, characterized by generalized convulsions (grand mal) or focal seizures (Jacksonian seizures) are common, while of the minor motor type, the petit mal variety of seizure is relatively rare. However, mixed varieties are frequent.

As a general rule, the earlier the onset of convulsions, the more likely are they to be the result of brain damage rather than to be idiopathic. Convulsions even when associated with high fever occurring in infants suspected of being developmentally retarded should not be taken lightly. A convulsion is often the first overt sign of cerebral malfunction! In cerebral palsied infants a sudden startle, a flinging of an arm, or a turning of the eye upwards may represent combinations of minor motor seizures rather than mass reflexes activity, such as the Moro reflex, or the extensor thrust reflex responses.

Electroencephalography. In cerebral palsy, the electroencephalogram may be completely normal, may show moderately slow activity generalized or localized, fast activity generalized, or a combination of slow and fast activity. The significance of an abnormal electroencephalogram record in cerebral palsy depends upon whether or not the child has or has not had clinical seizures. An abnormal electroencephalogram in a patient previously without seizures is a warning that seizures may occur.

Sensory Impairment. Many children with cerebral palsy have sensory defects: vision, hearing, kinesthesia, epicritic and proprioception. Recently attention has been drawn to the fact that frequently sensory impairment of the involved hand coexist with visual defects in older spastic hemiplegia children. These children are unable to recognize objects tactilely and have diminished two point discrimination. Loss of vision in the left half or right half of the visual field may be associated. Sensory impairments may contribute more to disturbed personality and integration than motor handicap.

Differential Diagnosis. Differential diagnosis is extremely important especially in infancy and early childhood since many conditions may masquerade as cerebral palsy or vice versa. An infant with avitaminosis, celiac syndrome, milk allergy, toxic or metabolic disturbances may simulate the signs and symptoms of cerebral palsy. The child with hydrocephalus, meningocele, subdural hematoma or even pseudo-retardation may be developmentally retarded. Brachial palsy, congenital dislocation of the hip, the residuals of post-poliomyelitis, muscle disorders, and bone and joint disorders, such as Morquio's or Arthrogyroposis, and other obscure orthopedic conditions may masquerade as cerebral palsy. The child with speech, vision, hearing disturbances, a brain tumor, or psychotic behavior may simulate athetosis, rigidity, or ataxia.

Repeated observations in a benign atmosphere may be the only means of differentiation.

Laboratory Diagnosis. Intensive laboratory investigation may be necessary to determine the reasons for the aberrant development in some cases. Pneumoencephalograms, electroencephalograms, x-rays of the wrists for bone age, blood sugar studies and subdural aspirations may be very helpful. Experience has taught that pneumoencephalography, though not recommended for routine use, may be of value in some difficult cases. In cerebral palsy, unilateral or bilateral cerebral or cortical atrophy, cerebellar atrophy, or relatively normal air x-rays may be found. Generally, the child with cerebral palsy with bilateral cerebral and cortical damage has a poorer outlook than the child with the relatively normal air x-ray or unilateral porencephaly.[12] In primary amentia the pneumoencephalogram may be normal while in mental deficiency due to brain damage, all of the above classifications except unilateral cerebral atrophy have been found. Clinical and psychometric test findings are valuable in further differentiation.

The electroencephalogram is helpful in cerebral palsy in that almost all of these children present dysrhythmia with convulsive or subconvulsive tendencies while children in other categories may or may not demonstrate electroencephalographic abnormalities.

Evidence of hypometabolism, delayed bone age, and/or increased blood cholesterol or decreased total protein bound iodine are found in approximately 20 per cent of cerebral palsied children.

Positive subdural taps characterized by blood tinged or yellow semi-viscid or gelatinous fluid with a high total protein usually indicative of cortical atrophy of a long standing duration were found in 19 infants of a group of 38 who were tested for this finding.

Summary. To summarize, the signs of neuromotor abnormality during infancy are variable. Sleeping and feeding disturbances are most likely to be the earliest symptoms of cerebral palsy. As growth occurs, characteristic physical attitudes develop which become manifest as spasticity, dyskinesia and ataxia. During the pre-school period, mental deficiency, behavioral disorders and seizures become more evident as well as speech, hearing, visual disturbances, and other sensory disorders. Laboratory tests are needed in the less obvious cases for prognosis and differential diagnosis.

PSYCHOLOGICAL ASPECTS OF CEREBRAL PALSY

Psychological aspects of cerebral palsy include (1) psychometric testing of the child, (2) the diagnosis and treatment of the behavior disturbances associated with the disease, (3) individual parent and group guidance, and (4) staff guidance. The child's psychological appraisal is done within the psychiatric team setting.

Psychometric Testing. Many special tests are advocated and specially devised for the intellectual evaluation of the cerebral palsied child. However, the experienced psychologist generally depends upon the use of the Stanford-Binet Tests, the Wechsler Intelligence Scale for children, the Wechsler-Bellevue Tests for Adolescents and Adults, the Cattel Infant Intelligence Scale, the Vineland Scale of Social Maturity, the Gesell Developmental Schedules, the Goodenough Draw-A-Man Test, the Bender Visual Motor Gestalt Test and Scale, the Rorschach Test, and the Thematic Apperception Test. Although the severely handicapped child may not be tested as accurately as the normal child when these standard test procedures are used, the experienced psychologist can obtain fairly accurate delineations of intelligence. Although the mentally defective children, that is, those with an I.Q. below 50 are relatively in the same proportion as the normal population (3%), approximately half of cerebral palsied children are mentally retarded (I.Q. below 90). The remaining cerebral palsied children with average and above intelligence are found in the same proportions as in the normal population.

As a general rule, intelligence scores which are accurately checked early in life, change little during the years. In some cases where sensory handicaps, such as hearing or vision disturbance, or behavior disturbance have complicated the early picture, marked improvement in intelligence ratings occurs when these handicaps are treated adequately.

Personality Characteristics. A cerebral palsied child may have the same personality problems as the normal child. These may be related to anxiety or to neuroticisms associated with his environment. However, the cerebral palsied child may have the additional handicap of the "hyperkinetic syndrome of behavior." Distractibility, poor attention span, hyperactivity, perserveration, mood swings, make up the syndrome. Recent evidence suggests that these behavior characteristics are the result of anoxic damage to the hypothalamus in the mid-brain. Either the hypothalamus functions poorly, or the subsidiary and intermediary pathways between the cortex and hypothalamus are disturbed.

Emotional problems usually occur because of the child's feeling about himself and his handicap or result from the attitudes of parent-family, teachers and neighbors. Ultimately, the child not only is disturbed by the hyperkinesis but also develops anxiety or acts out his feelings of oppression. The hyperkinetic behavior syndrome disappears at adolescence, but the secondary effects of a rejecting family or neighbors may persist for a lifetime.

Parent Guidance. A child's happiness is predicated upon his parent's reactions to his behavior. This philosophy embraces all children but especially the ones handicapped by cerebral palsy. Therefore, understanding the parents and their feelings about their handicapped child is an important psychologic function. The cerebral palsy team as well as the private physician must understand the fears, anxieties and doubts of the parents of the cerebral palsied child. On the other hand, these parents must understand that their child's needs can only be met in a warm, loving, home atmosphere. Parent-imposed non-realistic goals for their handicapped child often lead to anxiety and insecurity in the growing child. Since the cerebral palsied child's emotional development background is different from the normal child's, the problems are much more intense if unrealistic demands are made. The psychologist's function is to understand both the mother's and father's role in the family. He must be able to help guide these parents through the rigors of over-protection and rejection to realistic attitudes. Poor parent attitudes prove a stumbling block to successful treatment-training programs. In essence, the major number of problems of parents stem from the difficulty they have had with their child in the newborn and infancy periods. These parents often cannot understand the extreme responses to hunger, pain, warmth, cold of their handicapped child. As a result they became excessively rigid or over-protective.

Individual and group sessions with parents when their child is first diagnosed by the physician are important if the physician is to achieve success in the medical planning. This counseling must be done in an informal manner at first since many parents resent the psychiatric inference to their problem. Within the group conferences the physician can identify those parents who are sufficiently disturbed to need further guidance on an individual basis. The great majority of average normal parents endowed with a normal amount of tension and anxiety about their cerebral palsied child emerge somewhat the better for their experience in the group.

No matter how the parents are counseled, certain actions must be taken. First, the handicapped child must receive a detailed medical survey. Discussion about the findings with the parents must be factual and placed upon a positive level. In discussing babies and young children, stress should be made upon favorable developmental attitudes rather than on unfavorable medical criteria. The parents must be left with the feeling that medical and psychological tests are definitive only if all factors affecting the testing situation remain unchanged. The attitude of the family toward the child and the behavior of the child toward the family may make the ultimate difference between success or failure. If the clouds of guilt and guilt complexes that lie over many handicapped children are cleared a great deal has been done.

The next step for the psychologist is to guide the parents in methods of handling their particular child. This method may vary from family to family. Discipline of the cerebral palsied child is as essential as for the non-handicapped child. Discipline, however, should be in the form of guidance rather than in punitive measures. Overdependence is not condoned. Parents of such a child must be convinced that if the child is to compete in a normal society, the parents must be "tougher" than they would be with a normal child. Home developmental programs are the best practical measures to work out these early problems of discipline and guidance.

Staff Guidance. The psychiatric team must be equipped to assess the emotional attitudes of other workers with cerebral palsied children and be prepared to help them to understand their own particular attitudes toward the group or toward a specific child. Some staff workers unconsciously become over-protective, over-attached, or rejecting. The clinical psychologist, working with the team in its daily routines, is best able to guide the workers successfully through these psychological hazards.

Summary. The psychological aspects of cerebral palsy include mental, behavioral, and emotional evaluation of the child and staff guidance for the parents. Because psychologic factors more frequently interfere with social adjustment than do motor disabilities, a successful program for cerebral palsy rehabilitation must have heavy psychological indoctrination.

SPECIAL PROBLEMS

Speech and Hearing. Cerebral palsied children have the same speech and hearing problems as normal children but in higher incidence. However, communication is more difficult in cerebral palsied children due to the variety of additional sensory handicaps. Since a positive correlation exists between level of language and speech development, many cerebral palsied children are retarded in speech because of mental retardation. Although overall communication failure may be the result of widespread brain damage resulting in clinical conditions resembling aphasia, such defects are usually due to neuromuscular involvement. Defective hearing, vision, visual-perceptual difficulty, motor handicap, hyperkinesis, and emotional problems frequently interfere with the speech processes. In a recent New Jersey survey[9] 68% of 1,224 children studied had defective speech.

Hearing. The evaluation of hearing is obviously important since distortions in hearing reflect distortions in speech. Hearing evaluation in cerebral palsied children is especially difficult to achieve but is possible through a variety of definitive techniques. These techniques include such auditory stimuli as whistles, horns, percussion instruments, responses to amplification, and responses to psychogalvanometer testing. Early diagnosis and treatment, particularly through amplification hearing-aid techniques, is advocated at as early an age as possible. Varying estimates of hearing and speech impairment among samples of cerebral palsied children have been made. A recent study in New Jersey indicates that 13% of cerebral palsied children studied had a definite or questionable hearing defect. Athetoid children make up the largest group with impaired hearing.

Since mental and emotional disturbances contribute a good deal to the underlying problem of hearing and speech disturbances, treatment not only involves correction of the hearing deficit but also concerns proper stimulation of speech. Various techniques utilized by the speech therapist combined with exposure to as normal an environment as the child's development makes possible is needed in order to achieve a successful treatment program.

Summary Since the ability to communicate well reflects motor, sensory, mental, and emotional control, speech ability can be used as an index of improvement and adjustment.

MEDICAL TREATMENT

The treatment of cerebral palsy is based upon fulfilling simultaneously and as early as possible the physical, mental, emotional, and social needs of the child. To learn as early as possible which child will be capable of participation in an organized nursery group program when he reaches the necessary developmental age for participation is important in a home developmental program. This habilitation program can be done only through a team approach, an approach designed to give security, to promote relaxation, and to relieve anxiety in both the child and his parents. This term merely implies simplified therapy designed to keep the baby within his own developmental capacity, to give the parents the opportunity to get acquainted with therapists, and the therapists an opportunity to get acquainted with the child. Under medical guidance, motor re-education is attempted simultaneously through physical therapy, occupational therapy, speech therapy, and play therapy.

As the child develops under guidance, the team is able to identify the child capable of participating in the high-powered program designed for the habilitation of the cerebral palsied. For purposes of charting progress within the home developmental program, the cerebral palsied child is described by five developmental levels: (1) the unorganized stage of development (reflex activity); (2) the uncoordinated state of development (conscious "contact"); (3) the semi-coordinated stage of development; (4) the partially coordinated stage of development; and (5) the coordinated (physical self-sufficiency) stage of development. These descriptions permit evaluation of the child at his own developmental rate rather than comparing his progress against the chronological age level utilizing Gesell's criteria. Children capable of progress pass rapidly from one stage to another, whereas the severely handicapped or mentally handicapped child remains for long periods in the lower categories.

The pediatrician or general practitioner is charged with maintaining good parent-child relationships, with maintaining good nutrition, with preventing seizures, and with guiding the child properly through the home developmental program.

The physiatrist supervises muscle strengthening methods.

The orthopedic surgeon is responsible primarily for preventing contractures and enhancing motility by utilizing physical, mechanical, or operative aids which encourage walking and use of the hands. He may recommend braces to fortify good posture, to help gain strength, or to limit motion. Recently there is a trend to recommend early operative procedures which can overcome spacticity. Adductor tenotomy and tibial neurectomy, unilateral and bilateral appear helpful. At the age of three years procedures like these may encourage development in a child whose progress is being limited because of inability to overcome spasticity.

The opthalmologist evaluates and corrects vision and visual-perceptual disturbances, while the otologist clarifies hearing status.

The psychiatrist is utilized for parent and child guidance.

To prevent seizures or to minimize seizures when they occur is the role of the neurologist. A wide host of anticonvulsant medications are available, such as Dilantin® sodium, Mesantoin®, Phenobarbital, Tridione®, Paradione®, Mysoline®, Milontin® and Phenurone®.

To help overcome hyperkinesis, anxiety or acting out behavior, tranquilizing or ataraxic drugs are now available. Thorazine® particularly has been exceedingly helpful in these areas of behavior.[13] The Rauwolfia compounds and Dexedrine Sulfate® also help speed the way for the child's ability to participate in the therapeutic program.

Muscle relaxant drugs, such as Mephenesin® and Flexin® are frequently used to overcome spasticity. These appear helpful in approximately 30% of the cases used. Tranquilizers, such as Miltown® or Thorazine® have been effective in reducing athetosis through its favorable behavioral effects.

When seizures cannot be controlled and when deterioration appears likely, especially in the hemiplegic child with unilateral porencephaly, the neurosurgeon may advise cortical excision or hemispherectomy.

The dentist has assumed an increasingly important role in cerebral palsy, and knowledge is accruing on the best methods to prevent and treat oral disturbances. Currently techniques have been devised which allow dental repair to be done at one sitting under anesthesia.

Rounding out a Team. The physical therapist helps to achieve total relaxation for the child particularly of the lower extremities. The occupational therapist particularly works to achieve good movement and use of the upper extremities. Correction of the visual-perceptual disturbances lies within this area. Speech therapists help communication skills. The nursery school teacher encourages independence in daily activities, in addition to preparing the child for formal education. The social worker helps coordinate the parent program and acts as a trouble shooter for family problems. The clinical psychologist directs play therapy and gives parent and staff guidance under the supervision of the psychiatrist. To achieve success, all of these persons must learn to work cohesively and interchangeably as the occasion demands.

Summary. Medical treatment depends upon proper and early diagnosis. Control of seizures and achievement of motor and emotional relaxation is possible in some measure by the use of specific drugs. Orthopedic procedures to encourage developmental progress, eye and ear consultation to overcome sensory handicaps, and neurosurgical methods to prevent deterioration may be necessary. This coordination cannot be adequately achieved without the proper use of the team under medical supervision.

EDUCATIONAL PLANNING

Educational planning of the cerebral palsied child starts in the home developmental program, progresses through the nursery school, continues through the regular public school system, and considers special schools or special institutions depending upon the particular needs of the individual. Preschool training plays a much more important role in cerebral palsy than it does with normal children since the cerebral palsied child needs more preparation to overcome physical, mental and emotional handicaps. Nursery school helps him prepare for participation in daily living activities and to acquire pre-learning skills. When the child is mature enough to achieve success in these skills, he may go on to public school. Like the normal child there are many programs that are available for him. A regular school program should be prepared to provide special teaching methods for the cerebral palsied child with normal intelligence, with minor physical handicap, and with perceptual and behavioral handicaps. The intelligent cerebral palsied child with severe motor handicap and the moderately motor handicapped cerebral palsied child with mental retardation may require special classes or home teaching. The severely mentally-physically handicapped child usually requires custodial care. An educational program must distinguish between those with severe mental deficiency and those with severe physical disability and moderate mental retardation. Plans must be established for proper selection of cases. The criteria for selection are based on chronological age, maturation age, degree of the physical disability, personality and adjustment of the child, and the degree of development of self-help skills. An I.Q. of 85 may be taken as the minimal level of mental ability required for cerebral palsied children to profit from special education techniques. Not all children with this level of ability will profit from such experiences since much depends upon their emotional and behavioral capacities. Although mental ability should not be the sole criteria for selection for education, it is, nevertheless, an important one. Medical criteria alone, such as vision, speech, hearing, or convulsions should not stand in the way of selection or rejection. Teachers must be taught to understand the problems these children present and must not be frightened by them. Understanding teachers who are trained in special education techniques are necessarily a part of the educational plan.

Educational adjustment of the child depends a great deal upon his family attitudes.[14] The kind, realistic parent apparently can favorably affect the educational progress of his handicapped child in spite of distractibility, poor attention span, perserveration which are particular handicaps for learning. Many of these can be helped with parent understanding and medication. The family physician should be involved with these parents if educational success is desired. Children fail in school when their parents establish unrealistic goals, complain, and seek the "golden apple," rather than accept competent professional advice.

VOCATIONAL GUIDANCE AND PLACEMENT

The reason for education is vocational placement. Since the ultimate goal of a cerebral palsied person is to adjust into the community at his own particular level and to be able to participate and contribute to the welfare of the community, vocational placement must be realistic. In considering the vocational potential of the individual disabled by cerebral palsy, the physical disability, the capacity for self-care, the mental status, the emotional status, and the appearance of being normal as well as the educational status and motivation must be assessed. Community resources which include counseling services manned by people who are skilled in understanding adolescent and young adult problems are needed to guide the placement properly. Realistic placement of these young adults is difficult since in many cases intellectual ability has little to do with practical application. One may work out many possible plans for vocational guidance and placement but unexpected details, such as inability to cross a street, recognize a traffic light, to make change properly, all stand in the way of perfectly good programs. Sheltered workshops are important adjuncts to vocational planning. It is here that one may help overcome in a practical way the specific disabilities of the individual. Here, again, success depends upon good counseling. These young adults need support from strong and wise professionals who are willing to stand behind them.

Studies of the employment of cerebral palsied adults reveal that they can hold a wide range of positions, such as professional, managerial, clerical, sales, service, agricultural, skilled, semi-skilled and unskilled. Thus job placement with the cerebral palsied presents the same problems as with normal young adults, except for acceptability. To achieve this requires total community education of the problems of the handicapped.

Summary. Cerebral palsy is a public health problem since the community must be educated to have a rehabilitation awareness. Careful planning by medical, social, psychological, educational and other professional disciplines are necessary if one is to achieve this total service program. However, experience has demonstrated that in the final analysis success in the rehabilitation of the physically handicapped person depends not only upon the contributions of all the people, but first upon the contributions the patient and his family make.

BIBLIOGRAPHY

1. Minear, W.: Report Nomenclature and Classification Committee, American Academy for Cerebral Palsy, 1956, *Pediatrics*, to be published.
2. Cruickshank, W. M., and Raus, George M. (Ed.): *Cerebral Palsy— Its Individual and Community Problems*, Syracuse, New York, Syracuse University Press, 1955, Chapter II, Medical Aspects by Denhoff, E. Pg. 22.

3. Anderson, G. W.: Current Trends in the Pathology of Human Reproductive Failure, *Am. J. Public Health*, 45:10 (Oct.) 1955.
4. Wishik, S.: *Services for Children with Cerebral Palsy*, Am. Public Health Assoc., Inc., 1955.
5. *Ibid*. 4:
6. *Ibid*. 2, Pg. 23-27.
7. *Ibid*. 2, Chapt. VIII, Educational Planning for the Cerebral Palsied, by Cruickshank, W. M., Pg. 337-341.
8. Yamazak, J. N., Wright, S. W., Wright, P. M.: Outcome of Pregnancy in Women Exposed to the Atomic Bomb in Nagasaki. *J.A.M.A.*, *24:* 758-768, 1952.
9. Hopkins, W. T., Bice, H. V. and C. . . . . ., K. C.: Evaluation and Education of the Cerebral Palsied Child, Int. Council for Exceptional Children, 1954. Chapter I.
10. Denhoff, E., and Holden, R. H.: The Etiology of Cerebral Palsy, An Experimental Approach. *Am. J. Obst. & Gynec.*, *70*:274-281 (Aug.) 1955.
11. Denhoff, E. and Holden, R. H.: Unpublished data.
12. Denhoff, E., Holden, R. H., and Silver, M.: Prognostic Studies in Cerebral Palsy. *J.A.M.A.*, *161:* 781-784 (June 30), 1956.
13. Denhoff, E., and Holden, R. H.: The Effectiveness of Chlorpromazine (Thorazine) with Cerebral Palsy. *J. Pediat.*, *27:*328-332 (Sept.) 1955.
14. Denhoff, E., and Holden, R. H.: Family Influence on Successful School Adjustment of Cerebral Palsied Children. *Journal of the International Council for Exceptional Children*. Pg. 5-7 (Oct.) 1954.

THE CHILD WITH A CONGENITAL HEART DEFECT

Saul J. Robinson, B.S., M.D.

AND

Benjamin M. Gasul, M.S., M.D.

Remarkable strides resulting in a completely changed attitude toward the child with a cardiac defect have been made in both the medical and surgical management of patients who exhibit congenital heart disease. While the medical management of these children has been vastly improved, surgical cure is now available for some of the defects, and at least some benefit from surgery is possible in other lesions. This progress has stimulated a study of the entire role that the congenital cardiac defect plays in the child's growth and development.

NATURE OF THE HANDICAP

The cause of congenital malformations of the heart is not known. In a very small percentage, German measles in the mother in the first two or three months of pregnancy is known to be responsible. Familial and hereditary tendencies have been noted by the number of these defects in relatives or siblings. For the vast number of congenital cardiac defects there is still no plausible explanation. Whatever the cause of these defects, the injury to the embryo and the resultant defect must occur in the early weeks, since the formation of the heart is almost complete by the first nine weeks of pregnancy.

Congenital malformation of the heart is essentially a mechanical defect not associated with inflammation. Therefore, the child with a congenital cardiac defect has an intact myocardium, except where the defect exists. He may thus withstand insults to his heart which would be harder to bear for a child with an inflammatory cardiac condition, such as rheumatic fever with heart involvement.

The congenital cardiac defects are not hard to understand if one is aware of the simple anatomy of the heart as consisting of four chambers with connecting vessels to and from the lungs and body. The blood from the body, which has been deprived of nutriment and oxygen in its course through the tissues, enters the right atrium, passes through the tricuspid valve, then goes into the right ventricle and out into the lungs through a pulmonary valve and into the pulmonary artery, which branches to the right and left lungs. Here the blood gives up carbon dioxide and waste products and receives oxygen. The blood returns to the left side of the heart by means of pulmonary veins which enter the left atrium. The blood then enters the left ventricle through the mitral valve and goes out into the body through the aortic valve and into the aorta, which is a large vessel supplying the entire body, and to the heart itself through the coronary arteries (Figure 1).

The many defects possible can be postulated in the development of the heart. (1) There may be holes in the walls, or septa, which separate the two sides of the heart. This is called an interatrial defect if the hole is between the two atria, or an interventricular defect if the hole is between the two ventricles. (2) There may be obstructions to the flow of the blood out of the heart. If the obstruction is from the heart to the lungs at or below the pulmonary valve, it is called valvular or infundibular stenosis. If the obstruction is at or below the valve leading from the heart to the aorta, it is known as aortic or sub-aortic stenosis. If the obstruction takes place in the aorta at a more distant point, due to a narrowing of the aorta, it is known as a coarctation of the aorta. (3) In addition to these defects in the walls and obstructions through normal channels, there may be a persistence of channels which are present early in the development of the heart; such as a double aortic arch and those which are present at birth, but which usually cease functioning soon after birth. These are the opening between the two atria known as the foramen ovale, and the duct which connects the pulmonary artery to the aorta, patent ductus arteriosus. (4) There may be a failure of the various blood vessels going to and from the heart to connect with the proper chamber of the heart. The two great vessels, the pulmonary artery and the aorta, may thus be transposed and

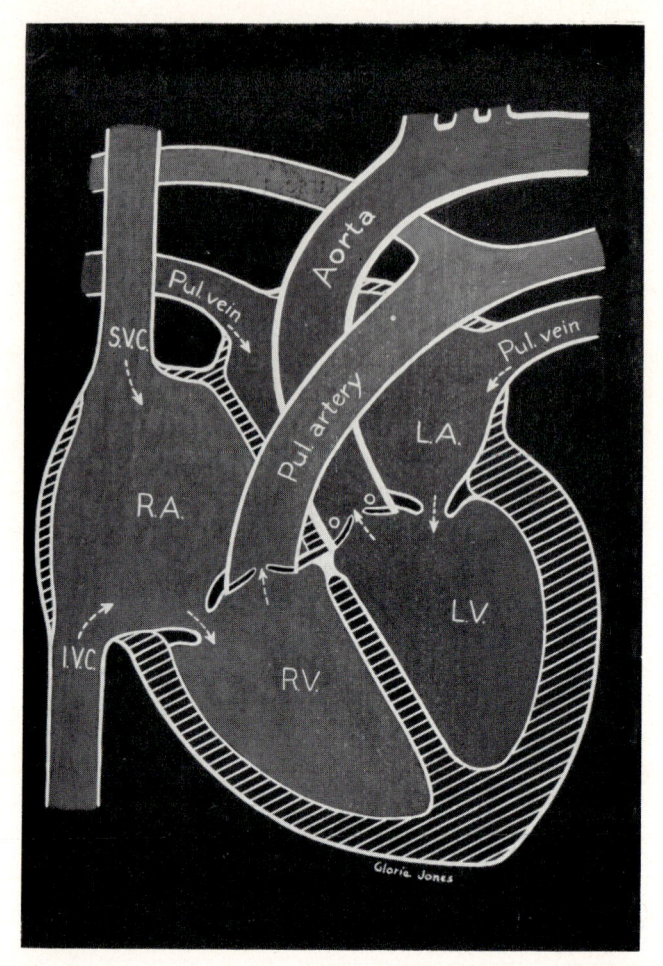

FIGURE 1. Diagram of heart showing the relation of great vessels to the chambers and location of the valves. S.V.C. Superior Vena Cava. I.V.C. Inferior Vena Cava. R.A. Right Antrium. L.A. Left Antrium. R.V. Right Ventricle. L.V. Left Ventricle.

come off of the opposite ventricle, or the pulmonary veins may enter the right side of the heart instead of the left side. The transposition of the great vessels may not be complete, and the vessels may then arise from both ventricles, or a portion of the pulmonary veins may properly enter the left side of the heart, while the remainder enter the right side of the heart, and finally (5) there may be thickening of the inner lining of the heart, the endocardium, or deposition of certain substances in the heart muscles such as glycogen which interfere with the proper emptying and nutrition of the heart and thus lead to early heart failure. The intricate manner by which the heart is formed explains how easily these malformations can occur.

METHODS OF DIAGNOSIS

The necessity for an exact diagnosis of the nature of the congenital cardiac lesion becomes paramount if proper treatment is to be instituted. The methods by which these accurate diagnoses can be made include: (1) A careful interview with the parents as to the symptoms referable to the cardiac defect. In many instances the symptoms may be obscure, and not directly related to the heart, such as eating difficulties, retardation of growth, rapid respirations, and frequent bouts of pneumonia. Other signs and symptoms more directly referable to the heart, such as the ability to keep up with other children, the tendency to squat when tired, and the presence of blue nails or lips (cyanosis) are all important in evaluating the child's lesion. (2) A complete physical examination is equally important and should include a notation as to the presence or absence of associated congenital lesions, deformity of the chest, estimation of heart size, determination of the blood pressure of the arms and legs, the presence of murmurs as well as their type and location, enlargement of the liver as an indication of heart failure, and any other unusual findings which are variations from the normal.

Associated with the history and physical examination there should be x-rays and fluoroscopy of the heart performed while the child is swallowing radio-opaque barium sulfate. Such examination determines the size and shape of the heart and of the great vessels and their branches, and the amount of blood flowing to the lungs, whether it is decreased, increased, or normal. An electrocardiogram tracing of the heart must be performed. In the congenital heart defects this is invaluable in indicating the specific chamber of the heart which may be enlarged. A complete blood count to determine if anemia or infection is present and an urinalysis to make certain that an associated kidney anomaly is not present are both important additions to the diagnosis.

While in most instances the above procedures are adequate to determine the nature of the lesion, in some cases special diagnostic aids must be utilized, particularly if surgical intervention is contemplated. A cardiac catheterization of the heart is the threading of a small hollow tube into an arm or leg vessel and so into the chambers of the heart. From a determination of the pressure in each of the chambers, as well as the determination of oxygen content in samples of blood taken from the heart and lungs under fluoroscopic observation, abnormal openings or obstructions can be located, and even to some extent their size can be determined. Another valuable procedure, known as angiocardiography, is the injection of a radio-opaque contrast substance into an artery or vein while a rapid series of x-rays are taken showing this substance coursing through the heart and vessels as well as its passage through abnormal or narrowed openings. In some instances both of these special procedures are necessary in order to determine an accurate diagnosis.

Some defects are so bizarre in their nature that even the use of all of these procedures may not give a clear picture of the lesion. Fortunately, the vast majority of defects follow a pattern by which they may be identified. In general, the congenital cardiac lesions group themselves into certain general classifications. (1) The child is blue or not blue. (2) The murmurs have certain timing in relation to the cardiac cycle, that is, either systolic or diastolic, and are maximally heard at certain specific locations. (3) The heart is larger in size than normal, smaller than normal, or normal in size and shape. (4) The x-rays indicate that the vascularity of the lung fields is increased or decreased over that of normal. (5) Examination of the x-rays indicates the specific chamber or chambers which are enlarged. (6) The electrocardiogram adds much decisive information of specific chamber enlargements. By classifying the findings in the above mentioned categories the physician can determine the nature of the lesion and can estimate the possibility of surgical cure or modification.

GENERAL CARE

The maintenance of the health of the infant or child with congenital heart disease makes more pleasant the lives of many children for whom no operation is possible, or needed, at this time. It is also important in the maintenance of children until they reach the best age for surgical intervention. Since the important aspect of general care for the child with a congenital heart defect is to attain an environment which best suits his individual needs and the needs of those about him, an orderly and rational environment should be the goal in any such program.

A murmur is not necessarily synonomous with the presence of a cardiac defect. An many as 70% of infants and children, but particularly children, may have a murmur over the heart which does not indicate heart disease, is not disabling, and has no relationship to any congenital or acquired cardiac defect. Such children should not be placed in any special category, restricted, or in any way prevented from leading a completely normal life by reason of having an innocent sound in the region of the heart.

There are children with congenital cardiac defects who have symptoms which require no special care, other than precautions to prevent complications. The following principles of care, however, apply to these as well as to those children presenting symptoms.

Proper Nutrition

While many children eat, sleep, and grow in a normal manner despite their cardiac defects, there are some, and particularly those with cyanosis, who, because they are poor eaters, may have problems related to their nutrition. They may refuse to take all foods other than milk. Since milk is not an adequate food in itself after the first few months of life, the diet must be supplemented by solid foods. A milk diet without supplement may result in a failure to grow. Such a diet may possibly result in the development of a severe anemia due to a deficient amount of iron in cow's milk. Because some infants tire with extreme ease, they require frequent small feedings during the day. Such feeding treatment requires understanding and extreme patience on the part of the parents if the child is to receive an adequate diet. Rarely, an infant with extreme cyanosis may develop an attack of unconsciousness if an extremely large quantity of food is taken at one time. An adequate quantity of the basic foods, including cereals, fruits, vegetables, meats, eggs, butter and milk, is necessary after the first few months of life. The usual vitamins, particularly

A, C, and D are necessary. Because children with congenital heart disease do not absorb fat soluble vitamins from the gastrointestinal tract with ease, one of the aqueous preparations is preferable.

Another frequent complaint of these children is constipation. The use of laxative fruits, such as prunes, one of the new wetting agents, or the addition of a mild laxative to the diet may be recommended.

Immunization

The need for protection during the early months of life is as important for the infant with congenital heart disease as it is for the normal child. While the fear of a violent reaction might lead one to defer immunization, these children usually develop little or no reaction. The immunizations should be administered at the usual time unless there is some other contraindication aside from the cardiac defect. When the physician feels that a severe reaction must be avoided, divided doses of the immunizing substance may be given to minimize such a reaction. In addition to the immunization for diphtheria, whooping cough, tetanus and smallpox, as well as the booster doses, other immune substances such as gamma globulin for the modification or prevention of measles, and poliomyelitis vaccine should be freely utilized when indicated. Although the suppression of measles may not be necessary, modification of the illness might well be indicated.

Protection from Illness

Protection from illness should not be considered to mean extreme isolation of the child with a cardiac defect from other children or from normal play. In many instances these children actually have an unusual ability to resist illness, but there are some who are particularly prone to severe respiratory infections. The administration of a small daily dose of penicillin or some other similar antibiotic as a prophylactic agent, particularly during the winter months, usually will give protection from these intercurrent illnesses. This administration of a small daily dose of penicillin has been particularly helpful for infants under the age of one year with lesions which are peculiarly associated with frequent bouts of pneumonia, such as those with an increased flow of the blood to the lungs.

Dental Hygiene

Carious teeth and dental infections are a highly dangerous source of infection to the child with a congenital cardiac defect. In the more severe forms of heart disease the teeth often fail to grow or develop well. Proper care of the teeth, including brushing, fluoridization, and regular dental care, is essential to avoid complications. Extraction of teeth may be complicated by subacute bacterial endocarditis, but this complication may be avoided by the routine use of penicillin or some other similar antibiotic by one of the schedules outlined in the paragraph on subacute bacterial endocarditis.

General Activity

In recent years the lessening of restrictions on the activity of children with congenital heart disease has been a very gratifying trend. In general, the child with congenital heart disease requires little, if any, restriction of activity. In late infancy it is certainly not necessary to carry them after they have reached the age for walking, as exercise will prevent atrophy of the muscles, increase the general tone, and help to prevent constipation. Experience has shown that the child with a congenital heart defect will limit his activity in a more effective way than can be measured by parents or the physician. When such a child is needlessly restricted, he tends to over-exert himself in rebellion. If the child is asymptomatic and the heart is normal in size, no limitation of activity may be indicated. With symptoms and cardiac enlargement, games and activities which may be strenuous enough to place a strain on the heart should be modified. Consultation with the parents, physician, and school authorities should be arranged so that the child may be channeled into activities which are less taxing without causing his resentment. The child with cyanosis will limit his own activity by the amount of functional incapacity which he has, either by stopping, squatting, or lying down until he acquires enough reserve to go on. Although competitive sports may be allowed some children, medico-legal rather than medical considerations may influence such decisions.

A functional capacity classification such as follows has been helpful in guiding teachers and physical education instructors in the limitation of activity. For medico-legal reasons, no child with obvious congenital heart disease is placed in the unrestricted category. Those children, however, with murmurs which are considered to be functional should not be considered to be in such a category and should be permitted unrestricted activity. A majority of the children with congenital heart disease may be placed in the first class. This classification includes virtually all school activities except competitive sports, either extramural or intramural, except that some activities, such as baseball, may be permitted on an individual basis at the discretion of the physician.

In the second class are children who have cyanosis and/or cardiomegaly which does not permit them to keep up with their fellow students but which does permit them to participate in games of slight activity and postural exercises. When tired such children should be permitted to drop out without comment by their supervising physical education instructor. Such understanding necessitates that the instructor be aware of the child's disability and his limitations, which are imposed by the lesion itself rather than by any restrictions placed by the physician.

In the third class is complete rest with no participation. This classification should rarely be used except in those instances where the physician is anxious to have the child mingle with his fellow students, but in which any type of exercise, as well as the fear of exposure by dressing and undressing into the gymnasium clothes, would be considered harmful. Such children should not, however, be used for errands or other school activities which require physical effort beyond their capacity.

The fourth class is restricted activity at home for a child of school age. Congenital cardiac conditions rarely necessitate this complete isolation of the child from normal relationship with other children his own age. In some instances where the danger of infection is to be avoided until such time as surgical correction is performed, or for an interval following such major surgery on the heart or great vessels, a child may be confined to his home, with special attention given to his education by means of a home-bound teacher, occupational therapy, and playmates, if at all possible.

Education

Schooling is actually more important to the child with congenital heart disease than it is to the normal child. Proper vocational guidance during the school years may do much to permit such an individual ultimately to earn his own livelihood within the limits of his own endurance. Schooling should be in as normal an environment as possible. The teacher should understand the nature of the child's defect, the degree of activity which is permissible, and the importance of his education. A special class for children with congenital heart defects is in most cases unnecessary, since it only serves to emphasize the patient's handicap. When the child reaches high school age, vocational counseling should be utilized to direct the child, without coercion, toward training for a type of life which is within the limits of his own capacity. So that the child will not fall behind his classmates or fail to attain the goal which will permit him to earn an independent livelihood, absences from school of any duration necessitating confinement at home should involve education by a home teacher.

COMPLICATIONS OF CONGENITAL HEART DISEASE
Congestive Heart Failure

Congestive heart failure in infants and children with congenital heart disease, although a serious complication, responds to treatment in a very gratifying way. Rest, oxygen, proper diet, restriction of sodium, the proper use of digitalis, and the use of diuretics are the essentials of treatment. Also important is the treatment of such conditions as infections or anemia, which cause an extra load to the heart, and which if properly treated will also relieve the congestive failure.

Anoxic Attacks

Infants with extreme cyanosis are susceptible to attacks of increased cyanosis, convulsions and unconsciousness, usually occurring following meals, bowel movements, or exposure to cold. During such an attack the child should be immediately placed in the knee chest position, with the knees sharply flexed toward the head, and oxygen, if available, should be administered by inhalation. Morphine sulfate in a dose of 1 mg. per 10 lbs. of body weight, or Demerol® in a dose of 1 mg. per pound of body weight, should be administered intramuscularly or even intravenously. If the respirations seem to be weak or have ceased, artificial respiration is also indicated. Children treated promptly usually recover from such an attack within a few minutes.

Cerebral Thrombosis

Children with cyanotic congenital heart disease show a remarkable increase in the red cells of the blood with an increased viscosity of this blood so that it flows more slowly than normal blood. If fluids are not adequately maintained in such children, blood clots may form in the small vessels of the brain. Such clotting may occur following brief exposure to extreme degrees of heat or following diarrhea and vomiting without adequate fluid intake. Blood clots may also be precipitated by a prolonged or severe restriction of fluids prior to or after surgery. The importance of adequate fluid intake in children with cyanotic heart disease must be uppermost in the minds of the parents and the physician.

Subacute Bacterial Endocarditis

This complication, peculiar to individuals with heart disease, is an infection of the heart valves by an organism which may not be dangerous to an individual with a normal heart. This insidious disease has very mild symptoms, such as fatigue, fever and anemia. Although the diagnosis is made by blood culture, in some instances the cultures may be negative despite the presence of the disease. While the successful treatment of subacute bacterial endocarditis is now possible, its prevention is much easier. Prevention of this complication is possible by the administration of penicillin or similar agents prior to any surgery, major or minor, any dental extraction, particularly of the second teeth, and by the vigorous treatment of intercurrent infections. Following are the prophylactic methods for preventing this disease as recommended by the American Heart Association in 1957:

PENICILLIN: Drug of Choice
Intramuscular and Oral—first choice:
    200,000 to 250,000 Units by mouth four times a day for five days beginning two days prior to surgery, AND 600,000 units aqueous penicillin intramuscularly with 600,000 units procaine penicillin intramuscularly shortly before surgery.
Oral—second choice:
    200,000 to 250,000 units four times a day for five days beginning two days prior to surgery.
CONTRAINDICATIONS: History of sensitivity to penicillin.
OTHER ANTIBIOTICS: For patients sensitive to penicillin and for patients undergoing surgery of urinary or lower gastrointestinal tract:
    Full dosage for five days, beginning two days prior to surgical procedure.

PROGNOSIS

The prognosis for children with congenital cardiac defects has changed markedly in the last fifteen years, and more particularly in the past ten years since the advent of the "blue baby" type of operation. In such lesions as the patent ductus arteriosus where the defect may be litigated or sectioned and thus completely obliterated, an apparently complete cure is possible. In a condition such as the coarctation of the aorta, where there is a narrowing of the large vessel leading from the heart, the resection of this area leads to almost normal circulatory dynamics. The operation for tetralogy of Fallot, or the usual "blue baby operation," is only palliative. New operations are now in existence which may well be virtually curative. Although the closure of defects in the septa, or walls between the chambers of the heart, is very new, the operation bids fair to be almost completely successful in obliterating these defects. Some of the newer operations are dependent on completely new methods of approach. The use of hypothermia, or of very low body temperature, during surgery has been successfully utilized to virtually stop the circulation to the heart for several minutes while the operation of the pulmonary valve, or a septal defect, can be performed under direct vision. The use of a parent as a substitute for the heart and lung for the child during the course of the operation, or the so-called cross circulation method, was used while direct intracardiac surgery was being perfected. At the present time it has been abandoned in favor of a machine which takes over the circulation of the child while the surgery is being performed. This has been accomplished by the successful introduction of various types of heart-lung machines which are capable of substituting for the heart and lung of the child for a sufficient length of time for the surgeon to open the heart and close the defect, or defects, by direct vision while the heart is empty of blood, and which may be stopped for a few moments by the injection of a drug, allowing the surgeon to operate on a heart which is absolutely still but whose beat can be restored after the operation is completed. This latter method has made it possible to substitute a curative type of surgery for some of the palliative procedures previously mentioned in the operative types of cyanotic heart disease in such a way as to restore the circulation of the blood within the heart and vessels to normal channels. This method, known as direct vision intra-cardiac surgery, has been perfected to the point where it is now used for the closure of holes in the wall between the upper chambers of the heart (interatrial septal defects); for closure of holes in the wall between the lower chambers (interventricular defects); to widen a narrowed valve leading into the aorta (aortic or sub-aortic stenosis); and for many other lesions previously considered inoperable. In addition there is now a type of surgery available for infants and children in whom the large vessels leading from the heart have in some way become crossed over so that they are connected to the wrong portion of the heart (transposition of the great vessels). The long term effect of this latter type of surgery has not yet been evaluated, but it offers hope where none was present before.

The future holds forth even greater encouragement for children with congenital heart defects. Methods are now available for the protection against and treatment of subacute bacterial endocarditis, a previously fatal disease. Not only palliative procedures, but also curative operations for children with both cyanotic and non-cyanotic defects are available. The remarkable advances of the past few years indicate that there will soon be methods which will promise a more favorable prognosis for those infants and children who at the present time are beyond surgical help. Proper care not only can make the life of the child with a congenital cardiac defect more pleasant but also can lead to a normal adulthood with marriage and children as a logical part of the normal existence for which these individuals strive and which with the proper guidance they can achieve.

THE CHILD WITH A CONVULSIVE DISORDER

Z. Stephen Bohn, M.D.

Although convulsive disorders may begin at any age, the great majority start early in life and, therefore, come to the attention of the pediatrician. Since the management of such patients in early childhood may have considerable bearing on their later life, much has been said regarding the development of a sensible attitude on the part of the patient, his parents, his school teachers, his friends, and even his physician toward this affliction. A great deal of psychic trauma can develop in a patient suffering from this illness, especially if its onset occurs during his early formative years. In view of the modern trend to consider the emotional as well as the physical aspects of the patient suffering from convulsive seizures, the pediatrician has a wonderful opportunity to help the patient to adjust to his future.

INCIDENCE

The community problem of epilepsy or convulsive disorders is much more extensive than most people realize. Approximately 1.5 per cent of the population in the United States suffer from some type of a convulsive disorder. Two million or more persons suffer from some form of this affliction, and of these the vast majority are children. At least 70 per cent of patients display their first symptoms before they are twenty years old. Although the peak age for the development of seizures is during the first two years of life, another high point occurs during adolescence. Only five out of a thousand adults display such symptoms. Because many children with very mild or fleeting attacks of petit mal are mistakenly thought to be having attacks of "syncope," "dizzy spells," "indigestion," or "lapses of memory" and since such attacks may seem unimportant to the family, no attempt is made to investigate further. Many cases of actual psychomotor epilepsy are not recognized as such. These conditions are judged as being manifestations of a "queer" or "not right" child, or are misdiagnosed as a functional illness such as a behavior problem, a neurosis, or an incipient psychosis.

ETIOLOGY

The etiology of convulsive disorders is still a subject of considerable discussion. The so-called "idiopathic epilepsies" have gradually been reduced over a period of years with the advancement of modern techniques in research and examinations. Investigations in the field of pathology, neurology, neurophysiology, neurosurgery, endocrinology, allergy, and clinical research have accounted for the reduction in the idiopathic category with a resultant increase in the "symptomatic" variety. Hereditary factors, however, are still an important consideration contrary to an apparent current trend of thought. All too often the development of a severe seizure state is obscured in a patient whose family history indicates that one of his parents had "out-grown" convulsions during childhood or adolescence, or that there were instances of "fainting" or "dizzy spells," "isolated convulsions" or "fever convulsions" in the genetic history. Even when no direct transmission of a convulsive disorder can be demonstrated, the predisposition for such a state does exist in positive family histories. Therefore, any "trigger" or precipitating factor in the individual patient's life becomes an important factor. Nearly every child sustains occasional head injuries, shows evidence of infestation by worms, develops foci of infections of a degree sufficient to be compatible with a seizure state, or is a product of an unhealthy home environment. Any of these conditions may be implicated in the onset of seizures. For this reason, the medical profession is urged to eliminate, if at all possible, prenatal, postnatal, or environmental factors which may precipitate such an affliction.

The pediatrician, for example, knows of the strong trend for children with seizures in families with diabetic parents. He also needs to be alert to early infantile diabetic attacks. These may result in brain damage and a seizure trend before the diabetic control is established. An uncontrolled diabetic episode may lead to brain damage and seizures which, in turn, may enhance the uncontrolled aspect of the diabetes. Occasionally, this pair of disturbances (brain damage and diabetes) become mutually perpetuating and lead to progressive deterioration. Finally, the prompt care and follow up observation of infectious diseases of childhood, of cerebral injuries, of serious operative procedures, and of undue emotional stress are the responsibilities of the vigilant and conscientious physician.

Irritation of the cerebral cortex due to intoxication has always been considered a prominent etiological factor in convulsive disorders. Even though the public has been educated regarding the dangers of intoxication from lead poisoning and even though proper steps have been taken to rectify conditions previously prevalent, the physician must include these possibilities in his differential diagnosis. A child still might have had access to chewing on old furniture covered with paint containing lead, and the usual test for the determination of lead intoxication is indicated in such suspected cases. Other possible sources of toxic cerebral irritation include that due to pertussis vaccination, to the various febrile states (fever convulsions) some of which may be of undetermined etiology, and finally to the usual conditions of avitaminosis leading to deficiency disease.

EXAMINATION

Regardless of the etiology, the sooner the patient with convulsive seizures is examined and investigated, the better the chances of adequate control or improvement of his illness are apt to be. The first consideration, and perhaps the most important to the individual, is an adequate history. Securing such a history may not be difficult for the physician in a rural area or where the family physician is well aware of the genetic background, but in the usual present day, big city practice this becomes a time consuming factor which should not be neglected. The usual careful general physical examination may uncover a precipitating factor or some puzzling finding which may require further examination or consultation. Laboratory procedures, such as x-rays of the skull, glucose tolerance tests, basal metabolism tests, examination of the stool, and tests for allergy may be indicated beyond routine office procedures.

Although not as important as in patients with seizures starting at a later age, a neurological examination is definitely indicated. Not only is the mechanical procedure of this examination to be desired, but, perhaps, more important is the neurologist's orientation in some of the more rare neurological disorders. This orientation is often of inestimable value since, otherwise, an infrequent etiologic factor might be overlooked. The existence of a convulsive disorder with sebaceous adenometa of the face along with a history of a regressing intelligence quotient could very possibly make for a diagnosis of tuberous sclerosis before x-rays of the skull and a pneumo-encephalogram corroborate that diagnosis. A history of head injury followed by somnolence, inequality of the pupils, and pyramidal tract signs might presage the onset of a subdural hematoma. Sudden loss of consciousness followed by nuchal rigidity and ensuing convulsions may indicate a ruptured cerebral aneurysm of the circle of Willis, confirmed later by the presence of subarachnoid hemorrhage and by angiography. Convulsive seizures following mastoid or sinus infections, a focus of infection elsewhere in the body, or encephalitis with or without meningitis might indicate an early cerebral abscess. Porencephalic cysts (verified by a pneumo-encephalogram), early hydrocephalus, congenital vascular malformations, or congenital cerebral anomalies with an associated mental deficiency also may be found. Even primary brain tumors, though rare in children aside from those found in the cerebellum which are associated with increased intracranial pressure, may be discovered by the neurologist. Other pathologic processes may be suspected and verified by proper special neurological tests to account for seizures. Needless to say, the presence of Jacksonian seizures, either full blown or fragmentary, may lead to a diagnosis of some organic condition after special tests or examinations are carried out.

SPECIAL TESTS

When to subject the patient to special tests is a matter of judgment. Though 90 per cent or more of the pneumo-encephalograms are normal in patients suffering from a convulsive disorder, the corroboration secured in the 10 per cent of doubtful cases justifies the testing procedure. Based on neurological findings, a pneumo-encephalogram is certainly justified when seizures are focal or

Jacksonian in type, when a congenital defect is suspected to account for the seizures, or when a brain tumor, some other type of expanding lesion, or other localizing organic lesions are suspected. A pneumo-encephalogram is also justified for patients who have experienced frequent, severe seizures over a period of years and who are showing signs of mental deterioration. If such a test shows evidence of cerebral atrophy, the physician is in a much better position to inform the family regarding the prognosis, not only for control of seizures but for possible custodial care.

Angiography has rapidly become an important special test in selected cases. This technique is not only the best means for determining the presence of vascular malformations but also is helpful in the diagnosis of a brain tumor or cerebral atrophy. In the hands of a skillful neuro-surgeon, the procedure is relatively innocuous.

Corticography is a recently developed test requiring the combined services of a neurosurgeon and an electro-encephalographer. Use of this method in patients who show evidence of a focal lesion or who fail to respond to adequate anticonvulsant therapy, has frequently uncovered and removed an epileptogenic focus. The technique consists of first performing a craniotomy over the site of the suspected lesion. The cortical surface, and to some extent the depths, can be explored by electrical recordings and electrical stimulation. If these procedures can clearly outline the areas which produce the patient's characteristic auras or seizures, then removal of one of these areas may be considered. In the hands of an expert team the results may be of considerable benefit.

PSYCHOLOGICAL INVESTIGATION

By the time the patient has been investigated up to this point, psychologic factors may be of importance in relation to the child and the convulsive disorder.

The individual epileptic child is frequently found to show certain kinds of intellectual and emotional disturbances. The most common intellectual disturbance is a demonstrable reduction in intellectual efficiency, i.e., he is not making adequate use of his basic intellectual capacity. This disturbance may be on an emotional basis, it may have some type of organic or physiological basis, or all of these factors may be present. In some cases, anticonvulsant drugs may be affecting the child's intellectual functioning. Actual mental deterioration may be occurring, either as the result of a high incidence of seizures or through deteriorating processes of the central nervous system. A certain percentage of children may actually have a primary mental retardation, in addition to the convulsive disorder on a hereditary or organic basis.

Although an "epileptic personality" as such has not been established, thorough investigation in a number of cases reveals the presence of certain personality trends or traits. In many instances, the epileptic child, having been infantilized, is not achieving adequate emotional growth and development. The child, becoming increasingly more handicapped in his interpersonal relationships, does not learn adequate ways to control and to discharge hostility and aggressive impulses. As an adult, characterological disorders of over dependency, infantilism, egocentricity, and over aggressiveness may result.

The psychological evaluation deals with intelligence and thought organization, with emotional organization, and with the influence of organic, physiological, and emotional factors on the functioning of the patient. The most useful battery of psychological tests includes the Wechsler-Bellevue Intelligence Scale for Children, the Rorschach Ink Blot Test, the Children's Apperception Test (CAT), the Bender-Gestalt, and the Drawing Tests.

The Bender-Gestalt and the visual-motor tests or the Wechsler can provide evidence of brain pathology, if present. The Rorschach can, at times, also throw light on the organic basis of symptoms.

The Rorschach is the main instrument for assisting in personality diagnosis, and the Story Telling Test affords understanding of the patient's specific personality problems and attitudes.

The intelligence test provides an evaluation of memory, judgment, attention, concentration and visual-motor functions, and a reliable overall estimate of intellectual functioning. Qualitative analysis will often reveal the presence of any discrepancy between basic capacity and functioning level. The value of psychological test results and interpretation is greatly increased when integrated with the other areas of evaluation and examination.

PSYCHIATRIC EVALUATION

From the psychiatric standpoint, the family, relatives, teachers, and friends frequently present varied problems. Tension, brought on by the preconceived ideas of one or the other parent as to the significance of "epilepsy," whether to treat it as a "hush-hush" disease or to consider the offspring abnormal and regard him as such in the presence of relatives and friends, sometimes exists between parents and patient. Too many times a domineering parent is observed overruling sensible suggestions made by relatives, teachers, spiritual advisors, and physicians as to limitations imposed on the child to say nothing of the patient's therapy or status in the community.

Parents are usually very guilty, extremely defensive, and confused concerning epilepsy in their family. They anticipate and actually feel the community stigma that sometimes does arise. In their minds lurk the fear that the child is or will become insane. They frantically rush the child from place to place looking for quick, magical ways to stop the seizures. They go to cultists for treatment by herbs and diets, to faith healers and cultists advertising complete and permanent cures, and to mail order concerns who send their own particular preparations without adequate, if any, examination, control or follow up of the patient. They sometimes express the desire openly to have their disturbed child committed even when need for such action is lacking.

A convulsive child can be helped to achieve emotional and social maturity. Epilepsy is a psychosomatic problem in which a very complex interplay of physical, emotional, and social factors constantly exert an influence upon the life of the convulsive person. The seizure itself is merely the symptom of an underlying disorder. The seizure can be explained as a massive physical discharge of accumulated energy, a most effective and primitive way to discharge energy in the shortest period of time. Non-epileptic persons have other ways of discharging pent-up energy, often more socially acceptable but not always as effective. Convulsive persons have a lower threshold for a convulsive type of energy discharge than other people, but anyone can convulse if the right combination of factors is present. A convulsive person is more likely to be predisposed to developing seizures. When adequate physical and emotional factors are present, seizures occur.

After a child develops seizures, the family and community continue to exert strenuous efforts to close off all avenues against this seemingly uncontrollable behavior. The child is out of normal classroom situations and put among other convulsive persons. He is restricted from too strenuous play or from swimming or boating. He cannot climb trees or ride a bicycle or drive a car. He has great difficulty in finding a job or getting married, and he is told he should not have children. Since epilepsy is a psychosomatic problem, the physician must be interested in the epileptic and his problems as a total person.

The psychiatrist, then, interviews the patient, the parents and other interested people. He evaluates the emotional status of the individual, emphasizes certain psychological testing that might be of importance, sizes up the environmental state of the individual, especially home and school, and prepares the patient and the family for future recommendations after the patient's case is completely studied.

TREATMENT AND MANAGEMENT

The proper therapy of patients with convulsive disorder should include management as well as treatment. The "team" approach to this psychosomatic problem involves the consideration of the patient as a whole. The general plan of treatment of epilepsy is divided into five main categories, viz., prophylactic, medical, surgical, social, and institutional.

The prophylactic approach consists of the prevention of natal and postnatal injuries whenever possible, the prevention of cerebral anoxia from whatever cause, the prompt diagnosis and treatment of the acute, infectious diseases of childhood, the elimination of foci of infections, and the avoidance of toxic encephalopathy by constant vigilance and by the education of the parents.

The medical phase of the patient's management may be divided into dehydration regimen, the ketogenic diet, drug therapy, and general improvement of the patient's overall health. The dehydration regimen, introduced in the 1930's, consists of hospitalization of the patient in order to measure adequately the intake of fluids, including that in food, and the output of urine. The diet is finally determined so that the total fluid content, including that in food, comes between 300 and 500 cc. for every twenty four hours. In addition, salt is eliminated from the food. Because of the advancement of anticonvulsive drugs, this somewhat cumbersome procedure has more or less gone into disuse. However, it still has merit in certain selected cases.

The ketogenic diet is very effective in the reduction of petit mal seizures, especially in children. This diet consists of an initial starvation period, followed by a high fat and low carbohydrate diet, in order to produce ketone (aceto-acetic acid) bodies. Seizures may be dramatically reduced by this regime, but unfortunately, not only the cooperation of the patient but the cooperation of the parents must be secured. All too often, painstaking explanations and attempts to obtain the cooperation of the parents fail. Quite often the assistance of a dietitian will be effective in helping the child stay on the prescribed diet, in helping to explain to the parents why such a diet is necessary, and to solve unforeseen complications regarding the type of food required.

Drug or anticonvulsant therapy of convulsive disorders goes back many years. The bromides were the first drugs used. Whenever massive doses were indicated to control the seizures, the patients usually became mentally dull and lethargic or developed evidence of bromide intoxication. This type of medication is now again becoming popular, but the therapy is interrupted approximately two days out of the week and salt is added to the diet. In addition, blood bromide levels are taken to prevent the onset of bromide intoxication.

Phenobarbital later replaced the bromides, but it too caused excessive drowsiness when high dosages were required in order to obtain adequate control. Furthermore, it did not control all types of seizures. Of recent years a variety of anticonvulsant drugs have been developed. Although none is a panacea, the judicious therapeutic trial of several drugs individually, and then the use of them in various combinations provides the best results. Serial electro-encephalograms help guide the therapeutist in his choice of medication in the average obstinate case. A recent method suggests the use of the EEG pattern to determine the effectiveness of possible medications. When there are many seizure discharges in the EEG, the influence of several drugs on these discharges can be determined after a brief period of massive dosage of each drug. The drugs which produce an absence of seizure discharges are the medications of choice. This procedure may be a time saver and of considerable help when medical management is difficult. A knowledge of the type of seizure prevalent in the patient, its response to the various anticonvulsant drugs, plus a review of the particular type of brain wave exhibited in the electro-encephalogram, will bring about the best results.

In a general way, one may group the following anticonvulsant drugs according to the types of seizures which they control best. In patients suffering primarily from grand mal seizures, Dilantin® sodium has been found to be generally the most effective and safe. Mesantoin®, another effective drug in these cases, tends to produce undesirable side effects in some cases. Mebaral® and Mysoline® may also be used in selected cases. Phenobarbital and the bromides complete the list. These drugs may be used separately at first and then in various combinations until the maximum therapeutic effect is achieved. Each drug should be pushed to the limit of the patient's tolerance before changing to another drug. Adequate time should be allowed even if no immediate improvement is obtained, pressure from the family notwithstanding. When one drug is being substituted for another, the initial drug should be gradually instead of suddenly discontinued while simultaneously increasing the second drug, also on a gradual basis. Sometimes these drugs tend to cause drowsiness when high dosages are required to control the seizures. In such patients the use of Benzedrene® with the anticonvulsant drug provides for a more wakeful state and allows the patient to carry on his duties in a normal manner.

Patients with petit mal seizures respond to Tridione®, Paradione®, and Milontin® most effectively. If, however, the patient is subject to grand mal seizures in addition to the petit mal seizures, the use of Tridione® and Paradione® is usually contraindicated. Although these drugs may reduce or control the minor seizures, they also tend to precipitate an alarming increase in the major seizures. In addition to these drugs mentioned for the petit mal seizures, phenobarbital, Mebaral®, and the bromides either alone or in various combinations are used. Dexedrene® or Benzedrene® alone or in combination with the other drugs sometimes improve these patients. These latter therapeutic possibilities have been created from recent theories developed from electrophysiologic measurements. These theories offer the thought provoking idea that a seizure discharge may be physiologically a state of over synchronization of the electric beating of many cerebral units in response to some pacemaker and its neuronal circuits. Ordinarily, this pacemaker and its circuits cannot dominate over a brain wave that is busy, and which is in a state of constantly fluctuating pattern of reaction. When repose, sleep, or some abnormal physiologic state supervenes, the busy state is lost and the more primitive system has a chance to dominate and produce the abnormal beat. Confirmation for this is that there is an increasing frequency and intensity of electrical seizure discharges in sleep, that many clinical seizures occur in sleep, that seizures occur in early morning hours or just after the excitement is over, and that healthy work decreases the incidence of seizures. The stimulating drugs potentiate the busy lines and reduce the possibility of control by more primitive systems.

In psychomotor (psychic equivalent) seizures the drugs of choice are Phenurone®, Dilantin® sodium, phenobarbital, Mesantoin® and Tridione®. Since some of these might produce side effects, response should be watched.

The side effects to drug therapy of this disorder include blood dyscrasias, fever, sore throat, epistaxis, hypertrophy of the gums, vaginal hemorrhage, dermal pathology, spontaneous ecchymosis, and hepatitis. Dilantin® sodium tends to cause gingival hypertrophy in a considerable percentage of cases. An erythematous skin eruption, drowsiness, and some ataxia may also be caused in an occasional case when the dosage is raised to a high level.

Mesantoin®, Tridione®, Paradione®, and Phenurone® may cause various types of anemias, some of which have been aplastic in type due to bone marrow involvement. Unless frequent blood counts are obtained, especially in the first weeks of therapy, and unless the patient is watched closely, rather serious complications may occur.

Patients who exhibit status epilepticus constitute a rather serious medical emergency and a problem all their own. Usually it is necessary to start with some form of intravenous medication, such as Sodium Pentothal®. This treatment is probably contraindicated in patients with lung pathology. The drug should be administered by an anaesthetist so that, should occlusion of the air passages occur, proper mechanical steps can be started immediately to alleviate the condition. Various other types of medication, such as sodium Amytal® and sodium phenobarbital may be given intravenously. Sometimes paraldehyde rectally, intramuscularly or intravenously, or ether in oil per rectum will control the tendency toward successive grand mal seizures. Seconal® per rectum also is often effective.

Surgical intervention in recent years has been resorted to in certain selected cases. The surgical removal of an epileptogenic focus has previously been alluded to after pneumo-encephalograph, arteriography, or corticography has demonstrated the presence and site of such a lesion. When the epileptogenic zone involves large areas, the removal of a part or all of the affected cerebral lobe may be accomplished. In patients with infantile hemiplegia even more radical procedures, such as hemispherectomies, have been performed without increasing the original physical disability. Following such surgical procedures some patients have exhibited a reduction in the frequency and severity of the seizures, and even an improvement in mental and physical performance over a period of at least five years.

SOCIAL THERAPY

Under the social therapeutic aspects in the management of these patients must be considered the attitude of the parents and patient to the disability. The relationship of the patient to the community and his training for productive work must be evaluated. The laws concerning the operation of motor vehicles should be studied. When necessary the possible resort to sterilization or the need for institutional care should be discussed with the family. The physician needs to discuss economic, religious and social fears as well as misconceptions. Further discussion should include the patient's own need to succeed as well as marriage and business prospects. He must try to help the patient understand himself. Recently a new facet has been added to the general overall management of this disorder. Pastoral psychology as practiced by spiritual advisors who are aware of the religious aspects, whatever the denomination, that may be helpful in the team management of these patients.

Psychiatric help is sought, perhaps more frequently than any other single aspect in the management of this disorder, except drug therapy. Placing not only the patient but one or both parents in treatment with a psychiatrist, (usually not the same physician for the patient and parents) who is well oriented in convulsive disorders, is frequently advisable. The family physician, however, who has made it a point to orient himself in the psychiatric aspects of this disorder, can be of immense help to his patients. Because he is well informed concerning the family history of the patient and other factors related to his illness, the patient's physician can automatically eliminate the usual time consuming efforts of the psychiatrist. He, furthermore, is the natural advisor to whom not only the patient and the parents, but the friends, teachers, spiritual advisors and relatives interested in helping the patient turn for counsel, information and guidance.

The parents should be advised that the usual epileptic child is normal. Activities need not be unduly curtailed provided that seizures are under control and good cooperation exists with the treating physician. Although each child's case must be individually evaluated, the controlled epileptic should not be denied participation in the usual activities and recreation, such as games (including contact sports), gymnasium work in the school, riding a bicycle, and swimming under supervision. However, climbing to undue heights is usually contraindicated. The child with an occasional seizure should attend a regular school, if at all possible, instead of being sent to a special school, such as those for epileptics. The pursuit of normal physical and mental activity actually seems to surpress the cerebral dysrythmia as seen in the EEG and, seemingly, militates against the production of seizures.

Institutionalization is inevitable in some patients whose seizures are excessively severe and frequent, who fail to respond to adequate and intensive therapy, who live in a home situation where adequate supervision is lacking, or when there is evidence of progressive cerebral degeneration. Commitment for institutionalization usually is authorized by the Probate Court of the County in which the patient resides. The family should be instructed to consult such facilities when the need is indicated.

Depending upon the severity of the child's problem and life situation, skilled professional help by a psychosomatic team may be necessary. Whether or not this is so, the child always needs understanding and help in his community life, his home, his neighborhood, his church, and, of course, his school. No professional help can be successful unless the epileptic child is in a social setting with an opportunity to secure most of the gratifications of average community living, and where he is expected to meet normal community expectations and regulations.

What can parents, educators, teachers, principals, counselors, and school nurses do to help the convulsive child achieve emotional maturity? Depending upon the physician, the child, the parents, the particular school, and sometimes the medical situation, a great deal may be accomplished. The school teacher may be of incalculcable help to a convulsive child in her class. Should such a child have a grand mal seizure in class, the teacher can set a wonderful example to the other pupils. By acting quickly, she can prevent the patient from harming himself by helping him to lie on the floor, by preventing him from biting his tongue, lips or cheeks, by loosening his collar or belt, by helping the patient to breathe properly, and by talking to the patient in a reassuring tone of voice as he begins to recover. She can later explain to the class that the patient has an illness for which he should not be shunned or condemned. Further, the teacher can explain that the patient cannot help such seizures, that he is not "crazy, insane or mentally ill," that his condition is not contagious, and that he cannot help being temporarily abnormal in his behavior even though he has no convulsive movements. A great deal of good, therefore, can be accomplished by a teacher not only for the afflicted child but in the prevention of psychic trauma to the other so-called "normal" children. Great prophylactic and therapeutic powers are within the grasp of well trained, informed teachers.

THE CHILD WITH DIABETES

ALVAH L. NEWCOMB, B.S., M.D.

WHILE diabetes mellitus is basically a hereditary disease, in the majority of instances the cause cannot be ascertained. Conditions predisposing to its development are acute infectious diseases, especially mumps, burns, severe emotional upsets, or an excess of hormones of other endocrine glands, i.e., pituitary, thyroid, and adrenal. Any of the above mentioned conditions or a combination of them may precipitate diabetes or aggravate an established case.

Characterized by the regular production of glycosuria and hyperglycemia by feeding dextrose, the symptoms of diabetes mellitus are a direct result of the inadequate production, or of the inert action of the hormone, insulin, produced by the beta cells of the islets of Langerhans of the pancreas. This deficiency of insulin allows the accumulation of sugar in the blood and its escape in the urine along with water and body salts. Such insulin deficiency leads to severe metabolic derangements, disturbance of carbohydrate metabolism with associated hyperglycemia and glycosuria, ketosis, metabolic acidosis, increase in cellular catabolism and dehydration, all of which contribute to a loss of intra and extracellular metabolites.

The incidence of diabetes among children under fifteen years of age has been determined to occur in about one per 2,500 children. 2.5 per cent of those who have diabetes are children. At the onset of the disease polyuria, polydipsia, loss of weight, anorexia, lassitude and fatigue are the cardinal symptoms. Nocturia and enuresis are commonly of sudden onset. The duration of mild symptoms in young children before the condition is diagnosed is only a few weeks; while in older children the symptoms may be of several months duration. Diabetes mellitus can be lived with best when thorough education of the parents and child in the management of the disease is conducted simultaneously.

Such education should center on an understanding of the ensuing six points:

(1) **Regulation of Insulin.** It is strongly advised that a diabetic child be admitted to a hospital for careful study so that the optimum diet and exact dosage of insulin may be determined. Single daily injections, in varied sites of the body, are ideal. One of the intermediate insulins, such as globin, NPH, or lente may usually be combined with regular insulin in proper proportion, so that no more than one dose is prescribed daily, except as infections or stress situations develop.

After the initial period of stabilization, begun in the hospital, a low dosage of insulin is usually required. A period of stability, once established, may last two or three years, but occasionally longer. The requirement for insulin begins to advance slowly, because of the increasing caloric needs of the growing child, until maturity (about 16 years in girls and about 18 years in boys). Tolerance for glucose and increased requirements of insulin may change rapidly with infections, especially septic, abdominal and diabetic coma. Although tolerance for glucose may return, such tolerance is generally impaired after such incidents.

The nurse is best equipped to teach the parents to measure and administer the proper insulin doses and to master the techniques of syringe and needle sterilization. She may teach and supervise the tests for glucose and acetone. Her patience in dealing with the family and her thorough understanding of the disease are necessary to help in the family adjustment.

(2) **Diet.** A weighed or measured diet is recommended. The diet prescription should be adequate in protective foods, minerals and vitamins. The prescription of protein should be generous, usually three to five grams per kilogram of body weight. The caloric requirements will vary from 80 to 100 calories per kilogram of body weight for the infant, to 50 to 80 for the older child.

The diet should be planned so that it will satisfy the patient and not burden the family unduly. Since too rigid restrictions affect both the physical and psychological well being of the patient, they should be avoided.

(3) **Urinalysis.** The parents, older siblings or other relatives in the home, who are responsible for the care of the very young diabetic child must learn to perform Benedict's qualitative glucose

test and the ferric chloride test for diacetic acid and/or the simpler tablet or paper tests for glucose, and the tablet tests for acetone.

(4) **Recognizing and Preventing Complications.** (*a*) *Hypoglycemic reactions.* The child and his parents should be taught to recognize the symptoms of oncoming insulin reactions, such as increasing hunger, pallor, weakness, lassitude, vertigo, nausea, vomiting, nervousness or inco-ordination. The imperative necessity of taking food immediately to raise the blood sugar must be completely appreciated. Since the small child is too young to recognize early symptoms of hypoglycemia due to omission of a snack or to increased exercise, adult understanding and supervision is particularly important. The parents or caretakers of a diabetic child must be trained to recognize their child's particular pattern and time of reaction with relation to the type of insulin being used. They must be prepared to avert severe reactions with glucose feedings. They should be instructed in the giving of epinephrine in emergency dosage. Three to five minums of epinephrine will usually free enough glucose from the liver to waken the patient so that oral feeding can be initiated. Since severe hypoglycemia may produce bizarre behavior patterns and deep and prolonged hypoglycemia which may cause cerebral damage in some instances, parent and child training must be thorough.

(*b*) *Ketosis.* The parents should be cautioned that two or three daily tests for glucose are important, at all times. An acetone or ferric chloride test should be made whenever there is excessive glycosuria, signs of an acute infection, diarrhea or vomiting and especially when these are accompanied by fever and excessive diuresis. Since the appearance of ketonuria is cause for alarm calling for prompt additional doses of insulin, parents must be thoroughly instructed in the emergency six-hour prescription of food and insulin until the emergency has passed.

(5) **Exercise.** Gradual increase of activity is encouraged while the child is still in the hospital. Some physicans recommend a constant amount of exercise, such as results from jumping rope. At home, however, no limitation of activity is advised. Experience with exercise will enable the observing parent to provide extra carbohydrate after or during such strenuous exercise as skating, tennis, or swimming. When both fast and intermediate insulins

are prescribed, a mid-morning, mid-afternoon, and bedtime snack are usually indicated to prevent hypoglycemia.

(6) **Mental Health.** The promotion of good mental health in diabetic children, as with all children, is one of the most important components of treatment. Helping them to have a wholesome attitude toward their illness, rather than an attitude of invalidism, is one of the most imperative contributions that all of the persons having contact with the child can make. Emotional tension decreases the diabetic's physical well being, as it does all people suffering with a chronic illness. The maladjusted diabetic child can use his illness as a tool for expressing his hostility or dissatisfaction, with disastrous results, if the basis for his unhappiness is not treated. Since severe emotional shock has seemed to be a predisposing factor in the onset of the disease in some patients, more research in this field should be undertaken.

The physician may find it necessary to spend long, but fruitful hours in the education of the patient, his family, and other custodians and friends. He must be ready to allow the family of the new diabetic to lean on him during the early days of the learning process. A sympathetic approach, availability, patience in the repetition of instruction, and praise for the child and the parents in carrying out the seemingly burdensome routine are necessary for the patient and his family in order to help them make a wholesome adjustment to living with the disease. The ability to instruct becomes a necessary responsibility for the physician in addition to the routine prescription of insulin and dietary formulae.

The teacher's interest in the diabetic child should be enlisted. Since an understanding of the disease and its manifestations is imperative, the teacher must be cognizant of the child's moods. The teacher must understand that acute disturbances of vision are usually due to insulin reactions. She must recognize the early symptoms of hypoglycemia. Knowing that fruit or lumps of sugar can usually prevent the onset of a severe insulin reaction she should be prepared to use this preventive measure. Failing to check the reaction she should immediately notify the school nurse, the parents and the physician.

Psychological testing, educational and vocational guidance are helpful aids in determining the wisest use of the child's potential abilities and in determining the most suitable opportunities for their development and use. Girls may be encouraged to prepare for careers in any field. Their knowledge of foods can be utilized in the form of a career in dietetics. Boys can plan for any career other than in transportation or where high speed machinery is involved.

Generally, juvenile diabetics may enjoy more freedom than was possible twenty years ago. Antibiotics and immunizations have dispelled some of the fears of infection. Diets are more liberal. Many free foods are now allowed. Since the development of the intermediate insulins, fewer insulin injections are needed. Each of these advances in the treatment of the patient has helped the diabetic child to feel less different from his friends than formerly was possible.

Camps for diabetic children provide an enriching experience which the child is unable to have otherwise, since most camps will not accept the diabetic child. They give an excellent opportunity for the child to become better acquainted with others in the "same boat," an acquaintanceship which tends to have a wholesome effect. Also, it is important to provide a "breathing spell" for parents who may be overanxious and over protective in caring for the child.

Fear and anxiety concerning complications may develop as the patient learns more about diabetes. Since most of the complications can be prevented, treated, or lived with, all questions by the parent should be answered honestly and the juvenile diabetic should be informed of the rewards of successful management and adjustment. A friendly, patient, optimistic outlook by all who care for the patient is most important.

Prognosis: The outlook for the cure of diabetes mellitus is in the future. At present hypodermic injection of insulin and diet regulation assure a healthy survival. Research on problems in diabetes including the investigations of oral preparations to supplement or replace insulin, continues throughout the world. The new oral sulfanyl preparations have not been highly successful in controlling diabetes in children. No harmful side effects have been noted.

With physician, parents, teachers and friends as helpful understanding advisors, the diabetic child has a consistent opportunity to live a reasonably normal life, to plan for a wide range of careers, and to be not much different from his non-diabetic friends.

THE CHILD WHO IS EMOTIONALLY DISTURBED

SHERMAN LITTLE, M.D.

IT has been facetiously said that today the only truly neglected child is one who does not have his own psychiatrist. Like so many things spoken in jest, this statement is evidence of the increasing concern over the incidence of emotional problems in children. Every physician who in his practice cares for children is impressed with the number of children whose primary complaint lies in the behavioral rather than the physical sphere. Additional numbers of children brought with primary physical complaints either have significant emotional problems or have their physical problems secondary to some physiological disturbance which has been set in motion by emotional turmoil.

Whether an actual increase in the number of emotionally disturbed children has occurred or whether the seeming increase reflects in part a greater social concern and public awareness is difficult to prove. A number of studies, however, attempt to get at the incidence of significant emotional problems in the adult population. Three recent ones report considerable agreement in the findings although they draw from quite different segments of population and geographical areas. The first is a study of the distribution of psychiatric symptoms in the population of a small town in Nova Scotia;[12] the second, a careful sampling of the population of the mid-town section of New York City;[15] and the third, a study of the incidence of personality disorders in two hundred randomly selected patients on the surgical service of the Cincinnati General Hospital.[20] These studies indicate that only about fifteen per cent of the population is free from symptoms of emotional disturbance and that about fifty per cent have minor psychiatric symptoms which do not seriously interfere with their adjustment. Of the remaining thirty-five per cent, five per cent have either spent some time in a mental hospital or their admission has been recommended; fifteen to twenty per cent more are so seriously disturbed as to be markedly handicapped in their adjustment; and a final fifteen to twenty per cent function reasonably well but have moderately handicapping symptoms. In other words, approximately thirty-five per cent of the adults over eighteen years of age have enough emotional disturbance to handicap them considerably in their personal, social, and economic adjustments. Although this conclusion may seem extraordinary and even startling at first sight, experienced clinicians are keenly aware of the tremendous number of people who need and who are seeking help.

The exact incidence of significant emotional disturbances in children is not reliably known. Disagreement as to the significance of various kinds of behavior in children is partially responsible for the lack of exact statistics. Some behavior—having imaginery companions, conversing with inanimate objects—which would be significant in an adult might be a normal component of growing up in a child. Among children even rather bizarre behavior may be quite usual or transient reaction in a particular situation.

One survey [16] made of the incidence of significant emotional problems in 755 "new" children in the pediatric out-patient department at Stanford University Hospital found that forty per cent of these children had "emotional problems to a degree which interfered with or prevented institution of somatic therapeutic measures which might otherwise be successful." This survey seems to be in substantial agreement with the studies previously mentioned on adults. While these studies are far from definitive, they do suggest that significant emotional problems in both adults and children are common. The studies further emphasize the need for developing many more clinical treatment facilities as well as broad, long-range programs aimed at both the social and individual forces which produce this significant emotional disturbance in large segments of the population.

The lack of confidence and satisfaction in the parental role of many modern parents appears to be related to the increased number of disturbed children. Increased industrialization, urbanization, and modern means of communication have brought the fearful problems of every part of the world into each individual's living room. Loss of confidence by the individual in his ability to manage his own affairs and to control his own destiny has resulted. This uncertainty, the increase in knowledge, and the corresponding desire for something which the individual can believe in has placed undue importance on information seemingly scientific. This condition has resulted in an increased attention to and dependence upon the "expert" in many areas, including that of bringing up children.

Stendler,[19] in an interesting study of this hypothesis points out that in 1890, bringing up children sounded relatively easy. Mother knew best, and she got results by having a good moral character and by setting a good example. She ruled supreme, and none challenged her authority and knowledge. In addition to this children were thought of as fairly reasonable, basically unviscious characters who could be indulged. Thumb sucking, for example, was encouraged as an important way of comforting the child. No one was worried about its being a devious manifestation of sex.

By 1900, a change in attitudes towards children had become apparent. That their natures were not essentially good and that they would grow up to be decent citizens only if they had a considerable amount of rigorous discipline and punishment came to be emphasized. Why this change in attitude has taken place is not entirely clear. Perhaps the religious attitudes of an earlier day, as expressed in the idea of infant damnation, were being reflected. Coming around 1900, perhaps the change reflected the community's awareness of the need for disciplinary controls of certain people and interests within the business community who were running roughshod over others less powerful.

From 1900 to 1920, a considerable emphasis on the need for discipline and for developing attitudes discouraging relaxed, flexible relationships with children was apparent. Concomitant, particularly during the first World War, was an increased emphasis on the science of nutrition which quickly spread to infant feeding. Mother, who had previously known best about how to raise her child and about what to give him to eat, no longer was an authority in these areas. The only person who seemed competent to manage the infant was one who knew all about the chemical composition of foods and their caloric value, knowledge that pretty well eliminated mother.

During this period psychology was beginning to come to the fore. In the 1920's, Watson's behavioristic psychology, which fitted into the new concepts of science, became popular. His psychology emphasized that mothers should suppress their warm, spontaneous impulses and to bring up their children as unspoiled but well-conditioned little automatons, an uncritical application of Pavlov's conditioned reflex work in animals. Strict feeding schedules and the stifling of maternal impulses to pick up crying children reflected not only the uncertainty of the individual but also a certain uncritical acceptance of the new information and theory concerning behavior.

Although much of the scientific understanding of nutrition and the beginning scientific understanding of human behavior was an important contribution to our general knowledge, many mistakes were made in applying this information to daily experience. In the process of learning how to use this information constructively, as well as at the same time adding to knowledge in areas only incompletely understood, parents were often made to feel that they could not and should not trust their own thinking and judgment. Not only did this attitude tend to confuse and paralyze parents, but it also took much of the pleasure and satisfaction out of being a parent. Resentment in parents against this uncomfortable role seriously interfered with the development of healthy parent-child relationships. The last years have been aptly described as "the age of the confused parent."

This emphasis was followed in the 1930's by a counter-reaction with the popularization and over-interpretation of psychoanalytic knowledge, particularly that which had to do with limiting or, as it was interpreted, frustrating children. The era of extreme permissiveness resulted. Today we are perhaps on the verge of another swing in popular reaction. If the rather extreme criticisms of our educational system and the frequently advanced suggestion that severe punishment is the chief preventive measure of juvenile delinquency are to be given serious consideration, the reaction of swinging back too far towards rigidity and irrational disciplinary measures may be developing. Need exists to recognize that this reaction should swing back only far enough to recognize the importance of intelligently applied limits which can have very important directive and constructive influences on children.

Although all areas of human growth are inter-related and essentially indivisible, growth can be considered as occurring in four major areas: physical, intellectual, emotional, and social. Social growth, slightly different from the first three, may represent the application of the other kinds of growth to varying living situations.

Emotion has been defined as a "mental feeling or affection that is distinct from cognition or volition," a "moving, stirring, agitation; a vehement or excited mental state."[14] Unfortunately, the word *emotion* often connotes weakness or instability and suggests a lack of self-control. For men, in particular, common usage of the word implies that to have emotion is to be feminine or at least unmanly. Although Americans probably have no more difficulty in striking a comfortable balance with their emotions than do people of other nations, frontier and Puritan tradition tend to limit the kinds of emotions Americans are supposed to have. Popularly, men are supposed to be brave and oblivious to pain, whether of a physical or an emotional origin. Only women, the so-called weaker sex, are allowed openly to show the more painful or tender feelings. Actually of course, both sexes have a full complement of feelings. While cultural or individual patterns of how such feelings may be shown may exist, the individual who attempts to deny or eliminate from his life certain areas of feeling does so at his own expense. Under some conditions, this cost may be excessive since the individual pays for it by limiting his energy and capabilities. He may find his behavior so controlled by emotions which he has attempted to eliminate that adjustment is seriously interfered with. He may develop a pattern of expressing feelings not as emotions but as physiological reactions. These reactions can result in a wide range of psychosomatic disturbances. The emotionally healthy individual is one who accepts and understands his emotions as essential and important parts of himself and who learns how to live constructively in equilibrium with them, neither giving way excessively, nor attempting to deny their existence.

Although relatively little is known about the innate capabilities of the child as they affect his emotional development, even less is known about his capacity to inherit these capabilities. Such studies as Fries,[17] however, do suggest an area of innate difference in reactivity. She observed that ten day old untraumatized newborns could be placed along a scale on the basis of their response to a deliberately provoked startle reaction and to sudden interruption of an unfinished feeding. She graded their responses from extreme hyperactivity to extreme unresponsiveness. The child classified as extremely hyperactive would become so upset when feeding was interrupted that it was almost impossible to get him to resume feeding. On the other extreme was the child who, although unfinished and still hungry, seemed to mind the interruption so little that he went to sleep. Usually, of course, he woke up much sooner for his next feeding, but even then did not make much of a fuss. Escalona,[6] in a report on the great variety of individual characteristic ways that children respond, suggests that babies differ both in sensitivity and in strength of impulse. She feels that these are components of the "congenital activity type" described by Fries.

The way in which an infant reacts to its mother's ministrations affect the mother's feelings and behavior towards the child. If, for example, a mother, scared and uncertain and even reluctant in her maternal role, is confronted by a hypertonic, colicky, relatively sleepless baby, the mother-child relationship is less satisfactory. Another uncertain mother who has a child who is so quiet and unresponsive as almost to seem to disregard her may feel unneeded and unnecessary. All kinds of variations can be observed. The important thing to recognize is that babies have characteristic patterns of reaction which are fundamentally neither bad nor good but which influence how they respond to the world and how the world responds to them. Current available evidence suggests that the relationship between mother and child is of great consequence to the way the infant thrives and develops.

Blauvelt,[2] in her work with goats, shows "the negative effects of even a few minutes separation of the animal mother from her just-born infant upon her interest in caring for him and the positive effects of her adequate responses upon the neonate's respiratory efficiency, oxygenation of blood, muscular activity, and strength". Blauvelt describes the early interchange between mother goat and kid as "survival patterns." Whether such comparable and important interchanges take place between human mother and newborn when conditions permit is currently the subject of studies being carried out by Dr. Blauvelt about the behavior of human mothers and their newborn infants.

Goat and human behavior cannot be compared directly. However, what effects modern obstetrical methods with routine anesthesia and subsequent physical separation of mother and child have upon the early development of comfortable and healthy mother-child relationships as well as upon such specific things as breast feeding are being observed. Serious thought is being given to "rooming in" and to some applications of "natural childbirth" as possible ways of counteracting some of the influences which interfere with women getting enjoyment and satisfaction out of motherhood. Such satisfaction is quite possible while at the same time recognizing the value of modern anesthesia and obstetrical skill and knowledge. These practices need to be examined not only in the light of their physical effects and possible benefits upon the mother and child, but also in the light of the way they may promote or interfere with the early development of sound mother-child relationships.

INFANCY

During the first year and a half of post natal life, many things happen. Erickson[4] has spoken of this period as being the time during which the infant develops his sense of "basic trust." Put more generally, this is the period of development of fundamental patterns of reaction upon which the individual's subsequent relationships with other people will be built. Erikson[5] speaks of the infant learning from his environment "how to get what he needs," "how to accept what is given," and "how to be a giver" through his experiencing being given. Infants who develop this trust have solid feelings of confidence in life and its experiences. This confidence comes from the interaction of the innate make-up with its relatively idiosyncratic needs with the environment which consists largely of mother and her ministrations.

Coincident and intimately related to this period of development, a wide variety of capacities and attitudes are being laid down. As the principal process which connects the infant with his mother, feeding and the handling that goes on around feeding determines the various conditioned reflex patterns between emotional reaction and the functioning of the infant's gastrointestinal tract. Infants initially experience feeling largely as a physical reaction. If the autonomic nervous system is frequently and forcefully stimulated in connection with some aspect of feeding, a pattern of upper gastro-intestinal tract response, such as vomiting, to subsequent similar emotional stimuli is possible.

The skin is the largest sense organ of the infant. The connection between cutaneous stimulation and various vital functions such as depth of respiration is clear. Careful studies of the important respiratory stimulating mechanisms at birth indicate that cutaneous stimulation is probably the most important. The pleasure or discomfort associated with the condition of and the care of the skin may influence the infant's interest in things in or outside himself. Lack of cutaneous stimulation, among other things, may play an important role in those extreme situations such as were described by Spitz[17] of the very withdrawn, apathetic, and maldeveloped infants who had been cared for by their mothers for the first three months of life and who were then left in the psychologically sterile atmosphere of a hospital to be cared for by competent nurses who divided their care among eight infants.

No one knows exactly the kind of care that a child needs in order to develop in an emotionally healthy fashion. But a variety of studies do indicate the need for a continuing contact between the infant and some one person who has a genuine interest in him. Goldfarb's[9] studies of the outcome of children institutionally reared point this conclusion out clearly. Lowrey[13] reported in 1940 on twenty-two children seen in a child guidance clinic on referral by social agencies because of the syptoms of aggressiveness, negativism, selfishness, feeding difficulties, speech defects, and enuresis. Their difficulties could be summarized by saying that they had an inability to give or to receive affection. Their histories indicated that twenty-one of them had been admitted to an institution or orphanage before their first birthday and had remained there until they were three or four years of age. Dr. Lowrey's somewhat pessimistic conclusions were that such children were almost impossible to work with psychiatrically and that it was extremely unlikely that these children would ever be able to make a good adjustment. Goldfarb's studies, which were the result of following such children into adolescence, suggest much the same thing. More recent evidence indicates that these conclusions do not apply to all children exposed to such experience. For reasons not well understood, some children weather such impersonal institutional experiences without permanent serious personality damage. Bowlby[3] feels that if the child has a series of disappointing, unsatisfactory relationships with mother figures, he is apt to develop into the "affectionless and psychopathic character."

The speed and facility with which the average child develops speech is greatly influenced not only by the amount of talking that the mother does to her baby but also by the satisfaction the child feels exists in the total relationship. If the relationship is one with a good deal of mutual pleasure, the child wants to respond by any means of communication. If his satisfaction comes too exclusively from eating and not from the total relationship, the individual later in life may turn to excessive eating, drinking, smoking or other oral activities in time of emotional discomfort. From the mental health standpoint even during infancy, the total experience of the individual is important, not certain techniques of infant care.

THE RUNABOUT CHILD

From the time that the child is approximately eighteen months to three and one-half years of age, another series of important and interrelated events take place. At the opening of this period the infant dimly begins to be aware of himself as a separate and discrete individual. During this time the child psychologically separates himself from his mother and begins to experience the joys and fears of independent existence. Many fears which are common in older children and adults are rooted in the uncertainties the child experiences as he reaches out and draws back from this inviting independence. Allen[1] reports, "In the very fact that he cannot keep his mother with him comes both a feeling of separateness and an awareness of not controlling all the movements of another person. Early he has an opportunity to discover what he can do, and cannot do, and in the normal growth process the doing and the limitation of doing, emerging together, lay the basis for creativeness in the new self of the child." Such separation is an important and sometimes difficult step not only for the child but also for the mother.

Many other attitudes develop concomitantly during this period of separation. Early in this period, sometimes before, parents begin toilet training. Out of this experience the individual develops attitudes toward his body and many of its functions, feelings about his physical competence, and attitudes toward himself as an acceptable or non-acceptable person, the basic attitudes upon which are built his subsequent reactions toward authority. These attitudes in large measure determine whether he will be able to accept authority without feeling crushed or whether he will be able to assert himself without needless rebellion. These attitudes are reflected not only in the obvious situations involving authority but also in situations such as the acceptance of the discipline of learning, especially the somewhat inexorable situations encountered in mathematics and spelling where little room for individuality is possible. During this period the child should develop a feeling of complete mastery of his body, a feeling of rightness and acceptability about all its parts. The child's feeling about the genital area will influence his attitude toward sexual activity in later life. Mixed with the child's attitudes toward himself as a person and how he relates to authority will be influences which may later determine whether he feels guilty and inhibited, inordinately interested, or aggressive and defiant in his sex activity.

As the child becomes aware of his separateness from his mother, he is likely to feel his beginning individuality as difference. This differentiation is puzzling and sometimes disturbing. In attempting to explain why he feels different, the child may use the obvious physical difference between male and female as a convenient explanation. If this difference is felt as bad, the child may imagine that the physical difference of boys from girls, with the lack of an externally visible penis in the female, has been imposed as a punishment. Although apparently many children entertain this notion at one time or another, it is not too disturbing except to those who have responded with considerable guilt to punishment or criticism of their behavior. These children may torture themselves with bizarre notions of what will or has happened to them. Drastic parental handling of the normal genital investigation of this and the somewhat earlier age is more likely to result in producing these disturbed fantasies.

If the experience of the child during this period is reasonably satisfactory, he emerges with a beginning healthy independence and yet a warm relatedness to his parents, with the feeling of mastery and pleasurable acceptance of his body, and with a way of relating to external authority which enables him to use his energies largely in productive ways. Because of wholeness and individuality in himself, the child is then able to accept other people even though they are combinations of attitudes and behavior all of which the child may not enjoy or like. Bowlby[3] speaks of this as the child's ability to see the mother "in the flesh."

PRE-SCHOOL

Building on the accomplishments of the previous period, and closely related to his developing intellectual capacity, the child now moves into an awareness of himself, not only as the separate individual he is but also as the kind of separate individual he can become. This awareness includes not only sensing his various endowments but also appreciating his beginning ability to think in abstract ways in such areas as what are socially acceptable attitudes toward other people and their property. He begins to think about and to be concerned with whether he is an acceptable boy or girl. If he feels reasonably good about himself and has good relationships with his parents, he begins to dare to aspire to become an acceptable man or woman. The beginning of his acceptance of using his mind imaginatively and creatively, the beginnings of conscience, and the basis upon which will be built his acceptance and satisfaction in whatever biological role in which he is cast originate during this period.

The innumerable questions and the insatiable curiosity of the child at this age can tax harassed parents. If parents can catch their breath and respond thoughtfully to these questions and support this curiosity, an open-mindedness and enthusiasm for more formal learning in the years will follow. The nature of these responses, both in words and reactions, has great influence on the attitudes and values of the child. If parents say one thing and do the opposite, the child will acquire a rather inadequately developed sense of values or conscience. If parents who speak of sharing and being considerate of others arbitrarily and violently punish the child for his investigational use of some parental property, the child's subsequent behavior toward his playmates may seem unduly assertive.

More subtle and serious problems can arise when a parent has strong anti-social or hostile drives of which he is not consciously aware, but which he unconsciously encourages his child to act out. These cases have been most completely described by Johnson,[10] who sees unconscious parental conflict result in delinquent behavior in adolescents. She feels that unconscious attitudes in parents are of the most frequent causes of delinquent behavior in children of middle class families. A four year old boy whose parents were concerned because of his very aggressive behavior with other children can be cited as an example. As this behavior was discussed with the parents, however, their concern lay not in his aggressive behavior. Actually, they seemed to enjoy it. They were concerned because his behavior caused them trouble with their neighbors.

Whether the child feels satisfaction in his role as a boy or a girl, and eventually as man or woman, is largely determined by the kind of acceptance and interest in the child by both parents, but especially by the parent of the same sex. What kind of man or woman he can accept being is again influenced by the way the parent of the same sex is able to accept and to live his own biological and social role. If, for example, the girl's mother finds all housework distasteful, the care of children unrewarding, and the bearing and nursing of babies degrading, the child who admires her mother will experience difficulty enjoying a more traditional feminine role. If the father treats his daughter as a doll to be displayed and dressed up, he can seriously influence the way in which she will eventually view herself in relating to men.

The ways in which each individual works out his role as man or woman is greatly influenced by the particular milieu or culture in which he lives. This influence is transmitted from one generation to the next, from parent to child. Fromm[8] speaks of this observation as follows, "The child does not meet society directly as first; it meets it through the medium of his parents, who in their character structure and methods of education represent the social structure, who are the psychological agency of society as it were."

THE SCHOOL YEARS

The years from six to thirteen should be constructive and creative ones. If all has gone well, the child will get along comfortably with his age mates and adults, will accept differences between himself and others, will be receptive to learning, and will have satisfaction in the creative use of his mind, his body, and himself as a social individual. Things, of course, do not always go well, not only because of left over, unsolved problems from the first six years, but also because situations may be encountered which are disturbing to his growing confidence and equilibrium. Illness, moving, a bad school situation, unavoidable parental separation from the children by war or economic necessity can be disruptive. The more common and more serious problems are usually evidence of persistent, unsolved earlier difficulties. The greatest numbers of children are referred to child guidance clinics during this age period. They come with learning problems, difficulties in relating to authority, and conscience problems such as stealing, firesetting, sex play. These residual problems usually demand direct help to the child with concomitant work with the parents. These problems are in contrast to the reactive problems which may show many of the same symptoms but which usually respond when excessive environmental pressures are alleviated. Since this child does not have unresolved problems from past experience, he usually does not need psychiatric help.

During the past thirty years the child guidance clinic has developed into a specialized agency to work with disturbed children and their parents. The child is helped by the therapist, usually the child psychiatrist, gradually to dare to bring out, sometimes only in actions, but often also in words, the unresolved area of difficulty. Slowly, through his relationship and trust with the therapist, the child dares to try to act in a more grown up way, a way more appropriate to his age. He dares to accept as a desired and necessary part of himself the emotions which he has felt a need either to deny or which he has previously felt he could not control. While this therapy is going on, specially trained psychiatric social workers help parents to examine their own relationship to the child, especially in the area of the problem. The parents are helped to find ways of supporting and encouraging the child as he tries out new and healthier ways of reacting so that parents and the child are enabled to go ahead satisfactorily on their own.

One nine year old boy who was brought by a rather forceful mother to a child guidance clinic because he had no boy friends and did not stand up for himself. When, through therapy, the boy obtained more confidence in himself and proceeded to manifest this confidence by defying a command of his mother's, the mother's reaction indicated that although a more assertive boy was what she said she wanted, this behavior was extremely difficult for her to accept. However, after a great deal of work, the social worker did enable the mother to accept and support the new, more healthy assertive self in her son.

Children possess a natural tendency towards growth and recovery. Many problems straighten out with time and living. In addition, many parents out of their own efforts think through and work out problems, either by themselves or with a little outside help.

ADOLESCENCE

Adolescence is a fascinating period of separation in many ways comparable to that which occurs during infancy. Building on the past, adolescence is an opportunity for testing many roles without a too early need for permanent commitment to any one. The adolescent asks many questions of himself. Am I capable of beginning really independent thought and behavior? Can I do this without going to extremes and totally denying my parents' advice and authority? What role am I capable of playing in life? Am I capable of becoming a wage earner, a mate, a parent, or citizen? If parents have built relationships solidly, they are not panicked by the intensity of their child's emotions and attitudes. They can stand their ground firmly and yet tolerantly.

If the relationship with authority has been in unstable equilibrium, the balance is likely to swing towards open and persistent defiance. All the unresolved problems of the past come to the fore with the heightened feelings which have produced them. Even the reasonably healthy adolescent can be a trial to himself and to his parents. His tremendous energy and little organization makes great demands upon his personality. His economy is for a time on a deficit finance basis. For those with some athletic skill and even for those who have none, physical activity in collaboration with others can be a valuable outlet. However, not all feeling can or should be handled by physical or even social activity. When the adolescent needs great support in facing and dealing directly with his turbulent feelings, he needs help to accept the pain of temporary defeat or humiliation.

The chemical changes accompanying physical puberty enhance and considerably strengthen all his feelings and impulses. This strengthening makes life both for the adolescent and his parents more trying. Although the adolescent who gets into serious trouble may be only unlucky, more often he is one who has had trouble handling his feelings in the past. The possibility of trouble may not have been obvious if manifested by too much control, too good behavior. The adolescent with this problem can have a really hard time. His feelings and attendant thoughts are now too powerful completely to repress. When these feelings come bursting through, they can make the unprepared adolescent wonder if he is becoming insane, This painful thought, and various mechanisms to defend against it, including, at times, delusions and hallucinations by which the individual projects his unpleasant feelings on others can be encountered.

Parents of adolescents are frequently worried about the ability of their children to cope with sex drives. If boys and girls have been helped to respect themselves and to feel reasonably comfortable in their sex roles, they have no major unresolved problems in their relationship to authority and in their attitudes toward their parents, especially those of the opposite sex. On the other hand, if a boy's relationship to his mother has been one in which he has been grossly over-protected and yet often unnecessarily physically stimulated or if the girl has learned to feel from her father that her only attractiveness lies in her physical appeal, trouble may ensue. Girls who have unhappy, rejecting home lives may seek sex as a substitute for genuine love and kindness. Yet for reasons not understood, some young people are able to work out satisfying ways of relating to the opposite sex without getting into any irretrievable trouble. Others do not. One bright, attractive, adolescent who when asked, perhaps somewhat naively, why she had gotten pregnant said, "I didn't think he would be interested in me for less," and then added, "I wanted to do the thing which would hurt my mother most." This is perhaps particularly difficult in this day and age when many parents do not know what to believe in and where there is often inadequate opportunity for youth constructively to blow off steam or test themselves out. Certainly many of our communities have not thought through nor provided enough recreational facilities for all children or enough special educational facilities for the intellectually average or below whose competence does not lie in academic achievement.

Emotions are the driving, controlling forces of our behavior. Each child needs help in learning how to accept and to live with his emotions in ways that enable him to get the benefit of their motive power. The relative ease or difficulty in accomplishing this acceptance depends upon his makeup, the circumstances he encounters in life, and, most important, upon the kind of relationship which exists between himself and his parents.

REFERENCES

1. Allen, F. H.: The Dilemma of Growth. *Arch. Neurol. & Psychiat.*, 37, 1937.
2. Blauvelt, H.: Quoted in, Patterns of Mothering, Brody, S., I.V.P., N. Y., 1956.
3. Bowlby, J., Robertson, J., Rosenbluth, D.: A Two Year Old Goes to the Hospital. *Psychoan, S. C., VII*: 82-94 I.V.P., N. Y., 1952.

4. Erikson, E. H.: *Childhood and Society*, Chapter VII, Norton, N. Y., 1950.
5. Erikson, E. H.: *New Perspective for Research in Juvenile Delinquency*, Witmer and Kotinsky, Eds., Childrens Bureau Publication No. 356, 1956.
6. Escalona, Sibylle: Emotional Development in the First Year of Life. *Trans, 6th Conf. on Problems of Infancy and Childhood*, 11-91, Josiah Macy Jr. Foundation, 1952.
7. Fries, M. E., Wolf, P.: Some Hypotheses on the Role of Congenital Activity Type of Personality Development, *Psychoan. S. C. VIII:* 48-62, I.V.P., N. Y., 1953.
8. Fromme, E.: Individual and Social Origins of Neurosis, in Personality in *Nature, Society, and Culture*, pp. 410, Kluckhohn and Murry, Eds., Knopf, N. Y., 1950.
9. Goldfarb, W.: Infant Rearing and Problem Behavior, *A. J. Ortho.*, *102:*18-33, 1945.
10. Johnson, Adelaide M.: Sanctions for Superego Lacunae of Adolescents in *Searchlights on Delinquency*, K. Eissler, Ed., I.V.P., N. Y., 1949.
11. Kauner, L.: Early Infantile Autism, *J. of Ped.*, *XXV:* 211-217, 1944.
12. Leighton, D. C.: Distribution of Psychiatric Symptoms in a Small Town. *A. J. Psychiatry*, *112:*716, 1956.
13. Lowry, L. G.: Personality Distortion and Early Institutional Care. *A. J. Ortho.*, *10:*576, 1940.
14. *Oxford Universal Dictionary*, 3rd Edition, Revised with Addenda 1955, Oxford University Press.
15. Rennie, Srole, Opler, Longner: *Urban Life and Mental Health. A. J. Psychiatry*, *113:*831, 1957.
16. Scull, A. J.: The Challenge of the Well Child. *Cal. Med.*, *77:*285-292, 1952.
17. Solomon, Seedeoman, Mendelson, Wexler: Sensory Deprivation, a Review. *A. J. Psychiatry*, *114:*357-363, 1957.
18. Spitz, R.: Hospitalism, An Inquiry into the Genesis of Psychiatric Conditions in Early Childhood. *Psychoan. S. C.*, *1:*53-74, I.V.P., N. Y., 1945.
19. Stendler, C. B.: Sixty Years of Child Training Practices: Revolution in the Nursery. *J. of Ped.*, *36:*122, 1950.
20. Zwerling, I. et al.: Personality Disorders and the Relationship of Emotion to Surgical Illness in 200 Surgical Patients. *A. J. Psychiatry*, *112:*270, 1955.

THE CHILD WITH FAMILIAL DYSAUTONOMIA

Conrad M. Riley, M.D.

Some handicapping conditions which produce only a slight degree of disability command attention because a large number of persons are affected. The milder cerebral palsies, diabetes, rheumatic fever with minimal heart damage, handicapping conditions for which mass planning can be made, are three examples. Other handicapping conditions which occur rarely but which produce severe disability must also command attention even though their infrequent occurrence requires an individual approach. Familial dysautonomia falls into this category.

First described in 1949, the condition has not yet received wide publication in medical literature. The 88 diagnosed cases reported by 1957 can be considered to represent only a fraction of the total number of persons affected. Despite the rarity implied by these figures, the potential havoc which this disorder can cause, not only to the patient but also to the entire family constellation, justifies its description and discussion. The term "dysautonomia" was adopted because some of the most striking disturbances of function are in the autonomic nervous system.

All forms of life possess mechanisms for receiving sensations and for initiating appropriate responses. In the lower forms, these mechanisms are strictly automatic. In higher forms, some of the automatic responses are affected by the voluntary nervous system. Nevertheless, the automatic (autonomic or non-voluntary) responses play an important role in maintaining, protecting, and reproducing life by autonomically controlling such activities as blood pressure, temperature, and sweating.

Familial dysautonomia is an inborn condition evidenced by a generalized disturbance of nervous system function. Fairly frequently more than one child in a family is affected. On the basis of characteristics observed among such patients, the dysautonomic child is almost always Jewish, is slightly more likely to be a girl, fails to produce tears in normal fashion when crying, perspires profusely, breaks out in red blotches with excitement, may drool, and emotionally is likely to be very unstable and unpredictable. Autonomic control of blood pressure and of body temperature is very disturbed and erratic. Such a patient may have recurrent episodes of broncho-pneumonia and severe recurrent episodes of vomiting. The child is usually slow in development both as to speech and general dexterity so that schooling is difficult. The degree of disability varies greatly from patient to patient. A particular child may experience recurrent episodes of physical illness and constant emotional instability. Another child may exhibit symptoms so mild that problems are minimal.

Although the cause of familial dysautonomia is not known with certainty, available data concerning its occurrence in siblings and to consanguinity of parents indicates a genetic disorder transmitted as a simple autosomal recessive gene. Such observations imply an appreciable risk that subsequent children of the same parents also could be afflicted. Even though the nature of the exact trait which could be so transmitted is unknown, investigators suspect a disturbance in some enzyme system concerned with nervous system function. No anatomical abnormality which might explain the diffuse disturbance has been found with any consistency.

Although the mortality rate is high, the outcome of the illness is variable. Out of the 88 cases known to the author, 27.2% are dead. Most of these deaths have occurred in the first five to six years of life, but a few have occurred later, the oldest patient dying at 17 years. Prognosis for those who survive is not fully known because the brief acquaintance with the condition has not provided the opportunity for very long follow-up periods. The oldest known patient is 24 years of age. Several are in the mid or late teens. On the basis of these observations, the fact that the physiological disabilities will persist can be expected. Since the patient, however, does seem with advancing adolescence to adjust to his handicaps to a varying degree, eventual improvement in the over-all picture may be predicted. The degree of affliction is infinitely variable. No one patient will have *all* of the manifestations, and some patients will have *none* of the severe ones.

NEWBORN PROBLEMS

Although difficulties are almost always apparent from the time of birth, diagnosis is uncertain much before the child is eight months or a year old. Many of the peculiarities could be the result of other disorders. If there has been a previous child with dysautonomia in the family or if several of the expected features are present, the diagnosis can be presumed.

Although the mother of such a child rarely reports that the baby was less active than expected before birth, some patients have had difficulty initiating normal respiration immediately after birth. Most have been inactive and limp-appearing. Feeding in most instances constitutes a real problem. Many such newborn babies have had to be tube fed for days, weeks, or sometimes months. Even those who are not so extreme are slow feeders, often taking up to an hour to finish the usual bottle.

A large proportion of such infants fail to grow at the usual rate. Parents are inclined to link this growth disturbance with the feeding problem, feeling that the lack of growth is due to the poor eating. Such an interpretation frustrates the parents even more. However, growth retardation is not limited to weight gain only but also affects height, and this observation is not readily explained on the basis of nutritional deficit. The small stature persists throughout life, even after feeding has improved. The failure of the infant to take much food is evidence of the fact that growth is minimal, that the usual infant intake is not necessary.

During the first year or two of life, other abnormalities appear. At the age when most babies begin to produce copious tears with crying (6 weeks to 3 months), these babies continue to cry without tears and never do produce them in normal amounts. This inability is not due to an inadequate lacrimal gland because they do produce moisture, and rarely, a proper tear or two. But they never produce tears comparable in quantity to a normal child when crying. This deficiency cannot in itself be considered diagnostic as a number of otherwise healthy children have been seen with a similar defect. Associated with this is a reduction of sensitivity of the cornea, the transparent part of the eyeball. This last feature is probably responsible for the fact that a few of these patients develop corneal ulcers which are slow to heal and difficult to treat. In a few cases the eyelids have been sewn together for several months to promote healing. In rare cases such ulcers have left permanent scars which have seriously interfered with vision.

Toward the latter part of the first year and throughout the second year a fair proportion of the patients start to run a fever. Such an abnormality may be a daily event with the temperature rising to 101 or 102 F. for a few hours. High fevers may occur intermittently without obvious explanation. Since more frequently than with other children these patients develop real bronchopneumonia, fever cannot be lightly dismissed as not being significant. As with any child, convulsions can occur with fever, but convulsions should not be considered a characteristic of dysautonomia. The patients probably never completely lose their abnormal temperature response to infection.

SKIN PECULARITIES:
SWEATING, BLOTCHING, MARMORATION

From earliest infancy the baby's skin shows a pattern of behavior which is different from normal. Practically all such patients tend to perspire profusely, particularly during times of excitement and crying. The perspiration on the head is most marked, a feature tending to persist throughout life. Because many such infants perspire remarkably at night, bed clothes have to be changed.

The appearance of evanescent red blotches is also a usual part of the syndrome, although it is a less frequent phenomenon in older children. These blotches are usually fairly sharply outlined red spots on head and upper trunk, sometimes spreading over the entire body and occasionally becoming confluent. The blotches usually appear while the child is eating or experiencing periods of excitement. They disappear a few minutes after the stimulus is withdrawn. Although such blotches are occasionally seen in normal people, their almost regular appearance in these patients should be considered a pathological exaggeration of a normal response.

Most of the babies will be discovered frequently to have cold hands and feet. This peculiarity is particularly evident when fever is present and while the body itself feels "burning hot." At the same time the fingers and toes are apt to be a bright pink. The extremities may show mottling or marmoration which is quite different from the red blotches of the head and trunk previously described.

INDIFFERENCE TO PAIN AND ITS CONSEQUENCES

As the baby grows older, the parents usually observe that he does not react as much to pain as most babies do. Perhaps he fails to cry when "given a needle" for immunization by the doctor, or perhaps he doesn't cry as might be expected from a child who is accidentally bruised. A few young patients have turned up with a swelling of the arm or leg without complaint, and then x-rays have shown a broken bone.

In infancy this unexpected reaction has given rise, in a number of patients, to a distressing complication. When the teeth come in, some infants develop a habit of rubbing their tongues over the newly erupted sharp object. Since no discomfort seems to result, the child continues the practice. In time, an ulcer appears which will not heal unless the tooth is capped or extracted. A few patients have actually chewed their tongues doing severe damage. Others have chewed the inside of their cheeks, producing non-healing ulcers. This phenomenon is not due to a lack of normal sensation since these children can readily distinguish painful (sharp-pointed) stimuli from non-painful (dull) ones as they grow older. They do not, however, experience the normal displeasure expected from such an experience.

DROOLING

Practically all children during the latter part of the first year and well into the second year of life go through a period of drooling which usually is associated with cutting teeth. For a three to eight year old child to persist with drooling is rare. Children with dysautonomia, in contrast, very commonly continue to drool as they grow older. Although they gradually overcome this difficulty, some of them, even in their teens, may revert to drooling when under excitement. The reason for this salivary overflow seems to be two-fold. First, there probably is some excessive production of saliva which most normal persons can dispose of without drooling. Secondly, the difficulty in swallowing which made feeding such a problem in early infancy seems to persist. Therefore, this normally automatic function has actually to be learned by these patients. The control of drooling can be expected to be slow and probably never to be perfect.

ACQUISITION OF SKILLS AND INTELLECTUAL POTENTIALITIES

Well informed parents and all persons trained to work with growing children have been taught to expect the appearance of new skills according to a reasonably predictable schedule. Considerable variability is compatible with normal child growth and development. Children with dysautonomia, however, frequently deviate to an alarming degree on the slow side of this schedule. Many of them do not learn to sit alone before ten to twelve months. Walking may not begin before eighteen months to two years. Talking is often delayed till three to four years. To a parent, already concerned with the physical difficulties, these delays may be indeed disturbing.

Counterbalance of this slowness in motor development is the fact that the child's comprehension of speech and recognition of the world about him may seem wholly disproportionate to his other accomplishments. Often a two year old patient will say no words at all but will respond to commands and instructions amazingly well. Tests of the older children suggest that mental deficiency is not a consistent part of the picture. Most of the patients seem to have average comprehension of abstract ideas. A few have even shown superior intelligence. Some have been frankly mentally defective.

This slowness of acquiring skills appears to be another manifestation of the diffuse nervous system disorder. In addition to the autonomic system dysfunction, the voluntary nervous system seems to mature more slowly and less completely than in a normal person. As dysautonomic patients grow older, their muscular coordination always remains poor. Running, throwing balls, bicycle riding may be beyond their abilities.

SPEECH AND EATING

The slow development of speech appears to be related to poor control of the muscles of the mouth, tongue, and throat. Even the older patients continue to experience difficulty with eating. Many have peculiar chewing habits, and some "mouth" their food for long periods before swallowing. Sometimes solids are better tolerated than liquids, or the reverse may be true. The muscles so essential both to speech and to eating usually fail to reach full maturity. When speech does develop, a persistent "nasal" quality something like that of a patient with a weak palate persists.

EMOTIONAL DEVELOPMENT

The features discussed up to this point have been related to the autonomic and voluntary nervous systems. Again and again the phrase "with excitement" or something similar has been used referring to some feature exaggerated under stress. Most observations suggest that deviations from the normal response to emotional stimuli can be expected. Whether the emotional peculiarities are secondary to the physiological peculiarities or whether they are primary, both factors play a role in the total picture. The unpredictable physiological responses to emotional stress must give the child a very peculiar view of himself and his environment.

In early infancy the baby is often a cranky, irritable child who is hard to please. Toward the end of the first year and through the second, many patients develop "breath-holding" spells during which they may turn almost black and even lose consciousness. When such an incident occurs, the parent will often try to avoid such episodes by trying to appease the child whenever possible, the usual rules for child-rearing understandably being totally disregarded so that secondary emotional problems are certain to arise.

In older children with dysautonomia, the emotional responses to situations appear to take on an "all-or-none" quality. Thus, at times, minor frustration is tolerated with no apparent concern on the part of the child. At other times, a similar frustration may lead to a major fear or anger reaction with a full-blown tantrum. Such unpredictability makes the parent-child relationship a very difficult one, leading some parents to live in a constant state of tension.

In addition to such extreme responses of a disagreeable sort, these children have extreme responses of an agreeable type. When in good health physically, they tend to be very dependent and affectionate. When moved to laughter, they may laugh inordinately. Sometimes they may even laugh themselves into a breath-holding spell comparable to one initiated by crying. Their relations with other children are usually unsatisfactory because of their lack of skills in playing, their small size, and their emotional immaturity. They play more happily in general with individuals younger than themselves because they find competition with their peers too difficult.

VOMITING

The last new major threat to the normal development and possibly the life of the patient with dysautonomia is the development of vomiting attacks. In early childhood many such children have spells of "gagging" or retching in the early morning. These attacks settle into a regular pattern and interfere with breakfast. Sometimes retching may actually progress to vomiting. Fortunately, in most children these attacks subside in frequency and intensity as the children mature.

In a moderate number of cases, at four to six years of age, recurrent severe vomiting attacks develop. These attacks may follow some obviously emotionally upsetting experience, they may be associated with a cold or other infection, or they may start with no apparent precipitating cause. In some patients such vomiting attacks occur once or twice a year; in others they recur as often as every two to three weeks. Although such attacks may occur over several years, they usually abate by early adolescence. Once the attack has started, the child vomits and retches repeatedly for two or three days. A marked personality change often attends these attacks: the patient becoming very withdrawn, occasionally maniacal, sometimes indulging in self-destructive acts such as scratching or hair-spilling. Often such attacks are severe enough to require admission to the hospital for management. Recent new medications have been discovered which control the severity and duration of the attack. Finally and quite suddenly the vomiting stops, and the usual personality returns.

ADDITIONAL FINDINGS

Normal individuals have an automatic response of blood pressure to changes in posture. When they rise to a standing position from lying down, a slight rise in pressure as if to compensate for the new position is measurable. In dysautonomic patients, the reverse happens, i.e., a fall in blood pressure, sometimes so great that fainting ensues, occurs. Blood pressure in such patients also rises extremely during periods of emotional stress, particularly with older children.

Another abnormality is the absence of deep tendon reflexes. With normal persons, tapping of the knee causes a reflex kick of the leg. In dysautonomic patients, this and other similar reflexes are not usually obtained, probably because of poor muscular control, although the relationship is not entirely clear.

One last abnormality which is more common in children with dysautonomia is the development of scoliosis or curvature of the spine. This development has been noted in mild degree in quite a number of patients but has only developed to a severe degree in a few. When such curvature does occur, it usually begins when the child is seven or eight years of age and progresses until the child reaches twelve or fourteen when it becomes fixed.

PROSPECTS FOR ADULT LIFE

By the time a patient reaches twelve or fourteen years of age, all of the difficulties, minor or major, will probably have declared themselves. For this reason death is less likely to occur after a patient survives these difficult years. After the teens have been reached, no new major developments need be expected; and some of the previously troublesome problems will begin to diminish. From this point on, the child can begin to learn to live with the handicaps he has and to move on into adult life with a reasonable hope that he will be able to make an adequate adjustment to the world of normal individuals.

MANAGEMENT

The immediate management of the patient with dysautonomia is obviously the direct concern of the parent. In the mild cases, little difficulty may be experienced since the youngster can be reared very much like any normal child. In the severe cases, both physical and emotional problems can give rise to enough difficulties so that outside assistance may be required. Nutrition, infection, ulceration, and severe vomiting may require frequent attention by a physician. Administration of special medication may call for the aid of a visiting nurse. Emotional and physical disturbances may demand the understanding support which can be offered by a social worker. Special training in speech may demand attention from a trained speech therapist. Educational difficulties may require the sympathetic help of an informed teacher. Muscular disabilities may be eased by a physiotherapist. The disruption of the entire family constellation may be somewhat ameliorated by the services of a psychiatrist or by a well informed religious counsellor. In many cases a whole "team" of interested persons may be required.

The day-by-day living with such children can emerge as a task of major proportions almost from the time the baby is brought home from the hospital. The feeding difficulties, the lack of growth, the failure of "normal" development may all be a source of justified worry to the uninformed parent. On top of this, if some of the possible physical complications develop, fear for the child's actual life can be superimposed. If temper tantrums and breath-holding spells are part of the picture, the tensions may indeed be almost unbearable. Under such circumstances parents may be completely controlled or manipulated by the youngster at a very early age. Although advisors may lay down the usual rules for rearing such a child to frustrated parents, parents may experience extreme difficulty in profiting by such advice. They must be reassured that the terrifying events of temper tantrums and breath-holding spells have never so far proven to be fatal and that these tantrums and spells must be tolerated for the sake of developing an over-all sense of security in the child. Understanding of the basic nature of the condition and sympathetic support can help a great deal. Specific problems in specific families have to be worked out on an individual basis.

Psychological and psychiatric studies of parents and children indicate that patients have difficulty in adjusting to new situations. Because of their physiological aberrations such patients react violently to changes which develop in normal daily routine, such as changing the time of awakening, of eating meals, of moving bowels, of going to bed at night. They find the adjustment to non-routine events such as going on a trip or paying a visit to the doctor's office even more difficult of management. The more "structured" or routinized that life can be, the less adaptation that the patients have to make, the better will be their over-all adjustment.

As the child grows older without developing speech, the question will arise as to the advisability of special speech therapy. Although such therapy has been attempted with several patients, observers have not determined whether the ability to speak is actually hastened by such assistance. Even without such aid the children do learn to talk. However, once speech has begun, its clarity can be improved by specific training.

Older children present problems of socialization and schooling. In those more serious instances where vomiting or other physical disabilities are frequent, schooling of the ordinary type becomes an impossibility. Homebound instruction, however, may be arranged in many metropolitan areas. Where school is possible, these children should join with other children of their own age in the learning process. The emotional immaturity of such patients may become painfully apparent, and their inability to play with children their own age may cause acute discomfort. Their small stature and lack of muscular coordination may further set them apart from the group. In classroom work, also, easy distractibility complicates the learning process. In spite of these difficulties, evidence indicates that effective therapy occurs when handicapped children attend regular school which has sufficient staff that is properly trained.

Management of children with dysautonomia can be difficult, frustrating, terrifying, and disheartening, but it can also be rewarding. Although the direct responsibility lies with parents, much indirect assistance can be given. In the New York area parents are meeting approximately monthly with a pediatrician, a psychiatrist, and a social worker. These group meetings are informal. Questions are directed to trained workers and to parents so that a forum for the exchange of information as to the kinds of problems encountered and as to techniques for dealing with them has been established. As a result, the medical and para-medical group has learned much about the nature of the disorder; but more important, the parents have developed a sense of corporate strength which seems to have added to their individual strength in dealing with their personal problems.

READINGS

Riley, C. M.; Day, R. L.; Greeley, D. McL.; and Langford, W. S.: Central autonomic dysfunction with defective lacrimation: I. Report of five cases. *Pediatrics*, *3:*468, 1949.

Riley, C. M.; Freedman, A. M.; and Langford, W. S.: Further Observations on familial dysautonomia. *Pediatrics*, *14:*475, 1954.

Riley, C. M.: Living with a child with familial dysautonomia (booklet for parents) obtainable on request from the Dysautonomia Association, 1201 Elder Avenue, New York 72, N. Y.

THE CHILD WHO IS A MONGOL

Heyworth N. Sanford, M.D.

Mongolism, a term used to describe a group of children who are deficient mentally, and who have similar physical characteristics, was applied to these children when they were originally recognized as constituting a distinct group. Their superficial resemblance to members of the Mongolian race caused the term Mongol to be applied to them. However, since such handicapped children are found among Negro, Indian, Chinese and Japanese peoples, their incidence is not confined to the white race.

(These handicapped children were not recognized as constituting a separate grouping until the middle of the 19th century. Langdon Down, an English physician, published the first description of them in 1866.) Ten years later another physician wrote that they were "rarely met with in asylums, but, nevertheless, not really uncommon." This comment is supported by the fact that Mongoloids have been found as subjects in old paintings. One of the best known, Le Satyre et Le Payson by Jacob Jordaens, a contemporary of Rubens, was painted about 1635.

(The Mongoloid child occurs in about three births per thousand infants.) Though the disease or condition is not new, some may not be recognized at birth. (Nevertheless, though their mortality during infancy is high, at least 60,000 of these children are estimated in the general population of the United States.) Research needs to be undertaken to determine whether these children are increasing in incidence. (Such research would consider the ability better to recognize these children as well as the fact that formerly their life span was short because of poor health and lack of resistance to infections.) Undoubtedly, improved general health contions and the use of antibiotics have increased the number of living Mongoloids.

Even though mongolism has been much discussed and studied, its cause has not definitely been established. Once considered as genetically inherited, investigators are now studying illness of the mother during early pregnancy as well as the possibility that genetic recessiveness may be a contributing factor.

Although these children are mentally deficient, the degree varies. Whereas, idiots do not progress past the mental development of a three year old child, many Mongoloid children will be in the imbecile class, reaching the mental age of seven years. A few may even progress into a low moron group and develop to a mental age of eight or nine years.

In families who have a Mongoloid child, no more mental deficiency, nervous or mental diseases, or malformations occur than in other families. The parents and brothers and sisters of Mongoloids are intelligent. Socially, some are usually above the average. Diseases such as syphilis, tuberculosis, and alcoholism are not a factor; neither are contraceptives nor abortive measures. The mother of a Mongoloid does very often show certain differences from the normal mother in this pregnancy Most conspicuously, the births of Mongoloids frequently occur at an older age of the mother. Everyone who has studied this problem is agreed that more mothers over thirty-five years of age bear Mongoloids than would be expected in normal pregnancies. The father's age, apparently, makes no difference.

When the first child is a Mongoloid, a longer interval between marriage and the pregnancy occurred than is usually expected. A longer pregnancy free interval also preceded and followed the birth of a Mongoloid than between normal births of the same birth order before and after the Mongoloid. Families who have a Mongoloid are not, as generally believed, large families. Rarely are there more than four children; often only one. These facts suggest a temporary depression in the ability of these mothers to reproduce.

The relatively uniform clinical picture of the Mongoloid, or as has been often noted, "they all look alike," would suggest that the same cause must always produce such a child. For this reason, any deviation from normal in the condition of the mother during pregnancy might offer a clue to the matter. Oster in Denmark, and Benda in this country have made careful observations on many Mongoloids, including the mothers' conditions during pregnancy. These studies covered many years.

While the largest group of mothers are over forty, almost as many are under forty (45%). In mothers under forty who give birth to Mongoloids, the most significant deviations from normal during pregnancy were inability to become pregnant and bleeding during pregnancy. More than one half of these mothers had menstrual irregularities. In almost all of them there was an interval of from three to twelve years between the last two pregnancies.

Benda also found that some of these mothers had thyroid disorders. Thyroid disorder was particularly noted in the very young age group (eighteen to twenty). Benda suggested that the factors which cause the development of a Mongoloid child interfere with the endocrine environment of the fetus, and that either the mother's pituitary gland or ovary is at fault.

Whatever the cause or causes of mongolism may be, they produce a deformity that appears to be an arrest in the development of the child who continues to retain fetal characteristics. Ingalls has shown that this damaging process may occur at about the eighth embryonic week of fetal life. Mongoloids appear as the result of some process that may be toxic, endocrine, or chemical that has caused a temporary cessation of their development and to their production as unfinished children. They are deprived of proper growth in body and mind.

This temporary cessation of their development results in the characteristic physical features that are so frequent, and that differ so much from those seen in other mental defectives and normal children, that science is justified in considering them as set apart from others. Of these physical features the most frequent centers in the eye region, and gives the condition its name. A lack of development of the orbital ridges gives a flattened appearance to the face. The eye sockets are small and slanting. This condition, further accentuated by a fold of skin in the epicanthus, gives the characteristic slant eyes. A tendency for this characteristic to become less apparent with advancing age has not been noted. The iris of the eye is frequently speckled.

The forehead is wrinkled, a condition which persists through adult life. The head, round and frequently flattened, also persists. The sutures and fontanelles are large at birth, and remain open much longer than in normal children. The hair of the head, which is very fine and silky in infancy and childhood, grows sparse and rough with age. The ears are frequently deformed and have a low position on the head. The mouth is invariably open, and the tongue is rough and furrowed. The teeth erupt late and are irregular. Mongoloids also show a high incidence of caries. The neck is usually short and the chest is frequently deformed. The abdomen is protruding. The genitalia are almost always small and underdeveloped. Congenital heart defects are present in almost half of these children. The skin, fine and soft during infancy, becomes dry and scaly later in childhood, and in older children is frequently cyanotic on the extremities. Very frequently the cheeks are red.

Two other signs are found with as great a frequency as the eye findings. The first of these is the extreme relaxation and flexibility of the joints. A lack of general muscle tone is distinctive in these children even in infancy. Frequently the nurse for the newborn will say, "This child feels like a rag doll." This limp condition is believed to be caused by a functional inferiority of the central nervous system. The second sign is the short, broad hand with a crooked little finger, and absence of the second line across the palm of the hand. The feet are also short and thick with a marked distance between the first and second toes. Webbed toes are common, and the crease on the sole of the foot persists.

Usually Mongoloids are smaller than normal for their age group. They weigh less at birth, gain poorly the first year, and often are only two thirds the weight of normal children. They remain smaller through childhood and adult life. Smallness of stature seems to be a part of their general condition, although it may in part be caused by malnutrition. Because they tire easily, have great difficulty in swallowing and cannot chew, they nurse poorly in infancy and take solid foods poorly. If solid foods are begun at the age they are usually given to normal children, and if Mongoloids are forced to take them, vomiting and diarrhea result. Consequently, their food intake is inadequate for their age and development. (They have a low resistance and contract frequent infections). In childhood they tend to have frequent colds, and eye infections. This tendency is overcome later in life.

Their skeleton is also delayed in growth, resulting in a slowness of epiphyseal centers to ossify, in delicate bones, and in lack of development of the middle phalanx of the little finger. The skull will occasionally show a failure to develop in length. (The blood, urine, and basal metabolism are all normal.) Sometimes the blood cholesterol will be elevated. Changes have been observed in the brain, particularly a demyelinization of the nerve cells, and in the pituitary body.

Mongoloid babies are very quiet and sleep most of the time. Since they cry very infrequently, many mothers remark, "It is the best baby we ever had." When awake they are apathetic and appear weak. This apathetic appearance is not due to lack of muscle power, but to an immaturity of the nervous system. Physical response requires a more powerful stimulation than is necessary for a normal infant.

They rarely sit up before the end of the first year, and do not crawl until about eighteen months of age. Walking is frequently delayed until three years of age, and even to five years. A normal child will spread its feet wide apart when it begins to walk. The Mongoloid will continue to spread its feet wide apart until almost ten years of age. Many will always walk in this manner, and their arm movements will continue to be clumsy and awkward. Since they never achieve good motor control, all are clumsy from the viewpoint of motor perfection.

Speech is also delayed, and develops usually one or two years after walking. Pronunciation is always clumsy, and indistinct. Mongoloids have difficulty in pronouncing certain letters. This faulty enunciation is further accentuated by their voices which remain harsh and low. Although the vocabulary will depend on the individual child, in the majority of cases it will remain at a two to three year old level. Others who have had training and good surroundings may acquire a larger vocabulary.

Emotionally they are lovable little children who are full of affection and tenderness. They play well with other children and exhibit no sadistic traits. Only if teased will they resort to any retaliation. However, they are invariably stubborn. They resent any deviation from their regular pattern. This resentment is caused by their inability to shift rapidly from any object or situation and to react to new impressions. This inability must always be borne in mind. While this tendency may be overcome in certain conditions by great patience, it remains a fundamental trait in all new situations.

Almost as characteristic as their stubbornness is their gift of mimicry. An attribute of the normal child between the ages of two and four years, in the Mongoloid it is a manifestation of protracted infancy. The wise parent may take full advantage of this attribute to use it to teach all sorts of useful and necessary manipulations.

In sensory development Mongoloids are frequently short-sighted and astigmatic. Their sense of smell is poor; however, they hear very well, and are particularly fond of music. Although they will listen to the same piece of music for hours, the rhythm, and not the tune, interests them. Their touch, pain, heat and cold sensations are not well developed, and they will easily burn themselves or acquire skin infections from not calling attention to their difficulties.

In their mental development the Mongoloids represent an example of infantilism and have been termed unfinished children. In the usual idiot or imbecile, mental development is arrested at a certain mental age. The Mongoloid is an infant or child who is never arrested at any mental age, but whose progression is so slow that he is still an infant during childhood, and only a child when development comes to an end. In other words, the Mongoloid is an infant for the first ten years of its life, and a child for the rest of it. The Mongoloid takes ten years to accomplish what a normal child does in two.

Although it may seem unfair to grade a Mongoloid by bare statistical examinations, intelligence is rated that way. The majority of these children will show an average I.Q. by the Binet method of from two to six years. The highest tests recorded are 10.8 years. The majority of Mongoloids will eventually reach an intelligence quotient of between thirty-five and forty-five, and only a few will go beyond a mental age of five to six years. Although administration of glutamic acid formulas and other treatments may produce a temporary increase in performance, permanent increase in intellectual capacity cannot be achieved. This fact should be fully explained to the parents so that they eventually will not be disappointed by the very slow progress made.

Present medical knowledge offers no satisfactory treatment to correct Mongoloid idiocy itself. Severe malformations with which these children are so frequently associated, such as eye cataracts and congenital heart disease make it more difficult to assess the results of earlier methods of medication and treatment. The earliest form of medication used was thyroid gland substance. Its success with the cretin or thyroid deficient child gave some hope for Mongoloids, but the results of this treatment have been disappointing. Some of these infants seem to be improved temporarily by the drug, particularly those that are slow and listless and have a tendency to constipation. Small amounts of thyroid usually, temporarily, will relieve the condition which produces these symptoms. Some of the thin and active, restless Mongoloid types will gain weight and become more quiet. Usually small quantities of the gland are sufficient.

Pituitary gland, extracts and whole gland, have been used. The majority of those who have used them feel that they are of no great value. Benda, however, who has had the most experience with such treatment, feels that it is beneficial if used over a long period of time. Although they may cause weight gain, adrenocorticotrophic substances also appear to have little influence on the general condition.

Glutamic acid, while successful in white rats who are able to perform maze tests more accurately and faster than those not given the drug, has been used in Mongoloids; but the general opinion is that it is not very helpful. Such large doses (24 to 48 gms.) are necessary that most children refuse to take the medication. Although intake of glutamic acid may raise the I.Q. performance slightly, to raise an I.Q. of forty-five to fifty-five does not cause much practical change. Only in the more intelligent Mongoloids who are able to receive some schooling is this treatment an aid. However, it must be emphasized again that these results are far below those achieved by a normal child.

[Actually, it is by general care that these unfortunate children can be helped most.] [Perhaps the most critical point in these children in infancy is their poor heat regulation mechanism and their poor resistance to respiratory tract infections.] They will have frequent colds and bronchial infections. They should be kept warmer than other children, and exposure to cold should be avoided. If respiratory or other infections develop, the infections can be controlled with sulfonamides and antibiotics which these children take very well. The chronic respiratory infections always cause an enlargement of the tonsils and adenoids. Most parents will want these removed, believing them to be a cause of the difficulty. Removal will have little influence on the infections, and may make matters worse. At about ten to fourteen years of age when the bridge of the nose develops, the nasal passages open up and the condition frequently is improved.

(Mongoloids always eat poorly and gain very slowly. It is a grave mistake to attempt to increase their food intake or give richer mixtures than average. Since Mongoloids usually will tolerate carbohydrates well, these can be increased to compensate for a reduction of the fats which are poorly digested.) They may require smaller feedings at shorter intervals than normal children. Solid foods should be introduced into the diet much later than with the average infant as they take a spoon and cup poorly.

(The decision whether a Mongoloid child should be placed in an institution or cared for in the home depends on the family situation.) Where formerly it was thought expedient to remove the child from the family at once, the present crowding of our mental institutions make this impossible for some period of time. (Re-examination of the problem has led many physicians to believe that these children may be better cared for in the family.) [Many also feel that if institutionalization is necessary, it can be done better at a later time.]

(Some difficulties are that parents may sacrifice the whole family in spending their money and time on the Mongoloid child. This neglect of the normal children is unfortunate. If it cannot be impressed on the parents that their duty is to all of their children, the Mongoloid had better be placed elsewhere. If the Mongoloid is the oldest child in the family, the younger siblings will surpass it in ability and present a difficult problem. Sometimes, if the Mongoloid is a younger member of a family, the older siblings may feel that their friends hesitate to visit them because of such a child. Older sisters may feel that their chances of marriage are lessened. These feelings should be recognized. If the Mongoloid is an only child, or if the age interval between the siblings is great, it can easily stay at home and benefit from the attention given it. Inasmuch as Mongoloid children learn from imitation and by the example set by others, their association in an institution with other feebleminded children, usually of lower intelligence, retards their development.

Continually during the early years it must be kept in mind that the child is developing more slowly and needs more time than the average child. Nothing is sadder than to see parents try to force a Mongoloid child to act up to the capacity of a normal child. Crying roughly at them and even using physical force will only make such children cower in fear and become incapable of doing anything. Such an attitude on the part of the adult is not only bad for the child, but it communicates itself to the older siblings and neighborhood children.

Up to the age of eight, Mongoloids must be considered as preschool children. Their development is about half that of the normal child. They cannot enter school at the usual age of six. Some may be at kindergarten level by six, and may even be at a first grade level by eight years. Since by this time they are too old for their class group, special training will have to be given them.

They have a good memory and can learn to spell and develop a fair speaking and listening vocabulary; however, reading is doubtful. Since Mongoloids have no conception of arithmetic, they never can handle money. The main goal for an attempt at education should be to train them for practical skills. They can learn to be helpful about the house, and in rural communities they can do many useful outdoor tasks.

That most of these children have a very short life span should always be kept in mind. However, if they do attain adult life, and it is apparent in their teens that they will have to be institutionalized, it is better to admit them then than to wait until they are twenty or over. At that time adjustment may be difficult

✱ (The Mongoloid child is influenced from an emotional standpoint by the same factors that are essential to the development of normal children.) (This child needs love, affection and patience. A lack of these will considerably influence its development. If the child is loved, it is trusting, quiet and lovable, and has no difficulty in establishing contact with its surroundings, and securing interest and affection from others. If the family will look on the child as a handicapped brother or sister who needs special love and consideration, a great deal can be accomplished.)

THE CHILD WITH PROGRESSIVE MUSCULAR DYSTROPHY

E. G. MURPHY, M.B., B.S., D.C.H.

INTEREST and research in progressive muscular dystrophy, a disease of the voluntary muscles, have increased greatly during recent years largely because of the efforts of the members of muscular dystrophy associations in the United States and Canada to publicize the story of this disease and to organize financial support. The emotional and financial help that the members of these associations have been able to provide not only has given aid and comfort to individual patients, but also has sustained continuing research in muscle disorders. The research data which have been secured encourages the hope that a rational treatment for the disease will be developed.

Muscular dystrophy is a slowly progressive disease of the voluntary muscles. Involuntary muscles, such as control the movements of the intestines, are not involved with one exception: the heart muscles in a form of muscular dystrophy whose incidence is slight. As the disease becomes more progressive, all muscles which normally can be controlled by voluntary action are finally involved. Slow degeneration of muscle structure occurs. This slow degeneration is manifested clinically by observed weakness and wasting and by contracture formation as the muscles become replaced by fat and fibrous tissue. The nervous system is not affected. The term, "muscular atrophy," is used to differentiate the weakness and wasting or paralysis which occurs secondary to diseases of the nervous system, to disuse, and to chronic debilitating illnesses.

The exact incidence of muscular dystrophy is not known. Since the condition is not an infectious disease, systematic reporting is not required. Results of various recent surveys suggest, however, that the incidence is approximately one case in twenty-two thousand in the general population. Such incidence appears to vary in different parts of the world. In the state of Utah, for instance, the known incidence is one case in five hundred. Estimates of the total numbers of cases in the United States vary between 100,000 and 200,000. More than half of the known cases of muscular dystrophy are children between the ages of three and thirteen. Most of these children die before reaching adulthood.

Muscular dystrophy may present itself in many different ways according to the type and age of onset. The following is a list of early diagnostic features:

1. History of falling frequently and inability to keep up with contemporaries physically.

2. Waddling gait and difficulty in climbing stairs.

3. The characteristic method of arising from a supine position.

4. Hypertrophy of the calves in the Duchenne type.

5. Typical facial appearance in the facioscapulohumeral and myotonic types.

6. A flabby baby with delayed physical landmarks in infancy and childhood.

The clearly recognized fact about muscular dystrophy is that the disease is genetically determined, not in any way acquired. Though the actual mode of inheritance varies with the different types of dystrophy, study of a sufficiently broad sample of cases indicates that the affected individual is born with a genetic defect which leads to degeneration of muscle fibres. Some metabolic error apparently produces a condition which does not allow muscles to sustain a normal state of health. Even though the disease may not become apparent for several years, thirty or forty per cent of the cases studied reveal an obvious inheritance factor. Although most cases fall into well defined groups, exceptions and variations occur quite frequently. Cases occurring in any one family almost certainly breed true to the type of the disease, to the mode of inheritance, and to other clinical features.

The classification of muscular dystrophy in six major clinical types is of considerable importance from a prognostic point of view. The Duchenne, a pseudohypertrophic type of muscular dystrophy whose onset of symptoms usually occurs during the first five years of life, is the most common. The facioscapulohumeral muscular dystrophy affecting both sexes equally, is inherited by a dominant factor which is not sex-linked. The limb girdle type, characterized by the development of a waddling gait during adolescence, is less common. The ocular type of muscular dystrophy which confines wasting to the external muscles of the eyes is familial, and develops during the first four decades of life. The familial distal type of muscular dystrophy, where the forearms and legs are affected before the upper arms and thighs, occurs usually after the age of thirty. The myotonic atrophies, which involve other organs beside the muscles in the clinical picture, form a sixth separate type.

The onset of the Duchenne type of muscular dystrophy is very insidious. The affected child may develop normally for the first two or three years. He may sit, stand, and walk as well as a normal child. He may be late or slow in his physical development, and he may be unusually awkward in his physical activity. Because the changes may not be conspicuous, the disease may not be detected for three or four years, or until the child is not able to keep up with his contemporaries.

Muscles which are earliest affected are the ones controlling the shoulders and hips. The upper arms are affected before the forearms and legs. The calves may appear bulky at an early stage of the disease, but they remain relatively strong. The child may develop a concave back, a gait waddling in character, and experience considerable difficulty in ascending stairs.

Since the progress of the disease is relatively rapid, the child may be severely crippled by adolescence. He may succumb to respiratory infection before the age of twenty because curvature of the spine and distortion of the chest may reduce the capacity to resist. Contracture formation, a feature of this type of dystrophy, occasionally may occur early to produce distortions and restrictions of movement. These contractures, particularly favored by inactivity and maintenance of fixed positions for long periods of time, most often occur in the lower extremities, drawing the feet downwards and inwards. Any injury or unrelated illness which necessitates confinement to bed or requires relative inactivity will hasten the process of the disease and contracture formation.

Males are affected much more frequently than females, and the disease may be transmitted by the female to appear in the male. This sex-linked recessive mode of inheritance is the same as occurs in hemophilia. This type of dystrophy frequently occurs sporadically where no family history has been evident. Remissions probably do not occur. Though periods may occur during which the disease seems almost static from the clinical point of view, objective testing and recording usually indicate some progressive dystrophy.

The onset of the facioscapulohumeral type of muscular dystrophy, a type where the muscles of the face, shoulder girdle, and upper arms are affected before there is a gradual spread finally involving all the voluntary muscles, is usually in adolescence. The course of the disease is slow and compatible with a normal life span. Occasionally cases are seen with an onset during the first few years of life. In these cases the progression of the disease is more rapid and the disablement more profound. Commonly, facial involvement with a flattening of features and with immobile expression occurs much earlier than the involvement of the muscles of the shoulder girdle. As the disease progresses, a striking wasting of the muscles of the shoulder and upper arm and a winging of the shoulder blades becomes noticeable. The size and strength of the forearms may remain satisfactory for many years. Cardiac involvement is said not to occur in this form of muscular dystrophy. Involvement of the respiratory muscles is not conspicuous. Disability gradually becomes quite considerable but ambulation is usually maintained.

Some individuals may be affected mildly and in a limited non-progressive fashion. Their only manifestation may be a flattening of facial features or a little shoulder girdle weakness. Recognition of these cases is important so that hereditary factors may be considered.

The limb girdle type of muscular dystrophy is more difficult to recognize. In early adolescence the patient develops a waddling gait though weakness and wasting of other muscles is not conspicuous. The rate of progression of this type of dystrophy is midway between the Duchenne and the facioscapulohumeral.

The sexes are equally affected, and severe disablement and premature death is to be expected. Inheritance is probably by a recessive factor.

The phenomenon which gives its name to myotonic dystrophies is characterized by prolonged contractions and slow relaxation of muscle fibres or muscle groups, and may be confined to some muscle groups or may involve all voluntary muscles. When an affected individual shakes hands, for instance, he is unable to relax his grip for a considerable time. The dystrophic process involves the face first of all. Distal limb muscles are next affected. The spread is central, the onset occurring in the first three decades of life. Observers have noted atrophy of the sex glands, low fertility rates, cataracts, and premature baldness. A high incidence of subnormal intelligence not associated with other types of muscular dystrophy, has been noted. Males and females are equally affected, and inheritance is by a dominant factor.

Since weakness and wasting of muscles may precede the myotonic phenomenon, these cases may have the appearance of a pure form of distal muscle disease or myopathy. However, the age of onset is earlier, and the family history is more positive. On the other hand myotonia may occur in infancy without conspicuous muscle wasting or involvement of other muscle systems. Such symptoms describe myotonia congenita or Thompson's disease. Though it is debatable whether these symptoms constitute a separate classification, muscle wasting and weakness and sex gland atrophy are claimed to occur eventually.

Many conditions may be confused with muscular dystrophy. In infancy and early childhood, progressive muscular atrophy of Werdnig-Hoffman may resemble muscular dystrophy though the condition is usually more rapid in its course and the muscular atrophy secondary to a disease of the nerves. Numerous conditions may cause a very flabby so-called hypertonic baby. Many of these conditions can be treated and recovery brought about. Some babies born with contractures and poorly developed muscles later on in life may present a picture which closely resembles the contracture stages of muscular dystrophy.

Probably the most important condition to differentiate from muscular dystrophy is an inflammatory disease of muscle called polymyositis. This myositis is not secondary to a virus or a parasitic agent, but is a disorder generally grouped with the collagen diseases such as rheumatism. The skin and the nerves may be affected in addition to the muscles.

Myositis occurring in childhood closely resembles the Duchenne or childhood type of muscular dystrophy. Although the clinical course is extremely variable, the onset of myositis is fairly rapid in childhood so that the child may become quite weak and disabled after three or four months. In addition the child may often appear ill and lacking in energy in contrast with the child with muscular dystrophy who at least for a few years will appear to be in quite good health and quite active within his limits. Skin involvement may not be conspicuous. When skin involvement does occur, a butterfly area over the face and bridge of the nose and reddened areas over the lower part of the neck and upper part of the chest and over the elbow regions may be identifying symptoms. Although polymyositis in childhood is quite often associated with spontaneous recovery, the use of ACTH and the cortisone group of drugs is indicated.

Myositis occurring in adults may resemble the facioscapulohumeral type of muscular dystrophy. The condition is more insidious and slow in its course than in childhood. Less liable to spontaneous remissions and less amenable to treatment, the condition responds to treatment successfully only in a certain percentage of cases.

Polymyositis must be differentiated from muscular dystrophy because of its different origin, its different prognosis, and its different amenability to treatment. Cases of polymyositis must be eliminated from trials of various forms of therapy on muscular dystrophy. Examination of a piece of muscle under a microscope will show signs of inflammatory changes rather than purely degenerative changes as seen in muscular dystrophy. In relatively early stages of the disease microscopic examination of the muscle will aid in differentiating muscular dystrophy from polymyositis and both these conditions from muscular degeneration secondary to nerve lesions. In late stages of these conditions microscopic examination may be less helpful because of replacement of muscle tissue by fat and fibrous tissue. So-called cures of muscular dystrophy and the few cases that have been reported in the literature of spontaneous recoveries from muscular dystrophy may really have been cases of polymyositis.

The electromyogram is also useful in differentiating nerve from muscle causes of weakness and wasting. Just as the electrocardiogram records the electrical activity of the heart and the electroencephalogram records the electrical activity of the brain, the electromyogram records the electrical activity of the muscle. Since surface electrodes are not so efficient, needle electrodes are usually placed in the muscle to detect the electrical activity The electromyogram of dystrophic muscles shows broken up and irregular small potentials on voluntary contraction. Myositis will give very much the same picture. However, disease or injury to the nerve supplying the muscle will give rise to spontaneous electrical potentials with the muscle at rest. Myotonia will give rise to runs of high frequency potentials. Since the electromyogram is difficult to interpret, the technique requires the assistance of an experienced electromyographer and the results must be aligned with the total clinical picture.

Because the chance of having another child affected with the same disease is frequently uppermost in the minds of parents of a child having muscular dystrophy, the Genetic Department of the Hospital for Sick Children, Toronto, attempts to secure a detailed family tree. On the basis of these investigations, about thirty per cent of the cases of Duchenne type of muscular dystrophy, the commonest type in the pediatric group, indicate a clear cut family history indicating that this type is inherited as a sex-linked recessive trait. The disease is transmitted by healthy women who are genetic carriers. On the average half of the sons of such carriers will be affected and half of the daughters will be carriers like their mothers. The pedigree in Figure I illustrated a family where the disease was transmitted in a sex-linked recessive manner. On the other hand, the majority of the patients with the Duchenne type of muscular dystrophy have a negative family history. In about 70% of all cases the patient is the only one in the family to be affected. An idea of the risk of having another child with the same disease may be determined by calculating the proportion of affected individuals among the brothers born after a sporadic

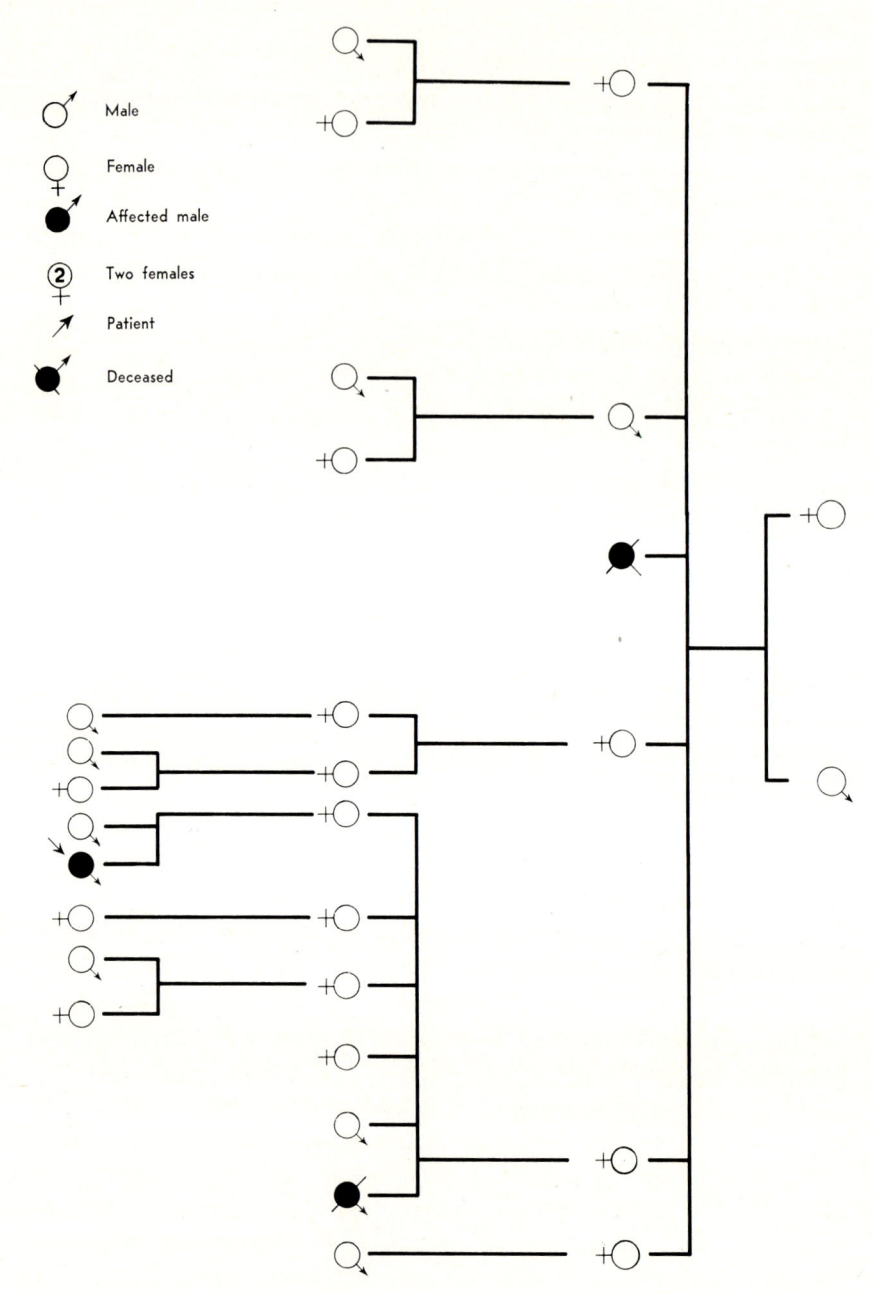

FIGURE 1. Inheritance of Duchenne muscular dystrophy. (*Hospital for Sick Children, Department of Genetics, Pedigree M113.*)

case of muscular dystrophy has been diagnosed. In a relatively small series at the Hospital for Sick Children the risk figure is about 21%. A woman has a chance of about one in five that any subsequent sons will be affected.

The facioscapulohumeral type of muscular dystrophy which is more commonly seen in late childhood and adult life is inherited by a dominant mechanism. About 60% of cases have a family history. As illustrated in Figure 2, the affected parent in a family where the disease has occurred previously stands half a chance of transmitting the disease to subsequent children regardless of sex. Owing to the relatively late onset of the disease, statistics are incomplete since there may be members of the family in whom the disease has not made itself manifest. As the disease is so much milder in its manifestations than the Duchenne type of dystrophy, from a practical point of view parents need not be so concerned. Other types of muscular dystrophy are so very rare that their mode of inheritance provides only academic interest.

As yet no specific treatment for muscular dystrophy has been developed. However, that the tremendous weight of research in muscle disorders will yield a useful specific therapeutic agent in the not too distant future is a justifiable hope. A great number of preparations have been given without producing any (statistically) significant effect on the course of the disease. These preparations have included vitamins, enzymes, amino acids, proteins, sugars, hormones, antibiotics, and various diets. That therapeutic trials should be very carefully controlled and rechecked and that the patient should be carefully diagnosed and investigated to exclude cases of myositis is clear. Allowance must be made for the transitory psychological benefits of any new form of treatment.

Personality difficulties and other problems in the child result mainly from family attitudes. The natural tendency for parents to be over-protective may lead to emotional immaturity in the child. The overprotected child tends to become inactive, to lose interest in his work and play, to lack independence and confidence. He may eventually become rather spoiled and display temper tantrums. The child does not require pity. He requires affection and understanding. Satisfactory personality adjustment as in normal childhood is dependent on secure family relationships.

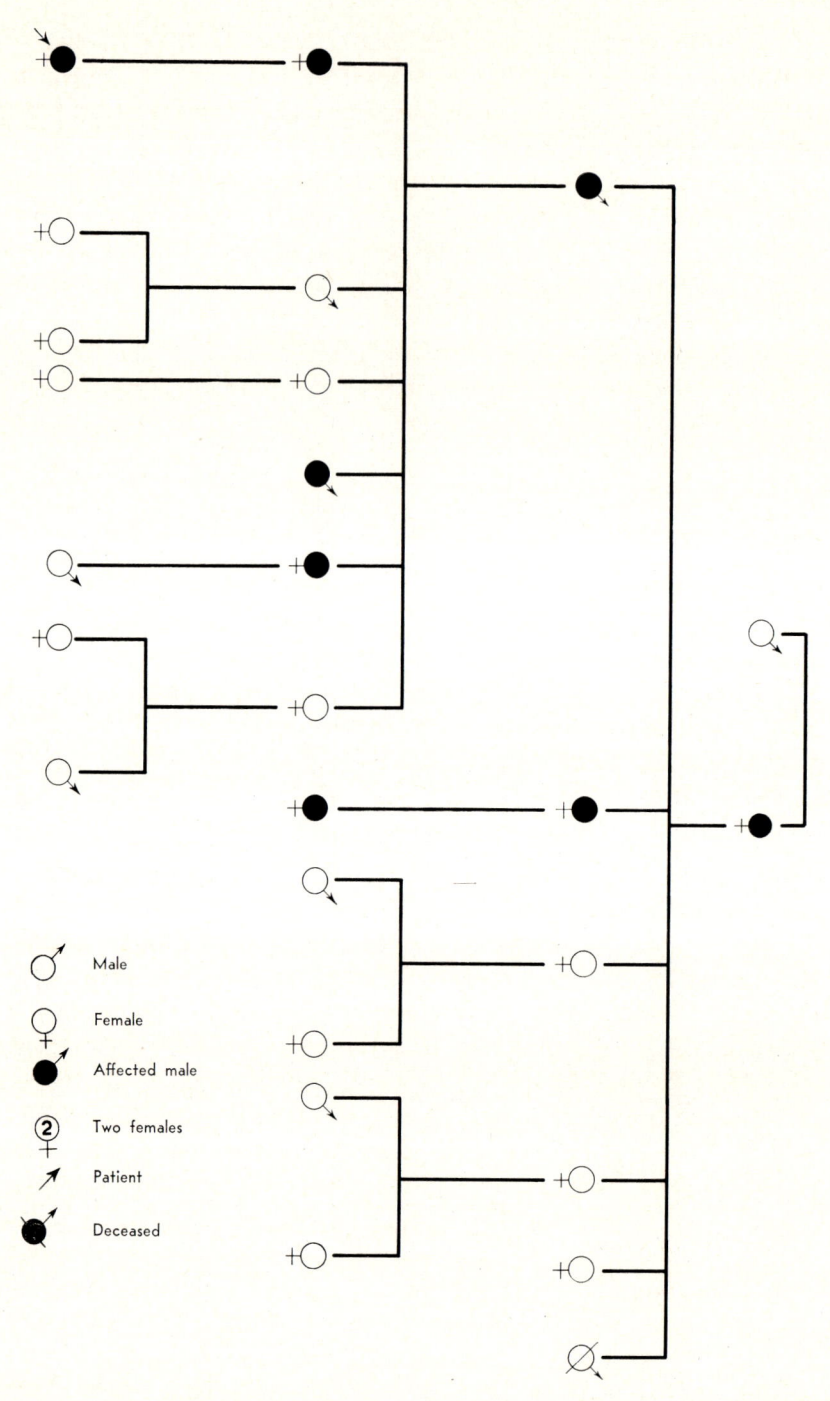

FIGURE 2. Inheritance of Facioscapulohumeral muscular dystrophy. (*Hospital for Sick Children, Department of Genetics, Pedigree M31.*)

The child's wish for independence should be respected and encouraged at all stages of the disease. Aside from special needs produced by his handicap, he should be accepted in a normal give and take relationship with the rest of the family. When the child is obviously disturbed by an inability to keep up with his contemporaries or when school attendance involves climbing stairs, he should be transferred to a school for crippled children. When lifting and nursing care become a problem, institutional or residential care is indicated. The child does not suffer directly from his disease. For the most part, he may be remarkably unaware of the nature or the significance of the disease process. Of course, some children do not adapt well. Some may require psychiatric help. The extent, however, to which most children adjust to their increasing disability is remarkable.

Although no specific treatment for muscular dystrophy has as yet been developed, the affected child and his parents may require a great deal of help and support. The mobility of the child may be maintained through physiotherapy. The formation of contractures can be slowed down and minimized to some extent. Disuse atrophy can be prevented by keeping muscles working to their capacity. In later stages of the disease, breathing exercises can maintain vital chest capacity, frequently found to be reduced by as much as 50%. Transportation may need to be provided. Special appliances, a wheel chair, or a lifting device may need to be purchased. Special arrangements to continue schooling through home to school telephone communication may need to be effected. Assistance with coping with the emotional factors may be most urgent. The happiness and the satisfactory adjustment of the family may require the concerted effort of the physician, the physiotherapist, the occupational therapist, the social worker, the teacher, and the resources of the local muscular dystrophy association. Each has a vital part to play in a comprehensive program. The medical profession and the community, working together, can help the child and the family to achieve a measure of happiness.

READINGS

1. Abramson, Arthur S.: *An Approach to the Rehabilitation of Children with Muscular Dystrophy.* Muscular Dystrophy Associations of America Inc.

2. Adams, R. D. H., Brown, Danny D., and Pearson, C. M.: *Diseases of Muscle*. Hoeber, New York, 1954.
3. Morrow, Robert S., and Cohen, Jacob: *The Psychological Factors in Muscular Dystrophy*. Muscular Dystrophy Associations of America, Inc., New York.
4. *Proceedings:* First, Second, and Third Medical Conferences, 1951, 1952, 1954, Muscular Dystrophy Associations of America, Inc., New York.

Literature pertaining to muscular dystrophy may be obtained from the Muscular Dystrophy Associations of America, Inc., 1790 Broadway, New York 19, New York.

THE CHILD WITH NEPHROSIS

Conrad M. Riley, M.D.

The term "handicapped child" is popularly reserved to describe the youngster with some visible deformity, such as a congenitally deformed limb, a persistent blueness resulting from a defective heart, atrophied muscles produced by poliomyelitis, or some other obviously incapacitating affliction. Until recently no state has included nephrosis in its list of acceptable diagnoses.

Child nephrosis is a condition which affects the general well-being of a moderate number of small children for periods varying from a year up to five to seven years. The outcome may be a complete return to normal health, a quiescent period of indefinite duration with only persistent abnormal laboratory findings, or a slowly progressive total deterioration of kidney function. At the beginning of the disease there is no way of being sure into which group an individual patient may fall.

Although the planning of the overall management of a child with nephrosis is primarily the responsibility of the physician, the long drawn out condition in which the patient spends much of his time beyond the direct purview of the doctor necessitates that most of the carrying out of the plans will have to be delegated to others. This delegation of responsibility to others emphasizes the importance of the widespread recognition of nephrosis as a handicapping condition by all persons dealing with children with handicaps. Such individuals who may render important assistance if well enough informed may range all the way from close friends of the family, through school teachers, to professional persons more closely allied to the medical profession, such as social workers and nurses.

The therapeutic value of well-informed parents is considerable in the overall treatment of the patient. The education of such parents should begin with the doctor, but the ability of any parent fully to grasp such a complicated subject at an interview or two may be limited. Further information will be sought from all sources which may be available.

NEPHROSIS DEFINED

The term *nephrosis* is one which by derivation does not have the same meaning as current usuage has given to it. Its Greek root *nephrosis* means simply a "condition of the kidney." In medical writings the term has been applied to kidney conditions resulting from chemical poisoning, from shock-like state following severe injury, from mechanical blocking of the outflow tracts for urine. The term is used in this chapter to refer to a disorder of unknown origin which causes the kidneys to leak a great deal of protein from the blood stream producing a lowered concentration of protein in the blood serum and associated with a tremendous increase in the amount of fat in the serum. In time: (1) this disorder; (2) this leakage; (3) this lowered concentration of protein; (4) this tremendous increase in the amount of fat, may give rise to damage to all the kidney functions, but this is characteristically absent early in the disease. The qualification that the condition is "of unknown origin" is important because there is a similar picture associated with several other known diseases or resulting from certain poisons.

The term *nephrosis* is most often confused with the term *nephritis*. Though in some instances the two conditions overlap and are difficult or impossible to separate, usually the conditions are quite distinct since they represent opposite ends of a spectrum. The very fact that they sometimes do seem to be on the same spectrum, however, justifies an inclusive terminology. Reverting to the historical name of "Bright's disease" has much to commend it.

DESCRIPTION OF NEPHROSIS

Nephrosis has always run a variable course in different children, but in the past 5 to 7 years it has become even more variable as the result of reasonably effective treatment. Nephrosis usually involves small children, rarely in the early months of life, most frequently in youngsters between 18 months and 3½ to 4 years of age (Fig. 1). However, the condition may develop at any

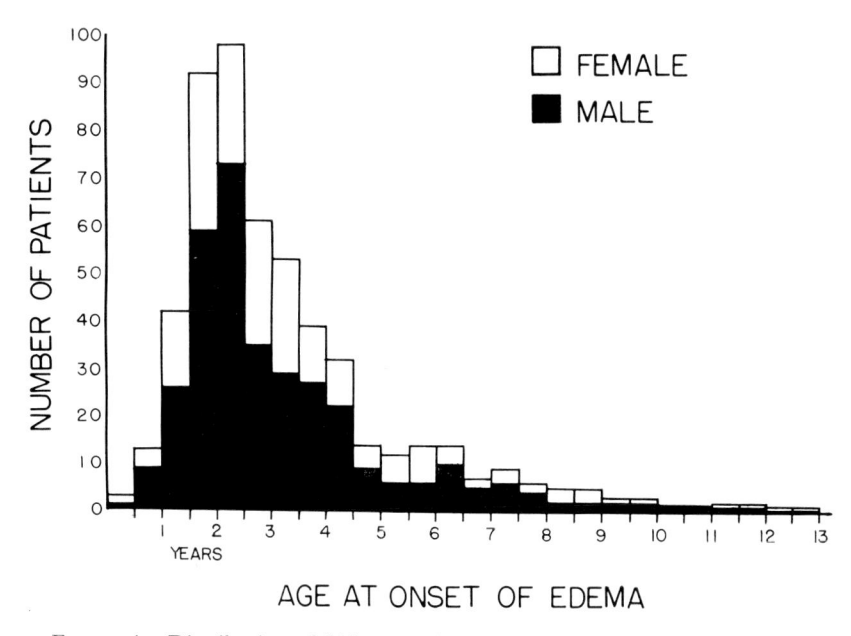

FIGURE 1. Distribution of 534 cases of childhood nephrosis by age and sex at time of onset of edema. (*Pediatric Clinics of North America*, August, 1955.)

time throughout childhood or adult life, occasional cases being seen to begin in 60 to 70 year old persons. For unknown reasons it occurs more commonly among boys than among girls, the ratio being approximately 2 to 1. No particular racial predisposition, geographical preponderance, or climate seems to influence its frequency. Though a slight tendency for nephrosis to repeat in families has been noted, the incidence is not great enough to label it as a familial disease, or to advise parents not to have more children if they have had one case of it. The estimated incidence of nephrosis in the general population is on the order of one new case per year per 200,000 total (adult and child) population. In contrast to this we see a second case cropping up in the same family 1–2% of the time. No particular body type among the patients has been noted. In fact, no real common denominator to help predict who is likely to develop nephrosis has been determined.

The first manifestations of the disease are signs of swelling, usually a little puffiness around the eyes appearing in the early morning and disappearing as the day progresses. As time goes on the eye swelling remains all day, and swelling of the feet and abdomen are next noticed. Associated with this, the particularly observant parent notices that the child's appetite has slackened, that the child tires a little more easily than previously, and that the child is more fretful. Sometimes all these conditions are ushered in by a cold or a minor infection, but the youngster does not seem very sick and does not run a fever. These early changes may be so gradual that the parents may not even seek doctor's advice for days or weeks after the first signs appear.

Occasionally the doctor will not take the first manifestations too seriously, attributing the puffy eyes to "an allergy" as, indeed, many transient swellings around the eyes really are. Fortunately, such a failure in diagnosis is not critical since, though early diagnosis is probably important with regard to starting treatment, such early diagnosis is measured in terms of weeks, or months, not of days. If the condition really is nephrosis and not an allergy, the swelling will increase to a point where no one could mistake it. The doctor can almost establish the diagnosis through a urine test. A large amount of protein not found in the urine of normal children will be present. To complete the evidence chemical tests will show a decreased amount of protein and in increased amount of fatty substances (particularly cholesterol) in the blood serum drawn from the vein.

Before the days of modern treatment, which has been effective in recent years, most patients affected by nephrosis progressed to marked generalized body swelling or "edema," their "tummies" ballooning out like a pregnant woman's. Patients often gained 25–50% more than their usual body weight. They presented a very distressing appearance with their eyes sometimes being swollen shut, or the scrotum of little boys ballooning out to the size of an orange or a grapefruit. With some patients the swelling came and went in periods of several weeks; in others it persisted, being relieved only by "tapping" the abdomen with a hollow needle at frequent intervals. Meanwhile, with the ingenuousness of childhood, the patient remained reasonably happy and only the parents would be distressed by the distorting swelling and the youngster's "bird-like" appetite.

Such a state of affairs often persisted for weeks, months, or even, in a few instances, years before the eagerly hoped for "diuresis" set in. Diuresis, a phenomenon during which the patient passed tremendous amounts of urine, saw the grotesque swelling melt away in the course of a few days. When this happened, the patient shrank from a bloated unrecognizable child to a sunken-eyed unrecognizable waif. Soon balance would be restored and the victim would appear normal. When this series of events occurred no one could be sure how long the remission or improvement would last. In some instances recovery was permanent; more often there would be respite for only a few weeks or months. In other cases death ensued after months or years of constant swelling.

In addition to the disfigurement produced by the swelling the sudden infection to which nephrotic patients are unusually prone, most often in the abdominal cavity (peritonitis), was an ever present hazard. Before suitable treatment for this complication was available, it was the commonest cause of death. Since the introduction of "sulfa drugs" in the late thirties and the later development of the modern antibiotics, death due to infection has become relatively rare. The ability to treat infections did not reduce the mortality from the disease in any significant degree. Another fatal complication, serious damage to the kidneys, became the most frequent cause of death. After a year or 18 months of the disease, many children began to show by their chemical tests that their kidneys were not functioning as they should. Death would supervene because of renal failure six months to a year later.

The clinical picture of the patient in renal failure was, and still is, a tragic one. Most often the time elapsed from the first signs of serious kidney damage to death was 6 months to a year or so. In such cases the patient retained his edema to the end and his decline was marked by increasing weakness, anemia requiring transfusions, and finally, near the end, vomiting. Terminally the heart appeared to become overtaxed so that death at last ensued. Rare cases existed in children, however, and more frequently in adults, where edema was lost as the failure of kidney function became apparent. When this occurred the decline was much more prolonged, and the patient may have lived several years. Under these circumstances growth was affected. Though he may not have suffered pain or major dis-

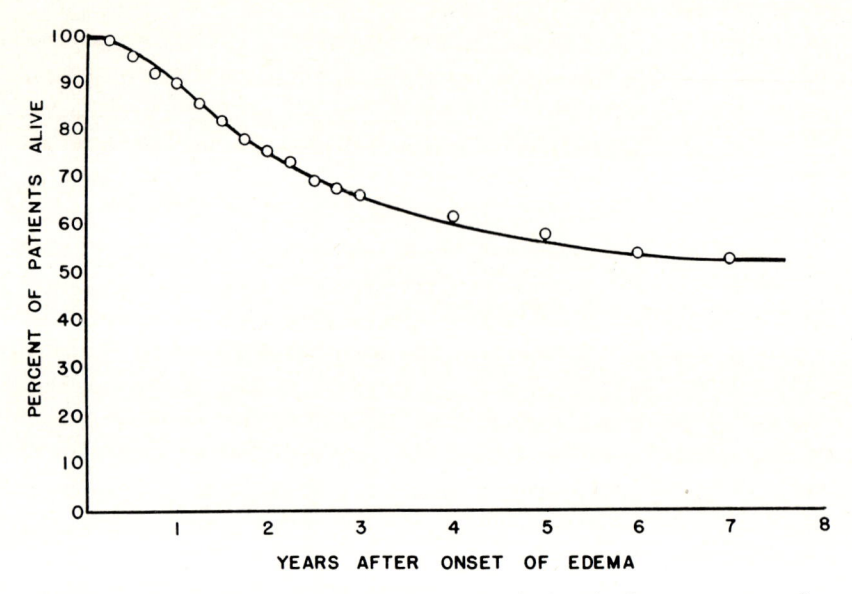

FIGURE 2. Cumulative percentage of survival during the first seven years after of onset of nephrosis in patients with no effective adrenocortical active hormone therapy. Total number of cases 429. Average population per year: 115. (*Pediatric Clinic of North America*, August 1955.)

comfort, his anemia and small stature were distressing to himself and to his family. Except for these features he may have remained quite comfortable until a few weeks before death.

The fate of a child who developed nephrosis in the period after the introduction of adequate treatment for infection—but before the use of modern, fairly specific treatment for the basic disease—could never be predicted in the individual case. The overall fate of a large group of such children is demonstrated by the graph in Figure 2. This graph indicates the per cent of patients living at varying intervals after the onset of the disease. Few deaths in the first year occurred, probably mostly from infection. In the second, third, and fourth years the survival per cent decreased rapidly as kidney failures began to take its toll. By the sixth and seventh years after onset, the survival rate had flattened out, and only about 50% were left alive. Of those living perhaps half had lost all chemical signs and clinical symptoms and could be considered cured, even though a few of them might later have shown a recurrence. Although the others might be free of all outward evidence of trouble, some patients would still have protein in the urine, showing that they were not entirely well. The future of these latter patients remained uncertain, with the hope that they might live out a normal life span, but with the real fear that life might be significantly shortened by early kidney failure.

Thus, only a few years ago, parents of a child with nephrosis could look ahead to a period of years of anguish with the ghastly spectre of continued or intermittent gross, almost incapacitating, swelling leading all too frequently to fairly early death. Though the swelling itself was known not to be harmful, terrifying as it was, it nevertheless was an outward sign of the unrelenting presence of the inward condition which could well destroy the child's kidneys and his chance for life. Even those patients who lived might be left with kidney damage, an uncertain future, and only a small proportion could be expected to be really well.

Until recently, innumerable types of treatment were tried and proved ineffective. These ranged from various types of drugs, through special diet plans, through deliberate induction of fever by various means, to dozens of highly illogical "nostrums." The one apparently irrelevant treatment which still seems effective was the deliberate exposure to measles; though a serious disease, measles was often followed by remission, sometimes even cure.

THE CHANGING PICTURE

With the most recent type of treatment, the use of an assortment of preparations which either stimulate the patient's own adrenal gland to greater activity (ACTH) or supply a synthetic substitute for the adrenal secretion (cortisone and steroid products), the picture has been radically changed. Just how great this change has been cannot be stated. Since use of these drugs, lumped under the general term "adreno-cortical active hormone therapy," frequently referred to less specifically simply as "hormone therapy," now seems to be able in general to arrest the disease process. There is certainly no suggestion as yet that use of these drugs can "cure" the disease. Such treatment does seem to be able to suppress it, and it is the hope that the process may eventually subside so that spontaneous cure can occur. Two reservations should be borne in mind. A small but appreciable group of patients which has had a rapid spontaneous remission of the disease has always been recognized. This group would have done well whether treatment had been given or not. Another small group of patients proves completely resistant no matter how soon treatment is started. In this group the disease progresses steadily and inexorably until complete kidney failure occurs. Between these two extremes, however, is the great majority of patients to which this "general" statement applies.

Although treatment with drugs has extended over a period of time too short to draw any real conclusions, Figure 3 indicates the change in the survival per cent of all patients with nephrosis in the first 30 months of disease in more recent years when the hormones have been used extensively in contrast to the pre-hormone days. If the promise of these early trends is borne out in the future, the overall mortality should be greatly diminished. On the other hand, since the disease is only suppressed, not cured, the period of uncertainty may be extended for years. In other words, the patient who formerly might have died in two or three years after the first signs of the condition appeared may now live an indefinite number of years with the disease recurring and becoming quiescent. Hopefully, he will eventually recover, but it is possible that a later death may merely be in the act of being staved off. To be reasonably confident that relapse will not occur, a period of at least 6 months in which the patient has received no treatment and has had no abnormal laboratory findings is demanded. Even under these conditions occasional relapses can be expected. Thus, though modern treatment has certainly brightened the outlook for the nephrotic patient, such treatment has simultaneously significantly extended the period in which he must be considered a handicapped child.

BASIC NATURE OF NEPHROSIS

The truly basic nature of nephrosis is not understood at present. The way the kidney functions is disturbed in that protein from the blood serum is allowed to escape into the urine. The normal kidney filters out water and other soluble small-molecule substances but holds back the protein. With time, and other factors which are not presently understood, other functions, more important as far as life is concerned, may become involved, and so

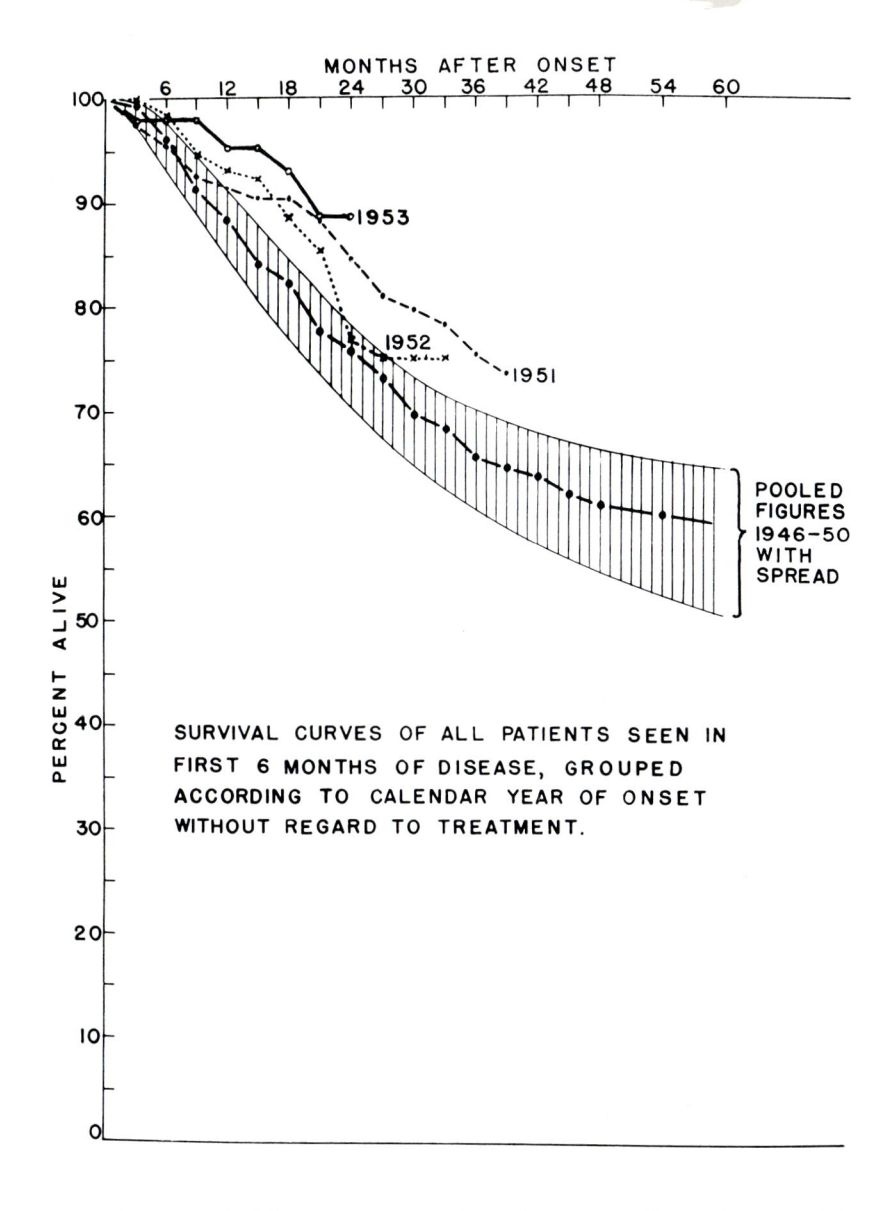

SURVIVAL CURVES OF ALL PATIENTS SEEN IN FIRST 6 MONTHS OF DISEASE, GROUPED ACCORDING TO CALENDAR YEAR OF ONSET WITHOUT REGARD TO TREATMENT.

complete renal failure may result. Thus, at first glance, this seems to be primarily a disease of the kidney. But there are other changes, such as the leakage of fluid into the body tissues, the reduction of proteins in the blood serum, and the increase of fatty substances in the blood. Some or all of these changes may

241

be secondary to the kidney disorder. On the other hand, the disturbance in the kidney may be merely part of a generalized disease of which the other findings are also a part. The correct answer to this question is not known, but in the medical world there are adherents to both points of view. Whatever the basic nature of the disease is, however, the kidney appears to be seriously and irreversibly injured.

RELATION TO OTHER KIDNEY DISEASE

The term "Bright's disease" arose from the early description by Richard Bright in 1827 of a condition often associated with body swelling in which protein was found in the urine. At autopsy the kidneys in such cases were found to be seriously diseased. Thus the term has come to refer to medical diseases of the kidney (in contrast to mechanical difficulties which might be corrected surgically) in which the above findings are present. Therefore, it is correct to consider nephrosis as one form of Bright's disease.

Nephritis is a term applied to other forms of Bright's disease. The name is applied usually to two fairly common conditions. Most frequent is acute nephritis (also called acute hemorrhagic nephritis and acute glomerulonephritis, a benign condition commonest in six to ten year old children, but seen occasionally at all ages. The condition often follows an acute sore throat or scarlet fever, is detected by the appearance of grossly bloody urine, and may be accompanied by a little transient body swelling. Some protein may be detected in the urine, but not a great deal; blood pressure may be elevated, sometimes to a dangerous degree; and general kidney function may be temporarily impaired. Rarely, it is severe enough to cause death in the acute attack. Ordinarily, however, the acute manifestations subside in a few weeks, but findings of red blood cells in the urine may persist for months. Many cases of acute nephritis are undoubtedly not recognized because the blood in the urine never becomes visible without the aid of a microscope. Many experts believe that almost everyone may have the disease in such a mild form without its being identified. In a few cases the urine fails to become normal and the disease progresses to what is called "chronic nephritis."

Chronic glomerulonephritis, a very insidious disease, is quite rare in childhood. Some doctors think it arises from an acute nephritis, either detected or undetected. Others believe that it may be an entirely distinct disease. A steadily progressive condition, sometimes over a few years, sometimes over decades, the condition gradually destroys functioning kidney tissue till death ensues, but until severe renal damage develops, it usually gives rise to no symptoms, being detectable only by the finding of red blood cells and a little protein in the urine. In occasional instances, however, more frequently in adults, a period of marked body swelling which is called the "nephrotic phase" of nephritis occurs. Many physicians feel that most nephrosis is in reality the "nephrotic phase of nephritis." Most patients who die after what started out as "nephrosis" show kidney changes much like the more typical instances of nephritis. To explain the examples, not infrequent in children, of complete recovery, these doctors cite a different category which they call "pure lipoid nephrosis." No good way of differentiating the two categories has been defined. All patients fit into the picture described earlier as simply having "nephrosis." The three conditions—nephrosis, acute nephritis and chronic nephritis—are usually quite distinct entities.

CAUSE

The cause of Bright's disease in general is not clear. Acute nephritis, from information accumulated in the past few years, seems most frequently to be a special delayed reaction to a particular type of streptococcus infection, hence its relation to a sore throat or scarlet fever. Chronic nephritis may be a continuation of acute nephritis, or if a separate disease, may have no presently known cause. Even if chronic nephritis is a result of acute nephritis, the reason why it occurs only in a small minority is not understood. Nephrosis in children is not regularly associated with preexisting infection, nor is it related to poor diet or bad climate. It is not associated with a strong family history of kidney disease—in brief, there is no known cause for it. Certainly, the many ideas that come to parents' minds: exposure to cold, fatigue, parental neglect, emotional upset, and a host of other possible precipitating factors do not seem to have any bearing on why it appears in some children. At this time the medical profession has no idea of the cause of nephrosis.

RESEARCH

In the area of understanding what the general nature of nephrosis is, the well informed but non-physician individuals should have some conception of the degree of hope offered by scientific research. Modern medical investigation along lines that are directly or indirectly related to this problem is extensive. Without really providing a solution as yet, the knowledge of renal function, the physiology of the production of edema, the anatomical changes in the ultramicroscopic appearance of the smallest units of the kidney and other tissue in allied diseases, the problems of altered metabolism of body proteins and fats, the reaction of kidneys to the injection of kidney anti-bodies into animals, the effects of hormones and other drugs on the progress of the disease are the subjects of intense study by various research laboratories throughout the world.

In the past ten years the number and quality of investigations that may have bearing on this disease have increased many fold. Many individual pieces of the complicated puzzle must already be in the hands of researchers. The remaining pieces and the fitting of them all together to give the complete picture may occur in the near future.

Many investigators believe that nephrosis is the result of an abnormal response in certain individuals to their own body tissues. Analagous situations in other disease conditions have been noted. Patients with nephrosis may be developing antibodies (normally materials which are protective against outside invading substances, such as bacteria) against their own kidney tissue, or perhaps a more generalized tissue (such as capillaries) which is peculiarly concentrated in the kidney. If this hypothesis should prove to be correct, future study may develop a means of interrupting this production of antibodies, or else rendering them innocuous, once formed.

HOSPITALIZATION

The amount of time that any patient will spend in the hospital will be dependent on the course of his particular disease. The practice in the Columbia-Presbyterian Medical Center is to admit a newly diagnosed patient to the hospital. This initial admission secures the necessary laboratory studies and careful observation of the patient through the first period of treatment. This first admission, often lasting a month or so, allows time to become acquainted with the parents and to try to help them to make necessary adjustments. By personal conversation and later by a special booklet written for the purpose, patient and parent learn what the disease is and what may be expected in time to come. The child gets accustomed to hospital life. Since he usually is not seriously ill in his own eyes, he is allowed free run of the wards. If future complications ever require readmission, he comes in with confidence and hope because of his initial happy experience.

Hospitalization may not necessarily fit all cases. Where there are no hospitals particularly suited for the care of children, to keep the patient at home may be wiser. In the more personal relationships of private doctor and family under such circumstances, the doctor may be able to consult and advise equally well at home.

After the first period of treatment is completed, the patient returns home to be followed at frequent intervals in the clinic or office. As time goes on, these intervals may be increased in length so that the burden on the family becomes less. Later admissions to the hospital are recommended only under special circumstances, such as severe infection complicating the picture or failure to respond adequately to home treatment. In some situations where home facilities may not be adequate, longer periods in the hospital may be necessary. Both parent and child should accept the thought that the hospital is a friendly and helpful place, not something to fear.

Upon return home, the patient may not find himself very handicapped if he is one of the many who respond successfully to treatment. The handicap to the parents and the family as a whole may prove to be much greater. If the initial educational program has been successful and if the parents are able to make a good emotional adjustment to their new problem, even this handicap may be minimal. The necessity for frequent visits to the clinic or doctor's office, the expense of costly medication, and the worry as to what the eventual outcome will be, remain.

At home the responsibility for the total care of the youngster now falls on the parents' shoulders. First, from the point of view of physical care the greatest task confronting them is one impossible of perfect accomplishment: that is the avoidance of infection. The common cold is often the trigger mechanism which sets off a recurrence of active nephrosis. Persons, particularly children with obvious colds, whose ideas of hygiene are rudimentary at best, should be kept away. If one of the parents himself develops a cold, he should take the precaution of wearing a mask when close to the child and should be particularly cautious about handwashing, especially when preparing food. The undue susceptibility of such patients to infection means that despite all the best practices, colds and occasionally more serious infections will develop from time to time.

Since such attempts at prevention are never certain, the child must be watched for early signs of infection and treated with suitable drugs without waiting for signs of serious illness to develop. For unknown reasons a badly swollen patient may have a prompt remission following measles. Occasionally such a remission may even prove to be permanent. Despite this, measles should not be taken too lightly. As serious complications can occur even with such a routine childhood ailment, the doctor should be completely informed.

Other types of precaution worth taking with regard to physical well-being include protection against chills. Sudden chilling drops resistance to infection. Unfortunately, many people frightened by this simple observation assume that everything which under uncontrolled conditions *might* give rise to a chill *will* under all conditions, actually do so. Such things as hair-washing, bathing, swimming and the like are often considered dangerous. In actual fact, if the hair is washed and dried promptly in warm surroundings, if the bath is given in a warm area and the body dried quickly and completely, if the swim is taken in not too cold water and the youngster dries quickly in the warm sun—no particular hazard is presented. Parents should remember what they are trying basically to guard against, not remember lists of specific activities which they cannot let their children indulge in.

Fatigue of extreme degree also is something which should be avoided. As with chilling, no specific activity needs to be foregone, provided none is indulged in to the point of real tiredness. Bicycle riding, running, baseball, and anything which a child might care to do can do no harm in itself. Fortunately, most young children are reasonably self-regulatory. That is, they will drop out of these activities when they have had enough, seldom driving themselves "until they drop." Therefore, if parents adopt the attitude that anything that the youngster wants to do, with only minimum supervision, the end results will not be far wrong. Obviously, there will be some instances when the parent's judgment will be better than the child's but this will not often be so.

Appetite is a function which can also be of much concern to the parent. The appetite of a nephrotic patient will frequently fluctuate as the disease fluctuates. If the parent can resign himself to these variations, everything will be much more peaceful. When the young victim "eats like a bird," it is reassuring to remember that this is a phase that will pass, and furthermore nothing anyone can do will make him eat more. Fortunately, no patient has ever gone on such a hunger strike to the point of seriously damaging himself. Patience and resignation on the part of the guardian adults will see this difficulty resolve itself.

Direction of the non-physical side of the patient's life is just as important as the care of the physical aspects. Nephrosis is not a brief and quickly forgotten episode in the life of the growing child but is something that will occupy a significant fraction of his youth. Therefore, any special attitudes which are adopted in the parent's mind "only for the duration" with the thought that there will be a "return to normal" when it is over will have a much more deep-grained effect than is desirable. When the youngster recovers from his physical illness, he may be left with the mental and emotional outlook of a chronic invalid which will hamper him all the rest of his life. For this reason the importance of the early indoctrination of the parents into thinking of this situation as a long-term affair and into thinking of it as something which is to be lived with naturally and normally, not as something which is a source of continual panic requiring constant pampering of the child, is to be emphasized.

The physical restrictions suggested in the foregoing section are things which we hope can be imposed without the child's being aware that anything special is being done for him. There should be no obvious, special exceptions made for him. When it comes to discipline, he should be treated like any other person of his own age. If he ought to be denied something he wants, no special case should be made of the fact that he has nephrosis. Thus the general rules of child rearing should continue to be applied.

Since most children with nephrosis are below school age when the condition starts, the problem of schooling does not raise itself. Since there are enough patients in the older age groups, the question deserves some mention. With the three to five year olds where school at most would be of the nursery or kindergarten variety, the advantages of the school experience do not seem to outweigh the risks of the almost constant exposure to infection. Therefore, this age group should remain at home. As age increases, however, the importance of school becomes greater. In first or second grade it may be wise to have them attend school during the fall and spring terms when the danger of infection is not too great, but to have a home teacher, if it can be arranged, in the winter term. As more advanced education is required, the school experience assumes enough greater importance. The calculated risk of exposure to the infections of such a group is one worth taking. These general rules must obviously be tailored to the particular individual concerned. If the patient is one who is doing particularly poorly and needs frequent treatment or if he has shown himself even more susceptible to infection than the usual run of nephrotic patients, then one should be more conservative than has been suggested above. If, on the other hand, he is doing particularly well and does not seem especially prone to infection, one can be more radical.

MANAGEMENT OF THE FAMILY

Implicit in the discussion has been the fact that a tremendous load—financially, physically and emotionally, falls upon the parents. Outsiders can do much, not directly for the child, but indirectly by giving understanding support to the parents. Such outsiders will include the group trained more or less in the medical field, such as doctors, nurses and medical social workers. It will also include relatives and friends.

The diagnosis of nephrosis usually connotes nothing to most parents, the term being completely new to them. With surprising rapidity they find friends who have known of a case or who have read an article in a magazine. More likely, they go to a library to look the subject up. As a result of this they rapidly acquire a good deal of information, or more often misinformation. Since the friends' stories usually are garbled and the library books are apt to be hopelessly out of date, the parents may immediately glean that this is almost certainly a fatal disease. They anxiously ask, "Is there any hope?" If they can be taught to put the emphasis the other way around, that is, "Is there any danger?" then, even though they are honestly told that there is a real danger, they may find the burden easier to bear.

When parents first learn of what a "mysterious killer" nephrosis is from popular articles, they are apt to feel completely lost, believing that nobody knows anything. If, on the other hand, parents can be given a reasonable picture of all that *is* known along with a frank admission of the parts of the picture which are still lacking, they can build up some confidence in their physician and other workers without having a childishly blind faith.

One of their early emotional responses, after the first reaction of terror has partially subsided, is often a strong unreasoning sense of guilt. This guilt is not always expressed. Since guilt is so often present the doctor should explain before parents ask how little is known about the cause of the disease. Parental worry that there is something wrong with the family heredity, that they have fed the youngster "wrong" foods, or have not fed him "correct" foods, that they let him get tired, that they allowed him to become chilled, that they gave him a bad psychological environment are brought up by persons newly meeting the disease. When it is realized that even the best informed physicans could not deliberately induce the disease in a child, even if they wanted to, it is fair to assume that nothing now known which the parent might have done or failed to do could have been responsible for the condition of the child.

Even after the first shock has worn off, the mother and father will have to learn to live with the knowledge that their child will be in an uncertain state of health for several years. Their instinctive reaction may be to overprotect and pamper the patient. If they can learn and come really to believe that only certain precautions, already discussed, seem helpful, they may be persuaded to let the child grow and develop in a more or less normal way. They should early come to realize that the danger of unnecessarily creating a mental invalid is really greater than any known danger of making the disease, nephrosis, worse, provided that they stick to the simple precepts laid down.

If the patient does prove to be one of the occasional ones who does not respond to treatment and whose condition gradually deteriorates, the difficulties become far greater. A realization again that this is not the result of negligence and that overbearing concern will not help, may prove valuable. Certainly, as such children grow worse they do not, until near the end, really feel sick. If they can be treated within their tolerance, as nearly like normal children as possible, they will have a happier time as the end approaches.

All these adjustments which the parents have to make cannot be made by them without help. The first help comes from the physician, but the physician is not always available when questions arise or ideas are sought. Therefore, all persons to whom the parent may turn can prove of much more value if they know in a general way what the nature of nephrosis is and what can be expected in helping the patient to weather the difficult period. Then when the hoped for "cure" or quiescent period comes, the child will be a well adjusted individual who will be able to meet the world of healthy individuals with confidence.

ORGANIZATION SPECIFICALLY INTERESTED IN NEPHROSIS

National Nephrosis Foundation
143 East 35th Street
New York 16, N. Y.

This organization is primarily concerned with the promotion of research. In some areas, however, the chapters are in a position to give limited aid in the care of patients. The National Nephrosis Foundation would like to have all cases reported so that they can keep an accurate roster.

Chapters currently are active in many locations. For the exact address, National Nephrosis Foundation may be contacted.

REFERENCES

Basic Research

Barnett, H. L.: *Advances in Pediatrics*, Vol. V, pp. 53-118, Year Book Publishers.

Squire, John B.: *Advances in Internal Medicine*, Vol. VII, pp. 201-241, Year Book Publishers.

Nephrosis Conferences (Proceedings of the Annual Conferences of the Nephrotic Syndrome) Sponsored by the National Nephrosis Foundation, New York, N. U., 1951-1955.

Clinical Management

Riley, C. M., and Davis, R. A.: Childhood Nephrosis, *Pediatric Clinics of North America*, 2:893-910, Aug. 1955.

Riley, C. M., Davis, R. A., Fergig, J. W., and Berger, A. P.: Nephrosis of Childhood: Statistical Evaluation of the Effect of Adrenocortical-active Therapy. *J. Chron. Dis.*, 3:640-650, June 1956.

For Parents

Riley, C. M.: *Nephrosis in Childhood—A Guide for Parents*, published by National Nephrosis Foundation.

THE CHILD WITH POLIOMYELITIS

Edward B. Shaw, M.D.

Poliomyelitis has been known since ancient times, but only in the last century has it occurred in epidemics and more frequently affected older children and adults. The theory is well sustained that under unsanitary living conditions the virus is ubiquitous in the population and is readily passed from one person to another. Under these conditions of almost universal exposure, paralysis occurs only in the very young ("infantile paralysis") and protective levels of immunity prevail to a considerable degree in older children and adults. The very factors which protect against exposure to many common communicable diseases have, thus, served to interfere with the natural method of immunization through recurring exposure. Whether artificial immunization with vaccines will successfully mimic this natural method of protection remains to be seen.

The results of virus research have been oversimplified to the public. There is no general appreciation of the intricacies of methods which have developed scientific knowledge of this disease. Ingenious tissue culture techniques have provided tools for better diagnosis, for the identification of the specific virus in large segments of the general population unaffected by actual disease, for serologic tests of immunity, and finally for attempts at artificial immunization.

COURSE

Poliomyelitis is an acute infection in which symptoms resemble many of the common febrile illnesses of childhood. The early course may give little warning of the muscular paralyses which may later ensue. The physician must establish the diagnosis on the basis of an influenza-like illness with minimal physical findings—slight stiffness and muscle tremulousness. Physical examination, otherwise, provides little significant evidence. Most of the laboratory studies are inconclusive with the exception of the spinal fluid which usually, but not invariably, shows an increase in the white cells and increased protein content.

The outcome of the disease is uncertain. Many patients who have typical early symptoms may escape paralysis entirely. Others may pass through the infection without any evidence of disease and proceed to develop immunity.

Usually the acute febrile course continues for about seven days. Muscular weakness appears during this time. The exact time of its appearance is capricious. Paralysis of cranial nerves appears somewhat early in the course, and signs of spinal nerve paresis appear relatively later. Muscle weakness is unaccompanied by sensory loss, and reaches its height in a very few days. It is to be expected that the patient will eventually recover some degree of his lost function. Early improvement has good prognostic significance.

At least 50% of probable recovery will be apparent within three months, and almost all of the final restoration of function will be present within six months. Many patients not only suffer from muscle weakness, but also lose the pattern of muscle function which must be painstakingly regained. Some degree of improvement may be found at a very late date. Early prediction regarding the final outcome which is either too optimistic or too pessimistic is unjustified. Although profound weakness may proceed to good functional recovery, relatively mild weakness may remain unaltered.

As acute symptoms of illness subside, and when consequent paralysis is definitely established, stiffness and soreness of the musculature appear which may not parallel the degree of muscle weakness. This feature is in decided contrast to most diseases with which this diagnosis might early be confused.

Many patients, whatever their precise involvement, will continue to feel and appear ill and depressed for four to six weeks even as other acute symptoms subside. These evidences of illness may originate in areas of the nervous system other than those governing motor nerve supply. Such evidences are more common in adults than in children. Probably these symptoms are not truly encephalitic in origin, and it is doubtful that they represent purely a period of psychic readjustment. At the end of this phase, and about the time that pain and soreness disappear, the patient's general condition may become greatly improved.

SPECIAL SITUATIONS

Few more bitter examples of the indignities to which a person must subject his body in the course of modern medical care exist than those which occur during paralytic poliomyelitis. Some of these are only annoying, but others, of lifesaving importance, may be most repugnant.

Disturbances of Bowel Function

Obstinate constipation almost always accompanies the first few weeks of poliomyelitis. This proceeds from obvious causes; the immediate effects of the infection, enforced inactivity and recumbency, weakness of the abdominal muscles, and atony of the intestinal musculature. Cathartics are useless. Intestinal lubricants are of slight value. Recourse must be to enemas, and, in severe cases, to digital evacuation. The wetting agents now available may be used to maintain the moisture content of the stools and avoid fecal impaction. Only careful management will avert impaction and symptoms of serious import.

Bladder Dysfunction

Difficulty in voiding, occurring commonly in the early course of the disease, should be expected to subside in a very few days. Dysuria is due to atony of the bladder wall, to the lack of expulsive force of the abdominal muscles, and especially to the weakness of the detrusor muscle with inability to open the sphincter.

This difficulty must be recognized promptly and dealt with appropriately. The patient may be repeatedly catheterized, or he may be provided with an indwelling catheter and periodic drainage. With the former method one may best determine when the patient is about to re-establish normal function. The use of the latter method makes it more difficult to tell when his spontaneous efforts will be effectual. Continued assurance that this function will return early and persistent encouragement of voluntary voiding will be most beneficial. Urocholin may be most *cautiously* tried after defervescence and in the absence of bulbar disease. Every effort to attempt to restore bladder function early is worth-while, for the longer dysuria persists the more difficult it is to correct, and the more surely will bacterial infection supervene. The use of antibacterial drugs is appropriate. I have never seen permanent impairment of urination.

Bulbar (Bulbo-pontine) Disease

Disturbances of cranial nerve function present great difficulties for the physician and may be terrifying to the patient. Minimal symptoms in this area may presage a serious threat to life for any of the centers involved are so closely adjacent to those which control vital functions that the least extension of disease may provoke a dangerous situation.

Eye Muscle Paralysis

Weakness of the extra-ocular muscles may early indicate invasion of the bulbo-pontine area. The greatest importance of such weakness is the evidence that there has been involvement of dangerous areas. Vision is unaffected, and function is nearly always eventually regained.

Paralysis of Muscles of Mastication

Fifth nerve involvement is relatively infrequent. The patient may be unable to close his jaws or to move his lower jaw from side to side. This weakness may be curiously intractable and may lead to permanent dysfunction, although ingenious surgical repair is a later possibility.

Facial Weakness

Facial paralysis is fairly common but is rarely bilateral. Inability to close either eye, to pucker the lips, to wrinkle the forehead, or to move one side of the face may lead to fears of permanent disfigurement. Almost invariably, however, there is gradual restoration of these functions and eventual disappearance of asymmetry.

Paralysis of Palate, Pharynx, Larynx, and the Central Mechanism of Respiration

Symptoms which proceed from weakness of the muscles of the palate, the constrictors of the pharynx, and the larynx must be recognized as an immediate threat to life. Although this weakness may be detected by observing the loss of movement of these structures by direct inspection, the alarming symptoms which ensue make it evident. Alterations in speech, inability to cough, accumulations of unswallowed saliva, choking and gradual drowning of the patient in his own secretions may supervene. Often progressive difficulty in respiration makes it impossible to determine whether the function most at fault is respiratory paralysis of central origin or simply the continued aspiration of saliva and administered fluids which obstruct breathing. The consequent filling of the lungs with this fluid produces pulmonary atelectasis and complicating pneumonia.

Inability to swallow, which is not readily controlled by the patient's own efforts in handling his secretions, by suctioning, or by postural drainage, calls for immediate tracheotomy. This procedure provides a free airway and helps to protect against aspiration of saliva and the development of atalectasis, progressive difficulties in respiration and pneumonia.

Tracheotomy is not the recourse for every single case of bulbar paralysis. Each patient must be carefully studied and repeatedly observed. Once a decision is reached that relief is necessary, surgical intervention must be promptly employed. Often the tracheotomized patient will have so much difficulty with breathing as to require the use of the tank respirator. Accordingly the tracheotomy should always be performed as high in the trachea as possible to permit the application of the respirator collar. That the patient who requires the respirator and has definite involvement of swallowing or speech must have a tracheotomy to provide a free airway to protect the lower respiratory tract, is axiomatic.

The polio patient who is unable to swallow must be fed by artificial routes. Immediately this calls for intravenous feedings with care to provide adequate intake but with the avoidance of excessive amounts of intravenous fluid. Continued maintenance by the intravenous route is an unhappy expedient. Some fluid and electrolytes can be administered rectally, the paretic bowel affording fairly good absorption. Within a very few days it may be possible to introduce an intragastric plastic tube through the nose by means of which adequate amounts of food, fluid, and electrolytes may be given.

Throughout this succession of ordeals and a period of complete dependence, the patient requires not only resourceful care, but continued reassurance. The physician must not be content to maintain nutrition indefinitely by artificial measures. The longer these are continued, the more difficult it is to re-institute deglutition. Function will almost inevitably return to these muscles of bulbar supply, but this requires constant suggestion and encouragement in re-learning the complicated muscle pattern necessary for swallowing.

The disturbances of deglutition, phonation, and respiration are frequently coincidental, and efforts to rehabilitation involve the education of voluntary action of any of the involved muscles. A variety of respiratory devices will help to re-train these muscles. Useful function may return before there is complete recovery of all the musculature.

Artificial Respiration

The necessity for aid to respiration previously referred to occurs more frequently in paralysis of the spinal muscles than in purely bulbar disease. The tank respirator must be available if one or both deltoid muscles are weakened, for this event warns of accompanying weakness of intercoastal muscles and the diaphragm. The patient may show restlessness and irritability and increasing inadequacy of respiratory exchange. Weakness of the intercostals and the diaphragm may lead to increasing rapidity of the pulse and respiration with progressive decrease in the depth of the latter. Progressive disorientation may point to anoxia. Actual cyanosis may appear only when symptoms are very far advanced.

The need for artificial assistance may be studied by spirometry and by various laboratory determinations. Clinical evaluation is equally significant. The ability of the patient to cough, to sniff, to count on one breath, and the sounds heard through the stethoscope applied to the chest and over the open mouth may provide an estimate of the amount of air which is being moved. Weakness of intercostals and diaphragm is more easily determined than disturbances of similar order in bulbo-spinal paralysis in which the airway is impaired and the exact source of irregular and ineffective breathing is difficult to determine.

It is a tenuous decision to establish the exact moment to admit the patient to a tank respirator. If this is done too early and before the patient feels the need of assistance, he may rebel and prove refractory to its continuation. If delayed until the patient has developed severe anoxia and cyanosis, atelectasis and pneumonia, the use of the respirator may be but a futile gesture.

The physician who introduces a patient into the respirator must accept the responsibility for attempting his eventual withdrawal from the machine. This device is designed to meet an emergency situation. Prolonged or lifetime dependency is so dismal a prospect that few would choose it, were theirs the choice.

No sooner has the patient been made comfortable in the respirator than plans should be initiated for eventual independence. The physician must not abstain from the inescapable risks involved. It is better to assure the patient of the temporary nature of the need for the respirator and to tell him that he will be able to come out in a day or so. To be sure, he may tolerate only a few seconds with the machine opened during the first few days. Gradually, however, he may be led to utilize minimal strength, to tolerate increasing periods without assistance, and to accept positive pressure devices, the chest respirator and the rocking bed, until his weakened muscles will re-establish independent breathing.

Few failures of functional recovery need occur if the patient can be sufficiently reassured to bring his own best efforts to the task. The longer complete dependence continues the more difficult is the problem of rehabilitation. Those who regain voluntary respiration most slowly may painstakingly be taught glosso-pharyngeal respiration, "frog breathing," which consists of inflation of the lungs by a curious pump-like action of the tongue and pharynx sufficient to produce speech and cough even though the intercostals and diaphragm remain extremely weak.

Spinal Muscle Paralysis

Weakness of the trunk and extremities once it appears rapidly reaches its height. The patient should not be fatigued by efforts to determine the exact extent of muscle involvement. This involvement can gradually be evaluated. Careful positioning in bed seeks to avoid maximum stretch or undue relaxation of affected muscles. Frequent turning and postural changes are necessary to prevent discomfort and pressure necrosis. No effort should be made early to stimulate voluntary activity. During this phase the program of slow and progressive rehabilitation must be planned, using every device of resourceful after care.

Pain and Muscle Spasm

About the time that weakness is maximal, the late oncoming soreness, pain, and stiffness of the musculature develop and may continue and increase for several weeks. These symptoms may not parallel the pattern of weakness but seem to be relatively independent of it. Even those who have little paralysis may be tormented by this late discomfort. Eventual disability may depend upon this phenomenon almost as much as upon essential weakness.

Minimal Paralysis

Severe forms of muscle weakness are readily observed. Lesser weakness is frequently ignored or overlooked. Only by careful and repeated follow-up examinations may minor degrees of paralysis be detected. Many patients who are early regarded as nonparalytic may proceed to later evidence of disability and deformity which might have been prevented by early and resourceful care.

Total Care

A great many of the unpleasant manifestations of poliomyelitis have been detailed in order now to consider the contributions which must be made to the successful overall care of the child thus handicapped. The problems are so complex and divergent that a team of experts is ideally a necessity for best results.

Early or late, the severely affected child may require the pediatrician, the otorhinolaryngologist, the respiratory physiologist, the cardiologist, the urologist, the psychiatrist, the orthopedist, the physical therapist, the nurse, the occupational therapist, the dietitian, and numerous other technical assistants. The problems of the entire course of the disease are so numerous as to tax every resource of the physician.

The best possible final restoration of function and rehabilitation can be achieved only when some one physician is in command and can mobilize these various technical skills as they are necessary. Ultimate success involves the whole child. It avails little to succeed in one aspect of the problem only to fail dismally in another. This one physician, whatever his particular specialty, must provide the child and his parents with advice that is not only wise but kind. He can rarely predict, least of all can he promise, the final outcome in the severely affected patient; but his infinite attention to every detail of care may be well rewarded by the end result.

The Parents

When most parents bring their child to the hospital with poliomyelitis, they come with mingled fear and incredulity. They want to be assured that these fears are unfounded, that the child does not have poliomyelitis. They hope, otherwise, to be told that he has a mild attack and will certainly escape paralysis. Initially they must accept the uncertainties of diagnosis and of prognosis. As the pattern of involvement emerges, they must tolerate the unpleasant procedures of care for the preservation of life. During the long uphill pull for survival and rehabilitation, they require the steady reassurance of the physician. They must understand that their child will benefit from the fortitude with which they meet this disaster. Some parents must finally face the problem of severe crippling and the realization that complete restoration of the child's health is impossible of fulfillment. A few can never quite accept this verdict, but the more fortunate child is the one whose parents will work with the physician toward the best possible outcome, who will accept the eventual limitations of his activities, and who will continue with the efforts to effect the best possible adaptation to his handicap.

The Patient

The child who realizes that he has poliomyelitis may be just as dismayed and frightened as are his parents. He may be terrified at the prospect of death or disability or of the unknown dangers which lie ahead. He may be frustrated by the restraints imposed by the disease and its complications, especially if he requires tracheotomy or the respirator. With curious frequency the child who has had little previous illness, who is very active, who is perhaps the potential athlete, and who is unprepared for limitations of activity, is the very one who develops poliomyelitis.

Children unerringly reflect their surroundings. Nothing is so reassuring to the child patient as steadiness and matter-of-factness in the attitude of his parents and of nursing and medical attendants.

With proper handling, children will accept with fortitude all of the discomfort and disability of the acute state and will adjust to handicapping sequelae. The prognosis for recovery from paralysis in the young is better than that the equally involved adult. Growth and repair are kindred phenomena, and the growing child may repair damage to an extent which might be quite impossible for an older person. The child is capable of re-learning patterns of muscle function, just as he readily acquires other skills, and is frequently able to develop useful activity even though he has considerable loss of strength.

The Nurse

The care of acute poliomyelitis demands nursing attention which is expert, resourceful, and kind. Much of this care will be directed to the comfort of the patient. Gentleness in handling, careful positioning, constant turning for the prevention of decubitous ulceration are a necessity. The nurse must be schooled in the many difficult procedures involved, in suctioning pharyngeal secretions, in the operation of the respirator, and in the detection and correction of mechanical difficulties which may develop in its operation. She must be adept in recognizing all of the danger signals in the progress of the disease. She must constantly attend to the child's nutrition, fluid intake, and the evacuation of bladder and bowel. She must supplement the latter efforts for the re-education of muscle function. The nurse who is adequate for the task is invaluable to the efforts of all the physicians and technicians concerned with total care.

Physical Therapist

Physical therapy has made a great contribution to the care of poliomyelitis. It should be instituted early, be painstaking and long continued. Although time consuming and expensive, its value is indisputable. The purpose is to maintain normal mobility of the joints and elasticity of the affected muscles within the range between contraction and optimum stretch. The return of any strength will thus not be opposed by loss of normal range of motion.

The theory of this may best be illustrated by what may happen to single muscles. Nerve supply may be so damaged that no voluntary contraction is possible, and a muscle may be so affected by soreness, tightness, and "muscle spasm" as to remain continuously in a position of extreme shortening. If either of these conditions is permitted to continue for very long, scarring and fibrosis may destroy any possibility of muscle elasticity.

Unless the nerve supply is completely destroyed, a few muscle bundles may retain their innervation. If normal muscle length and range of motion can be preserved by expert physical therapy, these few surviving fibers may be developed in strength (although new fibers will not be formed) to a point where some useful function is restored.

Attempts to maintain normal range of motion in the extremities and the trunk should be instituted as early, and continued as conscientiously, as pain and discomfort will permit. Nothing is known which will restore the function of motor nerves when they have been destroyed. The aim of physical therapy is to permit the return and detection of any power which has not been completely destroyed. The supplemental use of drugs and heat—such as the Kenny hot pack—is simply to relieve pain and tenderness to an extent which will allow the maintenance of normal motion.

Passive movements are gradually succeeded by the use of assisted motion in which the patient cooperates as much as he can with the additional use of such devices as Guthrie-Smith slings and underwater exercises. The final effort is not only to build up and strengthen isolated muscles but to re-develop, in the presence of some existing weakness, new patterns of muscle action to substitute for normal function.

The physical therapist must be well trained and indefatigable. It is manifestly and cruelly untrue that, no matter what the degree of involvement, function can be completely restored by expert care. The physician should decide when intensive therapy may be terminated, but at this point parents should be educated in carrying out a scheme of exercises and stretches which may be profitable for a long time.

The Orthopedist

The skilled orthopedist is helpful from early convalescence onward. He should assist with the supervision of physical therapy and with the efforts of late rehabilitation. Whether or not bracing should be applied early is a decision of great importance which must be individualized. Sometimes the early use of a brace will permit much more rapid restoration of function and the prevention of contracture deformities. The child and his family should not resign themselves to the idea that the application of a brace implies that no further improvement is to be expected. Many an appliance which is useful early may be discarded later. The care of persistent and severe disability, obviously, requires expert orthopedic care, bracing, and some later surgery.

The Occupational Therapist

The occupational therapist is an important member of team care. At first the child needs only diversion. Later various play activities can be developed in conference with the pediatrician, orthopedist, and the physical therapist to supplement other efforts in re-establishing function.

The Teacher

No impairment of mental capacity accompanies poliomyelitis. Early in convalescence education should gradually be resumed. The child who may have to forfeit certain of his potentialities should be helped to keep abreast of his contemporaries in every possible way. The teacher with special training can make a great contribution to after care. If she is wise enough not to add stress to the situation, she can guide the child in this normal activity without seeming to make any concession to his handicap.

The Social Worker

One of the most helpful components of the poliomyelitis problem is that this disaster for the family has become accepted as a community responsibility. The adept social worker can assist with many of the problems of the family; the mobilization of various resources for patient care; and the final adaptation of the child to his program of education, livelihood, and his place in society.

Conclusion

An intelligent and human approach on the part of the physician and the team of workers who surround the child must seek to be adequate to guide the child and his parents through the anxieties and the discomfort of the early stages of disease into the realities of late dysfunction and disability. Most children will accept these hardships philosophically. Neither the child nor his parents need ever accept an attitude of hopeless pessimism.

A time will finally arrive when, in many cases, plans must be made for a lifetime which is curtailed in one or another phase of motor activity. The entire program of care throughout the course of the illness must be such as to point the direction for this future planning. The child must be assisted not only in maximum rehabilitation of motor performance, but also in the adaptations of his aims and objectives toward a goal which will afford some measure of success.

Hardly a patient survives, no matter how severe his crippling, who cannot be guided into some accomplishment which will satisfy his ambitions.

THE CHILD WITH CYSTIC FIBROSIS

CHARLES D. MAY, M.D.

CHILDREN who suffer a handicap which is gradually apt to become increasingly severe, and is ultimately almost certainly fatal, require the most judicious management. A mature understanding coupled with a sensible desire to fill the child's limited life with happiness is a working challenge to be met by parents, friends, and teachers. After all, the future of any child is uncertain, and unforeseen tragedy may actually be more awesome.

Difficulty in breathing is as crippling to the full activity of children as is the loss of a limb; however, the limitations imposed are more subtle and not as easily appraised objectively. The burden imposed by chronic infection in the lungs and consequent labored breathing and weakness is much the same for most of the diseases affecting the lungs. However, the most common chronic lung disease in children is that accompanying cystic fibrosis of the pancreas. Consideration of this disorder will illustrate the general nature of the handicap of chronic lung diseases in children.

CLINICAL MANIFESTATIONS OF CYSTIC FIBROSIS OF THE PANCREAS

Cystic fibrosis of the pancreas is not, as the term implies, a disease involving the pancreas alone. The crippling effect is due to the almost regular appearance of a chronic infection and an obstructive process in the lungs. This inherited disorder may be expected in one in four of the offspring of parents who carry the abnormal genetic trait. Of course, this ratio does not actually occur in any one family. The ratio is an expression of the chance of the disease appearing among the children of an affected couple. At times, all of the children may be stricken, even nine in a single family has been observed. Fortunately one or two out of three to five children in a family is more usual. The condition usually becomes manifest at birth or within the first weeks of life. Although the cause of the disorder is hereditary, how this genetic fault produces the abnormal secretions and the consequent symptoms is unknown.

As the pancreas is almost completely destroyed by the cystic and fibrotic process, the digestive secretions which are produced in the pancreas are soon lost. These secretions are essential for the digestion of the basic food substances; protein, carbohydrates, and fat. However, only the so-called external secretions of the pancreas are lost. Since the internal secretion, insulin, is preserved, diabetes does not develop in children with cystic fibrosis of the pancreas. However, the nutrition of the child suffers, particularly when the manifestations in the lungs become pronounced. The faulty digestion is tolerated remarkably well because the child is led instinctively to eat ravenously to make up for the inefficiency in absorption of food.

The pathology in the pancreas and in the lungs seems to result from obstruction by excessively sticky mucous of the ducts of the pancreas and the finer branches of the ducts serving to bring air into the lungs (bronchioles). The ducts draining the liver may also become obstructed, adding a burden of chronic scarring of the liver. Most recent observation indicates that the sweat glands produce an abnormal secretion containing four or five times the normal amount of salt. In hot weather this salt loss may lead to heat prostration if extra salt is not given to the child.

Through the infection and interference with breathing, the lesion in the lungs is the major factor in determining the degree of malnutrition and crippling. The breathing is obstructed by the thick secretions accumulating in the finer branches of the bronchi. This accumulation provides favorable soil for the development of chronic infection deep in the lungs. This infection is virtually impossible to eliminate because of the thick secretions and the type of bacteria usually found. The bacteria (usually staphylococci) apparently quickly become insensitive to the complete array of antibiotics now available for treatment.

As may readily be imagined, when all of these organs are affected severely at the same time, the infant or child cannot long survive. Many of the children survive through the school years if the lesion in the lungs in only slowly progressive. Considerable progress has been made in treatment. Prior to the era of antibiotics an infant with cystic fibrosis of the pancreas usually died of the lung lesion before reaching an age of two years. Today although some children live to 16 years of age, survival beyond adolescence is still rare. Even though the lungs may be kept in good condition for long periods, most often the course is punctured with bouts of severe lung symptoms. Some disability from the lungs is common throughout the child's life.

The preceding considerations apply to the majority suffering from this condition who usually develop all of the possible manifestations in the pancreas, lungs, liver, and sweat. About 5% of the affected children, who may have symptoms from only one or two of these organs, may thrive surprisingly well if the lungs are not affected or only slightly so.

TREATMENT

Medical treatment is concerned with the infection in the lungs and the correction of malnutrition. Success in the former is a matter of repeated administration of antibiotics. Nothing presently at hand will thin the troublesome thick secretions (the really fundamental fault). Persistent attack on the infection is frequently rewarded by long periods of relative freedom from serious lung symptoms, depending primarily on the sensitivity of the offending bacteria to the available antibiotics and perhaps to some extent on the natural resistance of the child.

The digestion may be aided by pancreatic extracts which provide the missing enzymes. Restriction of the diet is not beneficial, but harmful, since these children need an increased amount of all foodstuffs to make up for the inefficient absorption. Children will take care of this malfunctioning by their ravenous appetite if provided an abundance of a well balanced diet, and if sensible eating habits are inculcated to avoid excessive indulgence in any one class of foodstuff.

The loss of salt in sweat is covered in hot weather by adding salt to the diet, and by permitting free access to salt. The lesion in the liver is not troublesome until late in the disease and until then requires no special measures.

EXTENT OF THE HANDICAPS IMPOSED

The majority of the children with this disease appear thin and chronically ill. The thick secretions in the lungs cause paroxysms of severe coughing. Exertion quickly leads to shortness of breath. Participation in more than mild exercise is difficult. Sometimes, blueness of lips and skin (cyanosis) will be conspicuous, and the fingers and toes will take on a clubbed appearance. Eventually the heart will be embarrassed by lack of oxygen, and heart failure with general dropsy will slowly develop. By this time the child will be bedridden.

A considerable number of children who exhibit a milder form of the disease may be able to attend school. Their nutrition may be no more troublesome than those associated with chronic bronchitis, asthma, or mild bronchiectasis. In this phase, the child will feel well and tend to ignore the minor handicap. Unfortunately, a relentless progression for the worse is in store for all but a few.

The considerable improvement in treatment which has enabled so large a number to reach school age gives sound basis for an optimistic mood. Active research in this disease offers promise of more dramatic success in treatment in the not too distant future. The most pressing need is for a means of restoring the thick secretions in the lung to a normal consistency. In all likelihood, the child would then eliminate the infection from the lung just as normally as human beings are continuously sweeping bacteria entrapped in mucous out of their respiratory tracts.

SIGNIFICANCE OF THE HANDICAPS

The lesion in the lungs constitutes a conscious handicap for children with this disorder. To have to eat more food in order to absorb enough nutrients is not a burden, the excessive salt in the sweat is not noticeable, and the loss is easily compensated. No symptoms from the process in the liver during its insidious development are noticeable. The lungs are truly crippling when the disease is advanced or uncontrolled. The problems then are those of the bedridden invalid.

The group of children of special concern are those well enough to be up and about and those attending school. These youngsters should be given the freedom of setting their own pace in activity and sociability. The impending doom does not force itself into their consciousness, nor should it creep in from the attitudes of those around them. Limiting activity or trying to prevent infection by avoiding joining others in play and school will not add significantly to survival. Most assuredly these actions will subtract from enjoyment while such enjoyment is still possible. Surprising improvement frequently follows in the wake of the most discouraging periods. Among children suffering from chronic illnesses, those with cystic fibrosis of the pancreas are singularly anxious to lead normal lives and are much less dependent or psychologically disturbed than diabetic patients. A less restrictive type of regimen, dietary as well as otherwise, in the management of patients with cystic fibrosis of the pancreas may be responsible for the fact that such patients are less likely to develop psychological complications.

Full activity and full attendance at school are recommended as long as desired by the child. Even part-time schooling is better than none. During periods when the symptoms make school attendance not feasible, teaching should be continued systematically at home. One cheerful aspect of this generally distressing condition is that seldom do other handicapping congenital disorders, such as congenital heart disease, occur simultaneously. Thus, when the therapy is more successful, and it may be any day, full advantage of the investment in schooling and normal rearing can be realized in those who will survive into adulthood.

In brief, in daily life and in school, the children with cystic fibrosis of the pancreas are safely and most wisely handled as normal children insofar as their own inclinations dictate and their strengths allow. The tendency for these children to ignore the handicap should be supported by a wholesome optimistic perspective on the part of all those surrounding them. Since most parents of an affected child soon achieve this philosophy to a laudable extent, they welcome a sympathetic mature response from everyone concerned with their child.

GUIDES TO FURTHER READING:

Di Sant' Agnese, P. A.: Cystic Fibrosis of the Pancreas. *Am. J. Med.*, *21:*406-422, 1956. An up-to-date technical review of current research with abundant references to the literature.

May, Charles D.: *Cystic Fibrosis of the Pancreas in Infants and Children.* Springfield, Thomas, 1954, 93 pp. Brief monograph providing an integrated account of the manifestations, pathology and diagnosis of the disease in language suitable for laymen as well as physicians.

THE CHILD WITH RHEUMATIC FEVER

Lee Forrest Hill, M.D.

Rheumatic fever is a prolonged chronic disease in which there may or may not be cardiac damage. Although only a few children out of each thousand contract it, the aggregate in the United States is large, constituting a major public health problem. Unlike many other diseases of childhood, one attack does not produce immunity. Recurrences are a possibility for a number of years, perhaps for life, with an increased risk of heart involvement with each recurrence. As would be expected, handicapping is greatest and most prolonged in the children with heart involvement. Even in those without cardiac damage, handicapping occurs, although to a lesser degree, because of the length of the acute and convalescent phases of the rheumatic attack itself.

Management of the disease process itself is a medical responsibility, but many problems of a sociological nature arise during the long-term course of the illness which require the services of other professions and groups. Thus, physicians, nurses, social workers, teachers, occupational therapists, physiotherapists, nutritionists and vocationalists constitute a team of experts, each with a special task to perform in the over-all job of rehabilitating the rheumatic victim to as full and useful a life as his capabilities will permit. Many organizations also exist, official and unofficial, governmental and voluntary, whose sole or main activities are devoted to the cardiac problem. In addition, these are physical facilities: diagnostic cardiac centers, rheumatic sanatoria, convalescent homes, heart hospitals, pediatric and general hospitals. All these people, organizations, and physical plants constitute a community's resources for meeting the challenge of rheumatic fever. Many states and communities have organized their resources into cardiac programs for greater efficiency and less duplication of effort. Whittemore[1] describes how this was accomplished in the State of Connecticut.

Before the specific handicapping effects of rheumatic fever and rheumatic carditis are described, a skeletal background about the disease itself will be outlined, although no attempt will be made to go into detailed medical descriptions. Assumed is the fact that most parents of a child with rheumatic fever want as much general information about the problem facing them as they can get. Informed and understanding parents are an extremely important asset.

The magnitude of the rheumatic problem should be understood. Between the ages of 5 and 19 the incidence of rheumatic heart disease ranges from 2 to 4 cases for 1,000 children. For each discovered case of rheumatic carditis, one or two others have had rheumatic fever but have escaped heart damage. The total number of cases of rheumatic heart disease in the United States for all ages is estimated at 500,000 and that over 1,000,000 have had rheumatic fever. Each year something like 25,000 persons in the nation become ill with the disease. The Statistical Bulletin of the Metropolitan Life Insurance Company published in August, 1954, shows that deaths from rheumatic fever and rheumatic heart disease between the ages of 5 and 14 rank second in the list of deaths from disease, being preceded only by deaths from malignancy. Most of the cardiac deaths among adults under 30 years of age are the result of rheumatic fever usually during childhood.

Rheumatic fever occurs infrequently before the age of 4. The greatest frequency occurs between 5 and 15 years, peak incidence of initial attacks occurring between 6 and 8 years of age. Adults, too, have rheumatic fever, some when they are well advanced in years, perhaps as recurrences of initial attacks in childhood. Most authorities are in agreement that infections of the upper respiratory tract, throat, sinuses and ears, with group A hemolytic streptococci are responsible for both initial and recurrent attacks. Usually a latent period of one to four weeks follows the "strep" infection. In this interval the child may not regain his customary zip and bounce. Loss of appetite, easy fatigability, paleness and perhaps fever of low degree may be noted. The observant teacher may be the first to detect something wrong in the changed attitude of the child toward his school work. Clear-cut evidence of rheumatic fever is present when painful inflammation in several joints (polyarthritis) occurs accompanied by a definite rise in body temperature, usually in the neighborhood of 102 to 103 degrees. Examination at this time may disclose a characteristic murmur at the apex of the heart. As was noted previously, however, approximately half the children with initial attacks of rheumatic fever escape carditis. On the other hand something like a third of the children discovered to have typical rheumatic carditis give no history and present no findings of rheumatic fever. In other instances the rheumatic process may take the form of purposeless involuntary muscular movements commonly known as St. Vitus dance. Here inflammation has occurred in the brain.

Just how the initiating streptococcic infection produces the pathologic changes recognized as rheumatic disease is not known. That the changes occur in the connective or cell-binding tissue of the joints, heart, and subcutaneous tissues is known. Little harm would result were it not for the structural damage to the heart. Such damage may occur to the heart muscle or myocardium, to the lining or endocardium, or to the covering of the heart, the pericardium. When all these areas are involved, the patient is said to have pancarditis. Jones[2] states that myocarditis is the most serious of the three types of heart involvement. A complication, sub-acute bacterial endocarditis, results when certain types of streptococcic germs propagate on damaged heart valves. Before the days of penicillin this complication was uniformly fatal. Today it can frequently be cured with intensive penicillin therapy. Better still, it can usually be prevented by adequate antimicrobial prophylaxis.

Why a few children develop the disease after a "strep" infection while the majority do not, is a problem for medical investigation. Increased familial incidence has led Wilson[3] to consider heredity a major factor. Hypersensitivity to group "A" streptococcic organisms has also been advanced as an explanation. Somewhat analogous is the situation in which children hypersensitive to ragweed pollen develop hay fever and asthma, whereas those not so sensitized do not.

Environmental factors, as well as inherited, are considered to have an important bearing upon the incidence of rheumatic fever, since the greatest frequency of the disease is reported in the poorer areas of large cities where crowding is great and living conditions are substandard. Although faulty nutrition as an etiologic factor has been suggested, this has not been proved. A more plausible explanation is that crowding favors the easy spread of streptococcic infections from person to person. Strong supporting evidence favoring this explanation was obtained during World War II. Epidemics of group A streptococcal infections among military personnel in camps were studied meticulously. A high incidence of rheumatic fever was found to follow these outbreaks. Altogether a total of some 40,000 cases of rheumatic fever were reported among servicemen in World War II.

In the past it has been held that rheumatic fever occurred with greater frequency in cold and temperate climates than in warm or tropical areas. In fact, it was a common practice for physicians to recommend to their rheumatic fever patients that they change from the cold climate of the north to the warm climate of the south, especially during the winter months. The practice has largely been abandoned at present for it has been found that streptococcic infections occur in all climates, facilitated, no doubt, by the great increase in travel incident to modern means of transportation.

The long-range outlook for children who become ill with rheumatic fever is of immediate interest to parents of such children and to all others who work in the field. Two studies may be cited which furnish information on this point. The first is a statistical report by the Metropolitan Life Insurance Company.[4] Some 3,000 children, ranging in age from 1 to 20 years who suffered their initial attacks between 1936 and 1938, were systematically followed during the next 15 years. The best results occurred in the children under 10 who had no recorded evidence of heart disease at the first observation. At the end of the 15 year period, 93 per cent of the boys and 94 per cent of the girls were living. Of those with evidence of heart disease at the first observation, 65 per cent of the boys were alive at the end of 15 years, and a slightly higher per cent of the girls survived. Deaths were highest in the years immediately after the attack, especially among those with heart disease. Rates given for boys was 66 per 1,000 in the first five years, 17 per 1,000 in the second five years, and only 8 per 1,000 in the third five-year period. The latter

274

low rate was thought to reflect the successful prevention of recurrent attacks by penicillin and sulfa drugs.

The other study was carried out by T. Duckett Jones[5] at the House of the Good Samaritan in Boston. One thousand children of an average age of 8 years when first seen sometime between 1921 and 1931 were followed for 20 years or longer. During the 20-year period, 301 patients died, the large majority from rheumatic fever and rheumatic heart disease. Of the survivors, 560 or 80 per cent, had little or no physical limitation, 122 had moderate limitation, and only 6 were classified as having marked limitation of activity. By the end of the 20-year period, all signs of rheumatic heart disease had disappeared in 16 per cent of the patients, and an additional 15 per cent were considered to have an improved cardiac status. Of the 1,000 patients in the study, 76 served in World War II. Of special interest is the fact that 421 children were born to the 709 female patients during the observation period.

Hopeful as the long-range outlook appears to be from these two reports, similar studies 10 years hence should be infinitely better. Even before the advent of the newer antimicrobial agents and the steroid compounds, mortality from rheumatic fever had been declining materially for many years. This decline was ascribed to improved economic and living conditions, a trend that can be expected to continue at an increasing tempo. Many believe that there has been a gradual decrease in severity of rheumatic fever over the years. This decrease in severity has been true for scarlet fever which is caused by group "A" streptococci and occasionally is the precursor of rheumatic fever. Important as are these natural trends, methods developed by man for his own protection would appear to be of even greater promise. Early and adequate treatment of streptococcic infections prevents most initial and recurring attacks of rheumatic fever. The most efficient drug for this purpose is penicillin. Furthermore, it has been demonstrated that streptococcic infections can be prevented in rheumatic persons by the daily ingestion of sulfadiazine or penicillin or by monthly injections of 1,200,000 units of Benzathine penicillin G. "All individuals who have a well established history of a previous attack of rheumatic fever or chorea or who show definite evidence of rheumatic heart disease should be placed on continuous prophylaxis."[6] By "continuous" is meant summer and winter throughout the year and, in the light of present knowledge, throughout life. So important to the control of rheumatic fever is this concept of the treatment and prevention of streptococcic infections that the American Heart Association has briefed every physician in the nation on the exact details of drug dosage and indications. In addition the Association has outlined a clinical description of the signs and symptoms of the usual streptococcic infection. To expect that all streptococcic infections in children can be recognized and treated with elimination of rheumatic fever is too optimistic. Cases will continue to occur, but it can confidently be predicted at a greatly lessened incidence.

For those children who do acquire the disease, a new form of therapy is being evaluated for its effectiveness in shortening the course of the illness and in lessening cardiac damage. This therapy employs the steroid compounds: ACTH, cortisone or meta-cortin. Although present reports are somewhat inconclusive, general agreement exists that patients with severe active rheumatic carditis should have this form of therapy.

Finally, surgery can frequently lessen handicapping from the effects of chronic valvular heart disease. Stenosed or narrowed valves in properly selected cases are being opened-up, thereby improving circulation and decreasing the work-load of the heart. Many patients formerly totally incapacitated, or nearly so, have been returned to useful active lives following such an operation.

Most of the tools necessary for fairly effective control of rheumatic fever are at hand. On the extent to which they are universally applied depends the degree of control secured. In the meantime, research is being conducted by a host of workers in an attempt to solve the mystery of the relation between the streptococcic infection and the subsequent pathological tissue changes. When this mechanism is known, as undoubtedly it will be, new methods of prevention and treatment may be discovered which will be vastly superior to those now available.

Handicapping Effects of Rheumatic Fever. Following the course of a hypothetical rheumatic child from the initial streptococcic infection to his eventual rehabilitation will emphasize the services and resources needed for his care.

With the acute streptococcal infection the problem facing the physician is one of diagnosis. In his daily work he commonly sees children with sore throats. To distinguish those due to streptococci from other organisms, often viral, is not easy. The American Heart Association[6] lists the common symptoms of streptococcic infections as sudden onset of sore throat with headache, fever varying from 101 to 104 degrees F, abdominal pain, nausea and vomiting. Common signs are red throat with exudate, swollen tender glands at the angle of the jaw, possibly a scarletiniform rash complicated at times by acute otitis media and sinusitis. The white blood count is usually over 12,000. A positive throat culture for hemolytic streptococci nearly always confirms a suspected diagnosis. The treatment schedule recommended by the American Heart Association for streptococcic infections is penicillin in amounts adequate to maintain effective blood levels for a period of 10 days, "even though the temperature returns to normal and the patient is asymptomatic." This can be accomplished by one intramuscular injection of 600,000 units of Benzathine penicillin G, by three intramuscular injections three days apart of 300,000 units of Procaine penicillin or by 250,000 units of oral penicillin three times a day for the full ten days. Prompt treatment carried out according to these recommendations should prevent initial or recurrent attacks of rheumatic fever.

But let us assume that for one reason or another our hypothetical patient failed to get adequate treatment for his streptococcic infection. After a latent period of some two to three weeks, the child develops symptoms which his parents fear may be rheumatic fever and he is taken to their physician for an examination. Or it may be that an astute school teacher has alerted the parents or the school nurse to the possibility. The diagnosis of rheumatic fever may be very simple or it may be difficult, perhaps impossible without several weeks of observation. Unfortunately there is no positive diagnostic test available for rheumatic fever as, for instance, the Wasserman test for syphilis or the Mantoux test for tuberculosis. Diagnosis is relatively easy if such signs and symptoms are present as migratory polyarthritis with fever, or chorea, or if there is definite carditis as shown by a blowing systolic apical murmur. There are referred to as major manifestations of rheumatic fever. Minor manifestations are leg cramps, abdominal pain, low grade fever, erythema multiforme, subcutaneous nodules, anemia, anorexia, leucocytosis and increased sedimentation rate. Such manifestations may be due to rheumatic fever; but unless accompanied by at least one of the major manifestations, a positive diagnosis cannot be made with certainty. Additional information may be obtained from fluoroscopic and x-ray examination of the heart, from electrocardiography, and from such tests as the anti-streptolysin titre and the C-reactive protein determination. Even with all these data at hand, a correct diagnosis may have to depend upon the good judgment and experience of the physician.

An understandable tendency both to "over-diagnosis" and to "under-diagnosis" of rheumatic fever occurs. The former is more common. Both should be avoided. Over-diagnosis results most frequently from mistakenly assuming that leg cramps, low grade fever, or accidently discovered innocent heart murmurs are due to rheumatic fever. Confirmatory laboratory and x-ray evidence is usually lacking. To remove these healthy children from school for a prolonged period of enforced bed rest is a serious error. Handicapping, with all its ramifications, can be just as real for such imagined illness.

Let us assume that in the case of the child we are following a positive diagnosis of rheumatic fever in the acute stage is possible, moreover, that clear evidence of rheumatic carditis is present. Of necessity the parents must be told of the diagnosis and a plan for the medical care of the child must be decided upon. Most parents have some information about rheumatic fever which they have gleaned from the wide publicity given to the disease. Some may have the impression that rheumatic fever inevitably means heart disease and possibly death, perhaps sudden death, or that the best they can expect is permanent cardiac crippling. Naturally these will be terror-stricken when told their child has rheumatic fever. Others may have a guilt complex, especially if the physician has probed rather vigorously into the family history and has uncovered the information that rheumatic fever has occurred in some of the relatives or in one or the other parent. The guilt feeling may arise from the parents' feeling that he or she is to blame, that the attack could have been prevented had the child been made to wear his hat or coat or rubbers or if he had been kept in out of the night air. Still another parental reaction is one of overprotection, over-solicitation, and of giving-in to every whim or demand of the child. This reaction, too, may be a cover-up for a guilt feeling. On the other hand, an occasional parent will react in an opposite direction, that of rejection of the child on the basis that the child's illness has added to parental burdens, is expensive, and has deprived the family of obtaining material or educational advantages. Thus, the physician faces his third problem in the rheumatic cycle, that of attempting to establish a rational-psychological-parental attitude about the child's illness. How well he succeeds may have an important bearing upon the child's progress throughout his acute illness, convalescence, and rehabilitation. Later, if his efforts have met with indifferent success, the services of a psychiatrist may be needed.

Next, the decision has to be made as to where the hypothetical child shall be cared for during the acute active phase of his rheumatic infection, at home or in the hospital. The hospital possesses advantages not obtained in the home. Complete bed rest will probably be necessary for a minimum of three months and perhaps for a year depending upon the seriousness of the attack. During the early weeks the needs of the patient will be largely of a service nature, medical management and nursing care. Frequent laboratory tests, roentgenographic studies, and electrocardiograms may need to be made. Unless the home and economic conditions are unusually good or the illness unusually mild with minimum requirements, these services are better provided in a hospital. Moreover, the attitude of the child toward his illness is likely to be better in the hospital atmosphere where there are other sick children than in the home where healthy siblings and playmates are present

A valid objection to prolonged institutionalization is the anxiety which may be created in the child's mind by enforced separation from his parents. Fortunately there is an active trend away from hospital regulations which permit visiting only once or twice a week or at most an hour a day. In the children's hospital with which the author is associated, essentially unlimited visiting hours have been in effect for the last three years. Although initially there were some objections on the part of the nursing staff and even of the house staff, these gradually melted away as the advantages of the more liberal regulations became apparent. In most instances parents are found to be a help rather than a hindrance. They help entertain the children, feed them and do many other chores that spare the nurses' time. The most important additional advantage is the increased opportunity liberal visiting hours give for parent education along many facets of child care, including, of course, a better understanding of the child's particular illness, in this case, rheumatic fever.

Prolonged hospitalization has been mentioned by some as increasing the risk of the child coming in contact with streptococci "A". If prophylaxis by one of the methods previously described is promptly instituted as soon as the diagnosis of rheumatic fever has been made, the objection should be neutralized.

When the acute active phase of rheumatic fever has subsided, a subacute convalescent stage begins which may last many months. During this period the need for medical and nursing service decreases materially, but other needs increase sharply. Chief among these are schooling, recreation, and a stable psychological attitude on the part of both the patient and his parents toward his disease. Again the decision has to be reached as to where the child shall be cared for during convalescence, at home or in an institution, such as a convalescent home, hospital, or a special rheumatic fever hospital. Most rheumatic patients, if not of too severe degree, can spend the convalescent weeks or months at home, providing, of course, home conditions are suitable. By suitable is meant a home that can provide a room for the patient's individual use, or at least a bed he can have to himself. The family's income should be such that food and medicines necessary for his proper nutrition and care can be purchased. Usually it is best for the child's mother to care for him. If it is necessary for the mother to work, a suitable responsible adult may be substituted.

Interruption of schooling with the risk of falling behind his peers is one of the most important concerns of the rheumatic patient. Several resources can be utilized to assist the child. The installation of a two-way radio between the child's classroom and his bedroom is one possibility. Consulting the visiting teacher employed by the public school system for this particular purpose is another. A third method, but not as satisfactory, would be to have the teaching done by the child's mother or some other competent person. Not only is maintaining the child in his proper grade a morale builder but also the time consumed in studying helps greatly to avoid boredom. Providing recreational outlets for the bed-fast child in the home was something of a struggle in the past but today the situation is vastly improved. Watching television, listening to radio, assembling of mechanical toys, such as airplanes, boats, and automobiles, and playing with a host of other modern devices pretty well solve the problem. Inability to engage freely in the physical and social activities of his siblings and playmates may create a psychological problem difficult for both mother and child alike. How much of a problem this turns out to be depends largely upon how a good job of parent and patient education has been done.

In contrast to home care for the convalescent rheumatic patient, institutional care possesses many advantages and only a few disadvantages. Properly equipped and staffed, the institution has a continuing well-balanced program designed to meet the expanded needs of the convalescent child as he is able to take on new activities. Planned meals by expert nutritionists meet the important nutritional problem. Most institutions have teachers connected with the public school system so that the education of the child can continue uninterrupted. Occupational therapists provide the recreational facilities necessary to keep the child occupied and interested. Physiotherapists are available to assist the child who needs such help to regain use of muscles weakened by inactivity. Finally, most children develop a good emotional adjustment to their handicap in the friendly but matter-of-fact atmosphere engendered by all the personnel responsible for their care and in the setting of other children with restrictions similar to their own. Several studies have been done to find out the preference of children who have had both home and institutional care. Bauer[7] reports a study on 50 such children. The majority favored the organized routine of the institution. Some even experienced difficulty in readjusting to the home situation after leaving the institution, the size of the home, the food and the way things were done being compared unfavorably to the way of life in the institution.

The services of the social service worker and of the public health nurse may be utilized to great advantage in the over-all planning for and carrying-out the care of the rheumatic child during the convalescent and follow-up course. Through the social worker's investigations, other community resources may be tapped to meet needs. The welfare agency may be able to secure more suitable living quarters for the low-income family living in a congested area or slum district. Financial assistance may be arranged to help families meet the added expenses imposed by the child's illness. Pencillin, still an expensive drug, may be obtained from some service organization for families unable to buy it for themselves. In addition to helping with the solution of problems such as these, the social worker keeps a case record of the rheumatic child which, along with the medical record, enables the physician at all times to have at his finger tips the complete story of the progress of his patient, psychological, social, economical and medical.

Eventually comes the day when the physician decides that the active stage of the rheumatic infection has subsided. The hypothetical child enters the chronic inactive infection phase which continues indefinitely unless interrupted by a recurrence. The physician must evaluate the degree of cardiac crippling the patient has undergone in order to establish the limitations of activity necessary for his education and for his protection as he resumes his place in society. Usually this is accomplished only after a series of tests which may include roentgenographic examination to determine heart size, electrocardiography, and other tests designed to measure functional capacity.

As a guide to the management of patients with carditis the functional and therapeutic classifications published by the Criteria Committee[8] of the New York Heart Association, Inc., and distributed by the American Heart Association, are reproduced here.

FUNCTIONAL CLASSIFICATION OF PATIENTS

Class I. Patients with cardiac disease, but without resulting limitation of activity. Ordinary physical activity does not cause undue fatigue, palpitation, dyspnoea or anginal pain.

Class II. Patients with cardiac disease resulting in slight limitation of physical activity. They are comfortable at rest. Ordinary physical activity results in fatigue, palpitation, dyspnoea or anginal pain.

Class III. Patients with cardiac disease resulting in marked limitation of physical activity. They are comfortable at rest. Less than ordinary activity causes fatigue, palpitation, dyspnoea or anginal pain.

Class IV. Patients with cardiac disease resulting in inability to carry on any physical activity without discomfort. Symptoms of cardiac insufficiency or of the anginal syndrome may be present even at rest. If any physical activity is undertaken, discomfort is increased.

The Functional Classification indicates the physician's estimate of cardiac capacity. It does not necessarily prescribe the amount of activity the patient should undertake. The Therapeutic Classification, on the other hand, is a "prescription for the amount of physical activity which is advised for those in each class."

THERAPEUTIC CLASSIFICATION OF PATIENTS

Class A. Patients with cardiac disease whose physical activity need not be restricted.

Class B. Patients with cardiac disease whose ordinary physical activity need not be restricted, but who should be advised against severe or competitive physical efforts.

Class C. Patients with cardiac disease whose ordinary physical activity should be moderately restricted, and whose more strenuous efforts should be discontinued.

Class D. Patients with cardiac disease whose ordinary physical activity should be markedly restricted.

Class E. Patients with cardiac disease who should be at complete rest, confined to bed or chair.

For our purposes here, patients in Class E may be excluded from further discussion, since it can be assumed that they would be continued at bed-rest at home or in an institution. What we are concerned with is whether our patient should attend regular school without restrictions of any kind, regular school with restrictions, a special class in a regular school, or a special school. The answer to this problem is not as simple as it might seem. Studies are lacking upon which valid conclusions can be drawn between educational placement in regular or special classes with respect to advantages or disadvantages of one over the other.

In general, opinion seems to favor regular classes whenever possible. Certainly there should be no question about children in Class A and Class B being placed in regular classes. Wallace, Wrightstone and Gall[9] state that the primary objective should be to return as many children as possible to regular classes in as short a time as possible. "Child life," they say, "lived apart from normal children is not considered to be conducive to the development of personality traits necessary for a shared social life. In so far as possible, handicapped children should participate in the normal school activities."

However, a few children will be left with such severe residual cardiac damage that special provisions must be made for them. Patients in Classes C and D might come in this category. The authors mentioned above summarize the specific principles which should govern the placement of children in special classes as follows: "Special classes should be provided for those children who need them and who otherwise would not be able to attend school; special classes should provide the necessary services essential to meet the individual needs of the children in them; medical criteria should be established by medical experts for the admission to, renewal of and discharge from placement in special classes in order to serve as a general guide for physicians responsible for the care of handicapped children; children should be placed in special classes and their placement renewed only upon recommendation of qualified medical specialists, and should remain under the guidance of well trained personnel in the various categories concerned, and with little or no segregation of children placed in the special classes. This principle is of major importance if children are to be given their opportunity of normal psychological growth and development. There should be a good record system to provide adequate data on each child's physical progress and emotional adjustment, and there should be easily accessible physical facilities for easy mobility of the children."

The main potential advantages of the special class for cardiac handicapped children are: (1) smaller size of the class permitting more individual attention to the needs of each child; (2) lessened opportunity for exposure to respiratory tract infection, and (3) closer supervision of the children by teachers, nurses and physicians. Potential disadvantages are: (1) psychological, from inability to attend the same school as neighborhood playmates and to share in their school experiences; (2) increased distance in traveling to and from the special school; (3) modification of the educational program made necessary by the wide age span in the class; (4) difficulties in transferring the child in and out of the special class, and (5) increased cost.

Most cardiac handicapped children can be placed in regular classes if the school building and facilities permit. For example, children with cardiac disease requiring considerable limitation of physical activity cannot climb two or three flights of stairs attending departmental classes, but can manage very well if the building is of the one-story type or if elevators are provided. In this respect, two final quotes from Wallace, *et al.*, seem appropriate. "Ideally", they say, "the regular classes should be smaller in registration and public schools should be one-story buildings or at least have elevators or ramps and easily accessible necessary physical facilities. It is possible that some of the problems in the education of handicapped children in schools are man-made, due to the lack of foresight in planning adequate physical plants and facilities," and ". . . it is suggested that any school have one room where children with any type of health problem requiring modification of the school program may be placed temporarily. This should be looked upon as a highly flexible and fluid plan with easy and quick movement in and out."

The decision for educational placement in a regular or special class as well as the degree of restriction of physical activity necessary is the responsibility of the physician. His instructions must be made clear to the child's teacher, to the school nurse, and to the parents. Follow-up visits must be made to the physician or clinic at regular intervals, fairly frequent at first, perhaps every one to two months; later every six months. Restrictions on physical activity should be as lenient as the cardiac status permits.

In the meantime, the most important goal for the rheumatic child is to attain all the education possible. Thus armed, a variety of vocations within the capabilities of his cardiac status will be open from which to choose. Wherever possible this course is to be recommended over the early selection of a vocation. For the rheumatic cardiac who may not be endowed intellectually for college and perhaps a professional education, a suitable vocation is advisable; but for those who can go on, every effort should be made to enable them to do so.

The physician may prescribe accurately and correctly what the cardiac handicapped child can and cannot do. But if his instructions are to be properly carried out, parent, patient and even teacher attitudes toward the child's handicap must be correctly established. An understandable parental reaction is to restrict the child's activities beyond what the physician has advised and otherwise to over-protect him for fear that he may have a relapse of his rheumatic fever. The child may not be required to do his share of the home chores, and in other ways be granted favoritism because he is "sick." Such favored treatment may arouse sibling's resentment and jealousies. Some children might make use of their illness to gain advantages for themselves.

Attitudes of children toward their cardiac handicap when they return to school has been investigated and reported by several authors.[10,11,12] As would be expected, these vary widely. Some children, perhaps the majority, are indifferent toward their heart disease and ignore it in their every day relations with other children. If restrictions on activity have been imposed, these are accepted and followed without resentment. Some children, on the other hand, conceal their heart disease so they will not be kept out of the games the other children play. In the reports mentioned above, an occasional child was encountered who appeared to be genuinely concerned about his condition. Most often this attitude was found in children who had shown signs of emotional instability before the onset of the rheumatic episode. Fear of death was usually related to knowledge on the child's part of some other child or person who had died from heart disease. Fear of the return of symptoms which had resulted in the original hospitalization was shown by some children. One child cited had been admitted to the hospital for evaluation of complaints on six different occasions, all of which were proven to be an emotional basis. Recently an attractive healthy nine-year-old girl who had had a diagnosis of rheumatic fever made three years previously was seen by the author because of complaints of leg and arm aches. Her first question was, "Do you think it's rheumatic?" On another occasion she reported pains in her jaws and demanded to know if she had tetanus.

These unsound emotional attitudes on the part of parents and patients, detrimental to rehabilitation, should be detected and corrected at the earliest possible time. Although this responsibility is best assumed by the physician, the social worker, public health nurse, teacher, or some other person who first becomes aware of the emotional instability, should bring it to the attention of the physician. Time-out at each visit to explain in a factual manner the nature of and necessity for limitations to activity is time well spent. Provided recurrences can be prevented, the time should come for the majority of rheumatic patients when all restrictions, except possibly those for the most active of competitive sports, can be removed.

Should a young woman with rheumatic carditis marry and bear children[4] This can only be answered by careful individual consideration of each case. Earlier it was pointed out in the study of the fate of 1,000 rheumatic patients by Jones that during the twenty-year observation period, 709 female patients gave birth to 421 children.

With all the advances which have been made in the last decade and with those that are certain to come in the next decade, a child who today contracts rheumatic fever has an excellent chance of not only surviving but of living a normal, productive and satisfactory existence even though cardiac damage has occurred. This goal can best be approached if each community has an organized cardiac program designed to make available to every rheumatic child whatever help he needs—medical, psychiatric, economic, educational, and vocational—to rehabilitate him to as full and useful a life in the community as his capabilities will permit.

In summary, the following points may be selected for emphasis:

1. Rheumatic fever is a chronic illness of unknown etiology which affects only a few children out of each thousand. Recurrences are common. Damage to the heart occurs with the initial attack in some children and increases in frequency in recurrences.

2. Rheumatic carditis is the chief cause of handicapping.

3. Early diagnosis of group A beta hemolytic streptococcic infections of the respiratory tract and adequate treatment with penicillin or other effective antimicrobial agents may prevent rheumatic fever and its recurrences.

4. In well substantiated rheumatic fever patients, prophylaxis against "strep" infections should be carried out for life.

5. Evidence indicates that the incidence of rheumatic fever as well as its severity is decreasing.

6. The diagnosis of rheumatic fever may require special tests and special knowledge. "Over-diagnosis" is common, but "under-diagnosis" also occurs. Both are to be avoided.

7. Psychological, emotional, and intellectual orientation of both parents and patient are essential to optimum rehabilitation of the child with rheumatic fever. Usually this responsibility falls upon the shoulders of the physician.

8. Rheumatic fever can be divided into an acute active stage, a subacute convalescent stage, and a chronic inactive stage. The first stage requires mainly medical service and is best spent in a hospital. The convalescent stage may be spent at home or in an institution. Children themselves appear to prefer the established routines of the institutions.

9. Interruption to education is one of the important handicaps in rheumatic fever. Institutions provide educational facilities. Convalescent children at home may keep up with their classmates via a two-way radio hook-up, a visiting public school teacher, or a competent teacher substitute.

10. The services of the public health nurse and of the social worker should be utilized wherever possible.

11. Each rheumatic child, at the conclusion of his subacute convalescent phase, should have an evaluation of his cardiac status according to the Functional and Therapeutic Classifications recommended by the American Heart Association.

12. Educational placement in regular classes, if possible, is recommended. Placement in special classes should be reserved for those who otherwise could not go to school or who are deemed by the physician to have special need for such placement.

13. Limitations to physical activity as prescribed by the physician should be scrupulously observed by parents, patient, and teachers; but in all other respects the child should be treated and accepted as a normal child. Over-protection and over-indulgence by parents and teachers are to be avoided.

14. Maximum education is the best form of rehabilitation.

15. The final goal is to achieve for each rheumatic person with or without cardiac damage as normal and useful a life in society as possible.

REFERENCES

1. Whittemore, Ruth: Group conferences in a cardiac program. *Pediatrics, 15:*620, 1955.
2. Jones, T. Duckett: *You and Your Heart.* New York, Random House,
3. Wilson, May G. and Schweitzer, M.: *Pattern of Hereditary Susceptibility in Rheumatic Fever.* Abstract of paper read before International Congress on Cardiology, Sept., 1954.
4. *Statistical Bulletin.* Metropolitan Life Ins. Co., August, 1954.
5. Jones, T. Duckett: *Rheumatic Fever.* Minneapolis, University of Minnesota, Press, 1 52.
6. American Heart Association, Prevention of Rheumatic Fever and Bacterial Endocarditis through control of Streptococcal Infections. *Circulation, 11,* Feb., 1955.
7. Bauer, Irving L.: Attitudes of Children with Rheumatic Fever. *J. Pediat., 40:*796, 1952.
8. *Nomenclature and Criteria for Diagnosis of Diseases of the Heart and Blood Vessels.* Criteria Committee, New York Heart Association, 1953.
9. Wallace, Helen M., Wrightstone, J. W., and Gall, E.: Special Classes for Handicapped Children. *Am. J. Pub. Health, 44:*1045, 1954.
10. Silver, Harry B.: Emotional and social development of girls with heart disease. *J. Pediat., 12:*218, 1938.
11. Lyon, R. A., Rauh, Louise W., and Carroll, Mary G.: The Social Adjustment of Children with Heart Disease. *Ment. Hyg., 25:* 3, 1941.
12. Josselyn, Irene M.: Emotional Implications of Rheumatic Heart Disease in Children. *Am. J. Orthopsychiat., 19:*87, 1949.

ADDITIONAL SOURCES OF READING MATERIAL

1. Smith, Mary Alice, A Community Program for the Prevention of Rheumatic Fever Recurrence, *Public Health Reports, 68:*16, 1953.
2. *What the Classroom Teacher Should Know and Do About Children with Heart Disease,* American Heart Association.
3. *Children with Cardiac Limitations:* Studies of Pupils Enrolled in Special Classes. New York, Bureau of Educational Research, Board of Education of the City of New York, Dec., 1952.

4. *Cardiac Classes and the Care of Cardiac Children.* New York, Board of Education, City of New York, 1941.
5. Nebelung, Raymond G.: The Value of Segregated Classes versus Regular Classroom Instruction for Post-Rheumatic Fever Children. *J. School Health*, *23:*139, May, 1953.
6. Fishbein, Morris. The Social Aspects of Rheumatic Fever. *Pediatrics*, *15:*610, May, 1955.
7. Taran, Leo M., and Hodsdon, A. Edith: The Social and Psychologic Problems Associated with Prolonged Institutional Care for Rheumatic Children. *J. Pediatrics*, *35:*648, 1949.

THE CHILD WITH A SPEECH AND HEARING DISORDER

Harriet G. Kopp, B.S., M.A. and
George A. Kopp, B.S., M.S., Ph.D.

Speech is a learned form of behavior. Children learn to talk by the simple process of imitation and trial and error. The world over children learn to speak the language they hear spoken by those who communicate with them during early infancy and childhood.

The birth cry is a signal that the infant has taken his first breath, that he has become an air breathing animal, that certain neuro-muscular connections are intact, that no primitive web veils the vocal cords, and that the infant has taken the first step, primitive and unconscious as it may be, toward the development of speech.

Beginning with the birth cry and extending with the cries and vocalizations of the first few weeks, the infant establishes coordination of muscle groups that are modified later in speech. In addition, he hears the sounds produced and feels the movements used in making them. During the first four months his vocalizations begin to portray comfort, discomfort, pain, frustration, "angelicness" and "cussedness." His mother soon is able to identify each type of vocalization. A stranger can differentiate the contented babble and coo from the yell for relief from pain or discomfort. During this period of oral play, the child makes most of the sounds used in the English language plus many that are not used in any language.

Vocalizations become more volitional and purposeful with age. The progression is from random vocalizations to less random and to some purposeful vocalizations. Although the sounds emitted during the first weeks develop into a code for communicating states of being or expression of wants, they are not stable enough in their phonetic composition to be classified as speech. As the infant develops such an auditory comprehension of oral language, he creates an auditory reference standard to control his own trial and error performances and to establish the automaticity of his speech patterns.

Although children may vary as much as two years in the acquisition of their first commonly accepted words, a child normally progresses from babbling to the use of a few words for persons or objects within the first eighteen months. For periods that vary in length with the individual child, he will use single words that stand for complete sentences or thoughts. His comprehension of the spoken language will exceed his use of it. By the time he is three years of age, he will have added verbs, some modifiers, and some prepositions to his language. By the age of six, his average spoken vocabulary may range from two to five thousand words.

Speech development is affected by many factors including racial background, prematurity, maturational potential, sex, number of siblings, motivation, intelligence, hearing, physical health and emotional development.

Children of some racial backgrounds tend to mature faster than those of other racial ancestries. Within every race the variation in the rate of maturation is considerable. If one or both parents did not learn to talk until the age of three it is possible their offspring will begin to speak at about the same age.

Premature birth may delay the acquisition of speech about a year for each month of prematurity, thus a seventh month premature may require two and a half to three years to catch up with a normal full term child.

Sex is a factor in the development of speech difficulties. Although we do not know the explanation disturbances in language occur over 50 per cent more frequently in boys than girls. In the area of stuttering four times as many boys are affected as are girls.

A child who can get his wants satisfied by making gestures, who has no playmates, who lives alone with deafened adults or with those who speak infrequently may be slow in learning to speak. The first child, if an only child, may develop speech at an early age, depending upon the attention given to him by his parents. A third or fourth child, however, because of the auditory stimulation he receives from his brothers and sisters and the motivation to keep up with them, may develop speech at an earlier age than a first child.

Health is also a determinent of the beginning of speech. A child who has had frequent illnesses or who has experienced a severe or recurrent illness during the first three years of his life may be expected to be slower in learning to speak than a child who has had no illness. Parental anxiety, worry and pressure to induce any child to talk before he is developmentally able to do so actually may delay the acquisition of speech.

A child speaks by modulating the flow of air which passes from the lungs through the trachea, vocal cords, throat, nose and mouth cavities. The term *modulation*, used to describe how speech is produced, expresses concisely what happens to the air as it flows from the lungs. The term *modulate* means to alter, vary, or regulate the flow of air. Four types of modulation in speech, start-stop, vocal cord, frictional, and cavity modulations, are of particular importance. The start-stop modulation, which may be produced either by the vocal cords or the articulators, starts and stops the air flow. Vocal cord modulation, produced by the vibrations of the vocal words which periodically interrupt the flow of air, converts the air flow into audible sound waves. Frictional modulation produced by the articulators being placed close enough together to form a small opening or constriction through which the air must flow characterizes the group of sounds like the *s*, *f*, and *sh*. Cavity modulation which is produced in the coupled cavities of the throat, mouth, and nose, acts on the overtones produced by both vocal cord and frictional modulation. Additional kinds of modulation such as stress, inflection, vibrato, and vocal quality determine general speech characteristics.

Good speech is characterized by a volume loud enough to be heard comfortably, by a tonal quality appropriate to age and sex, by a meaningful use of variation of stress and pitch, by intelligible articulation, and by symbolization of thought consistent with the development of the individual. These components of good speech are dependent upon the functional efficiency of the respiratory, phonatory, articulatory, and linguistic processes involved in the integrated act of speaking. Impaired function of one or more of these integrated processes will result in defective speech. Consequently, speech may be considered defective when the way it is used is detrimental to the purpose for which it is used.

The degree of perfection of speech performance expected of the child is related to the socio-economic status of the parents and friends and to the emotional stability and maturity of the familial interrelationships. If a child's inter-personal relationships are mainly with those who have speech defects, he will feel ill at ease and self-conscious if placed in a normal speech environment. A child with normal speech habits may be made to feel out of place with children who have defective speech. The urge to conform in dress, behavior, and speech is strong among children and since the large majority of children develop normal speech, the child with the speech defect is usually influenced adversely.

The severity of the influence of a speech disorder upon a child is evident in that child's total behavior pattern. The child may be hostile, insecure, moody, anxietous, withdrawn socially, aggressive, frustrated, discouraged, and fearful. He may evidence enuresis, nail-biting, sleep-walking, tantrums, refusal to talk, crying, and poor eating habits, common behavioral concomitants when the child is seriously affected. In addition, he may be retarded scholastically, especially with regard to language skills.

No objective guide exists to measure the effect of defective speech upon the child himself. Child A, who may distort a dozen sounds, may exhibit no adverse reaction should parents and playmates accept the speech as non-defective either because they make the same mistakes or because they do not display anxiety. Child B, who may produce one specific sound incorrectly, may be very self-conscious about his speech should he be teased and imitated by his playmates and repeatedly corrected by parents exhibiting parental anxiety.

Children with major speech disorders constitute one of the largest groups in our population of seriously handicapped youngsters. A 1952 Mid-Century White House Conference report of the American Speech and Hearing Committee on Speech Disorders and Speech Correction conservatively estimates that 2,000,000 children ranging in age between 5 and 21 or approximately 5% of this population are affected. An additional 5% is estimated to have relatively minor speech and voice defects, unimportant for most practical purposes but serious in their effects on personal and social adjustments and obviously significant for children destined for fields of work requiring good speech such as teaching, medicine, and law. As with other conditions handicapping children, early diagnosis and treatment are recommended. A total approach to diagnosis suggests the preparation of a comprehensive personal history, an evaluation of the child's speech, and an examination of the child himself.

The preparation of a comprehensive personal history of the child being examined should be an important phase of the evaluative program. Such a personal history should contain information concerning such varied items as the extent of the formal education of the parents, the use of more than one language in the home, the family neuropathic heredity, an evaluation of the vocal quality of parents and siblings. The health of the mother during gestation should be determined. Special reference should be made to nephritis, acute infections, measles, severe emotional shock, and similar factors if these occurred during gestation.

Relevant information concerning the child should continue with his birth. Whether the labor was unusually short, long, or difficult; whether the delivery was natural or with the aid of instruments; whether the birth was premature or delayed, and whether other complications occurred at birth should be determined. The history should continue with as complete a medical history during infancy and childhood as it is possible to obtain. Such factors as anoxia, convulsions, paralysis, congenital deafness, diseases, Rh incompatibility, injuries, for example, should be noted. A comprehensive estimate of the child's health (physical and emotional) should be secured. Anomalies of the skull, ear, hair, eyes, teeth, tongue, palate, skin, limbs, genitalia, and body should be noted.

The comprehensive personal history of the child should contain an accurate developmental record. The age of onset of walking, the age at which toilet training was established, the age at which the child began to feed himself, for example, should be established. The development of dressing, sleep, and play habits; the character of sibling, familial, and peer relationships; the appearance of fears or anxieties; the development of the child's attention span with respect to the ability to focus and to maintain attention and to shift attention appropriately and volitionally; the development of gait and general coordination; are all examples of factors which should be noted and considered both in relation to the usual normal reference standards and to the child's familial reference standards.

The evaluation of the child's speech should ascertain *what* parts of the language are omitted, substituted, or added, and what, if anything is wrong with the voice. Since respiration, phonation, resonation, articulation, and cerebration function simultaneously in the total act of speaking, functional efficiency of these integrated phases of the speech mechanism should be determined. Seldom, if ever, will the speech be so afflicted that a complete examination of each phase is necessary. However, the parts of the speech mechanism that are basic to the particular speech disturbance should be given careful attention since an evaluation of the articulation and the voice is necessary. To elicit speech from a pre-school child or a child who cannot read, sound games, toys, objects, and pictures of objects which include the various sounds of language, should be used. To elicit speech from a child who can read, both conversation and reading materials adapted to the vocabulary of the child being tested should be used. In any case, the materials selected should include the various sounds of the language in the initial, medial, and final position of words.

The examination of the speaker may ascertain why the speech is defective. A comprehensive physical examination may reveal anomalies of the skull, ear, hair, eyes, teeth, tongue, palate, skin, limbs, genitalia, and body. Because speech is seen as well as heard, such an examination may involve evaluation of cranial, cervical, and thoracic nerves as well as of the muscles of the head, neck and thorax. In any case, such an examination will place emphasis on the functional efficiency of muscles, nerves, and mental processes controlling respiration, articulation, and the linguistic process involved in the integrated act of speaking.

Respiration is the source of power for speech. In silence there is a rhythmic inhalation and exhalation of breath. In speech the inhalation phase is shortened and the exhalation phase is lengthened. The rate varies from 15 to 18 breaths per minute in silence, and from 8 to 14 in speech. Diaphragmatic, abdominal, thoracic, costal and clavicular breath support refer to the predominate types of muscular coordination during breathing for speech. The preferred type of coordination is that usually described as diaphragmatic or natural. The diaphragm contracts during inspiration and the abdominal recti muscles relax thus permitting a slight displacement outward of the viscera by the downward movement of the diaphragm. Laterally there is a slight outward movement of the lower ribs. During exhalation the reverse contractions and movements take place. The diaphragm relaxes and moves upward, the abdominal recti contract and move inward and the lower ribs move inward. Other thoracic muscles are used during forced respiration for loud speaking and shouting. Loudness, intensity, or amplitude, and breathiness of speech are related directly to breath support. The weak breath support characteristic of lowered physical vitality, of shallow breathing, of obstruction in the respiratory tract, or of certain varieties of psychological disturbance results in a weak, inaudible voice which may be breathy or aspirate because of insufficient power both for adequate vibration of the vocal cords and for resonation. Aspirate or breathing production of the last words of a sentence may be due to weak breath support or to inefficient distribution of exhaled breath. Spasmodic control of the muscles of respiration will result in jerky, irregular flow of speech. Occasionally speech is attempted on inhalation resulting in a distinctive type of gasping or sucking vocalization. Normal or adequate breath support for speech is indicated when the coordination of the musculature, the rhythm and strength of the movements of the musculature, combine to produce voice of appropriately controlled resonation, loudness, and rhythm.

In evaluating the functional efficiency of the larynx for speech, two functions should be considered. During speech the vocal cords move from the open position, to the affricative position, to the vibratory position, and to the closed position. The particular position the vocal cords assume depends upon the sound being produced at a given moment. They are in the open position for all voiceless sounds, such as the *f*, *th*, *s*, *sh*, *p*, *t* and *k* sounds. They are in the affricative position for the *h* sound, and move to the vibratory position for all voiced consonants, vowel and vowel-like sounds. A closed, or glottal stop, position is used chiefly in preparation for transition between sounds and termination of sounds. The primary action of opening and closing the glottis, or abduction and adduction of the vocal bands, is a function of certain intrinsic muscles of the larynx. A secondary action is performed by other intrinsic muscles of the larynx that tense or relax the vocal cords. Tensing occurs as the speaker varies the pitch upward; relaxation takes place as the pitch of the voice is lowered. Optimum pitch range and fundamental pitch vary with age for both sexes, changing continuously until maturity because of the change in the size of the larynx, the length of the vocal cords, and the size and shape of the pharyngeal, oral and nasal cavities.

Normal function of the vocal cords for speech is indicated when the child can make combinations of voiceless, voiced, and glottal fricative sounds with varying rates and amplitudes and with pitch variations appropriate to age, size, and sex. A careful laryngeal examination should determine whether the presence of a primitive web over the vocal cords, congenital papilloma, polyps, tumors, nodes, post-operative scars, partial paralysis of the intrinsic laryngeal muscles on one or both sides, developmental asymmetry, pressure from thyroid, inflammation, injury, or functional misuse is responsible for a dysfunction of the larynx. A functional examination of laryngeal action is helpful in verifying partial paralysis of the vocal cords or an asymmetrical closure of the glottis. While the child is vocalizing a vowel, pressure may be produced by placing the thumb and forefinger first on one side of the thyroid cartilage, and then on the other. Vocal quality will be improved as the mechanical pressure helps the deficient vocal cord to approximate its opposite at the midline. Functional examination for misuse of the larynx may contraindicate the presence of a growth or obstruction, especially when, after instruction and demonstration, a child can produce good vocal quality with variation in pitch. No known way of momentarily removing a growth or compensating for its presence to permit normal function of the larynx has been described. A trial period of vocal therapy is recommended before surgery for obstructions caused by misuse.

Resonation is the most individualistic of all of the components of speech. No two voices are identical in every respect. The anatomical structure of the speech mechanism of each individual is different from that of every other individual. Emotional, physiological, and psychological differences also contribute to the individualization of vocal quality. Normal vocal quality is determined primarily by the length of the vocal cords, which determines their rate of vibration, in relationship to the size and shape of the resonation cavities (pharyngeal, oral and nasal), the nature of the coupling or joining of these cavities and the manner in which the vibrated breath stream is channeled through them. In the process of selective amplification, certain frequencies generated at the vocal cords are selected for reinforcement or resonation in the coupled cavities of the vocal tract while other frequencies apparently are suppressed. This process of selectively amplifying certain frequencies and suppressing others is called resonation. The frequencies selected for resonation are determined by the size, shape, and coupling of the cavities.

Abnormal vocal quality may be caused by generation of frequencies at the vocal cords that cannot be resonated in the cavities, by improper coupling of the cavities and by inappropriate direction of the vibrated breath stream into the coupled cavities. To illustrate, if the vocal cords vibrate at frequencies too low to be resonated properly in the coupled cavities, a husky, discordant vocal quality will be produced. If the cavities are not coupled adequately, a predominately pharyngeal, oral, or nasal quality will result. This same effect can be produced also by improperly directing the vibrated breath stream into cavities that are adequately coupled to produce normal voice. When an abnormal vocal quality is present, each of these three determinants of vocal quality should be varied in an attempt to produce quality appropriate to the age, size, and sex of the child.

Special mention should be made of the nasal cavities that are coupled with the pharyngeal and oral cavities in the production of only three sounds of the English language, the *m*, *n* and *ng* sounds. All other sounds of the English language are made with the nasal port closed or approximately closed. The nasal port normally is closed by action of the soft palate or velum in relation to the pharyngeal constrictors, and the closure is referred to as the nasopharyngeal closure. Failure to effect this closure results in nasal quality of voice. The most frequently observed causes for insufficient action of the velum are the removal of one or both of the glosso-palatini muscles during tonsillectomy, the scarring or removal of the pharyngo-palatini muscles during tonsillectomy, the imitation of nasal voice, an inherited short soft palate, a partial paralysis of the soft palate, an injury to the velum, the cleft palate, and the enlargement of adenoids or tonsils.

A simple test to determine whether or not the velum is of sufficient length to make the closure may be made. The child is asked to blow out a match, to blow a whistle, or to close his mouth and to blow out on his checks. If he can perform these tasks without nasal emission of breath, his velum may be of sufficient length to make the nasopharyngeal closure. To eliminate the possibility that he uses the posterior part of the tongue to assist the velum in closing the nasal port, he should be asked to repeat blowing out on his cheeks and at the same time to move his tongue tip against first the inside of one cheek and then the other. The results of this tongue movement can be seen and felt by the examiner. If the child can pass this test without nasal emission of breath, and without closing the nasal port at the nostrils, the sphincteric function of the velum and Passavant's cushion may be assumed to be adequate to make the closure with the amount of breath pressure used. The breath pressure used in the test is much greater than that used in speech. A prognosis as to the rate of velar action and the extent to which the sphincteric function of the velum and Passavant's cushion can be utilized in speech can be made only from evaluation of the results obtained after a period of speech training, especially for the repaired cleft palate. Informed surgeons are constantly improving their techniques in an attempt to so repair the palate that it will be of adequate length and of potential mobility for speech. The nature of the surgical repair determines to a considerable degree the nature of the speech the cleft palate child will be able to acquire.

Articulation is the modulation of the voiced and voiceless breath stream in the production of sounds and combination of sounds in words of a language. The principal articulators include the muscles of the face that change the size and shape of the mouth opening, the muscles of mastication that raise and lower the mandible, the glossal muscles that in combination with the facial muscles and muscles of mastication change the size and shape of the orifice through which the breath stream is directed, the soft palate that regulates the coupling of the nasal cavities with the pharyngeal and oral cavities and thereby assists in directing the breath stream, and the teeth, dental ridges, and palate that serve mainly as walls and juncture points for the tongue and lip. In normal speech the articulators are present in normal size, shape, and alignment, and function with normal accuracy, speed and strength of movement. Disturbances of articulation are heard usually as sound omissions, distortions, or additions. Some of the more common causes of faulty articulation are imitation of poor models, or the presence of a hearing deficit, mental deficiency, dysphasia, unilateral or bilateral paralysis of one or more of the muscle groups, cerebral palsy, cleft lip and/or palate, tongue tie, and malocclusion.

In evaluating the functional efficiency of the muscles used in articulation, the examiner should observe their accuracy, rapidity, symmetry and strength of movement. Simple movements used to test the facial muscles include retractions of first one and then the other corner of the mouth showing the teeth, and rapid alternative movements from the lip positions used in saying $\bar{e}$ (eve) and $\bar{oo}$ (boot). The muscles of mastication used in speech to lower and raise the mandible are checked by alternately lowering and raising the jaw using varying rates and extent of movements. The strength of the muscles may be determined by the power of the bite. Deviation to one side or the other should be noted. Movements of the glossal musculature may be examined first for paralysis. Upon protrusion, the tongue will deviate to the side of paralysis if such exists. If bilateral paralysis is present, protrusion will not be possible. Retroflexing of the tongue is checked by having the child sweep the roof of his mouth with the top of his tongue.

A short frenum or frenulum may restrict the movements of the tip of the tongue to such an extent that sounds such as the *r*, *l*, and *sh* are distorted beyond recognition. From the speech point of view, the frenum should be clipped where the movement of the tip of the tongue is so restricted. Frenums clipped with one incision sometime result in a shorter frenum, with more restricted movement than prior to surgery. Using two clips, cutting a V shape wedge from the frenum, leaving sufficient tissue to hold the tongue forward, but at the same time freeing the tip of the tongue for speech movements is a technique that can be recommended.

The number, position and alignment of teeth are important especially in the articulation of the fricative sounds. A recessive or prognathic mandible makes compensatory articulative movements necessary to produce intelligible articulation of certain sounds. A child with a cleft lip may distort the bilabial sounds. Children with abnormal oral structures should be referred to a pediatrician, a pedodontist, a prosthodontist, or a dental, plastic, or oral surgeon for oral reconstruction essential to good speech.

No evaluation of the basic processes of speech and hearing can be complete without a consideration of its mental aspects. The mind is the center to which impressions go, in which the impressions are connected and associated with past experiences and retained, from which voluntary acts are initiated and appropriate muscular activity is coordinated. This power to receive stimuli, to retain it, to recall it, and voluntarily to act or not to act after receiving it, has led many workers in the field to believe that the psychological approach is all important. It is important. However, the nature of the central activity is determined and conditioned to a large extent by the interactivity of the peripheral end organs, other nerves, muscles, glands, and by the nature of the biochemical and neurophysiological functioning of the total organism.

Normally, a child learns to speak a language as he hears it spoken. Speech reproduction is dependent upon reception. The vital factor is the end organ of hearing and the nature of the transmission and association of auditory stimuli. Assuming the receptor (hearing) and neural pathways to be normal, that which is ultimately received through this sense may be changed by emotional states, fatigue, and other metabolic conditions. Similarly, on the motor side of mental activity, no motor skills can be developed by the thought processes alone. Muscle exercise is necessary in establishing muscular habits. Among the psychomotor acquisitions of the human being none is more complex than speech. Speech is more than a product of thought. Speech is the product of almost the entire organism. The total organism of a given individual is considered to function as a unit. Functional efficiency varies from birth to death. Basic to this continuous and ever-changing functional efficiency is an ever-changing composition or structure. In considering such phenomena as sensation, perception, association, volition, action and other so-called mental attributes that are interrelated in speech, the age, sex, maturation level, health and general metabolism incident to type of inheritance are important. To whatever degree intelligence is associated with metabolic conditions that influence the sensory input, the association of stimuli received, and the motor output, to that degree may intelligence be considered as being a relative function subject to considerable fluctuation.

However, intelligence is a word that has many meanings. Most tests of intelligence are based on psychomotor functions. Although certain kinds of organic brain disorder are assessable through the medium of the electro-encephalograph, the human organism has no recognized quantitative psychic manner of communicating thoughts and feelings. Therefore, expression of mental activity is restricted to some form of gesture, speech, or writing. A child who can neither speak nor write, who is afflicted with a peripheral or central hearing loss, or who has a dysphasic condition stands an excellent chance of being branded with an extremely low I.Q. and of being referred for institutionalization. Many such children after being trained to speak or to comprehend speech have been retested and have been found to be well within the normal range of intelligence. The major consideration in connection with intelligence is that intelligence tests and their results should be evaluated with respect to the total developmental, medical, and social history of the child.

Another aspect of cerebration or mental activity that underlies an increasing population with language defect is an aphasia-like (aphasoid) condition. In addition to the speech handicap, which may be characterized by many sound additions, distortions and omissions, general language development usually is impaired. Frequently, a child with this condition will have difficulty with vocabulary, language structure, spelling, reading, writing, and arithmetic. If given an intelligence test that utilizes any form of language, such a child may be classified as being unable to profit from elementary education. If a non-language intelligence test is administered to the child, he may be found to have normal intelligence provided that the receptive impairment is not so marked as to limit comprehension of directions. To evaluate the extent and nature of the disturbance, stimuli may be presented separately through each of the sensory avenues of vision, hearing, and feeling to elicit responses through each of the motor pathways of speech, writing, and gesture. Variations in the complexity of the stimuli should be introduced as required. The results should indicate the extent to which the problem is connected with reception, association, and expression of language and other symbolic forms. Special training for the aphasia-like child using the multi-sensory and multi-motor approach is recommended. Speech training alone does not solve the major problem because the oral use of the language is only one aspect of the total difficulty. Usual concomitants of the disturbance are behavior problems generated by feelings of frustration, inferiority, despondency, and frequently by hyper-activity, distractability, and poor emotional inhibitions.

Hearing is as important to speech as vision is to reading. A child born deaf does not learn to speak until trained to do so by special methods. In fact, his early education is dependent upon specially trained teachers. If there is no residual hearing, he may be trained to speak intelligibly but his reception of speech will be limited to lip or speech reading. A child with a 60 db to 90 db loss of hearing in the better ear has a loss severe enough to necessitate special training. With amplification (hearing aid) he may acquire more intelligible speech in a shorter time than the totally deaf child, and his reception of speech is not limited entirely to speech reading. A 40 to 60 db loss of hearing in the better ear is considered to be a moderate loss, but only excessively loud speech can be heard without amplification. With amplification a child with such a loss of hearing may acquire fairly normal speech and language. After initial training, such a child may be able to attend school with normal hearing children. The combination of amplification and training in lip reading usually results in relatively good reception of speech. When the hearing loss is between 20 and 40 db in the better ear, the loss is considered mild. A youngster with such a loss will acquire speech normally by imitation, but usually he will produce certain sounds incorrectly unless he receives special teaching. With amplification, reception of speech should be normal. A hearing loss of below 20 db in the better ear should not impair the development and use of speech or language. Accurate production of certain sounds may require special help and a seat near the teacher may be advisable for classroom instruction. No amplification should be needed. Where a hearing aid is desirable, the device should be selected after a careful evaluation by a reputable hearing clinic. If a hearing aid is to give optimum help to a child, a well supervised acoustic training, combining a home training program with available special education opportunities, should be developed in detailed consultation with the family.

Two kinds of hearing losses are recognized. One type of loss, designated by one of three terms: perception, sensory, or nerve, is caused by an involvement somewhere between the cochlea and the temporal lobe of the brain. The other type of hearing loss, called conduction deafness, is caused by a middle ear involvement and may be reversible if treatment be instituted promptly. Either type of loss may occur before the child has begun to acquire speech and language. Early diagnosis customarily initiates a home therapy program under supervision of an audiologist, followed by group training dependent upon age, nature of hearing loss, and availability of facilities. When hearing loss occurs after language and speech patterns have been established, a similar program is necessary to prevent loss or distortion of these patterns and to assure continued optimal development. Under any circumstance, the child should be maintained in an environment and under a type of management as close to that of a child with normal hearing as is consistent with his need.

Hearing deficit which frequently accompanies organic disorder such as cerebral palsy, organic brain damage, and mental retardation, may be masked by other symptoms. Such a deficit may have been due to inheritance, otitis media, high fever disease, brain injuries, meningitis, mastoiditis, ostosclerosis, or German measles. Whenever speech comprehension is limited, language development is delayed, or speech is markedly defective, hearing should be evaluated carefully despite the presence of a known organic disorder which may contribute to the observed symptomatology.

Behavioral concomitants of deafness vary with its severity, the age, the intelligence, and the environment of the child. These concomitants may include using vision to supplement or take the place of hearing, looking at the speaker's mouth instead of his eyes, responding to signs and gestures more than to auditory stimulation, failing to respond when the speaker cannot be seen, developing gestures instead of speech, and carrying the head to one side.

To test the hearing of children of all ages, to evaluate the test results, and to prescribe a hearing aid that will give the child the best reception requires equipment and training plus an understanding of children and an ability to work with them that can be acquired only by extensive training. To make a differential diagnosis among deafness, psychogenic deafness, dysphasia, and mental retardation or feeble mindedness requires the possession of an integrated body of information and clinical experience.

Foreign accent, oral inaccuracies, baby talk, lisping, and certain defects of voice, all due to influences of the environment, comprise from 70 to 80 per cent of all speech defects. The majority of these speech and voice defects could be prevented by pre-school home training. Principal members of the preventive training team are the child, his parents, their pediatrician, a psychologist, and a speech pathologist or correctionist.

Parents must assume the major responsibility for speech training as they do for other learning experiences of the pre-school child. The increase noted recently of functional articulatory and voice defects in the school age population may reflect the general population increase and of the greater awareness of speech defects. The increase may also reflect the apparent cultural shift away from parental acceptance of responsibility for language stimulation and development as evidenced in increased dependency upon such impersonal stimuli as television rather than story-telling nursery rhymes, and group family activities.

Prime determinants of normal speech development in normal children are love and security. An unloved or insecure child is usually a disturbed child. His speech efforts reflect the disturbance. Next in importance to affection and protection is the awareness of self or of ego development. A child, within limitations of his inherited potential, will strive to be what his parents and those around him expect him to be. If he is told that he cannot make certain sounds, he may not even attempt to make them. If favorable and commendable attention is given to inarticulations because these inarticulations are amusing or if the negative criticism given satisfies the need for attention, the child may continue to use faulty speech. If favorable attention without undue stress is given only to good speech performance and if no mention is made of the faulty articulation, the child imitates the speech that he hears because the emphasis is properly placed. The child who has good models to imitate, who is encouraged to talk when he is mentally, emotionally, and psychologically able to do so, who is included in conversation, who is listened to even though what he has to say is unintelligible, who is read to, who has had pictures, objects, and experiences explained to him, who is provided with the recorded auditory stimulation of music, rhymes, verses, and stories, who has playmates regardless of the distance involved to get them, and who has received toys and playthings that motivate speech and active creative play, has been allowed to mature in an enriched environment which should stimulate optimum growth.

Aiding the child and his parents in voice and speech defect prevention is a group of persons with special training. The chief role of the pediatrician on the team is that of guardian of health. Normal speech development is predicated upon normal health. Once the pediatrician is convinced that the child has a functional speech defect, he is justified in advising the parents that the child might outgrow this condition provided the parents understand and assume their responsibilities in the training program. The psychologist can evaluate the child's mental, emotional and social maturity. His consultive help in respect to behavior and interpersonal relationships are essential. The speech pathologist or correctionist provides diagnostic and consultive assistance. His major contribution lies in periodic reevaluation of the problem and in assisting the parents in assuming the necessary role. He may act also in a supervisory capacity where home therapy appears to be desirable.

After the child with a functional defect of speech or voice has started to school, the school teacher should become a member of the group, working at this time to correct faulty speech habits rather than to prevent them. The role of the public school correctionist is that of a teacher with the responsibility for integrating the remedial speech services for the child with respect to school personnel and curriculum. In general, the procedure for treating functional articulatory defects is to explain articulation at the comprehension level of the individual or group being taught, to provide sensory training including the visual, auditory, and kinaesthetic experiences designed to develop an awareness of differences and similarities of sounds that serve as references in training, to help the individual to detect his own articulatory defects, to determine the causes, if any, of the defect and to have them removed, to train the production of the correct sound in combination with other sounds with appropriate physiology and transitions, to correct the pronunciation of all words in the individual's vocabulary that contain the sounds that have been mispronounced, and to make the new habits automatic in conversation and reading. The same general procedure may be followed in working with functional voice defects except that the sensory training should be focused on quality, force, time, and pitch of the voice. The training to produce an appropriate voice should be centered on the muscle groups that control respiration, phonation, and resonation.

Organic disorders of speech and hearing are listed as disturbances of the psychosensory, psychomotor, psycho-somatic systems, and disturbances of metabolism. These disorders are primarily disorders of the organism that result in disturbances of speech and hearing. As such, the basic consideration is the total child and his affliction. The medical and paramedical services involved vary with the nature and extent of the disturbance. In a cleft palate habilitative center, the staff may include a pediatrician, a prostheodontist, a pedodontist, a plastic surgeon, a dental surgeon, an oral surgeon, an otologist, a psychiatrist, a speech pathologist and audiologist, a psychologist, a social service worker, and a nurse. Although the services of the physiatrist, orthopedist, neurologist, physio-therapist and occupational therapist are not indicated generally in the cleft palate habilitative center, such members are of major importance in a cerebral palsy center. Each area of medical service is needed in a habilitative or rehabilitative program. Among the paramedical services those of the speech pathologist and audiologist are indicated whenever speech or hearing is involved. Jurisdiction or supervision of the integrated diagnostic and training programs resolves itself when the interest of those working together is child-centered. No one professional group is qualified by training to provide all of the varied services needed by these handicapped children. The type of service provided varies somewhat with the orientation of the persons conducting it. The personnel may be oriented medically, educationally, or psychologically. As the team approach to working with the handicapped matures, a balanced orientation and functioning of personnel will evolve.

City, state, and federal governments are allocating increasing sums of money for the habilitation and rehabilitation of the handicapped. In addition, private donors are contributing millions of dollars annually for the same purpose. The distribution of the appropriated monies is so complex that directories of agencies and services are needed in most of the large population areas. From the speech and hearing point of view, many types of services are available. Speech and hearing programs exist in public schools, private residential and day schools, centers supported by community services, national organizations and leagues, rehabilitation centers in both private and public hospitals and in colleges and university clinics. Most of the state universities, as well as the larger private universities, offer diagnostic and remedial services for the speech and hearing handicapped. Because most of these institutions are professional training centers, the remedial training is usually conducted under supervision by students in training. In addition, workshops and consultation programs are provided in many states in areas where speech and hearing services are unavailable. Summer camps supported by public and private funds are offered. Finally, an increasing number of private practitioners have entered in the field.

In 1925 the American Academy of Speech Correction was organized by 23 men and women who were interested in the problems of the speech handicapped. The organization became the American Society for the Study of Disorders of Speech in 1927, the American Speech Correction Association in 1934, and assumed its present name, the American Speech and Hearing Association in 1947. The *Annual Directory of the American Speech and Hearing Association* shows a total membership of 3,974. This rapid growth of the association is indicative of the extent of the services of professional workers in the field.

In order to help parents, other professional workers, and the speech and hearing handicapped to obtain high quality rehabilitation programs and to maintain standards throughout the profession, the ASHA maintains a certification program for its members. Four certificates of clinical competence, Basic in Speech, Advanced in Speech, Basic in Audiology, and the Advanced in Audiology are granted. Persons holding Basic Certification have had training and experience which qualifies them to work under supervision in the area of their specialization. Holders of Advanced Certification have had training and experience which qualifies them to examine, evaluate, and treat all types of disorders in either speech or hearing, dependent upon the area of certification and to supervise the work of others.

A membership directory of the American Speech and Hearing Association is published annually. The directory lists the names, the addresses, the degrees held, the positions and kind of certification, the geographical distribution by states of all of the members. In addition, the directory prints the Association's code of ethics and the By-laws. It is obtainable at cost from the Secretary-Treasurer, American Speech and Hearing Association, Wayne State University, Speech and Hearing Clinic, Detroit 2, Michigan.

REFERENCES

(Selected on the Basis of Treatment of Subjects Discussed in this Chapter)

Berry, Mildred F. and Eisenson, Jon: *Speech Disorders.* Appleton, Century, Crofts, 1956.

Davis, Hallowell: *Hearing and Deafness.* Rinehart Books, Inc., 1947.

Goldstein, Kurt: *Language and Language Disturbances.* Grune and Stratton, 1948.

Hitsh, Ira: *The Measurement of Hearing.* McGraw-Hill, 1952.

Johnson, Wendell, et al.: *Speech Handicapped School Children.* Harper and Brothers, 1948.

Potter, Ralph K., Kopp, George A., and Green, Harriet C.: *Visible Speech.* D. Van Nostrand Company, Inc., 1947.

Myklebust, Helmer R.: *Auditory Disorders in Children.* Grune and Stratton, 1954.

Van Riper, C.: *Speech Correction* 3rd ed., Prentice-Hall, 1954.

Travis, Lee Edward: *Handbook of Speech Pathology.* Appleton, Century, Crofts, 1957.

West, Robert, Ansberry, Merle and Carr, Anna: *The Rehabilitation of Speech.* 3rd ed., Harper and Brothers, 1957.

THE EYES OF CHILDREN*

Albert D. Ruedemann, M.D.† and
Albert D. Ruedemann, Jr., M.D.‡

The eyes are the most important special sense that a baby has. Inspection shortly after birth will reveal whether the baby has both eyes present; whether there is some deficiency in lids or whether the baby has a marked disparity in size between the two globes. The eyes of the baby are extremely small especially in relation to later size and for this reason examination is not easy. The average anterior-posterior diameter of a baby's eyes is a trifle over 17 mm.; whereas at the age of approximately six or seven the youngster's eyes measure about 25 mm. The cornea in a newborn measures about 8 mm. in comparison to 10 or 11 in the adult. The baby usually has a rather vacant stare because of the lack of development of the visual fibers and pathways. Because of the very small size of the eye the baby is usually extremely farsighted and except for large sized objects and the baby's gross movements one cannot be made fully aware of a baby's sight. The thinness of the sclera sometimes gives the eyes a bluish tinge. This is not like the blue that one sees in the so-called blue sclerotics. The quantitative amount of vision cannot be estimated for a long while in a child; therefore, it is unwise to make a statement whether you believe the child sees or not. Any assurance that the youngster does have sight is of extreme value to the apprehensive mother. This apprehension can be allayed by telling the mother that seeing is a learning process. and that youngsters with extremely poor eyes can learn to see and make use of their eyes very well as they grow older. The

---
*The Hereditary Ocular Disease in Children portion of this chapter was written by Albert D. Ruedemann, Jr., H.D.
†Chairman, Department of Ophthalmology, Wayne State University College of Medicine.
‡Instructor in Ophthalmology, Wayne University College of Medicine

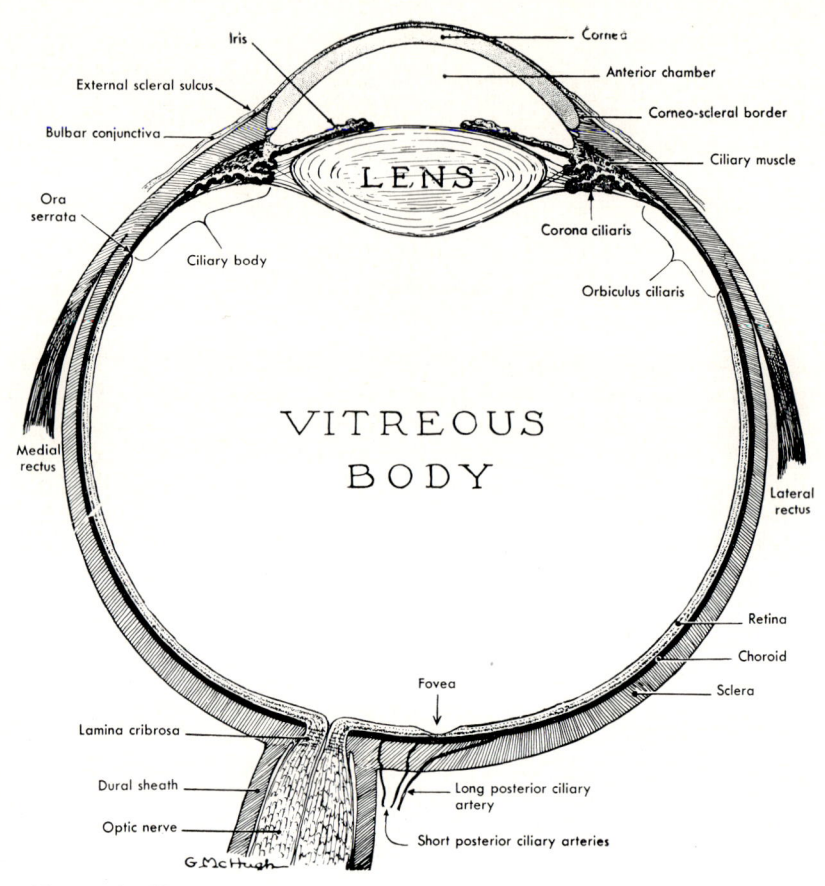

FIGURE 1. Horizontal section of a right eye (semi diagrammatic). *The Human Eye in Anatomical Transparencies*, Bausch and Lomb Press, Rochester, N. Y.)

newborn child may have hemorrhages in the orbit; may have hemorrhages in the conjuctiva; but he may also have retinal hemorrhages, especially in the region of the macula, and these usually take a short period of time to disappear. They are due to anoxia, minor birth trauma and in rare instances some maternal deficiencies showing at birth.

The premature may have a certain amount of difficulty and at the present time is being very carefully watched for any disturbance known as retrolental fibroplasia. This disease is produced by the use of oxygen over too long a period of time or too much oxygen over a shorter period of time. Later on it will be

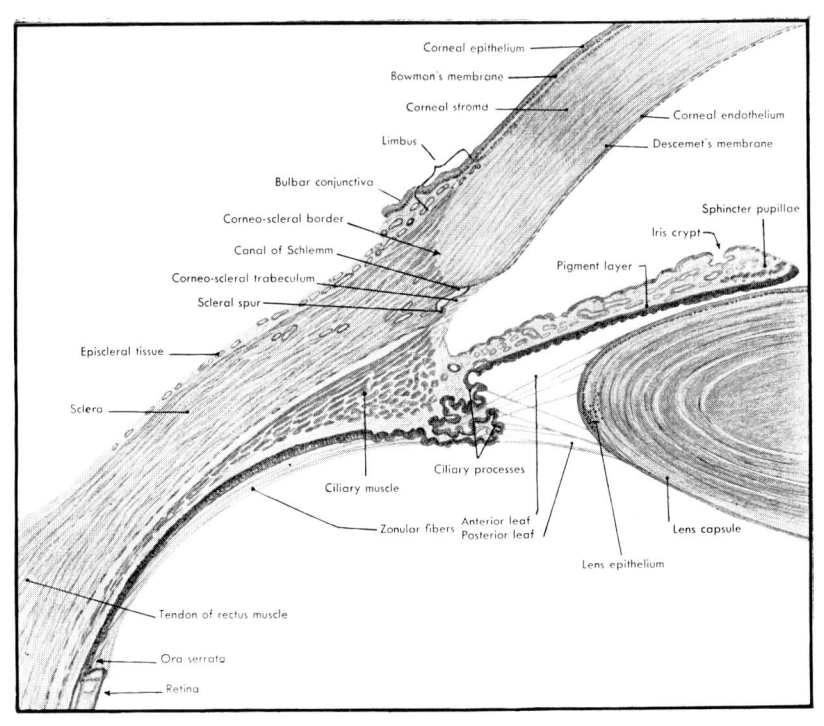

FIGURE 2. Antero-nasal portion of a horizontal section of a right eye (modified from M. Salzmann, semi diagrammatic). (*The Human Eye in Anatomical Transparencies*, Bausch and Lomb Press, Rochester, N. Y.)

found that the youngster has a retinal overgrowth due to a proliferation of the vascular portion of the retina. The story of the finding of retrolental fibroplasia by Terry in 1942 is now well known. During the next 10 years the disease or defect produced the major number of blind youngsters in America. At the present time, however, the disease is prevented by the proper use of oxygen although occasionally we are still seeing cases. Retinoblastoma and retrolental fibroplasia are frequently confused. The retinoblastoma does not commence until some time after birth and in the main does not have the same retinal picture that the retrolental fibroplasia does. It has a definite greenish-gray color. The history, weight and size of the baby are usually presumptive evidence of retrolental fibroplasia rather than that of retinoblastoma.

One might also have a persistent hyaloid artery or remnant that gives the superficial appearance of a retrolental fibroplasia. There is also the possibility of a retinal dysplasia. In the latter one may have also an associated cerebral dysplasia. Finally, there is evidence of severe trauma at birth. One could have proliferating retinopathy secondary to birth injury.

Blinking of the eyes is good evidence of eyesight and is quite common in children. No importance should be attributed to this phenomea except to evaluate it as to the amount of light that is being used at the time and to protect the youngster against excessive light whenever he shows evidence of having sensitivity to it. Usually it is quite amazing how much examination can be made on a very small child or baby and although the complete story cannot be found out in one examination, any evidence found or thought of that a youngster may be having some difficulty with his eyesight should be completely and thoroughly worked out early in life in order that the entire life program can be outlined. It is extremely important that congenital or other hereditary defects be elicited or worked out.

HEREDITARY OCULAR DISEASE IN CHILDREN

Each passing year presents the practitioner with new and valuable ways of controlling or preventing disease. Clues evolving through study of similar protoplasmic afflictions passing through individuals of similar genetic backgrounds have given physicians many aids in the diagnosis and possible treatment of patients. There are many hereditary diseases of the eye, for instance, where diagnosis of protoplasmic defect in the parent provides the physician with enough information to more adequately evaluate the abnormalities found in the children. We are all aware of the existence of a hereditary background in many diseases. Often times, however, in our concentration on the problem at hand we are likely to skip over some features of the case which might be of advantage not only to the individual but to relatives and progeny of the individual. Practical application of genetics in clinical practice can be of great benefit to all concerned.

Abiotrophic diseases are those in which an apparently normal tissue degenerates with the onset of a genetically determined abnormality. Retinitis pigmentosa, corneal dystrophies, macular

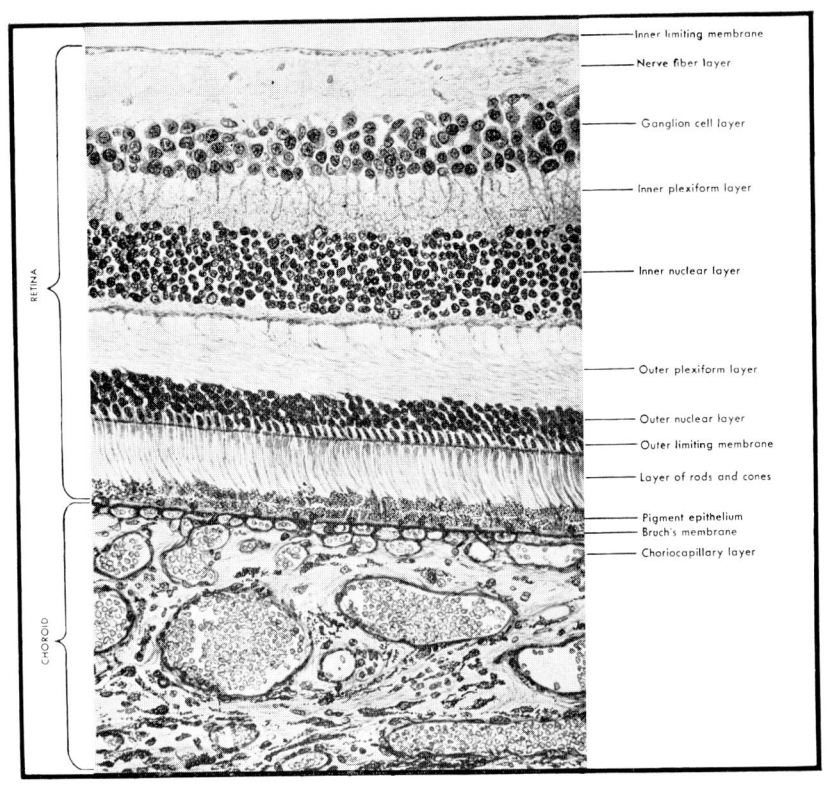

FIGURE 3. Cross section through retina and choroid near posterior pole of the eyeball. (*The Human Eye in Anatomical Transparencies*, Bausch and Lomb Press, Rochester, N.Y. (from S. Polyak, *The Retina*, University of Chicago Press. (1941.))

dystrophies, Leber's optic atrophy, glaucoma and cataracts are abiotrophic diseases. Familial stamp, similar onset, appearance and clinical course are requirements of these diseases. The symmetrical nature of the disease and the characteristic *clinical picture all point out* the hereditary nature.

1. **Retinitis pigmentosa** is a neuroepithelial degenerative process involving primarily the rods. The disease may come on very early in life and the child may be noted to have difficulty moving around in the dark. A similar process noted in the parents or relatives necessitates careful evaluation of the clinical picture. This disease is a progressive disease so that even though a child

315

may have apparently normal vision, the presence of poor night vision is an indication of future difficulties.

The characteristic clinical picture is bone spicule formation of pigment, gradual attenuation of the arteriolar vessels in the retina, and waxy atrophy of the optic disc. Naturally, evaluation of the peripheral vision of a child or infant is difficult; however, today electronic aides are coming along to help us. We now have a specific clinical test for retinitis pigmentosa, namely the electroretinogram. This may certainly be applied to children. The electroretinogram is an objective test of vision, particularly of rod vision which is specifically involved in this disease. Evidence of deficient response to light stimulus in children in the presence of a definite familial history is certainly cause for careful clinical follow-up and reasonable therapeutic trial. At the present time the Electroretinography Laboratory of the Kresge Eye Institute is following a family in which the parents were first cousins. The paternal grandfather had retinitis pigmentosa. Five of the eleven children of this particular marriage have retinitis pigmentosa (three girls and 2 boys). Obviously this is a recessive disease. Even though the chance of retinitis pigmentosa in the siblings of these particular individuals is remote, these children are being evaluated systematically for any evidence of deficient electroretinographic response. Another family presently being followed is that of a father who had retinitis pigmentosa and passed it on to half of his daughters. We have reasonable evidence that the daughters represent the carrier state and they may, in turn, have passed the disease on to their male sublings. This is an example of dominant sex-linked inheritance in which the daughters are like the father and so on. This is called criss-cross inheritance. Actually, eugenists are agreed on six possible variations in the transmission of retinitis pigmentosa: 1. Recessive, 2. Dominant, 3. Sex-linked recessive, 4. Intermediate sex-linked, 5. Dominant partial, 6. Recessive partial. The most common is recessive, followed by dominant and finally sex-linked. Careful evaluation of the family history of suspected children may yield enough information so that the physician can supply reasonable genetic advice to the parents.

Lawrence-Moon-Biedl-Bardet Syndrome or pituitary dysfunction is associated with retinitis pigmentosa. The child also will be obese, may illustrate polydactyly, hypogenitalism, mental

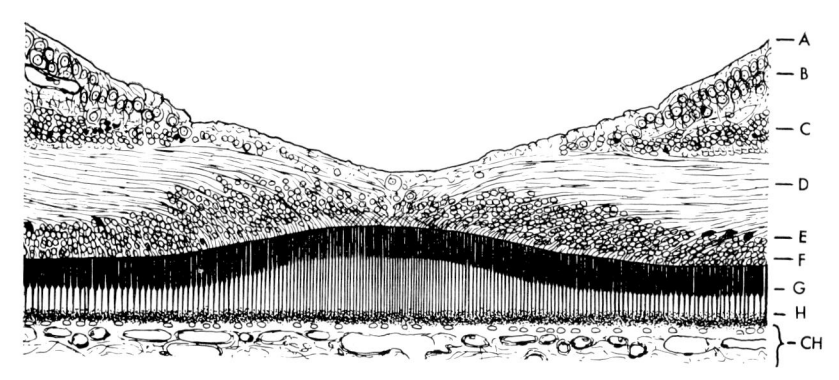

FIGURE 4. The fovea centralis of the human retina.

A = inner limiting membrane, B = ganglion cell layer, C = inner nuclear layer, D = Henle's fiber layer, E = cone nuclei, F = outer limiting membrane, G = cones, H = pigment epithelium, CH = choroid.

The Human Eye in Anatomical Transparencies, Bausch and Lomb Press, Rochester, N.Y. Number 38. (from S. Polyak, *The Retina*, University of Chicago Press, 1951.)

retardation to complete the syndrome. The disease is usually inherited as a recessive so that fairly optimistic advice can be given the parents in so far as further siblings are concerned.

2. **Hereditary macular degenerations** may present itself in the child and the classical form is noted as a recessive. The clinical picture begins with acute onset of sharply localized symmetrical mottling of both macular areas with concomitant loss of central vision. Fundoscopy reveals a pigmentary change, not unlike salt and pepper spots, in the fundus, which progress to gray, round bodies similar to colloid bodies. These conglomerate into large pigment clumps with an occasional halo. Sometimes there is cerebral involvement with progressive mental degeneration which would ally these diseases with the familial macular-cerebral degenerations known as Batten-Mayou or Infantile Amaurotic Idiocy.

Most of the other abiotrophic diseases usually present themselves in the late teens or at least the clinical features do not become really evident until these years have been reached.

Albinism is a common disease in children.

The eye finding may or may not be associated with systemic changes. Actually there are five types of albinism. The disease is evidenced by involvement of hair, skin or eyes, with one or all of the changes being evidenced in a single individual. The first type of albinism is nearly total lack of pigment. The hair is white, the eyes are red, due to pigmentation of the irides and choroid, the skin is very white. The second type is slightly less complete and the individual presents with straw hair and red eyes. These occasionally may develop some pigment in later life. The third type is called Albinoidism or leucism. It is seen only early in life and there is generalized pigment deficiency but pigment is definitely present. Albinoidism does not present any symptoms and is inherited as a dominant. The fourth type involves the eyeball alone and is usually inherited as a sex-linked recessive. The fifth type involves the retina only.

The ocular changes are usually as follows: 1. lack of choroidal and iris pigment, 2. underdevelopment of the macula with poor central vision, 3. nystagmus secondary to poor central vision. Usually, if the eye is involved alone, the disease is inherited as a recessive sex-linked, or a recessive or a irregular dominant disease. Albinism may be seen with many gradations and there may be other complications such as mental deficiency, and involvement of the peripheral retina so that the individual is night blind. These children may present themselves with marked photophobia, a bright red fundus reflex, nystagmus and poor visual acuity. They may well show some evidence of macular deficiency. Often children have normal peripheral vision and may claim to see better at night.

THE PHAKOMATOSES

1. ***Neurofibromatosis or Von Recklinghausen's disease*** may be present at birth but it becomes more evident at the stress periods of life, such as puberty. Inheritance is usually as an irregular-dominant with incomplete penetrance. The disease is characterized by the presence of subcutaneous nodules, cutaneous pigmentation and multiple tumors arising from the sheaths of cranial, spinal, peripheral, and sympathetic nerves. Bony abnormalities may be present as well as defective central nervous system development. From an ophthalmological standpoint one may see neurofibromatosis of the lids either as Fibroma Molluscum or Plexiform Neurofibroma. Neurofibromatosis may be

seen in the retina in the form of medullated nerve fibers. Neurofibromatosis may involve the orbital nerves causing proptosis with pulsation of the globe but no distress or bruit, no expansile pulsation. There may be some changes in the bony orbit but no enlargement of the optic foramen. Glioma of the optic nerve may be associated with loss of vision and proptosis. Cafe au lait spots and other cutaneous neurofibromata are also seen. Actually one can see neurofibromatosis of all the cranial nerves. An acoustic neuroma or cerebellopontine angle tumor may cause many characteristic changes, such as unilateral tinnitus with loss of hearing, vertigo, facial palsy, loss of sneeze reflex, homolateral V, general changes on the same side. The main ocular change is loss of corneal sensation. Advance in the disease may present cerebellar signs with ataxia, vertigo and hypotonia. Contralateral hemiplegia and hemianesthesia. is also noted

2. ***Tuberous sclerosis*** or epiloia is a disease seen in young individuals. The disease is inherited as a dominant with a high degree of penetrance and variable expression. Clinically the picture is one of epilepsy and mental deficiency associated with adenoma sebaceum. One may also see retinal tumors. The ocular lesions are mulberry-like nodular masses, like heaped-up drusen or hyaline bodies. There are actually four types of retinal changes described: yellow-red spots, pigmented spots, nevi or just pigmentary changes. Pathologically these have been found to be hyaline material with calcification and gliosis in the nerve fiber layer which may extend to the ganglion layer.

3. ***Angiomatosis retinae*** or Von Hippel's disease is a phakomatosis usually inherited as a dominant with variable expression. It is characterized by dilatations and tortuosities of localized retinal vessels, usually beginning in a large vein which dilates and becomes tortuous and this is associated with beading of the companion artery progressing after a time to a red-brown mass which is a hemangioma. Usually this is found in the lower fundus but may be anywhere. There may be multiple hemangiomata with a white exudate around the mass, and after a period retinal detachment, gliosis and edema may occur. Recurrent retinal hemorrhage is not uncommon. Angiomatosis retinae may be associated with cerebellar hemangiomata in which case the disease is called Von Hippel-Lindau's disease. Both segments of

this syndrome probably occur from maldevelopment of the vascular area in the second period of vascular development, when the primordial vascular plexus starts changing into arteries, veins and capillaries. At this time there is a rich capillary plexus in the posterior fossa as well as the retina. Actually this disease is very rarely, if ever, seen in young children, but the fact that it is a dominant should raise one's suspicion in dealing with the children of an involved parent or in giving genetic advice.

4. **Vasculo-Encephalo-Trigeminal Syndrome or Sturge-Weber Syndrome** is another member of the phakomatoses characterized by venous angiomata of the skin and brain with hemiplegia, angioma of the meninges, contralateral Jacksonian epilepsy, intracranial calcification, and unilateral glaucoma. The ocular signs are nevus flammeus and glaucoma. However, the glaucoma only occurs when the lids and conjunctiva are involved, and actually many of these cases show choroidal angiomata on the involved side associated with the facial nevus involving the lids and conjunctiva; the facial nevus flammeus or port wine mark. This disease is also inherited as a dominant with different members of the family showing lesions corresponding to the site of capillary angiomas.

CONGENITAL TUMORS OF THE EYE

There is only one congenital tumor of major importance insofar as the eyes are concerned; this is retinoblastoma. Retinoblastoma is a highly malignant primary tumor of the retina, almost always seen before five years of age. It is bilateral in 25% of the cases. Multiple origins of this tumor mean that the disease does not spread as a true metastasis. The heredity is described as dominant or irregular dominant. Survivors of the tumor pass this affection on to their children. Tucker, Steinberg and Cogan reported on pedigrees in eight cases of sporadic retinoblastoma. The affected parent has a one in four chance of transmitting the disease to 40–50% of his siblings. The heredity of this disease is extremely important because of the high mortality. Reese in his book on Tumors of the Eye discusses the frequency of the disease. He gave an incidence of 1–4% of siblings born of healthy parents with one child having the disease. He pointed out that 77% of the siblings of an affected parent had retinoblastoma. This series is undoubtedly weighted but it only points out the serious implications of this disease and the need for careful genetic counselling of parents. No child having retinoblastoma should grow up and produce young. Parents with one child having retinoblastoma can have more with reasonable safety. The treatment of retinoblastoma in infants is severe and at present three courses are open to the physician: 1. enucleation of the involved eye if the other eye is tumor free or if the other eye can be controlled on medical therapy. 2. Medical therapy consists of intensive radiation or 3. nitrogen mustards. In either case treatment should be supervised by an expert because the secondary changes may be severe insofar as radiation is concerned. The amount necessary for adequate treatment of the disease may be severely damaging to vision in itself and lead to blindness. If treatment is unsuccessful, enucleation is necessary. The physician is faced with a serious choice—to save the child for blindness or allow him to die.

LIPODYSTROPHIES
(RETICULOENDOTHELIAL GRANULOMATOSIS)

This is a defect in lipoid metabolism with reticuloendothelial reaction to the deposition of lipid. It may be a localized or primary metabolic disorder and six clinical entities may involve the ocular areas:

a. Tay Sach's or amaurotic family idiocy
b. Neimann-Pick disease
c. Hand Schuller Christian disease
d. Gaucher's diease
e. Dysostosis multiplex or Hurler's disease
f. Xanthomatosis

a. *Tay Sach's disease* is thought to be recessive in transmission. The clinical picture is notable in that the first sign is usually loss of vision. Ophthalmoscopically one notes a graying of the retina with a central red spot in the macular area. The infant becomes listless and may have difficulty walking. This, of course, is noted in a child who is otherwise normal and healthy at birth and up until ages 3–18 months. Usually the parents are Jewish.

Juvenile Batten Mayou's disease is associated with Tay Sach's disease but central involvement is not as extensive. Visual changes are usually first noted and come on between the ages 5–7 but the latest around 13. The child has difficulty seeing, there may be mental deterioration with speech defects, spasticity, difficulty in walking, and so on. Ophthalmologically, changes are not limited to the macular areas. There may be fine pigmentary deposits all over the retina with central red-black spots. Nystagmus and pale discs may also be noted. As one follows the eye changes, the first actual changes do not coincide well with the vision obtained. There may be a central macular spot with a reddish halo around it and some pigment spots which are symmetrical. The maculae may look like beaten copper or silver and actually the discs do not become pale until much later in the disease, nor do the peripheral retinal changes appear until later.

b. *Neimann-Pick disease or lipoid histiocytosis* has ocular and clinical changes similar to amaurotic idiocy. However the early cases are not blind.

c. *Hand-Schüller-Christian disease or diabetic exophthalmic dysostosis* may be notable in that there will be xanthomas of the orbit with proptosis and changes in the membrane bones of the skull. The lids, cornea and conjunctiva may have lipogranulomatous deposits.

d. *Gaucher's disease* in the child follows rather a chronic course. As the disease progresses there may be lipogranulomatous deposits with pigmentation in the sclera and conjunctiva in those areas exposed to light. These areas will be wedge shaped on either side of the cornea.

e. *Dysostosis multiplex, Hurler's Syndrome or lipochondrodystrophy* is a congenital lipoid disturbance involving cartilage, bones, skin, subcutaneous tissue, cornea, liver and spleen. The disease is characterized by dwarf stature, shortness of neck and trunk, kyphosis of spine, depression of the bridge of the nose, stiffness of joints, shortness of fingers, mental deficiency and clouding of the cornea. The disease is probably inherited as a recessive and the corneal changes may be the first noted. The corneas may appear large and hazy with a milk-glass appearance. Slit lamp examination reveals small granules in the parenchyma or Bowman's membrane and a careful differentiation from the interstitial keratitis of congenital syphilis or congenital glaucoma must be made.

HEREDITARY SYNDROMES

The various hereditary syndromes are of ophthalmologic interest for various reasons. Considering first the craniostenoses, these diseases are characterized by premature closing of the suture lines in infancy. This results in retention of the fetal position of the eyes for the orbits are laterally placed. They are also rather shallow. Characteristically, the child with craniostenoses has widely placed eyes or hypertelorism and exophthalmos due to the shallow orbits which may or may not be associated with optic atrophy.

Crouzon's disease is a typical example. Dysostosis craniofacialis is characterized by frontal bossing, exophthalmos, parrot beak nose, sunken maxilla and prognathic mandible. Often divergence of the eyes and primary optic atrophy is seen. It is inherited as a dominant as is oxycephaly proper (tower skull).

Mandibulo-facial dysostosis or Franceschetti's Syndrome is characterized by congenital defects of the ears, eyelids and malar bones. There is a lateral downward slope of the palpebral fissures with a temporal coloboma in the lower lid giving it an angular droop. These individuals also have a typical hair growth with a tongue shaped widow's peak. These individuals have a bird-like look and the changes are inherited as an irregular dominant with variable expression.

Generalized bone and mesodermal dystrophies also cause changes in the eyes. *Osteogenesis imperfecta* or brittle bones and blue sclerotics is a total mesodermal dysplasia characterized by retention of the immature collagen form, reticulum; in bone, epithelium, sclera, cornea and other mesodermal parts. The sclerae are unusually clear and thin due to the retention of the immature collagen. The choroid thus shows through this translucent tissue and appears blue. Most of the children do not live through childbirth since there are so many fractures of the bones and secondary changes.

Arachnodactyly or Marfan's Syndrome is a dominant disease characterized by spider-like fingers and toes, low subcutaneous fat, general muscular under development with hyperelastic ligaments, cardiac abnormalities, prominent ears, high arched palate, infantilism, kyphosis, scoliosis and sternum deformities as well as deformities of the joints, particularly of the feet. The major eye changes are due to dislocation of the lenses with myopia.

The reverse of this is *Spherophakia, Brachymorphia* Syndrome in which the involved individual has short stature, broad hands and feet with good development of the muscles and subcutaneous tissue. The eyes are also myopic because the lens is small and thick and often ectopic. This disease is also inherited as a dominant.

Waardenburg Syndrome is characterized by lateral displacement of the medial canthi combined with lateral displacement of the lacrimal puncta or blepharophimosis. The root of the nose is broad, there is a tendency for the eyebrows to extend across the root of the nose with hypertrichosis of the medial portion of each eyebrow. There is a white forelock with heterochromia iridis, deaf mutism or incomplete congenital deafness. This disease is inherited as a dominant.

One can not consider the ocular changes of infancy which are hereditary in nature without considering the various *colobomata*. Colobomata of the globe originate from non or faulty closure of the fetal choroidal cleft. They may vary from a defect in the iris and choroid to a nasal and inferior conus with circum papillary ectasia, coloboma of the lens and crater defect of the disc. The faulty closure may be of such magnitude that only a small eyeball remains but a large posterior cyst several times larger than the eye is found posteriorly. This disease is inherited as a dominant with wide expression and variable penetrance.

Pseudopapilledema is an important change in the optic nerve which looks exactly like papilledema. Often there are drusen bodies of the disc and a prepapillary membrane may be associated. These children are rather farsighted and usually changes are inherited as a dominant. The eyeball may be small in size, to practically absent. (Microphthalmos to anophthalmos.) These changes are inherited as a recessive and it means failure or degeneration of the optic vesicle. These children rarely live because there are so many other congenital defects. True anophthalmos is extremely rare; usually a small stump may be found.

Congenital glaucoma or buphthalmos is inherited as a recessive disease and in the primary form it may well be due to the retention of the mesenchymal tissue in the angle of the anterior chamber. These children have large eyes with deep chambers and corneal clouding and ruptures in Descemet's membrane. This is not an infection and the involved infant will undoubtedly have poor vision. In some cases a large cornea may be the only clue. Surgery is most often required as a means of retaining vision. The usual procedures are goniotomy or goniopuncture.

Heredity plays an important part in the ultimate *refractive power* of the eye and one must remember that the size and shape of the eyeball are not the only factors in the total refractive power. As a matter of fact there are several components of refraction: corneal curvature, thickness of lens, depth of the anterior chamber and axis length. Because of these various components refractive error is difficult to analyze in terms of heredity because one must consider more than one factor. Myopia is often seen in many members of a family. With such a history children should be examined before school age to determine a need for glasses.

Changes in the extra ocular muscles are not uncommon although the convergent and divergent squints may be inherited as a dominant. Often the amblyopia of one eye or the other in squint is seen in one or the other parent or close relative. Isolated ptosis which is often bilateral, is a dominant as is isolated involvement of the 6th nerve leading to the lateral rectus muscle. Superior oblique involvement through trochlear IV may be inherited as a dominant, also Duane's syndrome with fibrosis of the lateral rectus muscle, characterized by relative enophthalmos with ptosis on adduction of the homolateral eye. The child is unable to carry the eye beyond the midline laterally.

Marcus Gunn syndrome or jaw winking may be inherited as a dominant disease.

Nystagmus which may be a symptom of albinism or total color blindness or deficiency of the macula may also be inherited as a recessive sex-linked disease or as an irregular dominant with head nodding. Vision is reduced to 20/200 or 20/100 but the peripheral fields are full and these children get along remarkably well.

The changes in the *shape of the cornea* such as microcornea, cornea plana, keratoconus are inherited as a dominant while megalo-cornea is inherited as a sex-linked recessive.

Congenital cataract may well have a hereditary background and when all other factors are considered the disease may be found to have a dominant transmission.

Aniridia which may be seen in a wide variation of changes is usually inherited as a dominant. Often there will be aplasia of the macula with deficient central vision and glaucoma associated with the disease. Pathologically a stump of the iris usually remains in the most severe cases but the complications are severe and the chance for reasonable vision is slim.

OTHER EYE CHANGES

It should be stated definitely that the examination of a baby's eyes should be as thorough and complete as possible. If this is not done by examining the youngster in the office one should resort to the use of vinethane or ether for a thorough examination. The youngster should be definitely prepared for this examination, however; the pupils should be well dilated in order that a thorough examination of the eye grounds may be made as well as a good refraction under the cycloplegic. The surprising fact is that a very small number of babies and young children actually require an anesthetic for adequate examination. As was stated before it is usually at the end of about the first month or so that the interest in whether or how much a baby sees comes forth. There is sometimes apprehension as to the size of the pupils and this is of no significance unless they are maintained in dilated position. The reaction is rather an indifferent one in early life and excitement or fear will result in dilatation of the pupils. It might be stated that pupillary size should not be used as an interpretation of any disease process unless the pupils remain fixed.

As a baby does not have any tears at birth he fortunately maintains his lid fairly well closed and therefore the corneas do not dry out. After a short period of time there will be the appearance of fluid in the eye and then the actual tear formation, and the baby will express his displeasure frequently by the formation of a single tear. In the main the tears are well handled by the lacrimal apparatus and the patency of the lacrimal canal and duct into the nose becomes apparent very shortly after the tearing has started. Occasionally one eye remains fairly dry and the other may show a tear overflow. Shortly thereafter there will be a collection of mucus in the corner of the eye which mother thinks is pus or infection and slight pressure on the lacrimal sac will show some regurgence of mucoid material. Fortunately, these sacs rarely become infected in early years of life and unless the mother is too concerned one can defer probing the lacrimal duct until the age of 4, 5 or 6 months and usually a single probing suffices to open the duct. This is usually due to a small, valve-like structure at the junction of the lacrimal sac and the lacrimal duct. Occasionally pressure with a small piece of moistened cotton over the lacrimal sac and downward pressure into the nose will be sufficient to open the duct. On very rare occasions there is a congenital absence of the lacrimal drainage apparatus for which nothing can be done at this age. Irrigation of the eyes with a weak saline or boric acid solution is sufficient to keep the eyes clean. It is not necessary to use any antibiotic solution because the material does not become infected.

Congenital nystagmus or nystagmoid-like movements are not uncommon in children. When they occur in a very small baby, however, they are of definite significance as to the future eyesight of the individual. Because of the faulty musculature the baby may have nystagmoid movements in any quadrant and this is especially true on lateral gaze. Fine, fibrillary movements, however, and constant horizontal nystagmus must be considered pathological unless proven otherwise. A constant nystagmus is a tip-off that the individual may not be developing or have a central fovea and has a very low visual acuity. Evidence of macular defect should be sought for.

Seeing is the most important learning process that the individual posesses. This is a very compound-complex mechanism starting at the eyes and ending in the foveal center of the occipital lobe. Its importance starts at the time when foveal coordination begins to operate, at the end of the first month. The many factors concerned with the proper process of seeing which stimulates learning must be thoroughly studied to be completely understood. The primary stimulation comes from the eyes. It is a recognized fact that a youngster born without eyes can be taught by way of his ears or by way of the tactile sense. It is a painstaking, expensive process. It is also well known that a youngster born with one good eye and one bad eye can also be taught, can learn readily, and in most instances can get along equally as well as a two-eyed individual. What is not generally known is that a two-eyed individual must have equal sight in both eyes or sight that can be made equal with glasses, that both eyes must work together constantly and completely, and most naturally that he must have a cerebral center to go along with the ocular stimulation. The peripheral retina, that is the portion of the retina outside of the macular center, is used for the fixing of visual clues and the process of ambulation and gives wide area vision that becomes necessary in daily living. It is an entirely different matter in the learning process. This takes place by way of the macular area only or more generally basically. The first learning stimulation comes by way of the fovea. The light sense traverses the ocular pathways to the central areas in the occipital lobe and here the process of seeing commences. It follows that the central area in the eye and the central area in the brain must be both present and equal to the process of being stimulated and receptive. If we take this neuro-muscular visual mechanism up step by step one learns that the initial stimulation that comes by way of the ocular fovea flows along normally to the brain provided that the eye mechanism is completely intact and normal physiologically. This includes the optics of the eye, the central zones in the retina, the neural pathways, and finally the center in the brain.

The optical mechanism of the eye is a compound-complex lens system consisting of the cornea, the aqueous, the lens and the vitreous, forming a lens system in the neighborhood of 57 diopters. Like all human developments the eye may be imperfectly formed in that it may be too long or too short or not completely spherical.

Taking these up one at a time, the human eye is generally a trifle too short at birth. As was mentioned before, the anterior-posterior length is in the neighborhood of 17 mm.; whereas, the adult eye reaches a length of approximately 24-25 mm. It is also to be mentioned that the lens system anteriorly placed in the eye is not always in correct position as to its finality, and here again the length of the eye may be altered by the position of the lens or even the quality of the lens. If the eye is truly spherical and the anterior-posterior position is too short, we have the condition known as hyperopia. It therefore becomes imperative in hyperopia that if the image is to be properly placed in the fovea, there must be some method used to bring this image to clear foveal position. This is done by the ciliary muscle (accommodation).

A far-sighted eye must be in constant activity in order that all images are seen, even those at a fairly good distance, or there will be a blurriness on the fovea and the looking part of the mechanism will not be instituted properly. One can readily understand that when this is necessary the individual must make a constant effort to see and therefore nervousness, irritability and lack of interest eventually take over and these youngsters, because of this farsightedness, are in the main not interested in things that are actually necessary for learning. They have a subconscious indifference to everything that has to do with the use of the eyes and get away from a great deal of their nervous irritation by much sleep, at least the closing of the eyes. One can see that early in life this will have a material effect on the entire learning process. Add to this corneal distortion or lenticular distortion so that two meridians of the eye are unequal and add astigmatism to the farsightedness and one can carry this still further and have the astigmatism at an off axis or such that it is not the same in both eyes, and although the eye could correct for a certain amount of farsightedness, it does not and cannot correct for astigmatism. This is especially true if the astigmatism is not the same in both eyes, either in amount or in axis. Therefore, the size and shape of the eye are extremely important in the beginning learning process in a baby and should be one of the first physical mechanisms correctly examined if there is any tendency from the normal. Better than 80% of the youngsters are born farsighted or with some combination of farsightedness and astigmatism. As the eye develops the lens assumes its proper place and it approaches the zero mark in lens strength. The power of the lens system to focus an object on the fovea correctly in a single eye is known as accommodation. The accommodative strength of the average individual at birth is 14 diopters. In the farsighted individual the accommodation is in constant use. Because of this the individual has the constant eye effort of attempting to look.

The opposite is true in myopia or nearsightedness. The youngster is born with a large eye, one that is longer than the average of 17 mm. and because of this the images do not quite reach the fovea. These youngsters do not see well far off. Their accommodation is constantly relaxed. Their ciliary muscle does not progressively develop and except for the objects in close range they do not see. The vision may fall off precipitously at a very short distance and their lack of interest is one of lack of looking and seeing. Here again you may have a combination of nearsightedness and astigmatism, and again the eyes cannot correct for the mechanical defects or optical defects, and the youngster loses the effect of all the stimulation that comes from moving objects and seeing things in their proper relationships to one another. No amount of discussion can describe the loss of visual learning when there is interference by farsightedness or nearsightedness, especially in the very early phases of life.

Provided that the foveae are intact, that the neural mechanism is functioning properly, it then remains for the center in the brain to receive the stimulation from the eyes to put it into seeing. This stimulates the visual center and visual storage begins to take place. It is apparent that the stimulation of the fovea must take place equally and constantly so that both stimuli are of the same degree, and therefore the two eyes must be equal in the looking mechanism.

As is well known, the foveal area is made up of cone cells and each of these cells has its own nerve fibril to the foveal center in the brain. The entire reading process and in the main all learning that is done by way of the eyes must come by way of the fovea. With our present-day electroencephalographs it is possible to elicit the brain waves that give us a fairly good idea whether the central area is intact and with normal, intact, central, cerebral foveae it becomes imperative that we correct the stimulating mechanism in the eyes to allow the individual to learn by this most important process. Proceeding in order, we now have the central cerebral areas, we have the foveae in the eyes, we have the muscle of accommodation, including the lenticular optical system. In order that the two eyes might function simultaneously it becomes necessary that the extraocular muscles place the fovea in position to be activated and the muscles of accommodation have the images fixed on the foveae.

It becomes apparent that this neuro-muscular mechanism must be intact and must be functioning 100% in order to maintain constant foveal fixation. If the ciliary muscle or the muscle of accommodation is not equal to the entire task of maintaining foveal fixation, there must be some extra call made on the extraocular muscles or if the lenticular system is interfered with and there is some lens opacity, or if there is some faulty positioning of the fovea due to physical disparity of the eyes, then the extraocular muscle system has an extra duty to perform and may do this by excessive turning or use of one of the muscles. There may be defects in the neuro-muscular mechanism. These may be hereditary in origin, may be due to faulty development or some early disease process. It is most important that the extraocular muscle system put the two foveae in position constantly and completely in order that the individual may look without effort in order that the seeing part may function properly. The development of the ocular muscle system is a repetitive impact mechanism and commences very early in life and continues daily during all waking moments. The more repetitive the stimulation the more it will fit itself in a firm reflex manner. In my opinion these are all conditioned reflexes again produced by trial and error over preformed pathways and they require many, many stimuli in order that they become normal in their function. This does not begin in the fourth or fifth year but in the fourth or fifth month and by the time the fourth or fifth year has come around these reflexes are firmly established and in some instances cannot be altered. For example, in order that walking can be reflexly done without falling or tripping over every small object, the earth being the constant point of fixation for the body or the individual, it is required that the vertical position of the eyes, or the fixation of the eyes be constant. Any inequality or faulty positioning leads to clumsiness in walking, many falls and many bumps. The proper stimulation of the hand movements would naturally follow the proper coordination of the eyes, and again this coordination takes place by way of the fovea, getting its positioning clues from the peripheral retina. The process of looking to see how people move their mouths and how they eat and talk are also part of the seeing mechanism. If the two eyes do not function together consciously and completely, this disturbance will lead to disturbances of eating, use of the hand and listening.

To carry the neuro-muscular mechanism description to its conclusion let us assume that the extraocular muscles, because of their lack of capacity or lack of coordination, cannot completely put the foveae or the eye in proper position for constant looking. The neck muscles must take part in this neuro-muscular mechanism and this is exactly what happens. If you have fixed both eyes on an object, in order that you can maintain this constant foveal fixation the neck muscles take over and to maintain binocular foveal fixation it becomes a neck muscle process. Although this is not generally understood the primary purpose of the neck muscles is to maintain the position of the head in order that you can maintain position of the eyes. This becomes apparent to anyone in watching, say a tennis match, or having a stiff neck and attempting to drive an automobile. Twisting of the head or tilting of the head on the shoulder by way of the neck and producing a scoliosis is not an uncommon situation when we have a so-called vertical muscle error. The individual will assume any stance with the head and eye muscles in order to maintain as long as possible single binocular vision. Any deviation from this single binocularity leads to discomfort, so-called eyestrain, headaches, occasionally nausea, very infrequently vomiting, lack of appetite, nervousness and irritability, practically no span of attention and therefore no concentration, a faulty development of the visual memory, and in many instances a complete inability to learn to read. Any one or more of these signs or symptoms can be present in the same individual, and they depend almost entirely on the amount that the individual attempts to use his eyes for close work, how much stimulation is given to them in the way of small objects up close, and naturally how far off they are in the individual processes. Therefore, adding to the fovea, both central and peripheral, we have the muscle of accommodation and now the extraocular muscles and the neck and trunk muscles. I believe that they are of importance in this order.

It is not possible for me to stress too greatly the importance of this neuro-muscular mechanism consisting of the eye and muscles and nerve pathways in the learning process. Further, when one considers that this process begins very early in life and that by the time the youngsters are heading for school at the five or six year period, the entire system may be firmly entrenched and that the process may be so established that hardly anything else can be done to re-educate them in the proper eye-brain process. It also becomes apparent that surgery on the extraocular muscles is not the primary method of relieving the individual of faulty coordination. One must first establish normal vision in the two eyes. This can be done either by the proper use of glasses, and refractions can be done on babies with drops under anesthesia if necessary, but the importance of this should not be overlooked in the learning of an individual. Secondly, the entire future of the individual may depend on what he learns to do with his eyes during the first four years of his life. In the main I would say that 75% of the early and slight muscle errors, so-called, can be corrected by a pair of glasses. Add to this some proper regulation in the use of the eyes and some simple exercises in the establishing of binocular fixation and one can take care of 95% of all so-called muscle errors. There should be no effort in the process of looking. This allows the individual to put the effort in remembering, which is a second cerebral effort that allows the individual to develop visual memory and further thought processes.

If glasses and so-called orthoptic exercises do not re-educate and put the person in proper eye-brain relationship, it may be necessary to interfere mechanically or mechanically-psychologically with this by surgery and then by re-education to teach the individual the proper way to use his eyes or foveae together. The surgical interference must be done on the muscle that is showing the most tendency to be fixed in its processes, so-called spasms, for it is generally well known that the ocular muscles are not too weak or too strong; they are faulty in their coordination. If one has followed the sequence of events as outlined, it becomes apparent that by the time the youngster has reached school age his eye-brain system has been thoroughly established and that the schools should be made aware of this eye-brain mechanism in order that the youngster can be properly educated. Our basic education is designed according to the eyesight of the individual and 85% or more of our learning comes by way of the eyes, and it therefore becomes manifestly necessary that the eyes be as near perfect as possible when the youngster enters his educational field. It is obvious to me, therefore, that all babies and certainly children in the first and second year of their life should be studied from an oculist's point of view to learn whether certain things need be done in order to establish the normal eye-brain relationships. It is at this time that certain measures can be taken to correct the minor errors. The major ones may require either surgery and exercises or stimulation, but certainly it would give an interpretation of the future potential of the individual in the schools.

Every youngster should go to school with an eye record on which is stated his Visual capacity, which would be his vision, his foveal coordination, the condition of his retina, and to this might be added anything else that one is able to ascertain. Learning is in the main a seeing process. Any deviation from the normal is a handicap to the individual and at no time in life is this more important than during the first five years. Just as the pediatrician is able to examine and diagnose ailments in the individual, the oculist must become familiar with the early deviations that occur and must familiarize himself with the various methods used in the examination and prescribing of glasses and exercises for these children who are not completely coordinating. The reward is that of an individual who can learn completely by way of his eyes, does not have difficulty in reading and in school, and finally can go on to college for education. It is much more rewarding to an oculist than is the removal of a cataract in an 85 year old man who has less than one year to exist. In my estimation nothing is as rewarding, as important as the proper establishment of the correct foveal brain mechanism for eyesight and visual memory.

TRAUMA

Trauma in the child is quite common, especially when he reaches the second and third year of age. Trauma does not occur frequently to the child in his infancy; however, it does occur when there are brothers and sisters who, in their playing, might injure an eye with a pair of scissors or a fork; sometimes a kitchen knife happens to be too handy. This may lacerate the cornea. Here it has been our practice to sew these by direct suturing and unless the injury has been too extensive a fair result is obtained. Tetanus antitoxin is given and usually some antibiotic is carried along in order to avoid any deep infection. When the eyeball is contused by a baseball or a stick one is likely to have either a severe echymosis into the lids or the conjunctiva or to have a deep orbital hemorrhage. It is always possible to have trauma to the interior of the eye, retinal tears, choroidal lacerations. In severe contusion one sees frequently in the back of the eye in the region of the posterior third a severe commotic retinae.

Recurring hemorrhages are likely in the deep injuries to the posterior globe and a guarded prognosis should always be given because of the latent loss of vision or failure of the vitreous to clear. The extraocular muscles are rarely injured except an occasional case of a slicing wound with glass or a knife. They should be immediately reapproximated. It has been our policy to repair all lacerations and all trauma as near to normal as possible at the time of the injury. Delayed repair does not effect as good a cosmetic result and in the main subjects the youngster to a second procedure. Injury occurring because of automobile accidents and other severe trauma to the head may lead to a trauma to the extraocular muscles, the external rectus being the one most usually affected. As mentioned before we have occasionally the dilatation of the pupil, which usually clears up. Severe hemorrhage into the orbit with proptosis is rare but not entirely absent from head trauma. Very occasionally a retinal detachment is secondary to trauma but this is extremely rare. Direct injury to the optic nerve by compression at the time of injury may occur. Sometimes swelling at the angle of the eye may be due to insect bites that the youngsters picked up in the back yard. If there is much lacrimation and irritation of the lids sometimes a small insect has inserted itself beneath the upper lid, and by eversion of the lid one is able to find it in the upper cul de sac. Other foreign material gets into the children's eyes quite frequently, such as, small pieces of earth, chips of paint, pieces of straw. In looking for small foreign bodies on the cornea one must bring the light in by oblique illumination in order to highlight it. If the foreign body is not found on the cornea one should look over the pupillary space especially well. One prepares to evert the lid. This is done by holding the lashes between the thumb and first finger and with an applicator held in the other hand the lid is turned over on itself, and the applicator is now ready to remove the foreign body, which is usually found in the middle third, right in the tarsal groove. If one is prepared to do this in one maneuver, it is much easier on both the patient and the doctor as a second attempt will be definitely fought against. Finger nail scratches to the cornea may be inflicted by one child on another or the child, running along in groups of people, may be struck in the eye by a finger nail, or a child running through the garden may scratch his cornea on a sharp end of a bush. The cornea then should be stained with fluorescein to see the extent of the injury. An antibiotic unguent should be instilled and a patch applied. Small amounts of sodium salicylate should be given if there is pain. It is sometimes necessary to give these youngsters stronger sedation.

SWELLINGS AND NEW GROWTHS

All swellings in the neighborhood of the eye are of interest to the mother, and if they are progressive should be of interest to the medical man. First, if they are not inflammatory they can be an allergic state brought on by the use of a new soap or hair wash or the swelling may be due to some detergent used in washing the bed linens. Occasionally, one has a congenital new growth or a congenital malformation, and it is extremely important to differentiate between those that are progressively and potentially malignant and those that are benign and can be left alone over a long period of time. Dermoid tumors at the margin of the cornea or in the orbit are usually very slow growing and can be watched over a long period of time. If however they tend to go posterior and produce exophthalmos, early removal is advised.

PIGMENTED TUMORS

If pigmented nevi on the ocular conjunctiva (sometimes on the iris) show any tendency to extend they should be excised.

ORBITAL ABSCESS AND ORBITAL CELLULITIS

Following severe infectious diseases, pneumonia and other debilitating processes, one may see secondarily an orbital cellulitis which produces a low-grade inflammatory reaction, a painful socket, pain on movement of the eyes in the main, slight fever and an increase in the white count. This may continue and produce an orbital abscess, and as we have seen in one instance the entire orbit was filled with pus and dependent drainage was done through the lower lid at the outer margin. This usually occurs in youngsters who have not been well although styes and heavily congested chalazia can produce severe pain and severe inflammation in the lids.

The more malignant tumors include melanomas, neurofibromas, the gliomas of the optic nerve, sarcomas, chloromas, retinoblastomas and neuroblastomas. The progressive new growths in the eye orbit require careful differentiation, and the opinion of several men should be concurred in before any radical procedure is undertaken. This is especially true when there is any exophthalmos or tendency to protrusion of the eye. It is not advisable to do any exploratory procedures in the orbit in children, and therefore the differential diagnosis should be carefully made before the orbit is entered. The functional end result depends on the lesser amount of surgery that is done. It is advisable to remember that malignant tumors of the eye may result in death of the individual if the eye is not removed. There may be metastasis or extension to the brain.

Small vascular tumors along the eyelid and eyeball and in the region of the eye may be gently massaged according to a method outlined by Leuceutia, and unless there has been considerable progressive enlargement and a tendency to rapid infiltration, it is not necessary to remove them.

CONGENITAL GLAUCOMA

This is a very rare disease that occurs occasionally in infants and is entirely different from that which occurs in adults. The seriousness of this disease requires that it be constantly kept in mind because it results in total blindness for the individual; whereas, with proper early care it can be handled surgically. There are two types of congenital glaucoma that occur, up to three years of age the infantile, and from 3 years on, the juvenile. We have seen the juvenile type in the late twenties on several occasions. It has been my experience over a period of years that the glaucoma is usually bilateral, early surgery is much more satisfying than treatment with pilocarpine or other biotic drops, and though it may require several operations it is still the best method of procedure.

GLANDULAR DYSFUNCTION AND METABOLIC CHANGES

It is well to mention that hyperthyroidism may reveal itself in very small infants and may produce exophthalmos, which is usually bilateral and is first noted by increased tearing, levator recession and very slow oncoming exophthalmos, which also almost completely disappears on correction of the difficulty. Today medical management is probably better than surgical interference. This disease is frequently overlooked. One sees the low grades of hypometabolism in the children that we examine for muscle difficulties and those that are not progressing in school. They have gone unnoticed by the mother. They definitely have dry skin and short stubby hands. It is amazing how many muscle errors are associated with the glandular dysfunction. Mild forms of tetany in hypoparathyroidism are occasionally seen but are much more rare than are the hypometabolics.

Diabetic eye lesions are rarely seen in very small children except for the occasional complicated cataract that may occur. Most of the complications are associated with vascular disease. There is usually some kidney complication. Occasionally, there is an ocular muscle paralysis, usually the external rectus.

There are other deficiency diseases occurring in infancy and childhood due to the deficiencies of vitamin A or B or C that might occur at the time due to substitute feeding. On the removal of the baby from the breast the individual may have a sensitivity to the new food and not assimilate it. I have seen bilateral retinal detachments, keratomalacia and severe chorioretinitis associated with deficiency diseases, tuberculosis, toxoplasmosis, syphilis, etc.

Tuberculosis is a rare disease in children. It may produce interstitial keratitis and chorioretinitis. Careful X-ray of the chest will show any possibility of hilar glands and the skin test may reveal a sensitivity to the vaccine. Syphilis occurs frequently enough to warrant alertness in youngsters who show cloudiness of the cornea or a tendency to interstitial keratitis. Toxoplasmosis, which has recently been so thoroughly worked out has revealed itself as a fairly common disease in infants and requires considerable study to prove the diagnosis, but the ocular lesions are in most instances typical, and if in conjunction with small calcification spots in the brain are pathognomonic. In the sick baby it is always well to remember that, especially if there is inflammation in the eye, one may be dealing with a blood dyscrasia and this should be one of the first studies made. Thorough investigation and treatment of the general diseases is indicated.

OCULAR MANIFESTATIONS OF ALLERGY IN BABIES AND SMALL CHILDREN

Allergy is a common disease in babies and small infants. It usually occurs at the first instance of bathing with strange soaps ot the use of hair washes employed by the mother on the hair of very small babies. The youngster has a mucoid discharge, a great deal of blinking and watering and the lids may become swollen and have recurring chalazia. This is much more common with the modern detergents than heretofore. It requires that the individual be put back on simple soaps. This is a serious condition because it may lead to fine, punctate, corneal ulcerations or desquamation with subsequent secondary infection and severe corneal ulceration. A severe keratitis may result with loss of vision to one or both of the eyes. There is a tendency to recurrence, to photophobia and lacrimation, to the total absence of other signs of any infection, the possibility of getting a smear with some eosinophiles, to rapid clearance with the removal of the offending substance. It is well to bear in mind that any disease that may affect the adult may be seen in the infant, and it is important to arrive at a diagnosis as soon as possible in order that the tissues do not become permanently scarred. This is especially true in the allergic states around the eye where the continued use of antibiotics may result in permanent deep scarring of the cornea and may result in the loss of the globe. If one adds insult to injury the tissue responds very seriously with deep vascularization which results in a permanent scar. Early the tissue responds with edema and some capillary enlargement and repeated attacks of new vessels enter the territory and this is permanent change.

Recurring conjunctivitis in a youngster should be considered allergic unless organisms are found on smear and culture. According to the territory one lives in one finds either the pneumococcus or the Koch-Weeks bacillus.

Trachoma has not been present in any of our children in this territory and is almost a forgotten disease.

Vacinnia of the cornea and conjunctiva is frequent enough to warrant mentioning. Gonococcal ophthalmia (Neisserian infection) still persists in clinic patients and a baby with profuse discharge should be treated with extreme care because with present-day treatment with penicillin and the other antibiotics these youngsters are all salvaged. Any organism that will infect the rest of the individual may be found in the ocular conjunctival sac, but with the proper use of modern medication these are short-lived and should not lead to any serious damage. The use of general antibiotics in local conjunctival irritation is not warranted and unless the condition is too serious or too progressive it is better to limit oneself to the use locally in the eye.

Twenty-four hours may make the difference between eyesight and blindness in severe infection or in trauma and in other conditions around the eye. It is my studied opinion that although conservatism is indicated in many diseases this is not one area to practice watchful waiting. One must be alert, make early differential diagnosis, and treatment should be instituted with the idea in mind to get rid of the disease as soon as possible. As every pediatrician knows it is difficult to make the diagnosis in babies and infants, but the better the diagnosis the better the treatment and this certainly holds true around the eye.

GUIDES FOR DISCIPLINE

John C. Sullivan, Ph.D.

The knowledge of how children grow and develop gives adults the understanding which they need to assist an individual child to achieve happy adult living. This knowledge has no value, however, unless the adults in whose care the child is entrusted use it to develop limitations of the child's behavior to the end that he is increasingly able to help himself. The development of these controls, ever changing in the face of his increasing maturity, is commonly referred to as discipline. If discipline is thus defined as intelligent self-control, adults must see their role as setting limits in such a fashion that the child has the opportunity to internalize the guides to his behavior. In short, utilizing their knowledge of how children grow, adults must develop limitations on the child's behavior with him, and through him, to provide the understanding which will give him increasing control over himself.

Parents, teachers, and other professional workers find the control of the child's behavior their most arduous task. When they are dealing with a child with a handicap, the task seems doubly difficult. However, if they consider that all children, to some degree, are handicapped and that no child is without limitations, the task of controlling a child with an obvious handicap is not vastly different from that of controlling a so-called normal child. Often, however, in the case of the former, pity is confused with helpful assistance.

Adults working with children must determine each child's capabilities or limitations and design their controls of his behavior to develop his strengths and to minimize his weaknesses. No magic recipe or formula is available. Each child must be considered as a unique person. No child is helped except as he is given increasing skill in facing the problems with which he is confronted. Insofar as a human being is able to control his behavior in the face of the demands of the society of which he is a part, just to that degree will he be able to achieve a happy, satisfying life. In the face of their understanding of society, of the child's current stage of "self-control" and of his level of maturity, adults must determine a course of action for him to help increase his self-control. They need to ask, "Is this directly helping this child to help himself?" Those things which achieve this end over a period of time are good. Those which do not, require examination.

Although the place to start is with the child, adults must, as clearly as possible, determine the ideals, values and principles by which they live and by which they hope the child will live. Determining what these ideals, values, and principles are is of no value for the child until with and through him adults establish limits for his behavior which will help him to internalize a way of life.

Adults must struggle to work with the child and take him into their confidence. In whatever dimension possible, at his stage of growth, adults must work life's problems out with him. This working out of problems with the child must involve all adults who seek to further his growth, not only mother and father but also the doctor, nurse, teacher, in short, all adults who are directly concerned with the child. Unless the child understands to some degree why adults behave toward him as they do, he will not evidence the desired growth. The child himself must do his own growing. Adults can only assist as their controls help him to focus on and become involved in his own growing. All who seek the child's welfare must reach an accommodation so that the limits they enforce will be consistent with his best interest. The child who is torn by conflicting demands has little chance to achieve the controls necessary for happy adult living.

The first task confronting the parent or parent surrogate is the clarification of values or principles by which they expect the child eventually to live. What are the major values which they hope will govern the child's life? How shall adults verbalize or demonstrate these values? How do these values demonstrate themselves at this time in society? How shall adults help the child to hold his values in the face of his peer contacts without alienating him from the boys and girls with whom he must live? What can adults expect of him at his stage of understanding and development? These questions require a good deal of soul searching and an understanding of the time in which the child is living.

Adults cannot rely on what they think was true when they were young. Values express themselves differently in each generation. What is important and what is less important or superficial must be distinguished. Above all, adults must struggle from the beginning to make implicit as well as explicit the value behind the control which they are exerting. The objective is to help the child to accept intellectually and emotionally the values by which he must live so that he not only will understand but also will feel good about the way in which he behaves. A reasonable understanding of the values which determine the setting of limits allows adults to impose these limits. In short, parents hold the limit not because they are parents or in a position of authority, but because the authority rests in principle.

One of the most difficult skills to acquire is that of paying attention to the child. Adults are so busy doing things to and for the child that they fail to focus on him. They need to see the child's reactions (his behavior) and as best they can, appraise how he is thinking and feeling. Adults often pay attention to everything else, his disability, their own convenience, how his behavior strikes others, the clean floor, his failures. While these things are important, the real issue is the child. What their interaction with the child means to him determines how he will be affected in the long run. Parents cannot afford to allow their understanding of him to develop except through him. Therefore, they need to keep their attention on him as they deal with his behavior. Through their earnest attempt to attend to him, they will be able to judge the effectiveness of their handling of him.

Clear focusing of attention on the child allows the child to feel their love and acceptance of him. To grow well he needs to feel that even though his behavior may leave much to be desired, adults accept him as he is, that they are not rejecting him. The child with an obvious disability presents a problem since adults may confuse him through their action in that they may focus only on his disability. He may feel either that he is being accepted because of his disability or that he is being rejected for the same reason. Adults may avoid this difficulty if their concern is truly with the total child, and, as with any other child, with his potential.

They must examine their feelings to the end that their concern is with the child against their own pride, their clean floor, their comfort, their therapy. The child must be aware that in the eyes of adults he has real value as a person. Little of worth will accrue from their efforts unless the child feels unequivocal acceptance.

In order to promote the growth of a child, adults must help him to understand that he can effectively manage the tasks which life presents him. He must achieve this management through his own effort. The adults who love him must reinforce his feelings through their own genuine pleasure, no matter how minor the achievement. They must expend at least the same effort in helping him to understand the reasons for his achievements as they expend in helping him to understand his failures. He will have his failures, but the balance should be in the direction of success, real success which he feels in his very depths, not contrived success brought about by adults. Success is personal and cannot be felt except as a child truly senses achievement through his own effort.

The child with a disability needs to be encouraged and allowed to do as much for himself as is possible, no matter how painful this may be to the adult. His performance must be compared not with a child with less disability, but rather with what he himself has been able to do previously. The child with an obvious disability often traps adults into assistance which deprives him of the growth-producing feeling that he has achieved. This assistance results from adult impatience, mistaken adult pity, or unfortunate adult feeling of hopelessness. Any child's earliest attempts to do for himself should be encouraged, but it it crucial that the child with obvious disability be so encouraged. He must, up to the very limits of his disability, be able to do for himself in as many areas of living as possible.

Adults often assume that the child feels that he belongs to a group simply because the child is present. His feeling that he belongs is not necessarily true. Only as adults foster the behavior which contributes to group living can the child satisfy his need to belong. This need is satisfied as the group members truly feel that the individual's contribution forwards the purposes of the group. A child cannot survive well in a situation where he is treated either as the honored guest or as a poor relation. He must be helped to contribute to the ongoing welfare of any group of which he is a part, no matter how small his contribution. In the case of the child with a disability, adults must not cut off any avenue of service which he is capable of rendering, no matter how small. He needs to be supported in exploiting every opportunity of contributing to the group living open to him.

The child must have freedom to grow. The limits established by adults must not be so constricting that he does not have the opportunity to learn to manage his own life. Adults experience difficulty at first to allow a child the management of his life as dictated by his level of maturity and his background of experience. The child with a disability provides the adult with a seemingly obvious reason for protecting him from meeting the normal pressures of his age level through which he can learn the skills of living. Children have surprising capacities to manage when such management is expected of them; however, like human beings generally, they will take the easiest route. Within his capabilities, the child must be allowed to move in a normal fashion. Starting with the simplest things such as dressing himself, he must be encouraged to do for himself and take responsibility for his own behavior. He cannot be excused because he has a handicap. Only when adults discover that they have asked him to take too big a step, should his limits be readjusted. This readjustment of limits is not for the purpose of allowing him to avoid his responsibilities but rather of setting limits at a level which enables him to take responsibility. The child cannot be allowed to lean upon or impose upon his parents, his brothers and sisters, his teacher, his physician, or in short on anyone with whom he comes into contact.

Sympathy and pity do not help the child. Only the loving encouragement which allows him to grow can be of help. He should not be allowed to make slaves of his family and others with whom he must live. The conscientious parent must realize that, in the normal course of events, he will not always be available to protect the child and carry his burdens. Parents must help the child to build as much self-sufficiency as possible. To do this, they must set limits with enough freedom to enable him to gain increasing control of his own behavior.

Helping the child to help himself requires that he gain in his understanding of himself and the world in which he lives. To accomplish this through the way in which his behavior is controlled, adults must develop effective channels of communication. Most adults have little difficulty in talking at children with some degree of fluidity. Many adults need to practice the skill of talking with them. This skill can be developed into the high art of getting into genuine communication, that develops common understanding.

Perhaps the hardest thing to do in listening to what the child is saying is to go behind the words to understand what he is thinking and feeling. Action when full attention is concentrated upon what the child is trying to say, the current episode is kept under consideration and his words in focus, the whole understanding of the child is brought to bear on each discussion we have with him. Through the efforts of adults to listen and understand, they build our approach to the child not only in terms of what is to be said now, but also in terms of future work with the child.

When a partner in marriage is upset and indulges in a flow of words not altogether rational, some adults have learned from experience to let him "get it off his chest." They know that it is not good to "bottle it up." They also know they have to pay attention and not do other things as he talks. They know that he is aware of the stupidity of some of his remarks and that he has no intentions of carrying through on them. We quiet him carefully and gently only when he gets involved "over his head." Careful listening to the outburst provides the cues as to what is wrong and may need attention. In short, the outburst is not a loss at all, it is a necessary part of the individual's struggle to avoid conforming, changing his behavior, or accepting responsibility for his behavior. If such outbursts can be considered in this light for an adult, adults should be able to see how necessary this avenue of expression is for the immature child.

A strong tendency on the part of adults, especially in emotionally charged situations, operates to shut off the oral expression of children who are being "disciplined." Allowing a child to say something does not mean that the adult accepts the validity of the child's position. In a situation where the values underlying behavior are becoming increasingly clear, the child understands this as well as the adult. When the child shows signs of becoming frightened by his own outburst, the adult should step in. After the adult has heard a statement several times, he can suggest, if the child feels safe with him, that he's heard that and that both might wait until he (the child) wants to move ideas along. This suggestion implies that the adult is sincerely striving to help the child gain controls and is not engaged in imposing his solution upon the child.

In order to help the child to gain controls, adults have only the tools of communication to work with to achieve this objective. The child with a severe handicap may present special problems which seem almost insurmountable. If adults realize that words are only part of communication and that action which conveys rational intent is the background against which words take on vital meaning, they can courageously undertake their task. The life of Helen Keller should give them strength for their task. She became what she is through the work of her first great teacher, Miss Anna Sullivan. The break through to the child came as a result of the way in which this teacher worked to communicate with her. The struggle to help Helen understand was won through the way Miss Sullivan related herself to the child's total living.

Adults feel that they must set rules by which the child must live, limits designed to help the child internalize values to guide his action. This assumption is correct; but, as has been pointed out, a prior consideration on the part of the adults concerned with the child is to clarify for themselves the life values which they wish to inculcate. Many adults feel that, while this clarification may be important in working with the older child, such understanding is hardly necessary with young children. The very earliest controls exerted on children should be, at least in the mind of the controlling adult, clearly rooted in a basic value system. The expression of a value or values in the young may be very simple if not somewhat vague. However, unless adults start early, vital controls do not become part of the child in the firm dimension necessary for happy adult living. Through such clarification, distinguishing between those things which are fundamentally significant and those which are of lesser importance in the actions of the child is possible.

In setting up limits to help the child internalize controls, two factors must be recognized: (1) the level of maturity of the child—what controls could be exerted at his stage of development, and

(2) the times in which the child is living. Adults would like to believe that a child at a given age will always be able to control himself in a given way. While some evidence exists to support such a position, each child grows at his own rate as dictated by his particular nature and the particular set of forces to which he was and is exposed. In short, each child must be studied and in the face of what he is not and what he was, adults plan the next step, being concerned with the fundamental and not the superficial. Adults keep their focus on the child to gauge his ability to meet healthfully the frustration which holding a particular limit creates in him. This means—"can he take it?" Is it getting controls into him that he is understanding intellectually and beginning to feel good about? Because the child with a more or less severe handicap is hard to judge since he enlists our sympathy, adults working with him must be doubly cautious. As with all children, however, the adults must recognize that they are working for long-term gains, not for short-term results. The latter attitude is often just the wish for present comfort for themselves and for the child. This attitude is certainly true when the holding of limits may be relatively severe and unreasonable.

In order to carry forward their task, adults must involve the child. The rules and regulations must be worked out with the child, even though at an early age he can but dimly grasp what adults are driving at in their effort. Adults work things out in the face of what the child is like at the time in which he lives. Adults must truly find out what life is like in their generation. They often fall back on very inaccurate recollections of what they were like and what the world was like when they were young. Even if adults were more accurate in their recollections, the problems would not be solved. Fundamental values express themselves differently in different generations. Women wear lipstick in our generation, not so in grandmother's. In every generation, values must work in terms of that generation. These values can be internalized only as life is met in the child's generation. Adults work things out with the child when setting the limits as they help the child to understand that as he shows control he has freedom but as he shows lack of control, freedom is limited. Through this withdrawing privilege, the foundation, necessary for the child to grasp that a person is free insofar as he is responsible, is laid.

A need remains to deal with those things which are fundamental. While not ignoring those things which are less fundamental, basic concern should lead adults to keep the rules few upon which we hope to work. While avoiding rigidity, adults consistently hold limits on these few rules as lovingly and as honestly as possible. Inconsistency is the real foe adults must fight. Inconsistency tends to confuse, it signals uncertainty, and it provides the avenue by which the child escapes taking on the responsibility for his own behavior.

Ways of punishing a child have not been discussed since their "goodness" or "badness" rests on whether or not they help the child to understand the reasons why he is being punished. In dealing with the non-conforming child, actions which give the child increased understanding and which eventually lead to better feelings, are desirable. Those actions which confuse the child, which threaten his basic emotional security, or which allow him to escape the guilt he feels as the result of not conforming to realistic reasonable demands are bad.

Rules which are good at one point in the child's development will, of necessity, be out-grown. As the child shows ability to handle life's opportunities, as he grows in understanding, the limits must be changed to allow him further opportunities to grow. The goal is to set him up on his own controls internalized to a degree that he safely manages his life. Continuously giving him increasing control over his own behavior is necessary. While adults are at hand to "pick him up and set him on his feet to try again," they gradually remove external controls. Since adults cannot always take him through life by his hand, the child must learn to meet life. All limits must be examined to determine whether they have out-lived their usefulness. A limit which does not provide freedom to learn, stunts growth. Adults must, with intelligence and love, control the behavior of the child so that the child can ultimately grow to useful and happy adulthood.

When adults are as close to the child as parents, to seek the help of the professional people working with the child is wise. Few parents can see their own problems clearly. The help parents receive in understanding their child and setting a course of action through consulting professional personnel provides all the people working with the child a common base for action. The child who is controlled differently in the home from the way he is in school or in the clinic becomes confused; or, even worse, avoids the struggle of growing up.

Growing up is a long and hard process. Conforming to the demands of life is difficult. Parents owe their children their best effort. The controls they exert upon children must have as their purpose the establishing in the child of the ideals and values by which he is to live. The establishment of these values implies that parents continuously question their actions as to whether or not they are truly serving this objective.

The task of living with children is difficult, but the rewards are great. Growth cannot be hurried, and results do not show quickly. Single errors are not fatal, and as one of the writer's friends puts it, "You have to work hard to make a mess of a child." When the going gets tough, adults should look back a year to examine what they were struggling with then to detect positive signs in the child of good growth and helpful clues in finding a solution with a present problem. The way in which the loving parent or adult lives with himself, with others, and with the child is directly related to that child's developing the high ability of helping himself.

SUGGESTED READINGS

Baruch, Dorothy: *New Ways in Discipline*. New York, McGraw-Hill, 1949.

Hymes, James L.: *Discipline*. New York, Bureau of Publications, Teachers College, Columbia University, 1949.

Sheviakov, George V. and Redl, Fritz: *Discipline for Today's Children and Youth*. Washington, D. C., Association for Supervision and Curriculum, 1956 (revised edition.)

GUIDES FOR PARENTS

Elizabeth M. Boggs, Ph.D.

The conviction is firmly embedded in American culture that children grow up more effectively if the ultimate responsibility for their welfare remains with their parents. The kind of education, the character of their religious instruction, the type of medical care and attention children receive are characteristic of the broad range of decisions which are almost entirely left to the discretion of parents.

This parental right to make decisions concerning their children is well established in law. Although the culture supports the propriety of social and judicial concern for the welfare of each individual child, the right of others, even of official agencies, to interfere with parental choice is carefully hedged with safeguards protecting the right of decision by the parents. Only neglect, the failure to make or to implement decisions, or provable cruelty is allowed to justify the abridgment of parental jurisdiction.

Parents of atypical children are drawn, by the hand of chance, from the same ranks as those of "normal" children. They have the same kinds of strengths and weaknesses and above all the same diversity. They may be stable or unstable, conscientious or shiftless, intelligent or dull, economically comfortable or marginal, aggressive or meek, determined or aimless, happily or unhappily married, mature or immature, articulate or inarticulate, ambitious or placid. They exhibit these characteristics in all the myriad combinations and shadings which characterize other parents. Like these other parents they are entitled to the presumption that they can be entrusted with making decisions concerning the welfare of their own children.

You can gain the assurance necessary to play your role properly if as a parent you develop a plan which contains the following basic elements:

1. *Have a careful diagnostic study made as soon as you think "something is wrong."*

Where the handicap has resulted from an accident or an acute illness, once you are out of the acute phase, you will want an analysis of residual handicap. Try to develop a reliable prognosis, that is, a prediction as to the nature and degree of handicap which your child will have later in life. Such a prediction will be subject to revision as time goes on. Get its outlines early so that both you and your child will not waste time, effort, and hope preparing for the impossible.

2. *If you are not convinced of the accuracy of the first diagnosis, seek an additional expert opinion, preferably from a center offering specialized services in the area of handicap which is suspected in your child's case.*
No matter what the "presenting problem," the staff of such a center will want to make a complete physical, mental, and emotional evaluation of your child. After such an evaluation has been obtained, a member of the staff will be prepared to discuss your child's case with you in some detail. About some types of handicap doctors are able to be quite definite both in diagnosis and prognosis. About other types considerable research is still necessary. Try to get the whole picture and to understand his suggestions for action. Medical and surgical treatments may well be the least important. Some of the suggestions you can put into effect at home; some will depend on what is provided for handicapped children in your community.

3. *If your child's handicap is a long term one with implications for his adult life, establish contact with the most suitable agency in your home community which can offer you continuing practical counseling in planning for your child and in taking advantage of the resources of your locality and state.*
A family service agency is a good place to start, especially if no agency specializing in the handicapped is convenient. A social worker trained in family counseling will usually have more time to spend with you than your physician can give. See that the agency has all the information available about your child which you or the specialists possess so that you may be acquainted with all the special services, public and private, for which your child may be eligible. These services may be obtained through state agencies for the blind, through local cerebral palsy treatment centers, through state crippled children's services, through local visiting or public health nursing services, through clinics for the mentally retarded, through guidance centers for the emotionally dis-

turbed, and through local special school facilities. If no local family agency is available to help you, write to the national headquarters of the agency most directly concerned with your problem.

4. *Inform yourself about the general class of handicapping conditions of which your child's case is a particular example.*

Roughly speaking handicaps may be divided into two groups; those which interfere directly with the learning process, such as those which affect seeing, hearing, thinking, writing, and speaking, and those which present only indirect problems because the child is unable to get about in the regular school, is easily fatigued, or requires medical treatments or special therapy at frequent intervals. Schools may also find it difficult to handle children "whose behavior is dangerous to themselves or others." This description may include those with severe seizure patterns or those subject to violent emotional outbreaks. Our society attaches a particularly cruel form of approbrium to those defects which are presumed to be hereditary. Considerably more accurate scientific information than is currently in general circulation needs to be made available to the general public.

Genetic mechanisms must be sufficiently well understood to be of practical importance. Publicity pertaining to the hazards of "fall out" from atomic explosions has underlined the fact that every person is equally subject to the genetic effects of cosmic and other radiation which may occur in any generation. Parents must be able to shed the emotional resistance to identification of a defect as of genetic origin so that they can be free to seek out the specific details relating to the particular disorder in question and to make constructive use of the most recent discoveries.

5. *Make contact with other parents.*

Mutual exchange of practical pointers may lead you to form discussion groups and to understand the broad range of related concerns which affect people generally. Frequently the attitude of persons toward the birth of a handicapped child or toward the accident or disease which may have produced a permanent crippling condition is profoundly influenced by religious beliefs. To those persons for whom no sparrow falls but by God's design, so significant an event must somehow be placed in its religious context. Those individuals belonging to sects which stress retribution and the belief that the sins of the fathers are visited on the children may regard their own suffering as expiation. Those men or women for whom each adversity is part of "God's plan" may see its meaning as bringing to themselves a profounder understanding of spiritual values, as revealing to them their mission in life, or as a mystery to be accepted as an act of yielding to a higher will. Other persons may see their present suffering as preparation for a world to come. They may believe that God has singled them out for the special privilege of ministering to a special child or that the child himself has a mission, as in the Biblical story of the man born blind of whom Jesus answered, "Neither hath this man sinned, nor his parents: but that the works of God should be made manifest in him."

Most theological systems recognize pain and suffering and interpret its meaning for men. Many persons, however, not fully understanding the tenets of their own faith in relation to anguish of this kind, are ill prepared. For many the place of "natural law" has never been clarified. Confusion between scientific and theological explanations leads them to ask, "Why did this happen?" or, "Why did it happen to me?"

One parent wrote, "Max and I both come from homes of a religious background. For four generations our forebears had lived in the simple traditions of our faith. Perhaps it was because of this background that through all of this experience we never for one moment doubted the existence of God or His goodness and mercy to us as His children. This is not to say that in the initial stage of our grief for Stevie we were either wholly submissive or ready to accept the fact that we were parents of a retarded child. As all such parents know, this realization takes weeks, months, and in some cases even years to accomplish. But it does mean that throughout that period of our own lives because God was included in our thinking it became possible for us to say: How can God use me in this crisis? How can this mental and spiritual torture mold me into a person who can be more useful to Him? All of this seems very simple and easy to accomplish stated in so many words, but the struggle to abide by this philosophy instead of crying out, '*Why,—why* did this have to happen to me?' was a never ending one."[1]

---

[1]Murray, Dorothy G.: *This is Stevie's Story*. Brethren Publishing House, 1956.

Parents who are deeply religious must bring their experience into harmony with their beliefs before their energies can be fully liberated for constructive action. The advice of professional people—physicians, social workers, psychologists—does not always recognize the problems with which the parents may be grappling. In a country where freedom of religion is practiced, the professional counsellor may not be the final authority on guilt and innocence. An answer which may be a light to the path of the person may only add to the confusion of another.

6. *Get all the expert advice you need, but make your own decisions.* You will have to live with them. Take time to think things through at each stage, but don't let things drift indefinitely. Even after you have been able to minimize the unnecessary anxieties caused by the popular misinformation and prejudice you will have worries enough from real causes. Indeed what normal child grows to maturity without some anguish on his parents' part? Parents of the handicapped sometimes have to fight for the right to act like parents, for so frequently they are told that they are not objective about their handicapped children. And why should they be? No one expects parents of "normal" children to be entirely objective about their children. Parents should not only be partial to, but also should be partisans for their children. The right of the child to this special championship is no less real because he is handicapped.

7. *Have confidence in your own abilities as parents.*
You are the key to the situation. Much has been written about the "guilt feelings" of the parents of the handicapped child. What are sometimes called guilt feelings may in reality be a form of grief. Grief is a normal and appropriate human emotion whose suppression is unhealthy. Parents of a handicapped child must live with their continuing form of grief. As an individual he should be assisted by the knowledge that his emotions are respected. Moments of retrospection must not be denied. Human beings need the opportunity to explore fully the factors that cause them concern. Efforts to brush aside doubts with breezy superficial assurances that "of course the parents are not to blame" do not really assuage these doubts. "Blame" needs to be analyzed into the scientific, religious, and social components so that myths and folk tales are clearly identified.

8. *Keep step with each other in your learning and planning for your child.* The discovery of a handicapped child in a family accentuates already existing patterns. Family dissentions may become more pronounced in the face of a new distress. Equally significant, a basically stable family may go on to new strength and new unity in the face of a new challenge. If parents newly facing the fact of a handicapping condition could hear more about positive experiences, more about normal young people who look back upon their association with a mentally or physically handicapped brother or sister as an experience which added depth to their perception of life, they might be spared some unnecessary apprehension. Parents of handicapped children need specialized help but above all they need courage to play a difficult and essential role, the knowledge that no one else can quite play it, and the assurance that both they and those in supporting roles are properly cast.

9. *Get help in working out a program of home training in self care, safety, and activity for your child.*
Most physically and mentally handicapped children need to follow a pattern of their own, specific each to himself as well as to his handicap. Parents must find out what is important, when to try to teach it, and how. A child with diabetes, rheumatic heart disease, epilepsy, and certain comparable conditions needs to accept and take responsibility for his medical regimen. He needs as much of an explanation as he can comprehend for his own satisfaction and to enable him to explain to his friends why he may have to curtail some kinds of activity.

A child who is physically crippled, mentally retarded, or impaired in vision or hearing may require rather specific training in personal self care, locomotion in home and community, and communication in various combinations. "What to do" is obviously specific to the handicap and "when to do it" depends on the developmental stage of the child. Ideally the parent should have the guidance of the staff of a treatment center where the child has been studied and continues to be observed from time to time, or of a visiting nurse, teacher, or family counsellor. Most national organizations distribute articles or pamphlets with suggestions specific to the handicap. These suggestions can be adapted by parents who have some insight into where their child stands developmentally.

Whenever a child is attending a school, nursery, or treatment program make every effort to develop consistent and complementary patterns of instruction between school and home. A handicapped child has to work so much harder for everything he learns that it seems scarcely necessary to teach him two different approaches to tying his shoes just because mother and teacher didn't get together.

10. *Give thought to the modifications of the physical environment.*
The management of babies has been considerably eased by the invention of cribs, playpens, walkers, and diaper services. Recently a variety of designs of special furniture for the cerebral palsied have been worked out. Some publicity has been given to homes designed for adult paraphlegics. Relatively little help has been given to parents in the practical matters of adapting house and grounds to the needs of the handicapped child and to ease the mother's work load. Many parents, had they been able to foresee how things would have worked out as their children grew older, might have looked for different features when moving to a new house.

Any one can remove the scatter rugs that slip under the crutch, but houses differ enormously in the ease with which a crippled person can move in and out. Not so obvious is the importance of layout in the control and supervision of an active mentally retarded youngster whose physical ability to get about exceeds his good judgment. Can he play safely where you can see him while doing housework? Are storage areas exposed? More than the contents of the medicine cabinet must be kept from his grasp! Will the decor favor the partially seeing? Will the lighting be adequate for the deaf child where conversation is most likely to be carried on? Can the child who must be less active still be a participant, indoors and out, rather than left in seclusion to speculate on tantalizing noises? Will it be easy to transfer the child from house to car in any weather? A child must learn to live in a world which may not make many concessions to him. To learn to negotiate stairs when he has to is quite apart from having to spend ten hours a week laboriously on the same stairs because no one indicated how time and effort saving a one story house might be. While sparing their children, some parents do nothing to spare themselves. "No effort is too great if it helps

Billy" they say, not realizing that unnecessary or inefficient effort is paid for in time which could be more effectively spent. As children grow older specific problems change. Parents can help themselves as well as their children by trying to anticipate the new needs when buying and furnishing a house and by developing new arrangements from time to time.

11. *Begin early to accustom your child to the company of people outside the family circle and to being cared for occasionally by outsiders.*

Even the physically or mentally dependent person cannot be forever emotionally dependent on the same two or three people. Everyone needs emotional ties. The handicapped as well as the normal child must learn to establish new relationships. Your child will need these new relationships when you are gone. Encourage their development while you are living.

12. *Start working up an educational plan early, several years before your child will be ready for formal schooling, if possible.*

If you live in one of the larger cities, the chances are that a "director of special education" will be glad to explain to you just what your city offers in the way of special instruction. Generally speaking "special educators" prefer to keep your child with his agemates in a regular class, *if* your child can take advantage of most of the activities and can receive any needed special help on an individual supplementary basis. Speech problems are generally handled in this way. In some states and school districts, blind as well as partially seeing children attend regular classes and receive special instruction in braille from an itinerant teacher or in a special classroom. Children who use hearing aids may not be segregated although supplemental instruction in lip reading may be arranged on such a basis.

The special class or special school is more likely to benefit the totally deaf child, especially in his preschool and early elementary years. Such a school is recommended also for the mentally retarded, whether "educable" or "trainable," since the pace and content of all areas of learning have to be substantially modified. The cerebral palsied child also may be benefitted by special class placement, especially since he may have special handicaps in concept formation, speaking, reading, and writing, as well as in ambulation.

Parents can help by recognizing the advantages of these special facilities and by cooperating with the school when special placement is recommended. Even though special placement may be inconvenient for the parent or seem unduly to separate the child from his neighborhood companions, such placement may help children to mature into more capable adults.

Where it is impossible to get the child to a school or where there are not enough handicapped children to form a special teaching unit, home or hospital instruction should be arranged. Modern electronic devices, such as a two-way communication system may be arranged through the board of education and the telephone company. Although such arrangements do not give the child the full advantages of social interplay found in the classroom, they do represent a very real contribution to the life of the homebound child.

Special education opportunities are not by any means available today in every community for every type of child who may need help. With the increasing parental interest and with the passage of supportive or mandatory legislation in many states, educational opportunities for the handicapped of school age are multiplying rapidly. Since several years are required to get a new program underway, parents who arrive on the school's doorstep with a seven year old, without having lifted a finger in anticipation, may find the school unready.

In some sparsely populated areas special local facilities may not be practical for a small but heterogeneous group of atypical children. A realistic appraisal of the situation may lead parents to consider relocating or looking into the merits of residential schools. Many states maintain such schools for the deaf and blind, a few for the cerebral palsied; all but two states have residential centers for the mentally retarded of school age and beyond. Directories of private residential schools for the handicapped, including residential treatment centers for the emotionally disturbed, may be found in your local library.

13. *Don't overlook the importance of fun and change.*
All therapy and no play make Jack pretty solemn. Basic routines of living are fine for insuring that the essentials are included, but even the most severely handicapped child needs the stimulus of variety and choice. The importance of provoking or motivating spontaneous play and exploration in the very young handicapped

child is being increasingly recognized. Opportunities for group participation and adventure through organized recreation activities for older children are opening up for the handicapped. Today, for example, some suitable camping experience, either in a regular or specialized program, is available to nearly every type of handicapped child.

14. *Help your child to understand his handicap.*

The handicap is neither to be ignored nor to be exaggerated. Unless the child is very severely mentally retarded, he cannot escape discovering that he is different. He should find it out so early in his life that he does not remember *not* knowing it. He needs to know, in a matter of fact way and with increasing detail as he grows older, the scientific causes of the defect and the reasons behind the various kinds of special therapy or training. Help him to meet friendly curiosity as an expression of interest in him and as a desire to understand how he feels. When he is small, you can explain things for him to his friends. Gradually he may be able to do it for himself in a way that will make him feel more comfortable. One of the hardest things for a youngster to put across is the special limitations which he must observe and which are not self-evident, such as following a special diet, or responding quickly to an aura, or premonitions of fatigue.

15. *Do not let your child lean on his handicap.*

Expect and insist on performance up to his ability not only in the area of handicap but in others as well. Do not lead him to think that he will be able to get by in life on pity. Be sure he has family as well as his personal duties. Children of different ages in the family understand concessions or differentiations based on age. They will understand those based on special disabilities, too.

16. *Be frank with your children.*

Answer their questions truthfully and arm them with the fullest information appropriate to their understanding. This frankness is just as important when the handicapped child has been placed outside the home as when he is in it. Young children develop fears about the mysterious absence of another child. Older children are sensitive to overtones of reticence. Let brothers and sisters be partners in family planning, but do not ask them to assume responsibilities which are properly yours, particularly in relation to commitments for an unforeseeable future.

17. *Look your child's future squarely in the face and help him to do so.* Youngsters should be armed with knowledge as to how their particular handicap affects their hopes of parenthood. Many have been plagued unnecessarily with unjustified and long unexpressed fears which could well have been dispelled in childhood. A pre-adolescent whose chances of having healthy children have indeed been impaired should know where he stands. The physician or other skilled counsellor may be able to help.

Wherever communication is possible with the child and he is able to comprehend what it may mean to go away to school, ample time should be given by parents to preparing him for this eventuality. If possible the child should be allowed to participate in the advance visit of inspection and to share in the final decision. An understanding should be arrived at in advance about visiting and vacations. Being sent from home should *NEVER* be used as a threat.

If the child can become economically and socially independent, guide him in directions where he can succeed because of his capabilities. Don't urge a particular educational course just to "prove" something. A handicapped person who makes a fine academic record for himself in a profession which for reasons of impaired mobility or communication he cannot freely practice has not been helped. The physically handicapped can and do pursue a variety of different careers with distinction according to their intellectual gifts and bents. If the child is mentally handicapped but potentially able to maintain himself, start early to build respect for the kinds of employment which will be open to him.

If your school system has not established a close working relationship with your state vocational rehabilitation agency, find out for yourself what this state agency may have to offer. Most such agencies offer vocational evaluation and counseling but do not actually operate training and rehabilitation services. They can, however, subsidize such services in various ways. Parents may need to be forehanded in anticipating the needs of the community by promoting the establishment of a rehabilitation center or sheltered workshop in their locality.

If your child will be partially or wholly dependent, economically, socially or physically, your planning will have to be of a special kind. You will depend not so much on your own ability or inability to establish financial security as upon the continuity of enlightened concern in the state in which you or he resides, upon your status under social security, and upon such other factors which will require individual analysis in each case. The whole question of the care and support of the dependent adult is in a state of flux at present. Joint study and action by organizations and agencies, public and private, interested in the handicapped will probably be particularly productive in the next few decades.

18. *Take part in community action.*

No man is an island, least of all the parent of a handicapped child. The role of the individual parent in relation to his individual child is pivotal. Since ours is a highly organized society, the handicapped will not be part of it if he is not planned for cooperatively. The need for parents to take leadership in community planning has been well described by Eugene J. Taylor:

> "Fortunately, however, more and more parents are beginning to realize that rehabilitation and services to the handicapped have reached the stage where group action is necessary. True, each parent is rightfully interested primarily in the welfare of his own child, but only through concerted, organized group action directed toward the advancement of rehabilitation in all of its phases can the individual child be benefited. Realizing this, parents ask, 'What can I do as an individual to promote the general field of rehabilitation? How can I help to establish these services in my own community in order that my child will benefit from them?'
>
> "Social action, both nationally and on the community level, is admittedly a slow process, but before the parents of a handicapped child can justifiably criticize the apparent lethargy of society in meeting these problems, they must honestly ask themselves the question, 'How active was I in advancing the cause of the handicapped before my own child became disabled?'
>
> "In but a few cases, an honest answer is an embarrassed, apologetic 'I didn't know' or 'I didn't realize . . .' The same answer applies to our communities, 'They don't know' or 'They don't realize.' Before we can expect community action to improve services to the handicapped, they *must* know, and they *must* realize.
>
> "In any program of social action, the first step must be general education to the extent of the problem. National recognition of the problems of the disabled has been accelerated by the war. . . .

In our own local communities in most instances, however, few are aware of the number of disabled children and adults, and the opportunities that a community rehabilitation program would mean for them.

"Borrowing a page from the books of political pressure groups, action committees, lobbyists, advertising experts, public relations specialists, educators, and others who successfully influence public opinion, we must explore all possible paths toward a greater understanding by both professional groups and the general public of the rehabilitation needs of our communities. It is in promoting this understanding that parents can play the most effective role."

To evaluate how much you are now doing to promote such understanding, ask yourself these questions:

1. How well informed am I about the condition which my child has? Can I discuss the condition objectively and realistically with a minimum of emotion? Have I read available literature on the subject or is my knowledge based purely on my experiences with my own child? How well informed am I on my community's resources for rehabilitation? Has my interest and activity been directed toward improved services for all handicapped children or only those with disabilities similar to that of my own child? How well informed am I on the general subject of rehabilitation?

2. Have I ever discussed not only my child's problems but those of handicapped children in general with my child's teacher, school principal, superintendent of schools, or members of the board of education? With officials of local health and welfare agencies? With my physician? With my friends? City officials?

3. Have I supported health and welfare agencies in my own community? Do I belong to any such agencies? Have I attended their meetings? Have I attempted to direct their interest toward rehabilitation and services to the handicapped?

4. Am I familiar with the authorities in rehabilitation who live in my area? Have I suggested them as possible speakers at my civic club, church, parent-teachers association, and other groups to which I belong? Have I ever suggested films on rehabilitation to these groups for meetings?

5. Have I ever written a letter to my Mayor, Councilman, Governor, Representative, Congressman, or other government offi-

cials, commending him for any action on rehabilitation and services to the handicapped? Have I ever written such a letter to the editor of my local radio station about articles, editorials, or programs about rehabilitation? To National publications and networks?

6. As an employer, am I familiar with the selective placement program of my state employment service? Do I or have I ever considered employing handicapped workers?

"The primary interests of the average parent of a . . . handicapped child are services, facilities and research which may directly affect the health and happiness of his own child. Such services, to be of direct value, must be local, and local action results only because of local demands.

"The importance of membership, financial support, and active participation in national organizations to promote rehabilitation and services to the handicapped cannot be overemphasized. Such organizations are vital for the leadership which they provide. It is from them that we receive the guidance, publications, information, and other aids necessary to carry on an educational program to increase public understanding on the community and state levels.

"To solve the problems of translating national developments in rehabilitation and services to the handicapped to your own community, there must be cooperative action on all levels of activity—community, local, and national. You must help if you want help for your own child."[2]

During the last ten years there has been a dramatic increase in the opportunities afforded the handicapped child for education, for special training and rehabilitation, for recreation, for ultimate employment, and for participation in community life. Before a parent can use the openings, he must first have a plan of action for his own child. He must arrive at a pattern for daily living within the family which is consonant with that plan. Parents must have hope based on the clearest possible picture of the true situation, a recognition of the blocks which are immovable, and an appreciation for those factors which can be manipulated. Many parents, first alerted to the lacks and gaps in services for handicapped children, have gone well beyond the bounds of

---

[2]Taylor, Eugene J : *What About My Child. The Crippled Child,* June, 1948.

cooperative effort directed at their own child's problem. They have derived great satisfaction from what has become an altruistic community service in the interests of all children. In this larger work, as in that with their individual children, they are guided by a saying so apt and so often quoted, "God grant me courage to accept what I cannot change, strength to change what I can, and wisdom to know the difference."

FOR FURTHER READING

For Parents

Understanding Yourself and Your Child (pamphlet), National Society for Crippled Children and Adults, 1955.

The various national organizations listed on page 387 publish material designed to orient parents to specific handicaps and assist them with practical management problems. In the major areas the following reading lists may be helpful:

Physically handicapped (including blind, deaf, and speech handicapped:

Parent's Book Shelf and selected film list, National Society for Crippled Children and Adults.

Mentally retarded:

Windows of Understanding, National Association for Retarded Children.

By Parents

Many personal histories have appeared recently in book and magazine-article form. A small sampling:

Triumph of Love, by Leona S. Bruckner, Simon and Schuster, New York, 1954, (by the mother of a congenital amputee).

This is Stevie's Story, by Dorothy G. Murray, Brethren Publishing House, Elgin, Ill., 1956 (by the mother of a mentally retarded boy).

Karen, by Marie L. Killilea, Prentice-Hall, New York, 1952, (by the mother of a cerebral palsied girl).

My Child is Blind, by Lois T. Henderson, in *Special Education for the Exceptional*, Vol. II, by Frampton and Gall, Porter Sargent, Boston, 1955 (by the mother of a congenitally blind boy).

My Son's Story, by John Frank, Alfred Knopf, New York, 1952, (by the father of a child with a very severe brain defect).

About Parents (For professionals)

Rejecting Parents?, by James J. Gallagher, in *Exceptional Children* (22. 7:273) April, 1956 (International Council for Exceptional Children).

Parents' Problems with Exceptional Children, by Samuel R. Laycock and

George S. Stevenson, in *Forty-ninth Yearbook, Part II*, National Society for the Study of Education, University of Chicago Press, 1950.

Helping Parents Understand the Exceptional Child, Child Research Clinic, The Woods Schools, Langhoren, Pa., 1952.

The Role of the Parent in the Education and Training of the Mentally Superior Child. Kent State University Bulletin, Kent, Ohio, June, 1957. Price 50c.

GUIDES TO PLAY MATERIALS

Elenora Moore, M.A., Ed.D.

THE VALUE OF PLAY MATERIALS FOR ALL CHILDREN

Because the child uses play to express what he thinks and how he feels about emotionally significant events in his life, the reliving of his own experience is often more important than any mere imitation of what he sees adults doing. The play activities of the child afford him emotional release in situations where he may either play parts of his own life role with greater intensity or where he may reverse the usual role in which he is placed with adults. Through this process he can both express some of his own inner needs and, even more important, act out many of these tabooed impulses which he is permitted to express only in play. In addition the child develops motor coordination and gains satisfaction repeating those activities in which he has already developed a certain amount of skill.

Toys and play materials are useful in the process of socialization. They help the child to initiate and to carry out social contacts, to develop toward higher levels of social participation, and to express and share his own ideas with others. All play activity has been classified according to its social qualities. In new situations the child may be a mere watcher rather than an active participant. In solitary play the child may enjoy some toy or other play material by himself, without direct interaction with another. Parallel play may involve one child playing beside another instead of with him. In this kind of play little or no social interaction may occur. In group play, two or more children may either be playing together or planning for a common purpose in such play. Frequently normal and handicapped children may play together at several different social levels during the course of a single day. Younger children usually engage in more solitary play. In many homes and schools, too constant an emphasis is placed on pushing the young child's development toward cooperative play. All children, regardless of age level, need some opportunity for solitary activities.

THE SPECIAL VALUE OF PLAY MATERIALS FOR THE HANDICAPPED OR HOSPITALIZED CHILD

Appropriate play materials give the handicapped child not only opportunities for emotional release and incentives for the development of motor skill and language facility but also a means of socializing with normal children. Toys that enable him to play with other children help prevent the isolation of the handicapped child from his peer group. A child should have as normal a life as possible. Appropriate play equipment helps him to do this.

Play materials can make life more pleasant for the hospitalized child. They can give him opportunities to express his feelings about his illness and its treatment, make the separation from home easier, reduce his anxiety, and substitute interesting activity for boredom. Constructive activity with suitable play materials is always much to be preferred to the frequently mischievous behavior of the bored child. Much of the play of the hospitalized child will be individual both because it takes place in bed and because it often requires less effort than play with others.

THE SELECTION OF PLAY MATERIALS

A child needs toys and play materials that can be used to express many different types of play interest. He should have a well-balanced selection of play materials including those which will provide media for creative expression, which will give him an opportunity to experiment, to manipulate, to build, to construct and which will encourage physical activity, serve as stimulating media for dramatic play and dramatization, and foster social activity.

Too many parents select toys which they themselves prefer. Toys should be selected on the basis of their durability, their attractive appearance, and their appeal to the child. Obviously the toys must be safe for the child to use. Metal toys should be free from sharp edges, and wooden toys should have a smooth finish that does not splinter. The child should possess the necessary motor coordination to use the toys.

Only very general statements can be made about age level interests and preferences. Many toy companies now include suggested age levels on the labels of their toys. Such materials as paints can be used by a child from two years on up, but the manner in which he uses them will differ with his mental development and motor skill. As a child reaches the ages of six to twelve years, he develops a growing interest in more social play. Older children sometimes use toys suggested for younger children but in a different way.

SOME SPECIAL CONSIDERATIONS REGARDING THE SELECTION OF PLAY MATERIALS FOR THE HANDICAPPED CHILD

The handicapped child must have toys which he is able to use. If he is confronted with material that offers him nothing but frustration, he tends to become tense or to just give up. Durability is particularly important in selecting toys for children with handicaps involving lack of motor coordination. While normal children are upset because a toy breaks, a handicapped child may feel that he is personally responsible for breaking even a flimsy toy.

The child with cerebral palsy may continue to use toys usually popular with younger children because of his lack of motor skill, but many cerebral palsied children have been observed to show the same play interests as normal children. In such cases adapting the usual toys of their age group so they can use them is desirable. The parents should discuss specific play materials with those who provide therapy for their child. What the child can use effectively will obviously be related to his particular disability.

The mentally retarded child may prefer toys used by younger children, but he may also be interested in toys that children of his own age group enjoy. Some of each should be provided. The child with epilepsy needs play materials to help him live as normal a life as possible. Suitable toys designed to help the blind child to explore his world will reduce the amount of time he spends in such characteristic mannerisms of the blind as waving the arms and moving the head from side to side. The hospitalized and convalescent child often likes the types of toys he has at home. Sometimes he may prefer some of the kinds of toys more usual for younger children. Some of both types should be made available.

CREATIVE PLAY WITH ART MATERIALS FOR ALL CHILDREN

Art materials include different types of paint, crayons, clay, and dough. The purpose of creative play with art materials is to give pleasure, satisfaction, and emotional release to the child in the expression of his ideas and feelings. Adults should be more interested in the satisfaction the child receives from using the materials and less in the finished products made by him. The goal should be the joy of creating, rather than the narrow emphasis on the mere development of artistic skill.

Paints. Paint appeals to children of many age levels. In the child's use of such material, the parent should avoid looking for products which please only the adult eye. Parents frequently expect the child to make a picture that is almost a photographic representation of some thing, such as a house, an apple, or a person. Adults are sometimes disappointed to find seemingly meaningless blobs and daubs instead. Scribbling with crayons and daubing with paints are quite legitimate and helpful experimental activities for the young child.

Research and the observations of many teachers indicate that children go through several stages of growth in the use of paint and other graphic materials. While different investigators have called these stages by various names, substantial agreement on the way in which the child develops in the use of such materials has been reached.

In his first attempts, the child has a natural need to experiment and manipulate. The lines of paint that a young child puts on paper do not need to be called anything at all to give him rather complete satisfaction. The motor activity itself with the resulting visual effect is very satisfying to him.

Later the child begins to give names to his combinations of lines and scribblings. These names are usually related to experiences which he has had. Many five-year-olds make round heads and draw only two lines for the legs of a human figure. If the child refers to this figure by saying, "I am playing," the adult can ask such questions as, "What are you playing with?" "Where are you playing?" and "Is anybody playing with you?" Questions of this type stimulate thinking and are definitely to be preferred to making such specific suggestions as, "Why don't you make some pink flowers?" or "Put in a mother and a little brother."

In his early attempts at representation, the child makes each object according to the significance it has for him. The different objects in a picture do not necessarily have relationship to one another. Color is often used without regard to the actual color of the real object. A mother with pink hair and a father with green hair is quite acceptable to the child. Objectively correct proportions are not an end in these early attempts at representation. Children are about seven years of age before they begin to relate objects to a base line on the paper.

CREATIVE PLAY WITH ART MATERIAL FOR THE HANDICAPPED CHILD

The opportunities for self-expression offered by all art materials are particularly valuable for the epileptic child who has personality difficulties. Art materials such as paints and crayons help a deaf child to use his imagination.

Coloring books and painting books do little to help a child to think or to enjoy the satisfaction of creative activity. Since these materials tend to make the child too completely dependent upon lines, they often foster non-creative, mere repetitions of the pictures in the book. Some children can thus become so inhibited in their efforts to create that they will say, "I can't draw unless you make lines for me." Coloring book activities also demand eye-hand coordination which many younger or handicapped children do not have.

Paints. The mentally retarded child goes through the normal stages of development in the use of art materials, but he reaches each level at a later age. The highest level of development in the use of art materials reached by the mentally retarded child will be related to the extent of his retardation. The child with the lowest mentality may not develop beyond the scribbling-without-meaning stage. The child who is recovering from rheumatic fever or who has a cardiac condition can advantageously use paints and other coloring materials which require little physical exertion but provide needed opportunities for emotional release. The child who has motor disabilities which would make the use of brushes and crayons more frustrating than satisfying can find finger paint a source of very real pleasure. The blind child gets satisfaction from paints and brushes by feeling and smelling the paint and from the physical movement in using the brushes. The partially seeing child should paint on dull-finish paper. The color of the paint should not be glossy. Large paint brushes such as young children use should be used by the older partially seeing child. The child with cerebral palsy may be able to paint by using an easel. Directions for making such an easel are described in "A Manual of Cerebral Palsy Equipment" published by the National Society for Crippled Children and Adults.[1]

Powder paint has some special advantages over other types of paint because it can be mixed to different degrees of thickness. Even children in the primary grades can mix it for themselves. While measuring cups and spoons may be used, many children will prefer just mixing the paint to whatever consistency is particularly satisfying to them. If a child feels uncomfortable about using materials that seem messy to him, powder paint can be mixed to a thicker consistency so that he is less bothered by its tendency to drip. A good powder paint will not come off in flakes when it is dry as some poorer types do. Water color paint cakes are seldom suitable for children under seven or eight or for those with poor vision and/or poor muscular co-ordination. The free arm and finger movements used with the media are possible for many kinds of handicapped children. Although a commercial variety of finger paint or a homemade substitute may be used to advantage, a recipe for homemade finger paint is as follows:

> 2 tablespoons of gloss starch and a small amount of water to form a paste
> 1 cup of boiling water (cook until clear, remove from heat)
> ½ cup granulated soap (not flakes—beat until smooth)
> 4 tablespoons of powdered tempera. Heat.
> (Food coloring may be used)

Finger paint should be used on commercial finger-painting paper or on glazed paper. Since a child who has been rigorously trained to be very neat and clean may feel uncomfortable about using finger paint, he may avoid this medium at first. He may prefer to use brushes for painting. With brushes he does not have to get his hands or arms into the paint. After he has come

---

[1] *A Manual of Cerebral Palsy Equipment.* Chicago: The National Society for Crippled Children and Adults, 1952, p. 51.

to enjoy using brushes and powder paint, he may feel better about using finger paint. Easels or plastic-covered tables may be used. A serviceable painting smock can be made by cutting off the sleeves of one of father's old shirts. A smock of this kind permits the child to play in paint without worrying about having to keep his clothes free from paint spots.

Brushes. Large bristle brushes ¼ inch, or even ½ inch in diameter, and round size number 12 hair brushes with long handles may be advantageously provided for children two to seven years of age. Many older children still enjoy painting with these larger brushes on large 18 x 24 inch sheets of paper.

Crayons. Crayons provide opportunities for self-expression which require little or no effort in preparing the materials. Children develop, according to their levels of growth, from different types of scribbling to a more realistic type of drawing. The child's use of crayons is related to his total development. Again, the parent should be more interested in the satisfaction the child gets from using the materials than in the finished product. Since young boys often show less eye-hand co-ordination than do girls of the same age, they may have less interest in crayons because other materials are easier for them to use.

Children need not always use the points of crayons. They may roll and push crayons across newsprint paper after the covering has been peeled. This type of activity makes the crayon a different material, gives a different effect on paper, and provides a medium for the child who has difficulty in handling the crayon in the usual way. When good crayons are used, the child can get a satisfactory third color by overlaying one color with another as neither color comes off the paper. Young children need crayons about ½ inch in diameter.

The older partially seeing child needs the large crayons that make a dull finish and 18 x 24 inch off-white or unglazed manila paper. A "no-roll" type crayon or a crayon flattened on one side is desirable for the very young, convalescent, or hospitalized child. Some children with cerebral palsy may be able to use a drawing board with the crayon in a sponge rubber ball or a suitable tin holder as described in *A Manual of Cerebral Palsy Equipment.*[2]

---

[2]Ibid., p. 40 and 124.

Clay. Clay offers unlimited opportunities at that first level of the child's development in the use of art materials which he is merely manipulating or experimenting. In this process of trying out the material, children pinch, pull, pound, hit, feel, and smell the clay. Some even want to taste it. Occasionally the child accidently makes a clay object which reminds him of a real one. He then gives a name to his product and regards it as the actual article rather than as a mere representation of it. Young children pretend to eat and sometimes bite and chew the play cookies and doughnuts which they have made of clay. As children develop, they begin to realize that the objects are mere representations of the real thing. The clay objects, the conversations, and the use of materials indicate that many five and six year old children are in this level of development at least some of the time.

Clay is particularly useful for expressing aggressive feelings. The pounding and stamping which seems meaningless noise to adults can be a very satisfying means of emotional release for the child. Clay is an exceptionally good material because it gives the child an opportunity for expressing these destructive impulses. Because the clay is still there in a pliable state ready to be used again, he may make a product and destroy it without feeling guilty.

Many children do not wish to keep their clay products. They merely wish to enjoy producing them. If a child wants to save clay articles, the articles can be dried on paper plates and painted with powered paint. Powdered clay already mixed with water can be kept moist by keeping it in a plastic bag. The child's enjoyment of playing with clay should not be spoiled by worry about the scraps that fall on the floor. Helping to clean up these scraps can be fun for the child.

Clay is particularly good for the blind child because it has shape and texture which the child can feel. A blind child can learn to tell the difference in texture between clay, dough, plasticene, and paper maché. He may enjoy the varied experiences of playing with each of these materials. Hospitalized or convalescent children may use clay on a flat surface if the bed is protected by a suitable covering of plastic or other material.

Some children who for any reason do not like clay may enjoy using a homemade substitute such as dough which has a different texture. An additional experience may be secured by adding a few drops of food coloring to the different balls of dough so the child can have the fun of watching the color spread as he works it into the dough. The following recipe may be used for dough:

    1 cup of flour   ¼ - ½ cup of water
    ½ cup of salt   Vegetable coloring (as desired)
    3 teaspoons of alum

Water Play. Water is another interesting material to explore. Water play is particularly beneficial for children in their early years and for urban children who have few opportunities to play in sand and mud.

A pan of water with sponges, wash cloths, plastic objects, and soap flakes provides motivation for a hemiplegic child to open a tight fist. He needs to use both hands in playing with the water and toys.[6]

The culture of many social groups in American society does not permit young children to express their normal interest in playing with urine and feces. Water play can be a substitute material for such interests. Play with water is helpful in calming and soothing tense and aggressive children.

Pouring water in and out of containers is fun. A variety of experiences may be achieved by adding soap flakes, soap powder, or bubble bath materials. Small objects that float, toy dishes, wash cloth and sponges add to the enjoyment of water play.

Frequently preschoolers want to follow mother about the house to help her clean up. This interest in mopping and cleaning with sponges and other housecleaning utensils may not be a real interest in housecleaning so much as it is an interest in water play.

TOYS FOR MANIPULATION AND CONSTRUCTION

The earliest manipulative toys for children under two years of age should be made of washable, light-weight material. Stuffed animals and dolls should be of the soft cuddly type. Infants like to shake and bite strings and beads and use take-apart toys to satisfy their interest in manipulation. Beads and strings not only offer enjoyable possibilities for manipulation but also stimulate children from three to six to learn the different colors and to engage in counting and grouping activities. The first beads for stringing should be about one inch in diamater.

Puzzles. Puzzles for the young child three to six years of age should be made of wood ¼ to ½ inch in thickness. The pieces should fit into a wooden frame about 9 x 12 inches or larger. The puzzle picture can be of one object such as an animal to be put together in three to five or seven large pieces. When a child seems to be no longer challenged by such simple and easy puzzles, the pieces of two or more of them can be mixed together to provide the much more advanced enjoyment of picking out the pieces and putting together the two or more puzzle pictures.

Blocks. Dramatic play with blocks affords the child opportunities for expressing ideas and feelings. The child who has experienced too much pressure to keep clean may feel happier using blocks than using materials such as paint and clay. Children who are in great need of emotional release may want to bang the blocks together and to throw them around before they can even begin to build constructively. A child should be free to destroy his own block creations if he wishes. Animals, trains, cars, and trucks to go with the blocks often help to make the child's play more constructive.

Blocks may be of many sizes and shapes. Large hollow blocks provide needed physical activity and permit children to get into the larger structures which they have made. Large blocks frequently promote more social play than the small table variety. Blocks with curved pieces and arches help children to achieve more varied effects than they could get from rectangular pieces alone. Blocks can be used for either solitary, parallel, or social play.

TOYS FOR MANIPULATION AND CONSTRUCTION FOR THE HANDICAPPED CHILD

The slow-learning child will continue to enjoy the very simple puzzles and other materials suitable for younger children. The cerebral palsied child may be able to use puzzles if a piece of doweling is attached as a usable handle to each part of the puzzle.[3] If puzzles are used for a convalescing child, they should be used on a flat surface with raised edges to keep all the pieces within his reach. Manipulative toys such as puzzles, beads, strings, and

---

[3] Helen Craig, Toys for Children with Cerebral Palsy. *American Journal of Occupational Therapy,* March-April, 1951, pp. 50-51.

take-apart toys are good for the deaf child because they can be used without conversation and frequently foster parallel play. To help the small child who is blind, beads as large as an inch in diameter may be used. Strings with metal tips about an inch long should be provided.

Directions for making suitable large hollow wooden floor or table blocks are given in "The Manual for Equipment for Cerebral Palsied Children" published by the National Society for Crippled Children and Adults.[4] One of their leaflets also describes a wagon with rubber blocks especially adapted for such children's use.[5]

TOYS FOR PHYSICAL ACTIVITY

Play with push-pull toys, wheel toys, gym equipment, and balls provides necessary physical activity. Push-pull toys, such as animals on wheels and take-apart-and-put-together toys are particularly desirable for the child under 18 months. At the 18 month to three year old level, the child needs wheel toys, such as a low tricycle, a small wagon built to withstand hard usage, and trucks to ride. Low steps to climb, balls, a sand box big enough to get into, and a plastic wading pool offer additional physical activity. As the child grows during the three to six age period, he will need a larger tricycle. Some children will want and can use two-wheelers with auxiliary wheels before six years of age.

The development of motor skills is particularly important for the child during the years six through twelve. To some extent a child's acceptance in a social group is at least partially related to his effectiveness in participating in activities which involve motor skills. Both boys and girls are interested in wagons, bicycles, scooters, skates, skis, stilts, and parallel bars. Boys and some girls play games which they call baseball, football, or marbles. Frequently they make up their own rules for these varied types of competitive play. Girls enjoy jumping ropes and playing jack stones. At the nine to twelve age level children work to improve their skill in all games involving motor activity.

---

[4] *A Manual of Cerebral Palsy Equipment.* op. cit., pp. 10 and 11.
[5] Margaret Langdon, Cynthia Tunison Ream, Marilyn Hill Doebler, "Report of a Study on the Use of Toys in Work with Cerebral Palsied Children," Chicago: The National Society for Crippled Children and Adults, pp. 14 and 15.

TOYS FOR PHYSICAL ACTIVITY FOR THE HANDICAPPED CHILD

Because the child with cerebral palsy wishes to use his developing motor abilities, he is interested in the same type of toys that normal children like. He may use toys planned for younger children because of his limited motor development. Tricycles, wagons, pull-toys, take-apart toys, and manipulative toys have been used successfully with cerebral palsied children. The pamphlet, "Developing Crippled Children Through Play," gives the names of commercial toys and their manufacturers and ways in which these toys were found useful in various centers for work with cerebral palsied children.[7] A "Manual of Cerebral Palsy Equipment" shows pictures and gives directions for making modified steps and slides for these children.[8]

Toys for physical activity are desirable for the young deaf child. Many parents are apt to regard such a child as overactive. The child's intense activity is probably a substitute for speech. Evidence indicates that children with epilepsy feel more like normal children if they engage in the gym activities and games appropriate for their age level. Blind children especially enjoy push-pull toys more if they make musical sounds when played with. Hospitalized children of two to eight years enjoy pull toys providing they are well enough to pull them around the ward.

TOYS FOR DRAMATIC PLAY AND FOR DRAMATIZATION

Dramatic play is desirable for all young children and should not be confused with dramatization. In dramatization the child takes the part of a character in a story and knows just what that character did and how the story ends. Although occasionally younger children spontaneously play out bits of a well-known story, they do not usually enjoy the process of dramatization until they are old enough to remember the sequence of events in the story and the actions of the character they are to portray. In

---

[6]Isabel Pick Robinault, Occupational Therapy Technics for the Pre-School Hemiplegic. *American Journal of Occupational Therapy*, September-October, 1953, pp. 205,207.

[7]*Developing the Crippled Child Through Play.* Chicago: The National Society for Crippled Children and Adults in cooperation with the American Toy Institute, 1952, pp. 1-9.

[8]*A Manual of Cerebral Palsy Equipment*, op. cit., pp. 88-93.

dramatic play, on the other hand, the action evolves as the playing goes on. Children talk about this sort of play somewhat as the following: "I'll be the mother, and you be Aunt Jane. We'll go downtown. Now, let's play the company comes." In such dramatic play a very real need exists to communicate. This activity provides an excellent motivation for oral expression for children with speech difficulties.

Trains, trucks, dress-up materials, dolls, and housekeeping equipment give children both the fun of imitating adult activities and the opportunity for self-expression. The preschool child may be helped to adjust to an illness by playing out what he has experienced. Doctor sets, nurse sets, rubber dolls, unbreakable tea sets, and cooking utensils that can be immersed in water offer the advantages of both water and dramatic play. Such materials should be suitable for the hard usuage of an immature child. Similarly, toy cupboards and chests should have deep drawers that can be pulled out without upsetting the chest.

Such things as old silk scarves, old skirts, a father's coat, hat, and tie all help the child in playing family roles. Between the ages of six and nine children begin to want their dress-up costumes to look very much like the real thing. Indian and cowboy costumes, sailor, doctor, nurse, fireman, and policeman costumes are all popular. Children of school age often feel that they must have homemade or commercial costumes of this kind to participate in such group play. In some primary grades almost every child has articles of cowboy gear or Indian attire. The child may find it hard to be a part of this child society without some kind of costume. Even a red handkerchief may help a child feel more like one of the neighborhood cowboys. In many schools girls as well as boys have cowboy and Indian equipment and materials for space ship play. One seven-year-old expressed the situation by saying, "Daddy, there are too girl space ship men"[5] It is a good idea for the parent to know the current interest in his child's school. The current fad could be anything from Davy Crockett caps to space helmets. Some nursery school children have already begun talking about space helmets.

Nine to twelve-year-olds and some even younger children become interested in playing show. In this show play, children may either dramatize a well-known story or play one which they have made up. Playing show for the older child frequently provides opportunities for both oral and written expression. A great deal of social development takes place as a neighborhood group plans and enacts such a show.

Puppet shows are another variation of dramatization. A primitive sort of puppet can be made from tongue depressors and construction paper, from potatoes and sticks, from stuffed paper bags, or from stuffed socks. Younger children frequently use these almost as much as manipulative toys. Older children may also want commercially produced hand puppets and marionette sets.

SOCIAL GAMES

Between five and eight years of age children begin to be interested in group games. Picture lotto can be played by many children in kindergarten. Card games where children match and classify cards showing fruits, vegetables, and animals are popular. Dominoes and number games are another type of desirable social game. Children of normal mental development often make up their own methods of scoring for these games and for play with marbles and jack stones. At the eight to ten-year-old level, children of normal mental development enjoy games that involve spelling, arithmetic and geography. A handicapped child's social development is furthered whenever he can participate with his family or a small peer group in playing any of these games.

PLAY WITH HOUSEHOLD WASTE MATERIALS

Children work out their own ways of playing with such waste materials as wooden spools, typewriter ribbon wheels, attractive empty boxes of different shapes and sizes, large cardboard cartons, buttons of various sizes and types, smooth-edged tin cans, milk cartons, and old greeting cards. Many of these objects become satisfying toys for manipulation and construction. Boxes frequently stimulate dramatic play involving houses, stores, and other buildings. Old greeting cards may be useful in devising simple games involving grouping and classifying. Children like to touch and feel silk, velvet, tweed, wool, nylon, and plastic. These are good materials for children who need sedentary activity. The child without visual handicaps can also enjoy the colors and designs.

COOKING AS PLAY

Cooking can be fun for people who do not have to do it. When a handicapped child helps in cooking and preparing foods, he becomes more of a contributing member of his family group. Such activity helps the child acquire information regarding the name, appearance, and source of common foods. A child will obviously learn more if mother mixes her own eggs, flour, butter, sugar, and milk instead of using prepared mixes. Even if this may be only a watching activity for many of them, the process of cracking an egg and separating the yolk from the white is really interesting for pre-school children. Smelling, touching, and tasting such materials add to the child's fun and are of crucial importance for the blind child.

Such activities as frosting cookies with wooden tongue depressors or blunt knives are fun for the child of three to six. The whole family can have a good time making ice cream in an old fashioned freezer with a handle that has to be turned.

Children see the value of reading when they watch mother use a recipe book or file. A recipe book with pictures of the finished product adds to the fun. Children who are learning to read enjoy picture recipes which both name and picture the food and the measurements of its several ingredients.

GUIDES TO READING MATERIALS

Publications prepared by The Children's Bureau and Office of Education of the Department of Health, Education and Welfare.

These publications may be ordered from the Superintendent of Documents, United States Government Printing Office, Washington 25, District of Columbia.

CHILD HEALTH AND HYGIENE

Better chance for mental health for children in smaller communities. 1952. 10 p. il. 10c. Catalog No. FS 2.2:C 43.

Better health for school age children. 1952. 12 p. 10c. Catalog No. FS 3.202:H 34/2.

Emotional aspects of convalescence. 1948. 7 p. il. 5c. Catalog No. FS 3.207/a:C 769.

Emotional problems associated with handicapped conditions in children. 1952. 19 p. 20c. Catalog No. FS 3.209:336.

Healthy personality for your child. 1952. 23 p. il. 20c. Catalog No. FS 3.209:337.

DISEASES AND AILMENTS

Child who is hard of hearing. 1952. 14 p. il. 10c. Catalog No. FS 3.210:36.

Child who is mentally retarded. 1956. 24 p. il. 10c. Catalog No. FS 3.210:43.

Child with cerebral palsy. 1950. 14 p. il. 10c. Catalog No. FS 3.210:34.

Child with cleft palate. 1953. 14 p. il. 10c. Catalog No. FS 3.210:37.

Child with epilepsy. 1952. 16 p. il. 10c. Catalog No. FS 3.210:35.

Child with rheumatic fever. 1955. 14 p. il. 10c. Catalog No. FS 3.210:42.

Children with impaired hearing. 1952. 22 p. 15c. Catalog No. FS 3.209:326.

Preschool child who is blind. 1953. 24 p. il. 10c. Catalog No. FS 3.210:39.

MATERNITY AND INFANCY

Your premature baby. 1954. 14 p. il. 10c. Catalog No. FS 3.210:40.

Infant care. 1955. 106 p. il. 15c. Catalog No. FS 3.209:8.

Your well baby. 1948. 12 p. il. 5c. Catalog No. FS 3.210:9.

YOUR CHILD

Your child from 1 to 6. Rev. 1956. 110 p. il. 20c. Catalog No. FS 3.209:30.

Your child from 6 to 12. 1949. 141 p. il. 20c. Catalog No. FS 3.209:324.

Adolescent in your family. Rev. 1955. 110 p. il. 25c. Catalog No. FS 3.209:347.

MOTION PICTURES

Motion pictures on child life, list of 16-mm films. 1952. 61 p. 40c. Catalog No. FS 3.202:M 85/2.

—— Supplement 1 to above publication. 1954. 16 p. 15c. Catalog No. FS 3.202:M 85/2/supp. 1.

—— Supplement 2 to above publication. 1956. 12 p. 15c. Catalog No. FS 3.202:M 85/2/supp. 2.

BOOKS

Children's bookshelf, booklist for parents. Rev. 1953. 56 p. il. 25c. Catalog No. FS 3.209:304.

PLAY AND RECREATION

Home play and play equipment for the preschool child. 1946. 19 p. il. 15c. Catalog No. FS 3.209:238.

ELEMENTARY EDUCATION

How children learn to read. 1952. 16 p. il. 15c. Catalog No. FS 5.3:952/7.

How children learn to think. 1951. 19 p. il. 15c. Catalog No. FS 5.3:951/10.

How children learn to write. 1954. 24 p. il. 15c. Catalog No. FS 5.3:953/2.

How children use arithmetic. 1951. 13 p. il. 15c. Catalog No. FS 5.3:951/7.

EXCEPTIONAL CHILDREN

Crippled children in school. 1948. 37 p. il. 20c. Catalog No. FS 5.3:948/5.

Education of crippled children in United States. 1949. 12 p. il. 10c. Catalog No. FS 5.18:80.

Forward look, severely retarded child goes to school. 1952. 54 p. il. 25c. Catalog No. FS 5.3:952/11.

School in the hospital. 1949. 54 p. il. 25c. Catalog No. FS 5.3:949/3.

Some problems in education of handicapped children. 1952. 12 p. il. 15c. Catalog No. FS 5.17:112.

SCHOOL

Preparing your child for school. 1949. 24 p. il. 15c. Catalog No. FS 5.17:108.

RECREATION

Home play and play equipment for the preschool child. 1946. 19 p. il. 15c. Catalog No. FS 3.209:238.

GUIDES TO HEALTH EDUCATION MATERIALS

Sources and how health education materials may be obtained

In planning any health education activity the first step should be to outline the purpose of the program and the methods by which it is to be accomplished. When the outline of the program and the media to be used have been decided upon, a great deal of time and effort will be saved by a survey of the materials available through agencies engaged in similar health education activities.

The materials available may not always be exactly what is desired but frequently will furnish valuable suggestions which can be adapted to your special situation. In other instances such materials will supplement your materials and program. The extent to which such media is utilized depends upon a knowledge of what is obtainable.

The National Publicity Council for Health and Welfare, Inc., 257 Fourth Avenue, New York 10, N. Y., furnishes information concerning sources of ready-made educational materials. When a request for materials is made it is important to furnish detailed information concerning your plan. It is not enough, for example, to request materials on "Crippled Children." If the agency receiving your request does not know the purpose for which you wish to use the material, you could receive a pamphlet entirely unsuited for your needs, though it be an excellent pamphlet on the problem discussed. Such a pamphlet could outline the "Home Care of the Crippled Child," it might be a general discussion of the incidence of crippling conditions, or any other phase of the subject, whereas what you wanted was a pamphlet on games crippled children could participate in.

If you request printed material state the purpose for which you wish to use it; what points are to be emphasized, for example, prevention, early diagnosis, treatment, or community action; to whom it is to be distributed as well as any special requirements, such as size, cost, etc.

When radio programs are requested it is important to state whether a script or a transcription is desired; the main points the program is to cover; whether the time available is 5, 15 or 30 minutes. Is a talk, interview, round table discussion or dramatization most suitable for your needs? If the request is for a dramatization will the services of a director and professional cast be available or will it be an amateur production? Is the program one of a series? If so, what characteristics in the series should it match. Is it possible to pay the small fee some agencies charge for copies of their scripts?

When requesting a film one should state when, where and to whom it will be shown, as well as the type of film which can be used; for example, 16 or 35 mm., silent or sound, as well as the length of time available for showing. If a TV film is desired, is it for a 15 minute or 30 minute show? If a film is not available covering the specific subject, it is important to state what related subjects, if any, could be used.

If an exhibit is desired, state the type of audience that will view it. Will they be physicians, nurses, occupational therapists, industrial workers, parents, educators, or the public at large? Will the exhibit be a part of a group of exhibits or will it be a single exhibit? What type of space will be available—wall space, the amount in linear feet as well as height, a straight panel or is the space two or three sided including dimensions of each side? Is it to be a table top exhibit, window display, etc? What message is the exhibit to carry? If a suitable exhibit is not available, are there sufficient time and funds to build it if suggestions are made for creating one? Can the services of an artist, photographer or a sign writer be obtained?

It is essential to tell the who, what, when, where, and why in your request.

Local, county and state health departments in your community as well as other governmental and voluntary agencies have materials available which they will furnish upon request. On the national level federal departments, voluntary agencies and commercial companies are additional sources of useful materials.

The national sources listed in many instances have catalogues of materials available either free or at a nominal cost.

SOURCES OF MATERIAL

American Diabetes Association
1 E. 45th Street
New York 17, N. Y.
A.D.A. Forecast, bimonthly magazine, reprints, pamphlets.

American Foundation for the Blind
15 West 16th Street
New York 11, New York
Pamphlets, books, periodicals, films.

American Hearing Society
817 14th Street, N.W.
Washington 5, D.C.
Pamphlets, posters, reprints of articles from, *Hearing News*.

American Heart Association
Inquiries Section
44 E. 23rd Street
New York 10, N. Y.
Films, slide films, pamphlets, posters, exhibits, list of publications.

American Medical Association
Bureau of Health Education
535 N. Dearborn Street
Chicago 10, Ill.
Films, pamphlets, posters, exhibits, radio transcriptions, television scripts, packets, lists, and the magazine, *Today's Health*.

American Occupational Therapy Assn.
250 W. 57th Street
New York 19, N. Y.
Pamphlets, posters, radio scripts, slide films, exhibits, lists, movies, TV spots, technical reprints, manuals of professional interest.

American Physical Therapy Association
1790 Broadway
New York 19, N. Y.
Pamphlets, posters, radio and TV scripts, slide films, exhibits, catalogs, movies, magazine articles, monthly journal.

American Public Health Association
1790 Broadway
New York 19, N. Y.
Reports on education qualifications of health workers, community survey guide, list of publications and reprints.

Arthritis and Rheumatism Foundation
Director of Public Information
23 W. 4th Street
New York 36, N. Y.
Pamphlets, posters, radio scripts, transcriptions, film.

Association for the Aid of Crippled Children
Division of Publications and Public Education
345 E. 46th Street
New York 17, N. Y.
Pamphlets, reprints, exhibits, lists, movies, books.

Association for Physical and Mental Rehabilitation
1472 Broadway
New York 36, N. Y.
Pamphlets, reprints, a journal.

Better Vision Institute, Inc.
630 Fifth Avenue
New York 20, N. Y.
Pamphlets, slide sound films, Movies.

Center for Mass Communication,
Columbia University Press
1125 Amsterdam Avenue
New York 25, N. Y.
Films, pamphlets, posters, radio scripts, transcriptions, records, comic books.

Child Study Association of America
132 E. 74th Street
New York 21, N. Y.
Pamphlets, publication and book lists. Leaflet on organizing a parent education program.

Cleveland Health Museum
8911 Euclid Avenue
Cleveland 6, Ohio
Maintains workshops for creating exhibits to be loaned; Dickinson-Belskie life-size models on human reproduction, illustrations and photo-service.

Cleveland Junior Chamber of Commerce
400 Union Commerce Building
Cleveland, Ohio
Pamphlets—Speech and Hearing.

Encyclopaedia Britannica Films, Inc.
Public Relations
1150 Wilmette Avenue
Wilmette, Illinois
Slide Films, cartoons, movies.

Equitable Life Assurance Society of the United States
Bureau of Public Health
393 Seventh Avenue
New York 1, N. Y.
Booklets, posters, related material.

Films Incorporated
Public Relations
1150 Wilmette Avenue
Wilmette, Illinois
Cartoons, catalogs.

Health Information Foundation
Public Relations Director
420 Lexington Avenue
New York 17, N. Y.
Pamphlets, bulletins, transcriptions, films.

Hemophilia Foundation
175 Fifth Avenue
New York, N. Y.
Pamphlets.

Information Service Division
Department of National Health and Welfare
Ottawa,
Dominion of Canada
Pamphlets, films.

International Council for Exceptional Children
1201 Sixteenth Street, N.W.
Washington 6, D. C.
Pamphlets, films.

John Hancock Mutual Life Insurance Company
Health Education Service
200 Berkeley Street
Boston 17, Mass.
Pamphlets, lists.

Metropolitan Life Insurance Co.
Health and Welfare Division
1 Madison Avenue
New York 10, N. Y.
Pamphlets, exhibits, films, film strips, catalogs.

Muscular Dystrophy Association of America, Inc.
Public Information Department
1790 Broadway
New York 19, N. Y.
Pamphlets, reprints, films, radio scripts, exhibits, TV clips.

National Association for Retarded Children, Inc.
99 University Place
New York 3, New York
Pamphlets, periodicals, audio-visual materials, films, film strips, records, tape recordings.

National Epilepsy League
130 N. Wells Street
Chicago 6, Ill.
Quarterly newspaper, *Horizon.* Pamphlets.

National Foundation for Infantile Paralysis
Director of Public Education
301 E. 42nd Street
New York 17, N. Y.)
Pamphlets, booklets, films, film strips, exhibits, bibliographies.

National Health Council
1790 Broadway
New York 19, N. Y.
Pamphlets, reprints, leaflets, list of publications, health career materials.

National Heart Institute
Heart Information Center
Bethesda 14, Md.
Pamphlets, etc.

National Multiple Sclerosis Society
Public Relations
270 Park Avenue
New York, N. Y.
Pamphlets, radio scripts, radio and TV spot announcements, medical manuals, fact sheets.

National Publicity Council for Health and Welfare
257 Fourth Avenue
New York 10, N. Y.
Newsletter, library of health education materials.

National Society for Crippled Children and Adults
11 S. LaSalle Street
Chicago 3, Illinois
Pamphlets, radio scripts. Crippled Child Magazine, bulletin, books, News releases, film and transcription libraries.

National Society for the Prevention of Blindness
Director of Information Service
1790 Broadway
New York 19, N. Y.
Films, pamphlets, posters, exhibits, radio scripts, catalogs, vision testing charts.

Public Affairs Pamphlets
22 E. 38th Street
New York 16, N. Y.
Popularly written pamphlets on a variety of subjects in health and social welfare field.

United Cerebral Palsy Associations, Inc.
Public Relations Director
369 Lexington Avenue
New York 17, N. Y.
Pamphlets, posters, films, radio transcriptions, etc.

United States Department of Health, Education and Welfare
Washington 25, D. C.
1. The Children's Bureau
   Pamphlets, catalogs, lists.
2. The office of Education
   Pamphlets, catalogs, lists.
3. The Office of Vocational Rehabilitation
   Pamphlets, radio scripts, exhibits, lists, films.
4. The United States Public Health Service
   Leaflets and Pamphlets.

Volta Bureau
(Headquarters, Alexander Graham Bell Association for the Deaf)
1537 35th Street, N.W.
Washington, D. C.
Pamphlets, lists, movies—for deaf and hard of hearing.

389

GUIDES FOR COMMUNITY PROGRAMS

THE Committee on Child Health of the American Public Health Association in consultation with leading specialists in the medical, rehabilitative and public health fields has prepared a series of guides. The guides have been endorsed by leading professional organizations concerned with the health and welfare of handicapped children. Everyone interested in community programs concerned with handicapped children will find these guides valuable reading.

Among the guides which are available are the following:

    Health Supervision of Young Children
    Services for Handicapped Children
    Services for Children With Cerebral Palsy
    Services for Children With Cleft Lip and Cleft Palate
    Services for Children With Dento-facial Handicaps
    Services for Children With Eye and Vision Problems
    Services for Children With Hearing Impairment

$1.50 per volume

Available from:

    The Committee on Child Health
    American Public Health Association
    1790 Broadway
    New York 19, New York

DIRECTORY OF CAMPS FOR THE HANDICAPPED

Prepared cooperatively by

    American Academy of Pediatrics

    American Camping Association

    National Society for Crippled Children

Price, 50 cents

Copies available from

    American Camping Association
    Bradford Woods
    Martinsville, Indiana

    The National Society for Crippled Children and Adults, Inc.
    11 South LaSalle Street
    Chicago, Illinois.

DIRECTORY OF SCHOOLS, SERVICES AND OTHER FACILITIES

E. Nelson Hayes: Directory for Exceptional Children, Boston Porter Sargent.

ADDITIONAL BOOKS

ON HANDICAPPING CONDITIONS AND REHABILITATION

The interest in handicapping conditions and rehabilitation is manifested by the publication of increasing numbers of books for both lay and professional people.

This list has been prepared to enable those who seek additional information to select publications on any phase of the subject in which they are interested. It is a comprehensive list of recently published books which include material on almost all phases of handicapping conditions and rehabilitation. Equally important contributions may have been omitted because of a lack of opportunity to review them.

AJMONE-MARSAN AND RALSTON: *The Epileptic Seizure:* Its Functional Morphology and Diagnostic Significance. Springfield, Thomas, 1957, 264 pp., $6.

ALLAN: *Rehabilitation: A Community Challenge.* New York, Wiley, 1958, 263 pp., $5.75.

A.M.A.: *Handbook of Physical Medicine and Rehabilitation.* New York, Blakiston-McGraw, 1950, 573 pp., $4.50.

ANDERSON: *Functional Bracing of the Upper Extremity.* Springfield, Thomas, 1958, 480 pp., $9.50.

BENDER: *A Dynamic Psychopathology of Childhood.* Springfield, Thomas, 1954, 296 pp., $7.50.

BENDER: *Aggression, Hostility and Anxiety in Children.* Springfield, Thomas, 1953, 200 pp., $5.50.

BENDER: *Child Psychiatric Techniques:* Diagnostic and Therapeutic Approach to Normal and Abnormal Development Through Patterned, Expressive, and Group Behavior. Springfield, Thomas, 1952, 360 pp., $8.50.

BENDER: *Psychopathology of Children with Organic Brain Disorders.* Springfield, Thomas, 1956, 168 pp., $5.50.

BIERMAN AND LICHT: *Physical Medicine in General Practice*, 3rd Ed. New York, Hoeber, 1952, 832 pp., $12.50.

BOLTON AND GOODWIN: *An Introduction to Pool Exercises.* Baltimore, Williams & Wilkins, 1956, 48 pp., $1.75.

BOWLEY: *The Young Handicapped Child.* Baltimore, Williams & Wilkins, 1957, 127 pp., $3.50.

BRENNER: *Therapeutic Exercises for the Treatment of the Neurologically Disabled.* Springfield, Thomas, 1957, 73 pp., $3.50.
BRITTEN: *Practical Notes on Nursing Procedures.* Baltimore, Williams & Wilkins, 1957, 192 pp., $4.
BRYAN: *The Child That Nobody Wanted.* Caldwell, Id., Caxton Printers, 1957, 284 pp., $4.
BRYCE: *Physical Therapy After Amputation.* Madison, University of Wisconsin, 1954, 93 pp., $1.50.
BUCHWALD: *Physical Rehabilitation for Daily Living.* New York, Blakiston-McGraw, 1952, 185 pp., $7.50.
CLARKE: *Disabled Citizens.* New York, Macmillan, 1951, 235 pp., $3.50.
COLLIS: *The Infantile Cerebral Palsies.* Springfield, Thomas, 1957, 110 pp., $3.
COLSON: *Postural and Relaxation Training in Physiotherapy and Clinical Education.* Springfield, Thomas, 1956, 116 pp., $2.50.
CYRIAX: *Manipulation and Deep Massage*, 5th Ed. New York, Hoeber, 1957, 373 pp., $6.50.
DANIELS: *Muscle Testing*, 2nd Ed. Philadelphia, Saunders, 1956, 176 pp., $4.
DAVIS: *Clinical Applications of Recreational Therapy.* Springfield, Thomas, 1952, 136 pp., $3.75.
DAVIS: *Recovery from Schizophrenia.* Springfield, Thomas, 1957, 184 pp., $4.75.
DELORME AND WATKINS: *Progressive Resistance Exercise.* New York, Appleton, 1951, 256 pp., $6.
DENING, DEYOE, AND ELLISON: *Ambulation*: Physical Rehabilitation for Crutch Walkers. New York, Funk & Wagnalls, 1951, 188 pp., $3.50.
DIEHL: *Compendium on Stuttering.* Springfield, Thomas, due 1958.
DUNTON: *Prescribing Occupational Therapy*, 2nd Ed., 2nd Ptg. Springfield, Thomas, 1947, 164 pp., $3.
DUNTON AND LICHT: *Occupational Therapy*: Principles and Practice, 2nd Ed. Springfield, Thomas, 1956, 373 pp., $8.
DURKIN: *Group Therapy for Mothers of Disturbed Children.* Springfield, Thomas, 1954, 144 pp., $3.50.
ELLEDGE: *The Rehabilitation of the Patient.* Philadelphia, Lippincott, 1948, 112 pp., $2.50
ENGLER: *How to Raise Your Child's I.Q.* New York, Criterion. Due 1958.
EWARHARDT AND RIDDLE: *Therapeutic Exercise.* Philadelphia, Lea & Febiger, 1947, 152 pp., $2.50.
FIDLER AND FIDLER: *Introduction to Psychiatric Occupational Therapy.* New York, Macmillan, 1954, 224 pp., $4.
FISHER: *Lip Reading Practice Material for Children.* New York, Comet Press, 1957, 27 pp., $2.
FORD: *Diseases of the Nervous System in Infancy, Childhood and Adolescence*, 3rd Ed. Springfield, Thomas, 1952, 1216 pp., $18.50.
GALLOWAY: *Treatment of Respiratory Emergencies:* Including Bulbar Poliomyelitis. Springfield, Thomas, 1953, 112 pp., $3.
GARDINER: *The Principles and Practice of Exercise Therapy*, 2nd Ed. New York, Macmillan, due 1957.

GASTAUT: *The Epilepsies:* Electro-Clinical Correlations. Springfield, Thomas, 1954, 176 pp., $4.75.

GETZ: *Environment and The Deaf Child,* 2nd Ptg. Springfield, Thomas, 1956, 188 pp., $3.75.

GETZ AND REES: *The Mentally Ill Child.* Springfield, Thomas, 1957, 100 pp., $3.50.

GIBBS AND STAMPS: *Epilepsy Handbook.* Springfield, Thomas, 1958, 112 pp., $4.25.

GLASER: *Allergy in Childhood.* Springfield, Thomas, 1956, 560 pp., $12.50.

GRAHAM AND MULLEN: *Rehabilitation Literature.* New York, Blakiston-McGraw, 1956, 621 pp., $13.

HART: *Congenital Dysplasia of the Hip Joint and Sequelae:* In the Newborn and Early Postnatal Life. Springfield, Thomas, 1952, 216 pp., $5.50.

HASS: *Congenital Dislocation of the Hip.* Springfield, Thomas, 1951, 416 pp., $13.

HAWORTH AND MACDONALD: *Theory of Occupational Therapy,* 3rd Ed. Baltimore, Williams & Wilkins, 1946, 160 pp., $2.50.

HILLIARD AND KIRMAN: *Mental Deficiency.* Boston, Little, Brown, 1957, 517 pp., $10.

HUFFMAN: *Fun Comes First For Blind Slow-learners.* Springfield, Thomas, 1957, 176 pp., $5.

JEWRY-HARBERT: *The Importance of Physiotherapy in the Treatment of Sick Children.* New York, de Graff, 1956, 84 pp., $2.50.

JOKL: *The Clinical Physiology of Rehabilitation.* Springfield, Thomas, 1958, 208 pp., $8.50.

JONES: *Speech Correction at Home.* Springfield, Thomas, 1957, 138 pp., $4.75.

JONES: *The Postural Complex:* Observations as to Cause, Diagnosis and Treatment. Springfield, Thomas, 1955, 176 pp., $9.75.

KALKMAN: *Introduction to Psychiatric Nursing.* New York, McGraw-Hill, due 1958.

KANNER: *Child Psychiatry,* 3rd Ed. Springfield, Thomas, 1957, 800 pp., $8.50.

KANNER: *In Defense of Mothers:* How to Bring Up Children in Spite of the More Zealous Psychologists, 3rd Ptg. Springfield, Thomas, 1951, 170 pp., $3.50.

KARNOSH: *Psychiatry for Nurses.* St. Louis, Mosby, due 1958.

KERR AND BRUNNSTROM: *Training of the Lower Extremity Amputee.* Springfield, Thomas, 1956, 272 pp., $6.50.

KESSLER: *Principles and Practices of Rehabilitation.* Philadelphia, Lea & Febiger, 1950, 448 pp., $9.

KESSLER: *Rehabilitation of the Physically Handicapped,* 2nd Ed. New York, Columbia, 1953, 292 pp., $4.

KIERNANDER: *Physical Medicine and Rehabilitation.* Springfield, Thomas, 1953, 624 pp., $12.75.

KOVACS: *Manual of Physical Therapy,* 5th Ed. Philadelphia, Lea & Febiger, due 1958.

KRAMER: *Art Therapy.* Springfield, Thomas, 1958, 256 pp., $6.75.

KRAUS: *Play Activities for Boys and Girls* (six through twelve); a guide for teachers, parents and recreation leaders. New York, McGraw-Hill, 1957, 247 pp., $4.95.

KRAUS: *Principles and Practice of Therapeutic Exercises.* Springfield, Thomas, 1949, 309 pp., $7.50.
KRUSEN: *Physical Medicine and Rehabilitation for the Clinician.* Philadelphia, Saunders, 1951, 371 pp., $6.50.
LEVY: *Behavioral Analysis.* Springfield, Thomas, 1958, 416 pp., $9.50.
LIVINGSTONE: *The Diagnosis and Treatment of Convulsive Disorders in Children.* Springfield, Thomas, 1954, 329 pp., $9.50.
LONGERICH AND BORDEAUX: *Aphasia Therapeutics.* New York, Macmillan, 1954, 185 pp., $3.75.
LOWENFELD: *Our Blind Children.* Springfield, Thomas, 1956, 224 pp., $5.50.
LOWMAN AND ROEN: *Therapeutic Use of Pools and Tanks.* Philadelphia, Saunders, 1952, 90 pp., $3.
MALLISON: *None Can Be Called Deformed:* Problems of the Crippled Adolescent. New York, Roy, 1957, 224 pp., $3.
MCMURRICH: *Applied Muscle Action and Co-ordination.* Toronto, University of Toronto Press, 1957, 92 pp., $3.75.
MENNELL: *Manual Therapy.* Springfield, Thomas, 1951, 71 pp., $2.25.
MICHAELS: *Disorders of Character:* Persistent Enuresis, Juvenile Delinquency and Psychopathic Personality. Springfield, Thomas, 1955, 152 pp., $4.75.
MORLEY: *The Development and Disorders of Speech in Childhood.* Baltimore, Williams & Wilkins, 1957, 440 pp., $9.
MOSHER AND RICHARDSON: *Medical Social Worker in Rehabilitation.* Association for the Aid of Crippled Children.
NEUSCHUTZ: *Vocational Rehabilitation for the Physically Handicapped.* Springfield, Thomas, due 1958.
NOYES *et al.*: *Textbook of Psychiatric Nursing*, 5th Ed. New York, Macmillan, 1957, 423 pp., $4.75.
PATTISON: *The Handicapped and Their Rehabilitation.* Springfield, Thomas, 1957, 976 pp., $14.75.
PENFIELD: *Epileptic Seizure Patterns:* A Study of the Localizing Value of Initial Phenomena in Focal Cortical Seizures. Springfield, Thomas, 1951, 112 pp., $3.75.
PHELPS: *The Cerebral Palsied Child.* New York, Simon and Schuster. Due 1958.
PHELPS, KIPHUTH AND GOFF: *Diagnosis and Treatment of Postural Defects*, 2nd Ed. Springfield, Thomas, 1956, 198 pp., $6.50.
PINES: *Retarded Children Can Be Helped.* Great Neck, 1957, 159 pp., $5.
REYNOLDS: *Physical Measures in the Treatment of Poliomyelitis.* New York, Macmillan, 140 pp., $2.50.
ROMAN: *Reaching Delinquents Through Reading.* Springfield, Thomas, 1958, 144 pp., $4.50.
RUSK: *Rehabilitation Medicine.* St. Louis, Mosby. Due 1958.
RUSK AND TAYLOR: *Living with a Disability.* New York, Blakiston-McGraw, 1953, 256 pp., $3.50.
RUSS AND SOBOLOFF: *Cerebral Palsy.* Springfield, Thomas, 1958, 80 pp., $4.
SARGANT AND SLATER: *An Introduction to Physical Methods of Treatment in Psychiatry*, 3rd Ed. Baltimore, Williams & Wilkins, 1954, 371 pp., $4.75.

SARGENT: *Directory for Exceptional Children.* Boston, Sargent. Due 1958.

SARGENT: *Handbook of Private Schools*, 39th Ed. Boston, Sargent, 1958, $10.

SCHONELL: *Educating Spastic Children.* New York Philosophical Library, 1956, 242 pp., $6.

SCHUBERT: *The Doctor Eyes the Poor Reader.* Springfield, Thomas, 1957, 116 pp., $3.75.

SHIRLEY: *The Child, His Parents and the Physician.* Springfield, Thomas, 1954, 176 pp., $3.75.

SMITH: *Rehabilitation, Re-educational and Remedial Exercises*, 2nd Ed. Baltimore, Williams & Wilkins, 1949, 456 pp., $6.

SMOUT AND McDOWALL: *Anatomy and Physiology for Students of Physiotherapy*, 3rd Ed. Baltimore, Williams & Wilkins, 1956, 493 pp., $9.

SPEER: *The Management of Childhood Asthma.* Springfield, Thomas, 1958, 128 pp., $4.75.

SPEKTER: *The Pediatric Years:* A Guide in Pediatrics for Workers in Health, Education and Welfare. Springfield, Thomas, 1955, 760 pp., $12.50.

SPENCER: *Treatment of Acute Poliomyelitis*, 3rd Ed. Springfield, Thomas, 1956, 224 pp., $6.

TANNER: *Growth at Adolescence.* Springfield, Thomas, 1956, 224 pp., $6.50.

TIDY: *Massage and Remedial Exercises*, 9th Ed. Baltimore, Williams & Wilkins, 1952, 519 pp., $6.

TRUETA: *Handbook on Poliomyelitis.* Springfield, Thomas, 1957, 148 pp., $3.75.

WEST: *The Rehabilitation of Speech*, 3rd Ed. New York, Harper, 1957, 694 pp., $7.50.

WILLARD AND SPACKMAN: *Principles of Occupational Therapy*, 2nd Ed. Philadelphia, Lippencott, 1954, 376 pp., $6.

WILLIAMS AND WORTHINGHAM: *Therapeutic Exercises.* Philadelphia, Saunders, 1957, 127 pp., $3.50.

WILMER: *Social Psychiatry in Action:* A Therapeutic Community. Springfield, Thomas, 1958, 400 pp., $8.75.

WITTENBORN: *The Placement of Adoptive Children.* Springfield, Thomas, 1957, 224 pp., $4.75.

LISTS OF BOOKS FOR CHILDREN

The library in your community can furnish lists of books suitable for the child or children you wish to provide with reading materials. In addition there are lists available from other sources including the following:

Books for Children. Books about music, science, poetry for preschoolers and grade school children. Bank Street College of Education, 69 Bank Street, New York 14, N.Y. Free. Send self addressed envelope with request.

Guide to Books for Young People. A group of favorite stories. Stevens Publications, 139 E. 53rd Street, New York 22, N.Y. Single copy 25 cents.

Books for the Teen Age—1958. Subjects of interest for teen-agers. The New York Public Library, Fifth Avenue and 42nd Street, New York 18, N.Y. Single copy 25 cents.

Children's Books. A guide for selecting worthwhile literature from the low priced books available in bookstores and drugstores. Association for Childhood Education International, 1200 Fifteenth Street, N.W., Washington 5, D.C. 75 cents.

Suggested Reading for the Family. Books for all ages suitable for reading aloud. Barnes & Noble, Inc., Attn: G. R. Cosgrove, 105 Fifth Avenue, New York 3, N.Y. Free.

INDEX

A

Abiotrophic diseases, 314-5
Abnormalities
  classification of appendicular, 105-8
Acceptance
  in our culture, 30, 31
  of child with handicap, 20-1
  of parents by professional workers, 26
  parental attitude in, 21, 22
Adolescent
  reading list on, 383
Adoption
  attitude toward, 79
  and caseworker, 53
  and congenital heart disease, 78
  and congenital syphilis, 77, 78
  and epilepsy, 80
  and mental retardation, 80
  and pediatrician, 77
  inter-racial programs of, 80
  of amputee, 91, 99
  of cerebral palsied, 78
  of deaf child, 78
  of handicapped, 91, 99
  readings on, 81
  role of agencies, 74-81
Albinism, 317-8
Allergy
  ocular manifestations of, 339
Amputation, 90-127
  and congenital abnormality, 106
  arm, 93-8, 101
  child with, 90-127
  cineplastic, 114
  effect on long bones, 100
  leg, 98-9, 101
  level of, 93
  neuromata within stump, 103
Amputees
  adaptation to altered function, 91, 99
  age of, 99-105
  age for prosthetic fittings, 108-12
  and bursitis, 103

  and physical therapy, 119
  classification of, 92
  congenital, 92, 93, 105, 114
  follow up program for, 122
  growth of bony stump, 104
  nature of child, 91, 92
  non-congenital, 90, 92, 114
  number of, 90
  parental influence on, 92, 108, 112
  pelvis of, 101
  phantom limb, 103
  readings on, 392-7
  schooling of, 111
  training of, 107
Angiography, 167
Angiomatosis retinae, 319-21
Aniridia, 325
Anoxic attacks
  treatment of, 159
Arachnodactyly, 323
Ataxia, 135
Athetosis, 135, 145
Attitudes
  immature, 21
  in planning, 23
  maternal, 34
  of amputee, 92
  toward authority, 191
Audiologist, 308
Authority
  child's attitude toward, 191

B

Batten-Mayou, 317, 321
Blind
  and play materials, 371, 374, 378
  lists of reading on, 383
  see also Eyes of children
Body Image, 31, 32, 33, 39
Bone
  growth of in amputee, 100, 104
Books
  on handicapping and rehabilitation, 392-96

399

lists for children, 397
   see also Reading materials and lists
Brain-injured
   defined, 4
Bright's disease, 242, 243
   see also Nephrosis

C

Camps
   directory of for handicapped, 391
   for diabetic children, 181
   for handicapped, 51
Capacities vs limitations, 4
Cardiac,
   see Congenital cardiac defects
Care
   continuity of, 7
   see handicap under Child
   see under specific Handicap
Case finding, 6
Caseworker, 44-5
   assistance to parents, 47-56
Cataracts
   case history of congenital, 83-4
   see also Eyes of children
Cerebral Palsy, 128-49
   and adoption, 78
   and associated handicaps, 136, 142-3
   and behavior disturbances, 137
   and emotional growth, 34
   and parents, 140-2
   and sensory defects, 137
   and vocational guidance, 147
   and vocational placement, 147-8
   child with, 128-49
   convulsive disorders with, 137
   developmental diagnosis, 135-6
   defined, 128
   diagnosis of, 132-9
   education of child with, 147
   electroencephalogram in, 137
   genetic causes of, 130
   incidence of, 129
   in infancy, 132-4, 135
   in pre-school and older, 134-5
   paranatal causes, 131
   play materials for child with, 369, 373, 377, 378
   postnatal causes, 131
   prenatal causes, 130, 131
   psychometric tests in, 139
   readings on, 392-7
   school child with, 146-7
   symptoms of, 128
Cerebral Thrombosis
   in cyanotic heart disease, 160
Child
   and play materials, 367-81
   eyes of, 311-40
   needs of, 67
   reading list on health and hygiene of, 382
   who is emotionally disturbed, 53-4, 182-98
   who is a mongoloid, 211-20
   with amputation, 90-127
   with cerebral palsy, 128-49
   with congenital cardiac defect, 150-62
   with convulsive disorders, 163-76
   with cystic fibrosis, 255-70
   with diabetes, 177-81
   with familial dysautonomia, 199-210
   with nephrosis, 233-51
   with poliomyelitis, 252-64
   with progressive muscular dystrophy, 221-32
   with rheumatic fever, 271-90
   with speech and hearing defect, 291-310
   uniqueness of each, 371
Children's Bureau and office of Health, Education and Welfare
   some publications of, 382-4
Civic responsibility
   objectives of, 65
   see also Community
Cineplastic amputation
   age for, 117
   appraisal of, 116
   defined, 114
   location, 114
   post-operative procedure, 116-7
   preparation for, 115
   when used, 114, 115, 119
Cleft palate, 3, 86, 87
   reading list on, 382, 392-7
Clinics
   child guidance, 194-5
   heredity, 84, 89, 227
Community
   agencies, 7, 9, 17, 46, 352-3

and cardiac problems, 271
and school, 60-1, 70
and service for handicapped, 148, 353-66
and social worker, 44
guides for programs, 360
heredity counseling, 59
Congenital Cardiac defects, 150-62
  activity of child with, 157-8
  care of child with, 154-8
  child with congenital, 150-62
  cyanosis, 155, 157, 158, 159, 162
  diagnosis of, 153-4
  education of child with, 158-9, 284-6
  immunization of child with, 156
  nature of congenital, 150-3
  prognosis for child with, 161-2
  recovery from, 52
Congenital cataracts, 325
Congenital glaucoma, 324
Convulsive disorders, 163-76
  child with in school, 176
  etiology, 164-5
  incidence, 163
  need for examination, 165-6
  psychological aspects of, 167-70
  reading list on, 382
  social therapy in, 174-6
  treatment of, 170-4
Corticography, 137
Counseling
  in medical genetics, 78, 82-9
  location of institutions for, 89
  parents of cerebral palsied, 141
Counselor
  location of, 89
  medical genetics, 82
  physician as, 3, 8, 12-3
  policy of, 84
  value of, 84
Counselors, 18, 21, 22, 23, 24, 26
Crippled children
  state programs for, 45-6
Crippling
  externally invisible, 3
Crouzon's disease, 323
Cyanosis, 155, 157, 158, 159, 162
Cystic fibrosis, 255-70
  case history of child with, 85, 86
  child with, 255-70
  clinical manifestations, 265-7

handicaps imposed by, 268
readings on, 269-70, 392-7
schooling of child with, 268-9
significance of handicap, 268-9
treatment of, 267

D

Deaf child, 27, 28
  and adoption, 78
  play materials for, 371, 377-8
  see also Hearing, Speech
Decalogue for teachers, 66-71
Denial
  of emotions, 186
  of handicap, 36, 37
Dental hygiene
  in cardiac cases, 157
Dependence, 36, 38
Diabetes
  care of diabetic child, 178-81
  child with, 177-81
  defined, 177
  incidence of, 177
  prognosis for, 181
  readings on, 392-7
Diabetic exophthalmic dysostosis, 323
Diagnosis, 4
Discipline
  and achievement, 344
  and attention on child, 343-4
  and communication, 346
  and freedom to grow, 345-7, 349
  belonging, 344-5
  clarification of values, 342-3, 347, 350
  defined, 341
  guides for, 341-50
  inconsistency in, 349
  internalizing controls, 341, 348
  punishment, 349
  readings on, 350
Diseases and ailments
  reading list on, 382-3
Dysautonomia
  see Familial dysautonomia
Dysfunction
  in cerebral palsy, 128
Dysostosis multiplex, 322

E

Economic efficiency,

401

objectives of, 64
Education
   and population statistics, 59, 70
   and state, 61
   boards of, 62
   concept of, in United States, 57, 58
   for amputee, 111
   for cerebral palsied, 147
   objectives of American, 59, 70
   planning for, 358-9, 361-2
   reading material lists, 383-384
   responsibility of people for, 58
   United States Office of, 61
   see also Guidance, Rehabilitation, Schooling
Electrocardiogram, 227
Electroencephalogram, 227
   in cerebral palsy, 137
Electromyogram, 227
Electroretinogram, 316
Emotional development
   during infancy, 188-90
   factors influencing, 187-8, 190
   in early childhood, 190-2
   in pre-school years, 192-3
   in school years, 194-5
   of adolescence, 195-7
   of child with familial dysautonomia, 205
Emotional disturbance
   and role of caseworker, 54
   child with, 182-97
   readings on, 167-8, 197-8
   in cerebral palsy, 137, 229
   incidence of, 183-6
Emotionally healthy, 186, 189
Emotions
   and play, 367, 374, 376
   defined, 186
   denial of, 186
   inter-relationship of, 186
Endocarditis
   subacute bacterial, 157, 160, 162
Epilepsy, 85
   and adoption, 80
   seizure, 169
   readings on, 392-7
   see also Convulsive disorders
Eyes of children, 311-41
   and allergies, 339-40
   and learning process, 327-34

   congenital tumors in, 320-1, 336
   diseases of hereditary nature in, 314-22
   glandular disturbances and, 307-8, 337-58
   hereditary syndromes, 323-5
   hyperopia, 328-9
   in infancy, 311-4
   injury to, 334-6
   lipodystrophies, 321-2
   metabolic changes in, 337-8
   myopia, 329-30
   readings on, 392-7
   surgery on, 333, 336, 337
   tears of infants, 326-7
   tumors of, 335-6
Exceptional child
   list of reading materials, 384

F

Familial Dysautonomia, 199-210
   blood pressure, 207
   defined, 199-200
   diagnosis of, 201-2
   emotional development of child with, 205
   management of child with, 208, 210
   manifestations of, 201-5
   prospects for adult life, 207, 208
   readings on, 210
   schooling of child with, 209
   vomiting attacks, 206-7
Foster care, 53
Freedom to grow, 342-5

G

Gaucher's disease, 322
Genetic
   causes of cerebral palsy, 130
   causes of cystic fibrosis, 265-6
   causes of dysautonomia, 200
   cause in eye diseases, 314-20
Genetics
   counseling in, 19-20, 82-9, 320-1
   medical, 82-9
   understanding mechanism of, 353
Glomerulonephritis, 242, 243
Gonococcal opthalmic, 339-40
Growth
   complexity of, 66

Guidance
  for parents, 16, 19, 21
  vocational for cerebral palsied, 147
  see also Rehabilitation, Schooling
Guilt, 35-8, 40, 43, 47, 114

H

Handicap
  acceptance of children with, 20
  adoption of child with, 75, 79
  and basic needs, 33
  and dependence, 33, 34, 36, 38-9
  and freedom, 38-9
  and guilt feelings, 40
  and schooling, 41
  and social maturity, 36
  early definition of, 12
  educational, 6
  education of public concerning, 14
  emotional, 34
  further complications of, 32
  multiple, 3
  opportunities for child with, 12
  plans for child with, 14
  problems of, 30, 31
  single, 3
  tolerance of culture toward, 30, 31
  understanding of child with, 12
Handicapped child
  play materials for, 368-81
  books on, 392-6
Handicapping conditions
  books on, 392-6
  see also Child
Hand-Schuller-Christian disease, 322
Harelip, 86, 87
Health education
  guides to materials, 385-6
  sources of materials on, 387-9
Hearing
  behavioral concomitants in loss of, 305-6
  diagnosis of defects in, 306
  importance to speech, 304
  in cerebral palsied, 142-3
  loss of, 305
  reading list on, 310, 382, 392-7
  selection of aid for, 305
  training to improve, 308-10
  see also Speech

Heart
  see Congenital Cardiac defects
Heart disease, 3
  and adoption, 78
Hereditary syndromes, 323-5
Heredity, 82, 84
  and refractive power of eye, 324-5
  counseling in, 82-9
  see also Genetics
Heredity clinics, 84
  location of, 89
  policy of, 84, 87
  see also Genetics
Home
  as educative agency, 69
Human relationship,
  objectives, 64
Hurler's Syndrome, 322
Hyperopia, 328-9
Hypoglycemic reaction, 179

I

Immunization, 5
  in cardiac cases, 156
Incipient conditions, 5
In-patient services
  and prosthesis, 122-3
  in rehabilitation programs, 118
  see also Social worker
Infantile Amaurotic Idiocy, 317
Institutional care
  and caseworker, 52-3
Inspiration as motivation, 40
Intelligence quotient
  and adoption, 80
  evaluation of test results, 303

J

Juvenile amputee, 91
  classification of, 92, 93

K

Ketosis, 149

L

Lawrence-Moon-Biedl-Bardet Syndrome, 316

Learning
  defined, 67-8
  and eyes, 327-34
Limbs
  phantom of amputee, 103
Lipochondrodystrophy, 322
Lipodystrophies, 321-2
Lipoid histiocytosis, 322

M

Macular degeneration, 317
Mandibulo-facial dysostosis, 323
Marfan's syndrome, 323
Mendelian traits, 83
  see also Genetics, Heredity
Medical genetics, 82-9
Medical social worker, 45, 50
Mental health
  and diabetic child, 180
  and teacher, 68-9
  begun in infancy, 190
Mental retardation, 80
  and cerebral palsy, 136
  and social worker, 52-3
  in pituitary dysfunction, 316-7
  of mongolid, 216-7, 219
  reading on, 392-7
  play materials in cases of, 371
Midcentury White House Conference on Children and Youth
  pledge to children, 71-3
  report of speech and hearing committee, 294-5
Mongolism, 87, 88, 211-20
  defined, 211, 213
  emotional development in, 215-6, 219, 220
  factors causing development of, 212-3
  incidence of, 211
  life span in, 219
  medical care of, 217-8
  mental development in, 216-7, 219
  physical characteristics in, 213-5
  placement of child, 218-9
  readings on, 379-84, 392-7
  schooling of child, 212, 218
  sensory development in, 216
  siblings in family with, 212, 218
  speech in child with, 215

Mother and child relationship, 187-8, 193
  see also Parent, Parental
Motion pictures
  lists of available, 383
Motivation, 40
  for independence, 40
  inspiration as, 40
Motor development
  and prosthetic fittings, 108-111
Motor pattern
  of child with prosthesis, 92
Muscular atrophy, 221
Muscular dystrophy,
  see Progressive muscular dystrophy
Muscles
  hypoplastic, 117
Myopia, 329-30
Myositis
  differentiated from muscular dystrophy, 225, 226

N

Nephritis, 242-3
Nephrosis, 233-51
  basic nature of, 240-1
  care of child with, 244
  cause of, 243
  child with, 233-51
  definition of, 234
  description of, 234-9
  emotional adjustment of child with, 247-8
  management of family of child with, 248-50
  readings on, 220-1, 379-84
  relation to other kidney diseases, 242-3
  research findings, 244
  schooling of child with, 248
  treatment of, 239-40
Neumann-Pick disease, 322
Neurofibromatosis, 318-9
Nurse
  in poliomyelitis case, 261
Nursery school,
  and cerebral palsied, 146
Nystagmus
  and cerebral palsy, 133

O

Occupational therapist,

404

in poliomyelitis, 263
Oculist, 326, 334
Office of Education of Department of Health, Education and Welfare, some publications of, 382-3
Orbital abscess, 336-7
Orbital cellulitis, 336-7
Orthopedist
  in poliomyelitis, 262-3
Over-protection, 36, 37, 38
Out-patient services, 118, 121, 122
  see also Social worker

P

Paints
  uses of for child, 370-3
Paralysis of limb, 3
Parent (s)
  acceptance of child with handicap by, 20-1, 47-8
  and adolescence, 196-7
  and amputee at school, 122
  and child relationship, 185
  and consultations, 17
  and discipline, 341-50
  and educational opportunity, 60, 61
  and education of public, 14
  and financing treatment, 45
  and guilt feelings, 34, 35, 47
  and professional help, 47-8, 349-50
  and psychiatrist, 41-3
  and rehabilitation, 118-27
  and self-help organizations, 23-4
  and sex-linked traits, 86
  and social worker, 47-56
  assistance to, 15, 26, 47-56
  attitude toward child, 21, 22, 32
  guides to, 351-65
  marriage problems of, 19
  need of constructive help, 27
  need of early definition of problem, 13
  of atypical child, 351
  of cerebral palsied, 140-2, 147
  of child with convulsive disorders, 168-70, 174-6
  of child with diabetes, 177-81
  of child with dysautonomia, 210
  of child with nephrosis, 233, 248-50
  of child with progressive muscular dystrophy, 129
  of child with rheumatic fever, 278
  of child who is emotionally disturbed, 183
  of child who is a mongoloid, 217
  of pre-school child, 192-3
  physician as advisor to, 9
  plan for care of atypical child, 351-65
  readings for, 365-6, 392-7
  responsibility of after prosthesis, 117
  responsibility of in speech training, 306-7
  role of, 11-29
  stages of growth of, 23
  status of, 11
  unconscious attitudes of, 193
  understanding their problem, 14-7, 41
  working together, 18, 25
Parental
  adjustment, 15-16
  attitudes, 21, 22, 23, 33, 34, 105, 112
  concern, 33
  denial of handicap in child, 36-7
  dependence, 36, 38
  emotionally ill, 14, 15
  guilt feelings, 34-6, 37
  hostility, 37
  influence on amputee, 92, 108, 112
  maturity, 22, 24
  need for practical guidance, 15, 16
  need for professional counselors, 16-8, 82, 89
  rights, 351
Pediatrician, 16
  and adoption, 77
  and convulsive disorders, 162, 164-5
  in speech and voice defects, 307
  leadership role of, 16, 17
  see also Physician, Teamwork
Pelvis of amputee, 7
Personality characteristics,
  in cerebral palsied, 140
Phakomatoses, 318-20
Phantom limbs
  of amputee, 103
Physical therapist
  in poliomyelitis cases, 261-2
  see also Teamwork
Physician
  and assessment of child's needs, 6-7
  and cerebral palsied, 140-5
  and child placement, 8

405

   and convulsive disorders, 164-76
   and diabetic, 180-1
   and education of child, 8
   and family, 5
   and specialists, 4
   approach to total personality, 39
   as advisor to parent groups, 9
   as counselor, 3, 8, 12-3
   as interpreter to non-medical professional persons, 8
   confidence in, 13
   credo of responsibility, 3-9
   knowledge of resources for help, 17
   periodic examination by, 5, 6
   readings on, 9-10
   role of, 3-9
   utilizing resources, 19
Placement
   acceptance of, 21
   of cerebral palsied, 147-8
   of child, 15
   of handicapped, 361
   of mongoloid child, 218
   see also Adoption, Social worker
Plan
   for care of atypical child, 351-65
Play
   cooking as, 381
   creative, 370-5
   dramatic, 378-80
   paints in, 370-3
   parallel, 367
   reading material and lists on, 383, 392-7
   selections of materials for, 368-75
   social games, 381
   solitary, 367-8
   value of, 367
   with art materials, 371-5
   with household materials, 380
   with water, 395
Play materials
   creative, 370-5
   for hospitalized, 368
   for mentally retarded, 371
   guides to, 367-81
   purpose of, 370
   selection of, 368, 369
Pneumo-encephalogram
   use of in convulsive disorders, 166-7
Poliomyelitis, 252-64

   and the parents of patient, 260-2
   child with, 252-64
   course of disease, 252-4
   disturbances and dysfunctions caused by, 254-7
   manifestations of, 254-7, 258, 259
   need for occupational therapist, 263
   need for orthopedist, 262-3
   need for physical therapist, 261-2
   need for social worker, 263
   need for teacher, 263
   nursing care, 261
   prognosis for recovery, 261
   readings on, 379-84, 392-7
   tracheotomy, 256
   use of artificial respiration, 257
Professional workers, 4, 6, 14, 15, 16, 17, 25, 44
   and lay partnership, 24-8
   attitude of, 28
   counselors, 18, 21, 22, 23, 24, 26
   see also Teamwork
Progressive muscular dystrophy, 86, 221-32
   characteristics of, 223-5
   clinical types, 222-3
   conditions confused with, 225-7
   defined, 221
   diagnostic features, 222
   genetic factors, 222-3, 224, 227-31
   incidence of, 221-2
   personality adjustment in, 229, 230, 231
   readings on, 231-2, 392-7
   research in, 221, 229
   schooling of patient, 231
   treatment of, 229, 231
Prosthesis, 93-127
Prosthetic device, 93-9
   age for fittings, 108
   and amputation level, 93
   for lower extremities, 98, 99, 112, 113
   for upper extremities, 93, 98, 112
   need for proper functioning, 122
   training in use of, 120, 121
Prosthetic service, 117, 118, 122
Pseudopapilledema, 324
Psychiatrist, 30-42
   and cerebral palsied, 142
   and parents, 41-3
   guilt feelings, 34, 35
   helper in convulsive disorders, 174-5

related readings, 379-84, 392-7
role of, 30-42
see also Emotionally disturbed child, Teamwork

Q

Quadriplegia, 134-5

R

Race
  and adoption, 80-1
  and familial dysautonomia, 200
Reading materials and lists,
  books on handicapping conditions, 392-6
  guides to, 382-4
  maternity and infancy, 383
  motion pictures available, 383
  on child health and hygiene, 382
  on children's books, 383, 397
  on diseases and ailments, 382, 383
  on elementary education, 383-4
  on exceptional children, 384
  on play and recreation, 383, 384
  on school, 384
  on social worker, 56
  on your child, 383
Reality
  denial of, 36, 37
Rehabilitation
  books on, 392-6
  of amputee, 92, 105, 106, 112, 118-9
  of cardiac patient, 271-87
  of poliomyelitis patient, 264
Religion
  and adoption, 80-1
Retardation
  in pituitary dysfunction, 316-7
  mental plus orthopedic, 3
  see also Mental retardation
Reticuloendothelial granulomatosis, 321-2
Retinoblastoma, 313, 320-1
Retinitis pigmentosa, 315-7
Retrolental fibroplasis, 312, 313, 314
Rheumatic fever, 271-89
  and streptococci, 275, 276
  and surgery, 276
  characteristics of, 271
  child with, 271-89
  convalescent stage, 280-2
  diagnosis of, 277, 278
  emotional problems, 286, 288

functional classification of patients, 282-3
handicapping effects, 276, 277
hospitalization for, 279-80, 281, 288
incidence of, 272, 273-4, 288
manifestations of, 272-4, 277-8
prognosis for recovery, 274-5
readings on, 289-90, 392-7
research on, 276
schooling of child with, 280-1, 283-6
therapeutic classification of patients, 282-3
treatment of, 275-6, 287, 288

S

Safety, 5
Schooling
  and community, 60-1, 70
  away from home, 361
  determiners in quality of, 70
  experiences, 68
  for every child, 71
  of child with congenital heart disease, 158-9
  of child with convulsive disorders, 175
  of child with cystic fibrosis, 268-9
  of child with muscular dystrophy, 175
  of handicapped, 41, 358-9
  of rheumatic fever patient, 280-1, 283-6
  of young amputee, 111, 112, 122
  opportunities for, 60
  readings on, 383, 384, 392-7
Schools
  directory of for handicapped, 391
Security
  and parents, 51
  and speech development, 306-7
Seizures
  see Convulsive disorders
Self-pity, 23
Self-realization
  objectives of, 63
Sex-linked traits, 86
  see also Genetics, Heredity
Shame, 36
Sleep
  disturbances in infancy, 133
Speech
  and articulation, 300-2
  and behavior, 294
  and dramatic play, 378-9

407

and hearing, 302
characteristics of good, 293
child with disorder in, 291-310
defective, 292-4
development of, 291-3, 306-7
diagnosis of defects, 295-304
difficulties in familial dysautonomia, 205
incidence of defects, 294
larynx in speech, 297-8
mechanics of, 296-7
modulation in, 293
nasal cavities and, 299-300
of mongoloid child, 215
readings on, 310, 392-7
training, 306-10
Social growth, 186
Social participation, 7
of amputee, 111, 121, 127
of handicapped, 51
Social worker, 44-56
and adoption, 53, 76
and emotional problems, 53-4
and mental retardation, 52-3
and physically handicapped, 45-55
and poliomyelitis patient, 263
assistance to parents, 47-56
casework, 44-5, 46-7
foster care, 53
in group service, 49
in hospital, 48-9
in rehabilitation, 118
in voluntary agency, 55
medical, 45-50
readings on, 56
role of, 44-56
see also Professional workers, Teamwork
Spastic hemiplegia, 128, 134, 138
Specialists, 4
and cerebral palsied, 144-6
see also Professional workers, Teamwork
Spur formation, 102, 105
Strabismus
and cerebral palsy, 133
and personality disturbance, 3
see also Eyes of children
Streptoccic infections
and rheumatic fever, 275
treatment of, 277
Sturge-Weber Syndrome, 320
Susceptible, 5, 6

Sympathy, 345
Syphilis
congenital and adoption, 78, 79

T

Teacher (s), 57-73
and community opinion, 60
and convulsive child, 176
and diabetic child, 180-1
and poliomyelitis patient, 263
decalogue for, 66-71
of cardiac cases, 157-8
professional responsibility, 63
responsibilities of, 66
readings, 289, 392-7
role of, 57-73
Teamwork
and discipline, 342
and social worker, 44, 46
defined, 11
for amputee, 118-27
for diabetic, 181
in care of child with nephrosis, 233, 248
in care of child with poliomyelitis, 259-63
in cerebral palsy, 141-2, 143-5
in convulsive disorders, 175-6
in familial dysautonomic cases, 208-10
in progressive muscular dystrophy, 231
in rehabilitating rheumatic fever patient, 271, 279, 281-2
need of, 11, 117
with defects in speech, 306
Testing
psychometric in cerebral palsy, 139
Therapist, 40
see also Specialist, Teamwork
Therapy
physical, 118-9
occupational, 118, 120
Trauma, 90, 93, 163, 334, 337
Treatment of child and concept of self, 32
see also handicap under Child
Tuberous sclerosis, 319
Tracheotomy
in bulbar paralysis, 256
Tay Sach's disease, 321
Toys
for dramatic play, 378-80
for physical activity, 377-8

in socialization, 367-8
made of household materials, 380
manipulative, 375-7
see also Play, Play materials

V

Vasculo-Encephalo-Trigeminal Syndrome, 320
Vocational guidance,
see Guidance
Von Hippel's disease, 319

Von Recklinghausen's disease, 318-9
Vulnerable,
use of term, 6

W

Waardenburg Syndrome, 324

X

Xanthomatosis, 321